PSYCHOLOGY, PSYCHIATRY,

AND THE LAW:

A CLINICAL AND FORENSIC HANDBOOK

Edited by

Charles Patrick Ewing, J.D., Ph.D.

Faculty of Law and Jurisprudence
State University of New York
at Buffalo

Professional Resource Exchange, Inc.

Sarasota, Florida

Library of Congress Catalog Number: 85-60449
ISBN 0-943158-11-7

ACKNOWLEDGMENT

This volume is the product of many hands and many minds. The original idea for the book was developed independently but almost simultaneously by the editor and by Dr. Peter A. Keller, one of the founders of the Professional Resource Exchange, Inc. Dr. Keller was looking for someone to edit such a volume and I was seeking someone to publish it. Needless to say, we found each other and plans for this book began to take shape. I sincerely thank Dr. Keller for his confidence, encouragement, guidance, and friendship.

The book itself, of course, is largely the product of the contributors, all of whom have approached their contributions with creativity, cooperation, and tolerance for the editor. Getting to know and working with this extraordinary group of practitioners and scholars has been a true delight. I thank them all and hope that my editing and organization of the volume has done justice to their fine work.

The book was copy edited by Joann M. Bierenbaum, who is responsible for many improvements to its style and readability. Production of the volume was directed by Debbie Worthington, whose organizational skills, patience, and careful attention to detail are reflected throughout the book. Any errors which remain after their tireless efforts are the responsibility of the editor.

Finally, I want to mention that this volume, like all of my professional work, has been greatly encouraged and aided by my wife, Sharon Harris-Ewing. My contribution to this volume is dedicated to her.

C.P.E.

Buffalo, New York
April, 1985

CONTENTS

INTRODUCTION
TO THE VOLUME

Mention law and psychology or psychiatry in the same breath and most people anticipate a discourse on the insanity plea or civil commitment. For many, including those in the legal and mental health professions, these two issues have long been synonymous with the law-psychology/psychiatry interface. Until the past decade or so, there was more than the proverbial grain of truth to this stereotype. For many years, the issues of insanity and civil commitment did, indeed, dominate much if not most of the professional practice and clinical literature at the juncture of the disciplines of law, psychology, and psychiatry.

Recent decades, however, have been marked by a tremendous expansion of the role played by psychologists and psychiatrists in the legal process. In the criminal law arena, the traditional domain of forensic psychologists and psychiatrists, the insanity issue continues to be in the forefront, as the aftermath of the Hinckley trial has made clear. Yet today psychologists, psychiatrists, and other mental health professionals and behavioral scientists are directly involved in virtually every aspect of the criminal justice system, from arrest and trial to sentencing, corrections, and parole. It seems no exaggeration to say that the modern criminal justice system, as it has evolved in recent years, could not function without significant participation by mental health professionals and behavioral scientists.

At the same time, the role of psychologists and psychiatrists in other areas of the law has also grown tremendously. For example, civil litigation regarding personal injury, products liability, and other damage claims now routinely includes psychological and/or psychiatric expert testimony. And psychologists and psychiatrists have also found a significant and growing role in the adjudication of many Workers' Compensation claims.

Likewise, family law has become increasingly receptive to input from psychologists, psychiatrists, and other mental health professionals. Today, mental health experts are a standard fixture in divorce, child custody, and child/spouse abuse and neglect proceedings. Moreover, many mental health professionals have now begun to offer an alternative to traditional adversary modes of resolving divorce and custody disputes. Divorce mediation, a new and growing professional field, is clearly dominated by mental health professionals.

Civil commitment appears to be waning in recent years, but the role of psychologists and psychiatrists in this legal process has never been more important or visible. Recent precedent-setting judicial decisions have drastically altered civil commitment procedures in ways which have served to increase the need for psychological and psychiatric involvement. Furthermore, recent litigation over the "right" of committed patients to refuse treatment has called into question many traditional practices, thereby requiring the participation of countless mental health professionals in the task of formulating new standards of care.

While most of the increased interaction between law and the professions of psychology and psychiatry has involved mental health clinicians, in recent years academic behavioral scientists such as experimental and social psychologists also have begun to have a profound influence upon legal process. Research regarding sentencing guidelines, eyewitness identification, lie detection, and jury behavior and selection has found its way into the courtroom and other aspects of the legal process.

Finally, it should be noted that the relationship between law and the mental health professions has not remained a "one-way street." Just as psychology and psychiatry have come to influence many aspects of law and legal process, the law has begun to have significant influence upon many aspects of mental health practice. Today, more than at any time in the past, mental health clinicians are being required to conform their professional practices to the rapidly changing letter of the law. What were once strictly ethical issues (e.g., confidentiality, consent to mental health treatment, responsibility to nonpatients, and limits upon the doctor-patient relationship) have now become legal mandates. The ever growing spectre of malpractice suits makes it clear that no clinician can afford to be ignorant of the multitude of statutes and court decisions which directly define and limit acceptable mental health practice.

The purpose of this book, written by psychologists, psychiatrists, and lawyers, is to pull together in one handy resource volume many of the most recent and significant legal, theoretical, empirical, and clinical perspectives on the growing relationship of psychology and psychiatry to the law. The volume is intended to be used as a handbook for busy practitioners as well as others who need a concise, up-to-date, and readable briefing on current psycholegal theory, research, and practice. Given the wide diversity of the authors' backgrounds and experience in psychology, psychiatry, and law, the individual chapters vary in their orientation. Some chapters emphasize theory and research while others are focused more directly upon applications and practice. Yet, in every chapter, readers should find information and insights useful in everyday clinical and forensic practice.

INTRODUCTION TO SECTION I: PSYCHOLOGY, PSYCHIATRY, AND CRIMINAL JUSTICE

The relationship of psychology and psychiatry to the criminal law, though time-honored and deeply rooted in traditional concepts of criminal justice and jurisprudence, has never been an altogether happy one. Even the most ardent supporters of a highly individualized criminal process have long been skeptical of the ability of psychologists and psychiatrists to classify offenders in ways which truly further the ends of criminal justice. Met with such skepticism for so long, many mental health professionals and behavioral scientists have also become skeptics. Some have joined in the offensive, becoming openly skeptical if not critical of psychology and psychiatry, while others have responded defensively, asserting that their efforts on behalf of criminal justice have been undermined by a legal system which misuses their legitimate contributions. As a result, psychological and psychiatric input into criminal justice decision making, ubiquitous as it has become, is often both grudgingly given and received.

Perhaps the most unfortunate by-product of this unhappy state of affairs is the growing indifference of many of the best and brightest mental health professionals and behavioral scientists to the resolution of vital criminal justice issues. Skepticism and frustration seem to have led many practitioners and researchers to believe that they have nothing of value to offer the criminal justice system.

Psychological and psychiatric input into criminal justice decision making continues, but much of it is ill informed, out of touch with current thinking in the behavioral sciences and law, and given by those least qualified to represent psychology and psychiatry in this critical aspect of our legal system. The result, of course, is increased skepticism, a further widening of the gulf between the mental health professions and the criminal justice system, and a growing disengagement of qualified mental health professionals from the criminal justice process. This vicious cycle is played out not only in the literature of the professions but in legal agencies, courtrooms, and correctional institutions across the country.

The chapters in this section of the present volume make no pretense at resolving the fundamental issues which generate skepticism and fuel the conflicts between the mental health professions and the criminal justice system. The underlying common message of these chapters, however, is an optimistic one: Psychologists, psychiatrists, other mental health professionals, and behavioral scientists do have something of value to offer the criminal justice process *if* what they offer is firmly grounded in sound clinical practice, adequate empirical research, and a clear understanding of law, legal process, and public policy.

This section of the volume opens with John Monahan's chapter on the clinical prediction of violent behavior or "dangerousness." The prediction of "dangerousness," though required at various points throughout the criminal justice process, represents one of the most, if not the most, controversial aspects of psychological and psychiatric involvement in criminal law. Dr. Monahan, a psychologist and law professor who has written and practiced extensively in this area of forensic psychology, offers a guide to clinicians called upon to assess an individual's potential for violent behavior. This chapter is followed by four others which take the reader through the criminal justice process from pretrial assessments of competency and criminal responsibility to post-conviction problems of sentencing and corrections.

Competence to stand trial, addressed in Stephen Lawrence's chapter, is often confused with the issue of insanity. As Dr. Lawrence explains, however, competency is a separate and distinct issue related to the criminal defendant's ability to understand the charges against him or her and to assist in his or her defense, issues litigated much more frequently than insanity. Dr. Lawrence, a psychologist, critically examines the law, theory, research, and practice related to competence to stand trial. His chapter concludes with a description of a comprehensive competency assessment using the LAW-PSI and the LAW-COMP, two widely used clinical instruments he has developed over the course of many years of forensic practice.

Criminal responsibility, the subject of David Shapiro's chapter, encompasses the insanity defense, the issue of diminished capacity, and related concerns bearing upon individual culpability for criminal conduct. After describing the various existing and proposed legal tests of insanity and discussing the recent move toward abolition of the insanity defense, Dr. Shapiro explores a variety of issues which must be addressed in reconstructing a defendant's mental state at the time of the criminal act. Drawing upon many years of experience as a clinical and forensic psychologist, Dr. Shapiro offers clinicians a detailed guide to conducting the criminal responsibility assessment and effectively reporting and testifying to forensic findings.

Sentencing, the topic explored in the chapter by Jolene Galegher and John Carroll, is the subject of heated debate throughout the criminal justice system. In recent years, the broad discretion accorded judges and parole authorities in criminal sentencing has come under increasingly sharp criticism. Reformers have suggested, among other changes, a ban on plea bargaining, the review of sentences by a sentencing council, the imposition of mandatory minimum prison terms, the abolition of parole, and the use of sentencing guidelines, on either a statutory or voluntary basis. In their chapter, Drs. Galegher and Carroll, organizational and social psychologists, provide an overview of major issues involved in the construction and implementation of sentencing guidelines, emphasizing the importance of understanding legal process and issues of public policy in the development of workable guidelines.

This section of the volume concludes with Robert Levinson's essay on the role of the psychologist in correctional settings. Dr. Levinson draws upon 25 years of experience as a psychologist and administrator in the field of corrections to describe how correctional psychologists can function as change agents in the penal institutions they serve. Stressing that the correctional psychologist's "client" is not simply the individual inmate or inmate group but the prison community as a whole, Dr. Levinson advocates a community psychology approach in which the psychologist transcends traditional role stereotypes (e.g., assessment and treatment) and takes an active role in other institutional affairs such as administration, training, and research.

EVALUATING POTENTIALLY VIOLENT PERSONS

John Monahan

It is not without trepidation that a "model" format for the clinical prediction of violence is proposed. It is clear from the research literature that relatively few factors have proven their predictive mettle as antecedent conditions to violent behavior. Most of what follows represents nothing more (or less) than the professional judgments of persons experienced at the task of prediction. What is offered is a reasonable guide to performing a kind of assessment that increasingly is being sought from mental health professionals. This is not offered as a substitute for a careful reading of the clinical literature on prediction (particularly American Psychiatric Association, 1974; Cohen, Groth, & Siegel, 1978; Kozol, 1975; Kozol, Boucher, & Garofalo, 1972; Megargee, 1976).

The assessment proposed is solely for the purpose of predicting violent behavior and not for the purpose of diagnosing mental disorder. Violent behavior is not typically associated with mental disorder. Should the question of mental disorder also be of interest (e.g., for the purpose of civil commitment), an additional (or combined) examination would be necessary. Should the issue of violence arise in the course of ongoing treatment, many of the factors that are assayed here may already be known and need only to be made explicit. The procedures outlined here are necessarily idealized and could be superceded in the context of imminent violence. One

9

need not estimate the IQ of someone screaming "I'll kill you!" to restrain him or her from doing so.

Wherever possible, psychiatrists and psychologists should limit their role to providing an estimate of the probability of future violent behavior, substantiating that estimate with clinical and statistical evidence, and leaving to legislators or judges the decision as to whether preventive action should be triggered. Such a stance is not "passing the buck" to evade responsibility for difficult clinical decisions. It is forcing those in government to accept responsibility for difficult political decisions dealing with competing claims for freedom and safety. In matters of law, the buck must be permitted to pass until it stops at the doorstep of the legislature and the judiciary. Cohen et al. (1978) have put it well:

> It is a perilous, narrow path between the requirements of social order and the expression of individual freedom. To balance order and liberty properly is a sociopolitical, not a clinical, issue, and this must be done by society's courts and legislatures. The clinician should neither be given nor attempt to usurp society's right to determine the risks it is willing to take in resolving the conflict between safety and liberty. (p. 39)

QUESTIONS FOR THE CLINICIAN

IS IT A PREDICTION OF VIOLENT BEHAVIOR THAT IS BEING REQUESTED?

Shah (1978) has enumerated 15 points in the legal process at which estimates of future harmful conduct are taken. The first question to ask oneself is whether any questions of prediction are being raised in a given case and, if so, for what legal purpose. Such a question may seem excessively basic. Yet Geller and Lister (1978), in a study of psychiatric reports written for the purpose of determining competence to stand trial and criminal responsibility, found that 55% of the reports offered a prediction of "dangerousness" *even though one was not requested by the court.* At the same time, 65% of the

The ethical standards of both the American Psychiatric Association and the American Psychological Association support such honesty in the interests of client welfare. Without this openness, individuals being interviewed only for the purpose of assessing their violence potential, for example, may mistakenly believe that they are in the process of receiving treatment for their psychic pains.

GIVEN MY ANSWERS TO THE ABOVE QUESTIONS, IS THIS CASE AN APPROPRIATE ONE IN WHICH TO OFFER A PREDICTION?

Should one conclude that a prediction is not actually being requested, that one is not professionally competent to offer predictive judgments, or that one's ethical beliefs preclude rendering a prediction in this type of case, it is both appropriate and essential to decline to offer a professional opinion in the matter and to return the referral to its source with an explanation for the action taken.

Should the issue of violence prediction arise in the course of treatment and should the mental health professional lack confidence in his or her own abilities in this area, prompt consultation with a more knowledgeable colleague may be necessary.

Assuming that the case is one in which a prediction is appropriate, the following questions become germane.

WHAT EVENTS PRECIPITATED RAISING THE QUESTION OF THE PERSON'S POTENTIAL FOR VIOLENCE AND IN WHAT CONTEXT DID THESE EVENTS TAKE PLACE?

It is advantageous to be clear at the outset about precisely what the person did, or was alleged to have done, to have made someone (e.g., police officer, judge) concerned about his or her potential to be violent in the future, and the social context in which these events took place. A meticulous examination of the "precipitating incident" may yield much information of value to making a prediction. Knowing exactly who said or did what may provide clues to the situational contexts in which the individual reacts violently. Knowing, for example, that the assault of one person upon another took place in the context of a heated argument, but only after the victim had begun to cast aspersions upon the assailant's job performance, may raise the salience of job performance as an item worthy of further exploration. Thus, as Kozol (1975) has written:

> Of paramount importance is a meticulous description of the actual assault. The potential for violent assaultiveness is the core of our diagnostic problem, and the description of the aggressor in action is often the most valuable single source of information. The patient's version is compared with the victim's version. In many cases we interview the victim ourselves. Our most serious errors in diagnosis have been made when we ignored the details in the description of the assault. (p. 8)

WHAT ARE THE PERSON'S RELEVANT DEMOGRAPHIC CHARACTERISTICS?

Among the first and easiest factors on which one can gather information are demographic ones. In which relevant groups associated in a positive or negative way with violent behavior does the individual hold membership? There is evidence on the relationship between several demographic variables and violent behavior: (a) *age* (violence peaking in the late teens and early 20s); (b) *sex* (males tending to be much more violent than females); (c) *race* (nonwhites, and particularly blacks, committing proportionately more "street" violence than whites); (d) *social class* (the lower the SES, the more likely the street violence); (e) *history of opiate or alcohol abuse* (violence being more likely if such a history is present); (f) *IQ* (the lower the estimated IQ, the more likely the violence; (g) *educational attainment* (the less the education, the more likely the violence); and (h) *residential and employment stability* (violence being more likely among those who move or change jobs frequently).

The inclusion of some predictive factors may make others worthless in the clinical context. Thus, among persons with an extensive history of past violence, the significance of race as a predictor is eliminated.

WHAT IS THE PERSON'S HISTORY OF VIOLENT BEHAVIOR?

This is one of the most important questions one can ask in prediction, and obtaining a satisfactory answer may not be as easy as it seems. A very thorough probing of all forms of past violence should be conducted, paying particular attention to the *recency, severity,* and *frequency* of violent acts (Fisher, Brodsky, & Corse, 1977). It should be noted whether the person's pattern of violent behavior appears to be escalating or declining. At least five indices of violence should be considered: (a) arrests and convictions for violent crimes; (b) juvenile court involvement for violent acts; (c) mental hospitalizations for dangerous behavior; (d) violence in the home, such as spouse and child abuse; and (e) other self-reported violent behavior such as bar fights, fights in school, arson, violent highway disputes, and perhaps violence toward animals. It should be noted in this regard that an *attempt* to kill often differs from an actual murder only by occurring in close proximity to a hospital. Open-ended questions, such as "What is the most violent thing you have ever done?" and "What is the closest you have ever come to being violent?" may be helpful (American Psychiatric Association, 1974).

WHAT IS THE BASE RATE OF VIOLENT BEHAVIOR AMONG INDIVIDUALS OF THIS PERSON'S BACKGROUND?

The base rate of violence is the most significant information one can obtain in making a prediction of violent behavior. In some instances the base rate is published information. In other cases, one can compute the base rate for oneself from available records (e.g., the base rate of violence on a mental hospital ward may be ascertained from a sample of hospital charts). In many circumstances, however, base rates are neither available nor readily obtainable. What is the base rate of violent behavior among persons referred by the police for civil commitment as dangerous to others on the basis of a recent overt act? Surely, it is not the same as the rate in the general population. Unless someone is willing to deny commitment to a portion of these persons to see how often, in fact, they are violent, their base rate will remain unknown.

What, then, is the clinician to do when confronted with the knowledge that the base rate is the most important single piece of information to have and yet he or she does not have it? One is left with Meehl's (1973) advice that, when actuarial data do not exist, we must use our heads. The clinician must estimate as reasonably, as judiciously, as wisely as possible what the approximate base rate would be. In so doing, one should always ask why the base rate of violence among persons similar to the person one is examining should be any higher than the general population rate. Having committed a recent overt act of violence, for example, may be one indicator that a higher-than-average base rate reasonably could be imputed to the individual.

WHAT ARE THE SOURCES OF STRESS IN THE PERSON'S CURRENT ENVIRONMENT?

WHAT COGNITIVE AND AFFECTIVE FACTORS INDICATE THAT THE PERSON MAY BE PREDISPOSED TO COPE WITH STRESS IN A VIOLENT MANNER?

WHAT COGNITIVE AND AFFECTIVE FACTORS INDICATE THAT THE PERSON MAY BE PREDISPOSED TO COPE WITH STRESS IN A NONVIOLENT MANNER?

Stress is a concept that may provide an organizing principle for many of the issues in violence prediction. Stress can be understood as a state of imbalance between the demands of the social and physical environment and the capabilities of an individual to cope with these demands (McGrath, 1970; Mechanic, 1968). The higher the ratio of demands to resources, the more stress is experienced. Stress is thus to be thought of in terms of transactions between persons and their environments over time (Lazarus & Launier, in press). The voluminous literature on stress and its regulation has been masterfully reports did *not* address the issue of competency, and 93% did *not* address the issue of responsibility, which were the issues in which the court was interested.

Psychologists and psychiatrists are not alone in their confusion regarding questions to address. Farmer's (1977) study of presentence assessments performed for Federal court judges found that, in over 95% of the referrals to psychologists and psychiatrists, "judges consistently fail to communicate their objectives and questions" (p. 7) to the examiner. Judges surveyed found it difficult to say *why* they were requesting a mental health examination.

> Their answers suggested general and frequently nebulous concerns rather than a desire to have specific questions answered. For example, some would say that they just wanted to know more about the person, but could not readily explain what new information they sought. (Farmer, 1977, p. 7)

It would appear that the first task of the mental health professional is to be clear about whether anyone is interested in having a prediction made and, if not, what it is that they are interested in and what information is being sought. This may require going back to the source of the referral and requesting clarification of the task.

AM I PROFESSIONALLY COMPETENT TO OFFER AN ESTIMATE OF THE PROBABILITY OF FUTURE VIOLENCE?

Once the referral question is known to include a request to estimate the probability of future violence, the professional must consider his or her ability to answer it. The primary determinants of this ability are knowledge and understanding of (a) the theoretical and methodological literature on prediction and assessment in general; (b) the clinical and research literature on the prediction of violent behavior; and (c) the relevant legal framework in which the prediction would be offered (e.g., a state commitment statute). An adequate personal assessment of competence in these areas will require careful and candid introspection.

This introspection may lead to the conclusion that no one is competent to make the kind of prediction being requested; that some mental health professionals are competent to do so, but that the questioner is not among them; or that the questioner does indeed possess relative professional competence to address the issue at hand.

Competence in this type of assessment also involves the possession of a disposition that will allow objective evaluation of the facts at issue. Fisher's (1976) finding that psychiatrists and psychologists who score higher on the Rokeach dogmatism scale are more likely than others to predict dangerousness for a sample of clinical cases delineates just one dispositional trait that determines competence to estimate future violence.

ARE ANY ISSUES OF PERSONAL OR PROFESSIONAL ETHICS INVOLVED IN THIS CASE?

To the greatest extent possible, the clinician should defer to policymakers' questions of social and political value raised by violence prediction. These questions concern the definition of the violence predicted, the factors taken into account in predicting it, the degree of predictive accuracy necessary for taking preventive action, and the nature of the preventive action to be taken. They are questions for the legislature, the judiciary, and, ultimately, the voting public.

Two issues prevent this principled abdication of a policy role from being absolute. The first is that circumstances may arise in which the personal moral values of the mental health professional so clash with the accepted legal codes of society that the mental health professional, to maintain his or her own ethical integrity, should decline to participate in prediction altogether. Depending on the moral values of the mental health professional, the prediction of violent behavior for the purpose of imposing the death penalty, or the inclusion of certain variables (e.g., race) in prediction equations, may be examples of circumstances in which a clinician could decline, on principle, to participate in offering a prediction. (An analogy would be the refusal of physicians to perform abortions when to perform them would violate the physicians' moral beliefs.) Note that here one is *not* using science as a subterfuge for promulgating one's preferred moral or political beliefs, as would be the case if a clinician, believing an offender to have a high potential for violent behavior, testified otherwise in court in order to save the offender from execution. Rather, what is being advocated is a general presumption in favor of deferring policy questions to those whose formal role in a democratic society it is to answer them, with the mental health professional reserving the right to opt out of the process entirely if the results, or the process of arriving at them, would compromise his or her ethical integrity (see Loftus & Monahan, 1980).

The second qualification on an absolute abdication of a policy role by mental health professionals is that all too frequently policymakers have evaded their responsibility to provide a framework in which mental health professionals can operate. Thus, no state yet specifies the level of probability of violent behavior necessary to invoke civil commitment of a person as "dangerous to others" (Monahan & Wexler, 1978). In many cases, the mental health professional can simply state his or her judgment (e.g., "Due to the following factors, Mr. X has a 50% probability of committing assault within the next 2 weeks") and let the policymaker decide whether such a prediction is "high enough" to invoke legal constraints. In other situations, however, particularly "emergency" ones in which there is simply not enough time to force the policymaker's hand, the options for the mental health professional who concurs with the position being argued here reduce to walking out, muttering "When you people decide what you want, let me know" or reluctantly trying to fashion a workable framework within which to offer predictions, knowing full well the pitfalls involved. The crucial issue here would be to be explicit about what rules one was adopting and to follow them consistently. Thus, in a state in which the law simply held that a person could be committed if he or she was dangerous to others, a mental health professional in a psychiatric emergency admitting room could state in a letter to the local judge:

> Since I can find no guidance on how to interpret the statute and yet feel it necessary to take action

in many cases, I shall adopt this interpretation: "Dangerous to others" shall be taken to mean A, B, and C; the probability of such events occurring shall be taken to be D; and the time frame in question shall be taken to be E. If you believe any of these interpretations to be improper, please inform me and I shall modify my procedures accordingly.

While such a statement may fail to endear the clinician to the judge, it is one way of attenuating the problems created when policy decisions fall by default upon his or her shoulders.

There is one final issue of professional ethics that will arise in all cases in which a clinical examination is performed. That issue concerns what to inform the examinee regarding the nature of the examination. Should the individual be informed of the reason he or she is being examined (e.g., civil commitment, parole, etc.), the potential consequences of the examination (e.g., 2 weeks in a mental hospital, an extended period of imprisonment), or the *level of confidentiality* that applies to what the individual reveals (e.g., a complete report to the judge and opposing as well as defense counsel)? The answer to each question, I would argue, is "yes." It is yes, not for reasons of *legal duty* (although such duties have been proposed), but rather for reasons of *professional ethics*. As a Task Force of the American Psychological Association (1978) recently stated:

One crucial point in addressing confidentiality, as in addressing other dilemmas of the psychologist's loyalty, is that all parties with a claim on the psychologist's loyalty be fully informed in advance of the existence of the confidentiality, or lack of it, and of any circumstances that may trigger an exception to the agreed-upon priorities. The individual being evaluated...then has the option of deciding what information to reveal and what risks to confidentiality he or she wishes to bear. (p. 1104)

The ethical standards of both the American Psychiatric Association and the American Psychological Association support such honesty in the interests of client welfare. Without this openness, individuals being interviewed only for the purpose of assessing their violence potential, for example, may mistakenly believe that they are in the process of receiving treatment for their psychic pains.

GIVEN MY ANSWERS TO THE ABOVE QUESTIONS, IS THIS CASE AN APPROPRIATE ONE IN WHICH TO OFFER A PREDICTION?

Should one conclude that a prediction is not actually being requested, that one is not professionally competent to offer predictive judgments, or that one's ethical beliefs preclude rendering a prediction in this type of case, it is both appropriate and essential to decline to offer a professional opinion in the matter and to return the referral to its source with an explanation for the action taken.

Should the issue of violence prediction arise in the course of treatment and should the mental health professional lack confidence in his or her own abilities in this area, prompt consultation with a more knowledgeable colleague may be necessary.

Assuming that the case is one in which a prediction is appropriate, the following questions become germane.

WHAT EVENTS PRECIPITATED RAISING THE QUESTION OF THE PERSON'S POTENTIAL FOR VIOLENCE AND IN WHAT CONTEXT DID THESE EVENTS TAKE PLACE?

It is advantageous to be clear at the outset about precisely what the person did, or was alleged to have done, to have made someone (e.g., police officer, judge) concerned about his or her potential to be violent in the future, and the social context in which these events took place. A meticulous examination of the "precipitating incident" may yield much information of value to making a prediction. Knowing exactly who said or did what may provide clues to the situational contexts in which the

individual reacts violently. Knowing, for example, that
the assault of one person upon another took place in the
context of a heated argument, but only after the victim
had begun to cast aspersions upon the assailant's job
performance, may raise the salience of job performance as
an item worthy of further exploration. Thus, as Kozol
(1975) has written:

> Of paramount importance is a meticulous
> description of the actual assault. The potential
> for violent assaultiveness is the core of our
> diagnostic problem, and the description of the
> aggressor in action is often the most valuable
> single source of information. The patient's version
> is compared with the victim's version. In many
> cases we interview the victim ourselves. Our most
> serious errors in diagnosis have been made when
> we ignored the details in the description of the
> assault. (p. 8)

WHAT ARE THE PERSON'S RELEVANT DEMOGRAPHIC CHARACTERISTICS?

Among the first and easiest factors on which one can
gather information are demographic ones. In which
relevant groups associated in a positive or negative way
with violent behavior does the individual hold
membership? There is evidence on the relationship
between several demographic variables and violent
behavior: (a) *age* (violence peaking in the late teens and
early 20s); (b) *sex* (males tending to be much more violent
than females); (c) *race* (nonwhites, and particularly blacks,
committing proportionately more "street" violence than
whites); (d) *social class* (the lower the SES, the more likely
the street violence); (e) *history of opiate or alcohol abuse*
(violence being more likely if such a history is present);
(f) *IQ* (the lower the estimated IQ, the more likely the
violence; (g) *educational attainment* (the less the education,
the more likely the violence); and (h) *residential and
employment stability* (violence being more likely among
those who move or change jobs frequently).

The inclusion of some predictive factors may make
others worthless in the clinical context. Thus, among

persons with an extensive history of past violence, the significance of race as a predictor is eliminated.

WHAT IS THE PERSON'S HISTORY OF VIOLENT BEHAVIOR?

This is one of the most important questions one can ask in prediction, and obtaining a satisfactory answer may not be as easy as it seems. A very thorough probing of all forms of past violence should be conducted, paying particular attention to the *recency, severity,* and *frequency* of violent acts (Fisher, Brodsky, & Corse, 1977). It should be noted whether the person's pattern of violent behavior appears to be escalating or declining. At least five indices of violence should be considered: (a) arrests and convictions for violent crimes; (b) juvenile court involvement for violent acts; (c) mental hospitalizations for dangerous behavior; (d) violence in the home, such as spouse and child abuse; and (e) other self-reported violent behavior such as bar fights, fights in school, arson, violent highway disputes, and perhaps violence toward animals. It should be noted in this regard that an *attempt* to kill often differs from an actual murder only by occurring in close proximity to a hospital. Open-ended questions, such as "What is the most violent thing you have ever done?" and "What is the closest you have ever come to being violent?" may be helpful (American Psychiatric Association, 1974).

WHAT IS THE BASE RATE OF VIOLENT BEHAVIOR AMONG INDIVIDUALS OF THIS PERSON'S BACKGROUND?

The base rate of violence is the most significant information one can obtain in making a prediction of violent behavior. In some instances the base rate is published information. In other cases, one can compute the base rate for oneself from available records (e.g., the base rate of violence on a mental hospital ward may be ascertained from a sample of hospital charts). In many circumstances, however, base rates are neither available nor readily obtainable. What is the base rate of violent behavior among persons referred by the police for civil commitment as dangerous to others on the basis of a recent overt act? Surely, it is not the same as the rate in the general population. Unless someone is willing to deny commitment to a portion of these persons to see how often, in fact, they are violent, their base rate will remain unknown.

What, then, is the clinician to do when confronted with the knowledge that the base rate is the most important single piece of information to have and yet he or she does not have it? One is left with Meehl's (1973) advice that, when actuarial data do not exist, we must use our heads. The clinician must estimate as reasonably, as judiciously, as wisely as possible what the approximate base rate would be. In so doing, one should always ask why the base rate of violence among persons similar to the person one is examining should be any higher than the general population rate. Having committed a recent overt act of violence, for example, may be one indicator that a higher-than-average base rate reasonably could be imputed to the individual.

WHAT ARE THE SOURCES OF STRESS IN THE PERSON'S CURRENT ENVIRONMENT?

WHAT COGNITIVE AND AFFECTIVE FACTORS INDICATE THAT THE PERSON MAY BE PREDISPOSED TO COPE WITH STRESS IN A VIOLENT MANNER?

WHAT COGNITIVE AND AFFECTIVE FACTORS INDICATE THAT THE PERSON MAY BE PREDISPOSED TO COPE WITH STRESS IN A NONVIOLENT MANNER?

Stress is a concept that may provide an organizing principle for many of the issues in violence prediction. Stress can be understood as a state of imbalance between the demands of the social and physical environment and the capabilities of an individual to cope with these demands (McGrath, 1970; Mechanic, 1968). The higher the ratio of demands to resources, the more stress is experienced. Stress is thus to be thought of in terms of transactions between persons and their environments over time (Lazarus & Launier, in press). The voluminous literature on stress and its regulation has been masterfully systematized by Novaco (1979). Novaco presents a model of anger arousal as one form of reacting to stress, and his model, with some modification, may provide a vehicle for explicating many (but not all) of the factors to be assessed in violence prediction (cf. also Levinson & Ramsay, 1979). It is presented in Figure 1 (p. 20).

Stressful or aversive events such as frustrations, annoyances, insults, and assaults by another are seen in this model as filtered through certain cognitive processes. Novaco conceptualizes these cognitive processes as being of two types: appraisals and expectations.

Appraisal refers to the manner in which an individual interprets an event as a provocation and, therefore, experiences it as aversive. Perceived intentionality is perhaps the clearest example of an antagonistic appraisal (e.g., "You didn't just bump into me, you *meant* to hit me"). How a person cognitively appraises an event may have a great influence on whether he or she ultimately responds to it in a violent manner. Some persons may be prone to interpret seemingly innocuous interactions as intentional slights. The chips on their shoulders may be precariously balanced.

Expectations are cognitive processes that may influence the occurrence of violence in several ways. If one expects a desired outcome (e.g., a raise in pay, an expression of gratitude for a favor done) and it fails to occur, emotional arousal may ensue, and, depending upon the context, such arousal may be perceived as anger. If one appraises an event as a provocation, the occurrence of violence may still depend upon whether one expects violence to be instrumental in righting the perceived wrong or whether one can expect violence to be met with a counterforce. One may, for example, regard having sand kicked in one's face as a deliberate affront and yet, upon learning that the agent of provocation is built like a football linebacker, have such low expectations for successful retaliation that violence is no longer under consideration. Alternatively, should the provacateur resemble Woody Allen, one's expectation that violence will prevail may rise accordingly.

Both expectations and appraisals may be reflected in the "private speech" or self-statements a person uses regarding violent behavior (e.g., "Anybody who insults my

A MODEL OF SOME OF THE FACTORS TO BE ASSESSED IN THE PREDICTION OF VIOLENT BEHAVIOR*

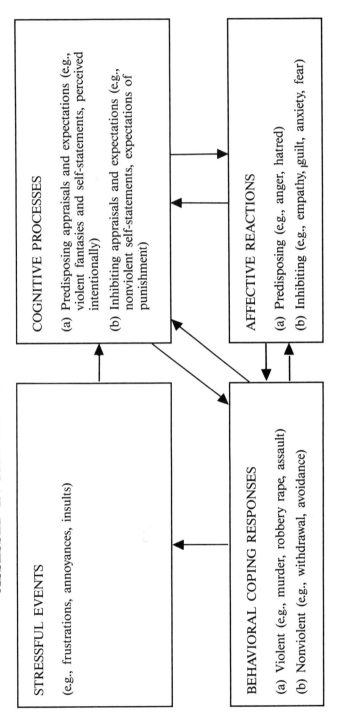

Figure 1.

*Adapted from Novaco (1979)

wife gets hit"). Violent delusions and fantasies may be thought of as extreme forms of such private conversations and statements of intention that are directly verbalized (i.e., threats of violence) may be particularly significant. For our purposes, appraisals and expectations may both be categorized as cognitive factors that "predispose" toward or "inhibit" violent behavior. These cognitive processes, in turn, may either give rise to certain affective or emotional reactions or may directly propel a behavioral response.

One need not be emotionally aroused to commit violent acts (e.g., the stereotypic "hitman" of *Godfather* fame). If, as is more typical, affective reactions intervene, they may be of a predisposing or an inhibiting type. Affective reactions predisposing a person toward violence would include the emotions of anger and hatred. While anger is not necessary for the occurrence of violent behavior, its arousal is a significant antecedent to aggression (Rule & Nesdale, 1976). Fortunately, excellent work on the clinical assessment of anger is currently available (Novaco, 1975, 1976, 1978, 1979). Affective reactions inhibiting violence (or, to put it more positively, predisposing toward peacefulness) include what have been called the "moral emotions" of empathy for the source of a frustration and guilt about injuring another, as well as anxiety reactions about engaging in violence or about the victim's possible retaliation. The lack of capacity for such affect has been viewed as the hallmark of the "sociopath" (Dinitz, 1978).

When an individual is in a state of alcohol or other drug-induced intoxication many factors that ordinarily would serve to inhibit violence may be suppressed. The likelihood of such suppression should be estimated.

These affective reactions are then behaviorally expressed in terms of a coping response which, for our purposes, may be dichotomized as violent or nonviolent. The type of response chosen may go on to influence further stressful events, as when a divorce eliminates interaction with a frustrating spouse or murder precipitates the stresses of imprisonment. Whether a given coping response attenuates or exacerbates further life stresses would have relevance to whether a given level of violence potential could be expected to increase or decrease. As Toch (1969) emphasized, violence may be thought of as interactional in nature. If one person's coping response (e.g., insulting a person perceived as a threat) leads the other to escalate his or her provocations, violence may eventually ensue.

Several of the relationships expressed in Figure 1 are *bidirectional* (as indicated by the arrows). This is meant to indicate that affective reactions can influence cognitive processes (e.g., "I feel so upset that I must be really angry") and that behavioral responses can affect both cognitions (e.g., "I hit him, therefore, I must want to hurt him") and emotions (e.g., "I avoided her, therefore, I must be angry at her").

The Novaco model of anger, as adapted here, is not exhaustive of the factors that influence violence. Demographic and historical factors, for example, are not addressed (hence, we inquire into them elsewhere in the assessment). But as a depiction of the cognitive and affective factors involved in violent behavior, the adapted Novaco model seems to capture well the essence of much of what must be assessed in violence prediction.

The kinds of stressors in which we are interested are those likely to be met with violent coping responses. While the kinds of stressors (e.g., frustrations, annoyances, insults, injuries) likely to result in violence are dependent upon the ways in which the individual cognitively and affectively processes them, and in fact may be thought of as fundamentally idiosyncratic in nature (see the next question), some general commonalities may exist among the kinds of situational demands likely to lead to violence. Based on an analysis of the situational correlates of violent behavior (Monahan & Klassen, 1982), at least three broad areas of concern suggest themselves.

1. *Family stressors.* The frustrations and annoyances attendant to husband-wife and parent-child relationships, as many have noted, appear particularly susceptible to violent resolution. An assessment of the individual's current living situation and the quality of social interactions involved would appear to be a priority.

2. *Peer group stressors.* Analogous to the family as a source of stress, the relationships of the individual

to persons he or she considers, or until recently has considered, friends may be germane. The disruption of friendship patterns can instigate stress. In addition, the role of peers as models for violent behavior (Bandura, 1969, 1973) and as sources of social support for violent and nonviolent life styles (President's Commission on Mental Health, 1978) suggests that peer relations be carefully investigated.

3. *Employment stressors.* While often overlooked, the stress associated with unemployment or with aversive employment situations may have a significant effect upon criminal behavior. These stressors may take the form of a recent firing, disputes with superiors or co-workers, or dissatisfaction with the nature of the work performed or the level of compensation paid for it.

HOW SIMILAR ARE THE CONTEXTS IN WHICH THE PERSON HAS USED VIOLENT COPING MECHANISMS IN THE PAST TO THE CONTEXTS IN WHICH THE PERSON LIKELY WILL FUNCTION IN THE FUTURE?

The prediction model suggested by Bem and Funder (1978) would lead a clinician to assess two things: (a) the characteristics of the situations in which the person tends to react violently; and (b) the characteristics of the situations in which the person is likely to be functioning in the future. The third step (c) would then be to estimate the degree of similarity between these two kinds of situations. The greater the similarity, the higher the probability of violent behavior occurring. It was noted that this approach is conducive to offering differential predictions, such as that the person has X probability of violence in situations typified by A, B, and C, and Y probability in situations typified by D, E, and F. Such predictions may prove useful in deciding among various forms of placement.

Another way of making the same point may be to reconstruct the pattern of violent behavior in the individual's past and to ascertain whether it is likely to repeat itself. Did the person become violent in the past when he or she was ending a relationship, or in a "manic" state, or when unemployed for several months, or when under the influence of alcohol or other drugs? If reliably so, is he or she now or in the near future likely to be ending a relationship, or in a "manic" state, or unemployed for several months, or under the influence of alcohol or other drugs? Note that one is here individualizing the situational and personality bases for prediction. It is not that all people or even most people react violently in the given situations, but rather that this *particular* person, when confronted in the past with this *particular* constellation of events, has evidenced a pattern of violent behavior. Likewise for dispositional states: It is not that psychological disorder is associated with violence, but rather that this *particular* person, when experiencing this *particular* disorder, has tended to react violently in the past. While individualizing predictions in this manner may be a researcher's nightmare, it may also constitute an occasion in which the value of clinical judgment is maximized.

IN PARTICULAR, WHO ARE THE LIKELY VICTIMS OF THE PERSON'S VIOLENT BEHAVIOR, AND HOW AVAILABLE ARE THEY?

In line with the above, one may wish to single out for special attention the likely victims of a person's violent behavior. As an initial step, the demographic composition of the past-victim pool (e.g., women, the elderly) should be ascertained and, to the extent possible, an account constructed of the cognitive and affective factors motivating the individual to choose them rather than others as victims. For example, the past-victim pool may have been limited to males who cast aspersions upon the individual's sense of masculinity, to a particular person such as a spouse or child, or it may have been the indiscriminate choice of the next person encountered (Shah, 1978).

One would then wish to know how likely the environments in which the person will function in the future are to contain persons of similar characteristics. In situations in which a large class of persons forms the potential victim pool (e.g., women in the case of a rapist), there will surely be many persons at risk for potential victimization. But where only one or a small group of persons is the target of potential violence, the unavailability of those persons may preclude violent behavior. Thus, a father guilty of forced incest may desist from violence when his daughter is older. Removal of the potential victim (e.g., spouse or adolescent child) from the family through separating residences may decrease the frequency of interaction and, hence, the probability of violence.

In ascertaining the likely victims of an individual's violence, much attention should be given to those who are the expressed targets of fantasized, threatened, or planned violence, or who elicit strong negative emotions such as anger. In particular, it should be noted whether or not the potential victims are family members.

As Toch (1969) noted, the reaction of the potential victim of violence may distinguish a verbal altercation from a murder, and in certain circumstances this reaction may also be foreseeable (e.g., if the potential victim, as well as the potential offender, is likely to be armed).

WHAT MEANS DOES THE PERSON POSSESS TO COMMIT VIOLENCE?

As in the case of assessing suicide potential, the availability of lethal means of stress reduction may be noteworthy. Both the person's dispositional capability to do harm (e.g., physical strength, expertise in combat or the martial arts), and his or her proclivity to make use of access to external aids for harm infliction (e.g., guns, knives) should be inquired into. In particular, the recent acquisition of a weapon in furtherance of violent cognitions or in response to violent affect may be significant. The deluded person who has just bought a gun for protection against fantasized aggressors, or the easily enraged person who purchases a hunting knife to deter further annoyances, may require special attention.

SUMMARY

The 14 questions comprising a "reasonable guide" to predicting violent behavior are present in Table 1 (p. 26).

TABLE 1: QUESTIONS FOR THE CLINICIAN IN PREDICTING VIOLENT BEHAVIOR

1. Is it a prediction of violent behavior that is being requested?

2. Am I professionally competent to offer an estimate of the probability of future violence?

3. Are there any issues of personal or professional ethics involved in this case?

4. Given my answers to the above questions, is this case an appropriate one in which to offer a prediction?

5. What events precipitated the question of the person's potential for violence being raised, and in what context did these events take place?

6. What are the person's relevant demographic characteristics?

7. What is the person's history of violent behavior?

8. What is the base rate of violent behavior among individuals of this person's background?

9. What are the sources of stress in the person's current environment?

10. What cognitive and affective factors indicate that the person may be predisposed to cope with stress in a violent manner?

11. What cognitive and affective factors indicate that the person may be predisposed to cope with stress in a nonviolent manner?

12. How similar are the contexts in which the person has used violent coping mechanisms in the past to the contexts in which the person likely will function in the future?

13. In particular, who are the likely victims of the person's violent behavior, and how available are they?

14. What means does the person possess to commit violence?

After having considered these 14 questions, it would be appropriate for the clinician to review the answers obtained with four "reliability" questions:

Can I be sure that the information I have obtained is accurate?

It is advisable to corroborate as much of the information as possible. This can be done, within the limits of confidentiality and legality, by verifying the factors elicited in the clinical examination with other sources knowledgeable about particular facets of the case. The police may have the individual's arrest records, the hospital may have his or her commitment record, and a spouse or friend may confirm, refute, or add detail to what has been said by the individual being examined. Without such corroboration, the trustworthiness of the information upon which a decision is to be based may be questionable. "In this sense the telephone, the written request for past records, and the checking of information against other informants are the important diagnostic devices" (Scott, 1977, p. 129).

While no formula can be offered as to how to score and combine what a person reveals on the various dimensions of the examination, the several admonitions given previously should be kept in mind during the process of arriving at a clinical estimate of violence potential. The following three questions may help in doing this:

Am I giving adequate attention to what I estimate the base rate of violent behavior to be among persons similarly situated to the person being examined?

What evidence do I have that the particular factors I have relied upon as predictors are in fact predictive of violent behavior (e.g., are illusory correlations being avoided)?

Am I giving a balanced consideration to factors indicating the absence of violent behavior, as well as to factors indicating its occurrence?

Finally, while professional peer review is becoming accepted practice for psychiatric or psychological treatment, there appears to be less emphasis on the peer review of clinical assessments. The development of some formal means for obtaining the opinion of colleagues in difficult cases of violence prediction appears a highly worthwhile endeavor. How do others rate the sources of stress in the person's environment? What is their best estimate of the relevant base rates? Consultation with colleagues on such issues may do much to improve the reliability of clinical predictions of violent behavior and may be a source of mutual professional education.

Particular attention should be paid to organizational contingencies and their associated demands which may bias clinical assessments in a conservative "better safe than sorry" direction.

A CASE STUDY

To illustrate how the questions presented above might be used to facilitate the clinical examination of a given case, a case will be described, the questions answered, and a report presented. The case is hypothetical. It should be noted that the examination and report are for the purpose of predicting violent behavior *only*. Additional issues that are often addressed by a mental health professional, such as the presence of psychological disorder or recommendations concerning treatment, are not considered (see Roth, 1978). The examination and report should be modified to consider such questions when they are of concern.

The case is that of Mr. Smith, a person who was civilly committed as "dangerous to others" under an emergency commitment statute, and who, several days later, desires his release on the grounds that he is not, in fact, "dangerous." The hospital staff, believing otherwise, wishes to have him remain in the hospital for an additional period of treatment. A judge requests a mental health professional not on the hospital staff to assess the individual's potential for violent behavior and to submit a report of the findings. The specific facts of the case are as follows.

Mr. Smith is a 20-year-old male who has never married and who dropped out of school in the ninth grade. His IQ is estimated to be in the dull-normal range. He has been residentially unstable, living at six different addresses since being discharged from the Marines 2 years ago.

The police report accompanying the commitment form states that they received a call from an employee of the N T Company saying that Mr. Smith had gone "berserk" and was threatening his supervisor. When the police arrived they found Mr. Smith with a crowbar in his hand threatening to kill Mr. Brown, his supervisor. Mr. Smith appeared to be either drunk or otherwise "high" and was described as "incoherent and bizarre." When Mr. Smith broke the window of the office into which Mr. Brown had fled, the police forcibly subdued him.

During the evaluation interview, Mr. Smith stated that Mr. Brown had told him when he was hired that he could progress rapidly through the ranks of the company. At the time of the incident, 1 month after being hired, Mr. Smith was still on the assembly line and felt that he had been deceived. When Mr. Brown criticized Mr. Smith for arriving at work several hours late and being in a state of intoxication, Mr. Smith became enraged. Thereupon, Mr. Brown fired him, and Mr. Smith picked up the crowbar.

Mr. Smith appeared very frustrated that he had not achieved a higher level of responsibility at his job. He wanted both the prestige and money that would go with advancement and felt cheated that he had not received them.

During the interview, Mr. Smith stated that he would like to get even with Mr. Brown, and that he would love to get him alone for just 5 minutes. He stated that he had thought about nothing else while in the hospital and that he did not know how he could give Mr. Brown "what he has coming to him" other than by physically assaulting him.

Mr. Smith appeared very agitated at the mention of Mr. Brown's name and readily volunteered that he was still enraged at how Mr. Brown had treated him.

Mr. Smith stated that he did not want to go to jail or return to the hospital for injuring Mr. Brown. He also stated that he realized Mr. Brown "had a job to get done" at the plant but that he did not think his arriving late for work on occasion should bother Mr. Brown as much as it did. He stated that he felt sorry that he had threatened some of his co-workers in his attempt to reach Mr. Brown.

His police record revealed that Mr. Smith had been arrested three times during the past 4 years, once for aggravated assault, once for simple assault, and once for public intoxication. He received a suspended sentence for the first incident, charges were modified to "disturbing the peace" in the second incident, and he served a few days in the county jail on the final charge. When asked to describe the previous assaults, he stated someone tried to "push me around and put me down in front of my friends." He admitted that he had been drinking heavily prior to both assaults.

Now let us apply the questions to the clinician in this case.

Is it a prediction of violent behavior that is being requested?

I am clearly being requested to offer an assessment of the likelihood of violent behavior toward others and not, for example, of competence to stand trial or criminal responsibility.

Am I professionally competent to offer an estimate of the probability of future violence?

In addition to being knowledgeable about the general topic of the clinical prediction of violent behavior (e.g., I have read the American Psychiatric Association, 1974, report; Cohen et al., 1978; Kozol et al., 1972), I have read Monahan's (1981) monograph on the prediction of violent behavior and several current articles on the topic in professional journals. I recently attended a continuing education seminar on civil commitment procedures in my state and believe I understand them. I am unaware of personal biases that would compromise my abilities to evaluate this case. In all, I believe that offering a prediction in a case like this is within the realm of mental health expertise and that I am professionally competent to do so.

Are there any issues of personal or professional ethics involved in this case?

To participate in a short-term civil commitment decision does not threaten to compromise my ethical integrity, nor are the factors I will clinically rely upon to predict violent behavior in this case morally problematic.

I *am* bothered by the fact that neither statutory nor

case law provides me with a definition of violent behavior, a statement of the time frame of concern, or a threshold probability of violence necessary to invoke civil commitment. Therefore, I will specify that what I am predicting is "serious, unjustified bodily harm" within the next 2 weeks, and I will simply state the probability figure I arrive at. It will then be up to the judge to do with this information what he or she will.

Given my answers to the above questions, is this case an appropriate one in which to offer a prediction?
Offering a prediction in this case does indeed appear to be appropriate.

What events precipitated the question of the person's potential for violence being raised, and in what context did these events take place?
He was picked up by the police for threatening his supervisor. This took place while the examinee was intoxicated and after he had been reprimanded for poor work performance.

What are the person's relevant demographic characteristics?
He is a 20-year-old, never-married male high school drop out. His IQ is dull-normal. He has a history of alcohol problems but no involvement with other drugs. His residential and employment history have been unstable.

What is the person's history of violent behavior?
His history, with two arrests for violent acts in addition to the current incident, is fairly extensive.

What is the base rate of violent behavior among individuals of this person's background?
To my knowledge (and I have sought such information), no base rates of violent behavior among persons with whom I would group Mr. Smith are available. Extrapolating from the most relevant pieces of research and based on my own clinical experience, my best estimate of the base rate of violent behavior among persons such as Mr. Smith is in the range of 30%.

What are the sources of stress in the person's current environment?

He is frustrated at not being able to achieve unrealistically high job advancement with little effort on his part. He feels bitter and cheated by his lack of advancement and attributes responsibility for this to Mr. Brown.

What cognitive and affective factors indicate that the person may be predisposed to cope with stress in a violent manner?

He is in an acute state of emotional arousal which he labels as anger. He readily expresses violent fantasies toward Mr. Brown.

What cognitive and affective factors indicate that the person may be predisposed to cope with stress in a nonviolent manner?

He expresses fear of being institutionalized if he assaults Mr. Brown and some empathy for his co-workers who were threatened during the precipitating incident.

How similar are the contexts in which the person has used violent coping mechanisms in the past to the contexts in which the person likely will function in the future?

Mr. Smith's past assaultive behavior occurred in contexts that could be characterized as including the presence of an authority figure, a reprimand or humiliation in the presence of peers, and a state of intoxication on the part of Mr. Smith. These factors are likely to be present in the immediate future, since Mr. Smith is intent on returning to his former place of employment to confront Mr. Brown as soon as he is released.

In particular, who are the likely victims of the person's violent behavior, and how available are they?

Plainly, Mr. Brown is the likely victim, and both his place of work and home address are known to Mr. Smith.

What means does the person possess to commit violence?

Mr. Smith, as an ex-Marine, is trained in methods of assault.

A CLINICAL REPORT

The following is the form a report might take based upon the above examination:

Judge Jane Doe
County Court House

Dear Judge Doe:

This letter reports my evaluation of the likelihood that Mr. J. Smith (Case No 1234) will inflict serious bodily harm upon another person during the next 2-week period. This evaluation was done in response to the court's request for information relevant to the issue of whether Mr. Smith's petition for release from the County Medical Center Psychiatric Unit should be granted. Mr. Smith has been involuntarily committed for a 72-hour observation period under Section 5150, and the hospital wishes to continue his commitment for an additional 14 days of intensive treatment. Mr. Smith, through his attorney, contests the allegation that he constitutes a continuing "danger to others."

I interviewed Mr. Smith at the Medical Center for approximately 1 hour on Monday, August 14. I informed him of the purpose of the examination before it began. I also read Mr. Smith's hospital records and the written police report on him. I discussed Mr. Smith's case with the ward staff.

Mr. Smith is a 20-year-old, never-married, male who appears to be of dull-normal intelligence. He has been intermittently employed as a factory worker since dropping out of high school in the ninth grade several years ago. At the time of his commitment, he had been working on the assembly line at the N T Company for a period of 1 month.

His police record reveals that he has been arrested three times during the past 4 years—once for aggravated assault, once for simple assault, and once for public intoxication. He received a suspended sentence for the first incident, charges were modified to disturbing the peace in the second incident, and he served several days in the county jail on the final charge. His hospital record reveals no prior hospitalizations. He admits to several school suspensions for fighting and several barroom altercations that did not result in an arrest.

The police report filed for the incident precipitating his commitment states that the police responded to a call from a supervisor at the N T Company on Friday, August 11. When they arrived they found Mr. Smith with a crowbar in his hand threatening to kill a Mr. Brown, his foreman. Mr. Brown had barricaded himself into an office. Mr. Smith appeared to the officers to be intoxicated from alcohol or some other substance and his screaming at Mr. Brown was described as "incoherent" and "bizarre." The officers failed to talk him into putting down the metal bar, and, when he broke the window on the door of the office into which Mr. Brown had fled, the police forcibly subdued him and brought him to the Medical Center.

During the interview, Mr. Smith was clearly upset at the incident. He raised his voice frequently and began to pace the room. He stated that Mr. Brown had told him when he was hired that he could progress through the ranks of the company "all the way to the top," if he had the ability and the energy. Now, 1 month later, he was still on the assembly line "going nowhere." He blamed Mr. Brown for his predicament and said that Mr. Brown was deliberately "holding me down" so that his superior talents would go unnoticed and not become a source of competition to Mr. Brown himself. When Mr. Brown criticized Mr. Smith for arriving at work several hours late and appearing in a state of intoxication, Mr. Smith states that he "just saw red" and told the foreman that he could do a better job drunk and in half the time than the foreman could ever do. Mr. Brown thereupon fired Mr. Smith and ordered him out of the plant. At that point, Mr. Smith said that he "went wild" and began chasing Mr. Brown with the iron bar.

During the interview, Mr. Smith repeatedly and with much anger referred to his former foreman as "that _____." He states that Mr. Brown "has not heard the end of this—not by a long shot" and that "nobody makes a fool of me and gets away with it." When asked directly whether he intended to harm Mr. Brown, Mr. Smith was evasive and would only reply "we'll see, we'll see." He intends to confront Mr. Brown at his first opportunity. He denied owning a gun but stated that he had easy access to the gun of a friend. The ward staff confirmed his state of acute agitation.

Based upon the above data, in particular upon his demographic profile, his history of violent behavior including a recent overt act of violence, his currently stressful employment situation, his alcohol-suppressed inhibitions, and his acute and clearly unresolved hostility toward Mr. Brown, it is my professional opinion that Mr. Smith is more likely than not to inflict serious bodily harm upon another person within the next 2-week period. That other person is likely to be Mr. Brown.

CONCLUSION

A study recently published in the *Stanford Law Review* (Wise, 1978) surveyed over 1,200 psychologists and psychiatrists in California concerning the issue of "dangerous behavior." Eighty percent of the responding mental health professionals saw at least one patient per year whom they considered to be "potentially dangerous." The mean number of potentially dangerous patients seen per year was 14. Despite the prevalence of violence prediction as an issue of clinical concern—arising an average of more than once per month for psychiatrists and psychologists throughout the state—the clinicians "found it difficult to articulate their standards. Typically, they said that they based their decisions on 'clinical judgment that the threat was serious' or that they 'believed' the patient was 'clearly dangerous' and likely to 'act on the threat' (78.2% of those stating their criteria)" (p. 181).

It was to assist in articulating standards that this chapter was written. Yet, even those most adept at prediction will be hard pressed not to let themselves be influenced by the contingencies operating in the clinical situation. The Stanford survey tried to assess the effects of the *Tarasoff* decision (*Tarasoff v. Regents of the University of California*, 1976)—that psychiatrists and psychologists may be liable for the violent acts of patients they predict, or *should* predict, to be violent—on the clinical practice of the 1,200 therapists who responded to their survey.

One quarter of the therapists who responded to the survey said that they were now giving more attention in their therapy sessions to the possibility of their patients' violent behavior. Almost as many said that the ruling led them to focus more frequently on less serious threats made by their patients. One-third of the psychiatrists and psychologists surveyed increased the frequency with which they consulted with colleagues concerning cases in which violence was an issue, and over half reported an increase in their own anxiety concerning the entire topic of dangerousness as a result of the *Tarasoff* decision. Unfortunately, the survey also revealed that as a result of *Tarasoff* almost one-fifth of the respondents had decided to *avoid* asking questions that could yield information bearing on the likelihood of violent behavior by their patients. Even more reported that they had changed their record-keeping procedures in an effort to avoid legal liability they might otherwise incur as a result of *Tarasoff*. "Some therapists ceased keeping detailed records; others began keeping *more* detailed records, including information that might justify any decisions they made and thereby trying to create a favorable evidentiary record for future litigation" (Wise, 1978, p. 182).

The prediction of violent behavior is difficult under the best of circumstances. It becomes more so when powerful social contingencies pull and push the clinician, now in one direction, then in another. But such is likely to be the case for the foreseeable future, until the patient's right not to be a false positive and the victim's right not be set upon by a false negative are balanced in the courts and legislatures of the land.

John Monahan, Ph.D., a psychologist, is Professor of Law, Psychology, and Legal Medicine at the University of Virginia School of Law and Associate Director of the University's Institute of Law, Psychiatry, and Public Policy. Dr. Monahan has been a Fellow in Law and Psychology at the Stanford and Harvard Law Schools and was a member of the Panel on Legal Issues of the President's Commission on Mental Health and the Panel on Offender Rehabilitation of the National Academy of Sciences. His most recent book, *The Clinical Prediction of Violent Behavior*, from which the present chapter was adapted, won the Manfred Guttmacher Award of the American Psychiatric Association in 1982.

RESOURCES

American Psychiatric Association. (1974). *Clinical Aspects of the Violent Individual.* Washington, DC: Author.

American Psychological Association. (1978). Report of the Task Force on the Role of Psychology in the Criminal Justice System. *American Psychologist, 33,* 1099-1113.

Bandura, A. (1969). *Principles of Behavior Modification.* New York: Holt, Rinehart & Winston.

Bandura, A. (1973). *Aggression: A Social Learning Analysis.* Englewood Cliffs, NJ: Prentice-Hall.

Bem, D., & Funder, D. (1978). Predicting more of the people more of the time: Assessing the personality of situation. *Psychological Review, 85,* 485-501.

Cohen, M., Groth, A., & Siegel, R. (1978). The clinical prediction of dangerousness. *Crime and Delinquency, 24,* 28-39.

Dinitz, S. (1978). Chronically antisocial offenders. In J. Conrad & S. Dinitz (Eds.), *In Fear of Each Other: Studies of Dangerousness in America* (pp. 21-42). Lexington, MA: Lexington Books.

Farmer, L. (1977). *Observation and Study: Critique and Recommendations of Federal Procedures.* Unpublished report, Federal Judicial Center, Washington, DC.

Fisher, B., Brodsky, S., & Corse, S. (1977). *Monitoring and Classification Guidelines and Procedures.* Unpublished Report, Department of Psychology, University of Alabama.

Fisher, R. (1976). *Factors Influencing the Prediction of Dangerousness: Authoritarianism, Dogmatism, and Data Quality.* Unpublished doctoral dissertation, Department of Psychology, University of Alabama.

Geller, J., & Lister, E. (1978). The process of criminal commitment for pre-trial psychiatric examination and evaluation. *American Journal of Psychiatry, 135,* 53-58.

Kozol, H. (1975). The diagnosis of dangerousness. In S. Pasternack (Ed.), *Violence and Victims* (pp. 3-13). New York: Spectrum.

Kozol, H., Boucher, R., & Garofalo, R. (1972). The diagnosis and treatment of dangerousness. *Crime and Delinquency, 18,* 371-392.

Lazarus, R., & Launier, R. (in press). Stress-related transactions between persons and environment. In L. Pervin & M. Lewis (Eds.), *Internal and External Determinants of Behavior.* New York: Plenum.

Levinson, R., & Ramsay, G. (1979). Dangerousness, stress, and mental health evaluations. *Journal of Health and Social Behavior, 20,* 178-187.

Loftus, E., & Monahan, J. (1980). Trial by data: Psychological research as legal evidence. *American Psychologist, 35,* 270-283.

McGrath, J. (1970). *Social and Psychological Factors in Stress.* New York: Holt, Rinehart & Winston.

Mechanic, D. (1968). *Medical Sociology: A Selective View.* New York: Free Press.

Meehl, P. (1973). *Psychodiagnosis: Selected Papers.* Minneapolis: University of Minnesota Press.

Megargee, E. (1976). The prediction of dangerous behavior. *Criminal Justice and Behavior, 3,* 3-21.

Monahan, J. (1981). *The Clinical Prediction of Violent Behavior.* Washington, DC: U. S. Government Printing Office.

Monahan, J., & Klassen, D. (1982). Situational approaches to understanding and predicting individual violent behavior. In M. Wolfgang & N. Weiner (Eds.), *Criminal Violence* (pp. 292-319). Beverly Hills: Sage.

Monahan, J., & Wexler, D. (1978). A definite maybe: Proofs and probability in civil commitment. *Law and Human Behavior, 2,* 37-42.

Novaco, R. (1975). *Anger Control: The Development and Evaluation of an Experimental Treatment.* Lexington, MA: Lexington Books.

Novaco, R. (1976). The function and regulation of the arousal of anger. *American Journal of Psychiatry, 133,* 1124-1128.

Novaco, R. (1978). Anger and coping with stress. In J. Foreyt & D. Rathjen (Eds.), *Cognitive Behavior Therapy: Theory, Research, and Practice* (pp. 133-195). New York: Plenum.

Novaco, R. (1979). The cognitive regulation of anger and stress. In P. Kendall & S. Hollon (Eds.), *Cognitive-Behavioral Interventions: Theory, Research, and Procedures* (pp. 241-285). New York: Academic Press.

President's Commission on Mental Health. (1978). *Report to the President.* Washington, DC: U. S. Government Printing Office.

Roth, L. (1978). Clinical and legal considerations in the therapy of violence-prone patients. In J. Masserman (Ed.), *Current Psychiatric Therapies* (pp. 55-63). New York: Grune & Stratton.

Rule, B, & Nesdale, A. (1976). Emotional arousal and aggressive behavior. *Psychological Bulletin, 83,* 851-863.

Scott, P. (1977). Assessing dangerousness in criminals. *British Journal of Psychiatry, 313,* 127-142.

Shah, S. (1978). Dangerousness and mental illness: Some conceptual, prediction and policy dilemmas. In C. Frederick (Ed.), *Dangerous Behavior: A Problem in Law and Mental Health* (NIMH, DHEW Publication No. ADM 78-563, pp. 153-191). Washington, DC: U. S. Government Printing Office.

Tarasoff v. Regents of the University of California, 131 Cal.Rptr. 14 (1976).

Toch, H. (1969). *Violent Men.* Chicago: Aldine.

Wise, T. (1978). Where the public peril begins: A survey of psychotherapists to determine the effects of Tarasoff. *Stanford Law Review, 31,* 165-190.

CLINICAL EVALUATION OF COMPETENCE TO STAND TRIAL

Stephen B. Lawrence

Competency to stand trial and insanity are two completely separate legal concepts and refer to a defendant's specific mental capacity at two separate points in time. In criminal cases in which the insanity issue has been raised, the legal question asked is: "What was the defendant's state of mind at the time of the commission of the alleged offense?" In cases involving competency to stand trial, two different legal questions are asked: (a) Does the defendant presently have the mental capacity to understand the nature and purpose of the proceedings taken against him or her? (b) Does the defendant have the mental capacity to collaborate with his or her attorney in his or her own defense or to prepare and conduct his or her own defense? An individual who meets the specific legal criteria for insanity may or may not be currently mentally competent to stand trial, and vice versa.

Most jurisdictions allow the issue of incapacity to be raised at any point in the criminal proceedings by either the defense or prosecuting attorneys or the presiding judge. Typically, two qualified mental health professionals are then either selected or appointed by the judge to examine the defendant and render an opinion as to whether the defendant is currently mentally competent to stand trial. On a split decision, a third forensic mental health expert may be appointed to "break the tie." Should the presiding judge then rule that the defendant is so intellectually or psychologically impaired as to be incompetent to stand trial, criminal proceedings are suspended and the defendant is remanded to an appropriate mental health facility until competency has been restored.

HISTORICAL PERSPECTIVES

The issue of competency to stand trial had its origin in early English law. In the 9th century, criminal trial judges adopted the practice of excusing deaf mutes from trial on the ground that to try individuals who could neither hear the charges nor make a plea would detract from the dignity, decorum, and symbolic value of the proceedings and violate the protection against unfair or inhumane prosecution (Walker, 1968). Under this early standard, the decision to excuse the defendant from trial depended upon others, usually the family, demonstrating to the court that the defendant had been unable to hear or speak from early childhood. Typically, the testimony of an expert examiner was not required.

In the 18th century, English courts broadened the incompetency standard to include individuals judged to be insane at the time of the trial. With this revision, which equated incompetency with insanity, English courts began the practice of basing their decision upon information provided by mental examiners. Following the legal practice of their time, physicians equated incompetency with insanity and established the practice of inferring competency from an assessment of the accused's mental processes of perception, thinking, and memory.

Early in the 19th century, English judges again revised the common-law standard for competency. The new standard defined competency as the ability to understand the nature and purposes of the proceedings and to rationally assist counsel in conducting the defense (Walker, 1968). This revision represented a significant departure from the earlier standard which simply equated incompetency with insanity. Under the new definition, additional aspects of the accused's cognitive status entered into the determination and it became legally

.

possible for an individual to be viewed as psychotic and competent, or not psychotic but nevertheless incompetent. This 19th century standard has now been adopted in virtually all American criminal jurisdictions (Janis, 1974). Despite this significant revision of the competency standard, however, many mental health professionals have continued to equate incompetency and insanity.

McGarry (1965), for example, concluded from a study of incompetent hospital patients that mental health examiners uniformly viewed psychotics as incompetent to stand trial. Roesch (1979), in a study of procedures for evaluating competency, found that incompetent defendants were typically viewed as psychotic or mentally retarded, whereas competent defendants were usually viewed as nonpsychotic. Both McGarry and Roesch found that reports of mental health professionals typically described a defendant's symptoms of mental illness and then generalized from the symptoms to inferences about competency. Robey (1965) and Bukatman, Foy, and DeGrazia (1971) have reported that mental health professionals often fail to mention competency in their reports to the court and refer only to the presence of mental illness and the need for hospitalization.

In 1960, the United States Supreme Court attempted to clarify the issues involved in competency matters and to provide mental health examiners some guidance in conducting competency evaluations. In *Dusky v. United States* (1960), the Court stated that:

> It is not enough...to find that the defendant is oriented to time and place and has some recollection of events. [T]he test must be whether he has sufficient present ability to consult with his lawyer with a reasonable degree of rational understanding and whether he has a rational as well as a factual understanding of the proceedings against him. (p. 402)

This statement has been interpreted to mean that the presence of psychosis or mental retardation is not a sufficient criterion for a finding of incompetency and that the accused's rational and factual understanding of the proceedings and ability to assist counsel in a rational manner must be the focus of assessment (Comment, 1967; Eizenstat, 1968; Pollack, 1973).

THEORETICAL PERSPECTIVES

Traditionally, Anglo-American courts have turned to mental health professionals for help in deciding which set of legal rules to apply in criminal trials involving the issue of competency. Although often unrecognized, the question asked by courts in their requests for competency examinations is not whether the accused is mentally ill or mentally retarded, but whether the accused differs sufficiently from other accused individuals, with respect to the criteria specified in the legal standard for competency, to warrant the application of a different set of rules to the proceeding (Morse, 1978). In making such requests, courts presume mental health professionals will apply special methods of observation, not ordinarily available to the judge or jury, which will reveal information concerning whether the accused does or does not differ from other accused individuals.

From a psychometric point of view, two theoretical approaches might be taken in conceptualizing competency. The first, suggested by Roesch (1979), involves a construct validation approach. From this perspective, competency to stand trial, like intelligence, may be viewed as a hypothetical construct which postulates a trait or attribute possessed by people and differentially demonstrated in performance (Cronbach & Meehl, 1955). The empirical question here would be the extent to which the construct of competency constitutes a valid inference or hypothesis in explaining differential performance among defendants. This approach would be appropriate to determining whether or not competency to stand trial is a valid psychological construct and to the task of psychological theory building.

The second approach to conceptualizing competency derives from an analysis of the legal definition, which states that competency consists of an understanding of the nature and purposes of the proceedings and the ability to assist counsel in a rational manner (*Dusky v. United States*, 1960). This definition focuses on cognitive variables

(Group for the Advancement of Psychiatry, 1974) and emphasizes knowledge, understanding, and skills (Bloom, Englehart, Furst, Hill, & Krathwohl, 1956). From this perspective, competency may be viewed as a body of knowledge and understanding regarding the nature and purposes of legal proceedings and of the role of counsel in conducting a defense. The task of assessment would be to sample this domain of content to determine whether the defendant differs from other defendants (Nunnally, 1967). Under this approach, an instrument which compares a subject's knowledge and understanding of courtroom procedures and the role of counsel with that of other criminal defendants might be expected to provide the type of information needed by courts in making discretionary judgments in competency matters.

EMPIRICAL PERSPECTIVES

Long overshadowed by the philosophically attractive issue of criminal responsibility, the adjudication of competency to stand trial has been a low visibility aspect of the judicial decision making process and has received little attention in the professional literature (Group for the Advancement of Psychiatry, 1974; Morris & Hawkins, 1970). Yet, in terms of the frequency with which the two issues are raised in criminal trials and the number of individual lives affected by them, competency is a considerably more significant issue. Stone (1975) has characterized competency as the most frequent mental health issue pursued in the American legal system. Morris and Hawkins (1970) have reported that the insanity defense is raised in less than 2% of all criminal cases that come to trial. Scheidemandel and Kanno (1969) have reported that in 1967, 52% of all persons committed to state mental institutions were there for assessment or treatment of incompetency while only 4% were there for reasons relating to criminal responsibility. In a Massachusetts study, McGarry (1971) found that during 1970 there were no commitments involving the insanity defense but that 2,101 persons were committed for pretrial assessment of competency.

In a field study for the American Bar Association, Matthews (1970) conducted a comprehensive survey of legal and mental health practices regarding competency in selected American criminal jurisdictions. Matthews noted large discrepancies between legal principles and actual practices as well as a lack of uniformity among jurisdictions. Other studies have focused on the use of the competency rule for purposes other than determination of the accused's fitness to stand trial. Hess and Thomas (1963), Matthews (1970), and Cooke, Johnston, and Pogany (1973) have all found that competency proceedings have been used to find dispositional alternatives in cases involving individuals viewed as somehow deviant and as a "catchall" for cases where competency was not a valid issue but there seemed to be no other dispositional alternative.

McGarry (1969) and Pollack (1973) have noted that competency proceedings have been used to achieve preventive detention without having to comply with the more rigorous rules governing civil commitment. In a study of 148 men committed as incompetent, McGarry (1971) found that the average length of hospitalization was 14.9 years and that three individuals had been in the hospital for 40, 36, and 17 years respectively. Both Szasz (1963) and Ennis (1972) have reported case studies of individuals whom they felt had been detained in mental hospitals for long periods of time under the guise of incompetency in order to avoid the more difficult issue of civil commitability. It should be noted, however, that in *Jackson v. Indiana* (1972) the United States Supreme Court ruled that incompetent individuals may not be confined for more than a reasonable period of time to determine their potential for restoration to competency. The legal implications of this decision have been discussed in detail by Pollack (1973) and Janis (1974).

Eizenstat (1968) has alleged that attorneys often invoke the competency issue as a means of gathering information about the accused or as a substitute for trial on the sanity issue. In a questionnaire survey of judges and attorneys in North Carolina, Roesch (1978) found that many attorneys did, in fact, initiate competency proceedings in order to obtain mental health data useful in such diverse areas as laying the foundation for an insanity defense, obtaining a plea bargain, identifying dispositional alternatives to sentencing, and preparing a motion to dismiss the charges. In another study, Roesch (1979) found that defense attorneys were more likely to raise the competency issue when the probability of conviction was high.

A few empirical studies have been done in an attempt to determine what effect competency proceedings have on subsequent trial outcome. In an early study, Vann (1965) found that defendants sent for pretrial competency assessments and subsequently returned to court for trial tended to receive longer prison sentences than control defendants not sent for pretrial examinations. McGarry (1971), however, found that of 71 defendants previously found incompetent to stand trial and subsequently returned for trial as restored to competency, charges were dismissed against 24, and 14 were found not guilty by reason of insanity. Of the 33 who were found guilty, only 14 were actually sentenced to prison. Roesch (1978), in a study comparing 126 previously incompetent defendants returned for trial and 131 competent defendants, found that previous determinations of incompetency had little influence on the type or length of sentence and that previously incompetent defendants charged with violent crimes were more likely than controls to be found innocent.

CRITICAL LEGAL PERSPECTIVES

Eizenstat (1968) has outlined a three-part legal rationale for the competency rule: First, the ban on trials *in absentia* implies that an accused must be mentally as well as physically present at trial. Second, trial of an incompetent might result in conviction of an innocent person due to an inability to present relevant facts, explanations, or arguments. Third, to proceed against a defendant who cannot participate in the trial process traditionally has been viewed as inhumane. Another commentator (Comment, 1967) has suggested that the competency rule is needed not only to protect against inaccurate or unfair prosecutions, but also to preserve the dignity and decorum of the trial process, and to insure that the accused, if found guilty, knows why punishment is being rendered.

Other commentators, however, have pointed to conflicts and inconsistencies between rights supposedly protected by the competency rule and various due process guarantees. Kaufman (1972) and Stone (1975), for example, have noted that bail—which is usually available to criminal defendants—is ordinarily denied during the period of competency assessment. Szasz (1963), Comment (1967), and Steadman and Braff (1974) have argued that requiring an accused to submit to pretrial competency assessment violates the privilege against self-incrimination. Kaufman (1972) has observed that if found unlikely to be restored to competency in the foreseeable future, an accused may be civilly committed irrespective of his or her guilt or innocence. Pollack (1973) has argued that such a commitment jeopardizes the accused's right to a speedy trial.

Additionally, there is the question of whether one adjudicated incompetent to stand trial is competent to execute waivers of other rights necessary to facilitate legal resolution of the competency issue. This question has not been directly addressed in the legal literature, but a recent study by Grisso (1980) may shed some light on the matter. In an empirical study of juveniles' capacity to waive their *Miranda* rights in the context of police questioning, Grisso found that younger juveniles and those with IQs below 80 were not competent to make such waivers.

Legal commentators (e.g., Comment, 1967; Eizenstat, 1968) have long argued that determination of an accused's fitness to stand trial requires a deeper and more comprehensive evaluation than either judge or jury can make through courtroom observation. This view reflects the theory, translated into a forensic perspective by Ray (1874), that aberrant behavior is the result of a disease or illness which requires a trained examiner to detect.

The pervasive influence of mental professionals in the adjudication of competency is readily apparent from the results of a number of studies. Matthews (1970), for example, has reported that judges rely almost exclusively upon the opinions and recommendations of mental health professionals in decision making regarding competency.

Roesch (1978) found that 38% of the judges in their sample never disagreed with mental health professionals' recommendations and 65% rarely or occasionally disagreed. Fifty-nine percent indicated that they typically did not hold a formal hearing and relied only on the recommendations of mental health examiners.

Yet commentators from both the mental health and legal professions have long been skeptical of the law-mental health interface in the competency context. Szasz (1963, 1965) and Leifer (1963), for instance, have argued that despite the legal emphasis on the scientific nature of mental health professionals' testimony, much of the information courts seek from mental health experts is of a moral and legal rather than scientific nature. These critics argue that mental health professionals, lacking objective methods of assessment, offer legally conclusive opinions rather than scientific data. This argument has received empirical support from studies by McGarry (1965) and Matthews (1970) which found that mental health professionals' reports to judges in competency matters often lack objective data and are typically conclusory rather than advisory.

In a recent attempt to clarify professional boundaries, Morse (1978) has urged mental health professionals to recognize the limits of their expertise and confine their participation in legal matters to answering questions for which they have objective data.

CLINICAL PERSPECTIVES

A significant theme in legal and psychological literature on competency to stand trial has been the allegation that mental health professionals persistently confuse mental health criteria of psychosis with legal criteria of competency and, in so doing, fail to provide courts with the type of information they need to make legally valid decisions. Research dealing with this issue and recent attempts to develop objective methods of assessment are summarized briefly below.

In one of the earliest attempts to incorporate the contemporary legal standard for competency into clinical assessment, Robey (1965) devised a brief checklist of areas to be reviewed in evaluating competency. Although this checklist provided some standardization of assessment, reliability and validity studies were not reported.

More recently, McGarry (1965, 1973) has developed the Competency Assessment Instrument which attempts to combine the legal criteria of competency with an ego psychological perspective. The instrument consists of 13 functions, derived from legal literature and clinical experience, which are thought to cover all possible grounds for incompetency. Validation studies of this instrument have not been done and raters using the instrument have often failed to elicit relevant information.

Lipsitt, Lelos, and McGarry (1971) have taken a different approach to the assessment of competency. They devised the Competency Screening Test, consisting of 22 sentence completion items focusing on courtroom situations. Being a self-administered test which requires reading ability, the Competency Screening Test may not be appropriate for illiterate or intellectually subnormal subjects.

Most recently, in an unpublished doctoral dissertation, Sheffield (1981) developed a Competency to Stand Trial data collection instrument by selecting from a review of the competency literature items that had apparent relevance to the legal definition of competency to stand trial and could be verbally administered to subjects. This instrument has 26 open-ended questions under the heading of "Understanding the Nature and Purpose of the Proceedings" and includes items purporting to tap understanding and knowledge of the range of possible penalties in the case, roles of key participants in a trial, legal proceedings, and legal rights. Seventeen questions are included under the heading of "Defendant's Ability to Assist Counsel in a Rational Manner" and are designed to tap the defendant's understanding and knowledge of facts surrounding events at the time of the offense, legal defenses available, relationship to counsel, and self-interest. Sheffield administered the Competency to Stand Trial data collection instrument to 60 individuals, 30 of whom had been adjudicated incompetent to stand trial and 30 of whom were awaiting trial on criminal charges and had not had their competency questioned.

Fifteen response records from each group were randomly selected and scored by three raters who worked independently and used a Q-sort technique. A combination of nine items was found to optimize the discriminant function. Using scoring guidelines developed by Sheffield, two raters, working independently, scored those nine items selected by the discriminant analysis on the remaining response records of each group. A one-way analysis of variance disclosed significant differences between groups on all nine items. Sheffield concluded that the Competency to Stand Trial Assessment Scale and its scoring guidelines do discriminate between competent and incompetent criminal defendants.

A COMPREHENSIVE COMPETENCY ASSESSMENT APPROACH USING THE LAW-PSI AND THE LAW-COMP

In 1978, after a number of years of development, this author published a handbook for clinical forensic assessments entitled *The Lawrence Psychological Forensic Examination*, known as the LAW-PSI (Lawrence, 1978b). The manual has been updated on a yearly basis and was designed to aid both the experienced and beginning mental health professional in conducting comprehensive forensic assessments, reaching precise legal judgments, and producing legally appropriate written reports in cases involving juvenile, criminal, and civil justice clients. The LAW-PSI has guidelines and worksheets for obtaining a client's mental status and a clinical history in 14 critical life areas along with interpretations of psychological test results, basic personality traits, intervention procedures, and recommendations. The document also includes critical summaries of the criminal/antisocial personality; probation alternatives; factors in sentencing; guidelines for workers' compensation, social security, child custody/visitation evaluations; excerpts from jury instructions; report evaluation forms; and frequently asked forensic questions.

During the development of the LAW-PSI, the author wished to include practical guidelines for use in competency assessments and report writing. There are, of course, many areas under the law where legal competency is required. In civil matters there is competency to make a contract, care for oneself and property, vote, drive, receive benefits (such as social security or veteran's administration funds), sue, be sued, make a will, consent to treatment, or give a release or waiver. In domestic law there is competency to marry, adopt, and act as a parent. In the criminal justice system, there is competency to entertain specific intent or premeditation, to enter a plea, to make a confession, to be responsible for criminal acts, and to stand trial.

In practice, however, 99% of competency evaluations assigned to mental health professionals will involve competency to stand trial. In considering the development of guidelines for competency evaluations, it was obvious to this writer that previously developed competency instruments were inadequate, primarily because the data base provided was too meager to produce a comprehensive, logical, and meaningful written report to the courts. The results of previous instruments failed to address both the pertinent legal issues under consideration and the practical dispositional problems in individual competency cases.

Long practical experience, as well as frequent consultation with juvenile and criminal justice professionals, indicated both judges and attorneys needed and preferred written competency reports which presented a *complete* picture of the defendant. Attorneys and judges want to know the defendant's life history and background, present mental status, level and degree of cognitive functioning, personality profile, diagnosis, and prognosis. Simply addressing the issue of legal competency to stand trial is too narrow a focus. Justice professionals, then, want not only a comprehensive psychological evaluation of the defendant, but a rigorous, factual, and legally precise data base from which they can make realistic judgments regarding treatment and disposition decisions as well as competency.

The author also recognized that competency reports placed in a defendant's legal files follow that defendant for years, if not indefinitely. When mental health professionals assess a defendant's competency to stand trial, they have a unique opportunity to present a complete psychological history and profile of the defendant, as well as to address competency issues in these reports which accompany the defendant throughout his or her involvement with the criminal justice system. Such complete reports can be of great practical, therapeutic, and legal service to defendants in custody in various criminal justice and mental health facilities. Those who have reviewed justice system files on competency defendants are most frequently struck by the fact that no matter how voluminous such files are, they very seldom give a realistic and comprehensive picture of the defendant.

COLLECTION OF BACKGROUND DATA

In most mental health facilities, data gathering on a client may be assigned appropriately among a number of multidisciplinary staff members and information usually can be collected at a relatively leisurely pace. Typically, however, competency evaluations are assigned by the court primarily to independent practitioners who are expected to submit a written report within a very brief period. Hence, the individual practitioner usually must gather, organize, and integrate all of the data and write the assessment report alone, generally under severe time restraints. What appeared to be needed first in competency evaluations, then, was an overall assessment data collection strategy.

Through a decade of practical experience, the author has developed such a strategy. The first practical steps after receiving a court order or independently requested competency examination entail consultation with both the defense and prosecuting attorneys in the case—which often can be done by telephone. The attorneys often can explain the critical issues of the particular case, and may also have specific and focused questions regarding defects or disorders in the defendant's intellectual, neurological, emotional, or personality functioning. Ordinarily both the defense and prosecuting attorneys will freely give vital information and opposing opinions as to the critical competency issues in the case, which then can be recorded by the clinician.

The second step in gathering data for competency evaluations is to review and summarize the case files available from each attorney. Generally, both attorneys will provide access to the files, and although the files will have some overlapping data, often an individual file will contain unique information. Data from these sources may lead to the names, addresses, and telephone numbers of institutions and individuals who have valuable information about the defendant.

Depending upon the amount of time and resources available to the clinician, some or all of these leads may be followed and developed into valuable data sources. This may involve interviews in person or by telephone with the defendant's relatives, spouse, friends, supervisors, co-workers, social workers, probation officers, counselors, and the like. Telephone and personal contacts also may be made at local institutions in which the defendant may have been held such as jails, hospitals, mental health facilities, juvenile detention centers, halfway homes, and so forth. Within a few hours, a resourceful clinician can amass a wealth of pertinent historical data and have an excellent understanding of not only the referral questions and unique qualities of the case, but the personal and legal opinions of all the significant persons and professionals involved in the case.

This author has found it critically important to have all such data systematically organized and recorded *before* making a personal contact with the defendant. The LAW-PSI includes worksheets specifically designed for this purpose. Since competency defendants are frequently psychotic, developmentally disabled, or suffering from severe mental or emotional disorders, they are often not reliable historians. If the defendant is incarcerated in a jail, hospital, or mental health facility, it is often also very valuable to interview appropriate institutional staff who have recently observed the defendant and to review staff records before actually interviewing the defendant. Unless most of the above actions are taken by the clinician prior to examining the defendant, an assessment of competency to stand trial is likely to be inadequate.

MENTAL STATUS EXAMINATION

Although the mental health evaluator may have a wealth of others' opinions as to the defendant's mental and emotional status, the referring source is asking for a final professional judgment by the clinician. Such a judgment must, of course, be based upon a face-to-face evaluation. Such an evaluation generally begins with a mental status examination of the defendant. Most of the mental status information can be obtained indirectly during a life history interview and other face-to-face contacts with the defendant during the evaluation. The LAW-PSI has interview behavior and mental status guidelines and worksheets which may be used to record mental status data throughout the entire assessment process. The guidelines cover the defendant's physical appearance and grooming, dress, motor activity and perception, speech, mood, and affect. Items covered under sensorium-intelligence relate to degree and efficiency of consciousness, orientation, attention, concentration, memory functions, abstract abilities, fund of knowledge, stream of thought, and intellectual factors. Also covered are mental, emotional, and characterological defects, major mental symptoms and disorders, and the defendant's insight and judgment. In the final report, this information should present a picture of the defendant's functioning, which is comprehensive, succinct, and written in a manner easily understood by justice system personnel.

LIFE HISTORY

The next step in a comprehensive competency evaluation is to interview the defendant with regard to his or her life history and contrast the defendant's version with statements of others who have already been interviewed. Certainly the defendant should be given ample opportunity to refute or explain allegations or criticisms made against him or her.

The clinician may choose to include in the final report his or her own opinions or observations on some of these issues, especially where there are significant discrepancies. Generally, an appropriate mixture of facts, opinions, and direct quotations from various sources makes for a well-balanced, interesting, and readable competency report.

The major life history categories found to be most useful have been included in the LAW-PSI guidelines and accompanying worksheets. In gathering life history information for the LAW-PSI, the examiner will inquire into family history, educational background, marital status, and occupational and military experience. The defendant will be asked about his or her medical and psychiatric history, sexual functioning, abuse of alcohol and drugs, record of criminal and/or violent behavior, and significant relationships with other persons and groups. Depending on the nature of the case, one or more of these categories might be more detailed or specific than others.

PSYCHOLOGICAL TESTING

Psychological test results in competency evaluations are not only useful as an adjunct to other collected data, but are often indispensable and sometimes mandatory. For example, if the issue in question is one of developmental disability, mental retardation, or psychosis, psychological test procedures specifically designed to assess such impairments are often needed. Experience has also demonstrated that the justice system responds more positively to forensic reports which include psychological test data, rather than just the clinician's opinions and judgments. A specific intelligence quotient number from a standardized intellectual testing instrument, for example, often carries much more weight in competency determinations than a clinician's estimate of a defendant's intelligence level. Test results, therefore, should be included in a competency report as data which confirm or refute historical information and/or the opinions and judgments of significant others in the case.

DIAGNOSIS

Any well-done professional mental health assessment report should include a diagnosis from the *Diagnostic and Statistical Manual* (3rd ed.), known as the *DSM-III*

(American Psychiatric Association, 1980). Competency examinations are a part of the legal process, and precision and exactness are qualities well respected by the court and justice systems. Of course, diagnostic data in the competency report should be consistent and logically equivalent to the precise *DSM-III* definitions and descriptions. Consistency in diagnostic data is especially important should the clinician be required to support any diagnostic judgments through in-court testimony.

SPECIFIC ASSESSMENT OF COMPETENCY

At this point in a competency evaluation, the data amassed by the clinician include direct and third party observations and judgments, subjective and legal opinions regarding the defendant, life history, mental status, psychological test data, and *DSM-III* diagnosis. What is needed next are the defendant's responses to a specific competency evaluation instrument. In designing such an instrument, the author intended that it should first be applicable to the complete *DSM-III* classification and cover the full range of possible competency defendants (including psychotics, retardates, developmentally or neurologically handicapped, etc.). Secondly, the author felt that such an instrument should be flexible enough to meet all or nearly all of the unusual and special cases presented by competency defendants. Finally, it was felt that the instrument should also be acceptable to and have face validity for both legal and mental health professionals.

After a decade of conducting hundreds of competency evaluations with a full range of defendants, the author decided that an interview guide would be the most practical and effective vehicle. In developing the instrument, critical legal concepts judged necessary for competency to stand trial were placed in categories, under which a total of 250 questions were grouped. The questions were both specific and open ended, and the wording could be varied depending on the cognitive, intellectual, and emotional status of each defendant. Interviewing guidelines and a simple scoring system were developed to evaluate the defendant's individual answers and to provide total scores for each legal concept category.

The result of this effort was the *Lawrence Present Mental Competency Test* (known as the LAW-COMP, Lawrence, 1978a), which was published in 1978. McGarry's (1965, 1973) legal criteria for competency were first divided into two major classes: (a) "Factual Criteria for a Defendant's Present Ability to Understand the Nature and Purpose of the Proceedings Taken Against Him" and (b) "Inferential Criteria for a Defendant's Present Ability to Cooperate in a Rational Manner with Counselor in Presenting a Defense and/or Conduct His Own Defense in a Rational Manner Without Counsel."

Under the "First Major Class" were grouped the following six categories: capacity to understand (a) the current legal situation; (b) the charges; (c) legal rights; (d) legal issues and procedures in the case; (e) the role of defense counsel, prosecuting attorney, judge, jury, and the adversary legal proceedings; and (f) the range and nature of possible pleas, verdicts, dispositions, and penalties. Under the "Second Major Class" were grouped the following nine categories: capacity to (a) cooperate and collaborate with counsel; (b) understand and disclose to counsel available pertinent facts surrounding the alleged instant offense(s); (c) collaborate with counsel in maintaining a consistent legal strategy; (d) comprehend counsel's instructions and advice and make decisions based on this information; (e) follow court testimony for contradictions or errors, so inform counsel, and realistically challenge prosecution witnesses; (f) testify relevantly, if necessary, and respond appropriately if cross-examined; (g) protect himself or herself and utilize available legal safeguards with a self-serving rather than a self-defeating motivation; (h) identify, locate, and evaluate possible defense witnesses; and (i) avoid substantial mental deterioration under the stress of waiting for, and participating in, the legal proceedings.

Next, for each of the categories, the author developed a series of specific and open-ended questions exploring the defendant's knowledge, understanding, or capacity.

For example, Major Class I, Category 1 (Capacity to understand the current legal situation) includes the following questions:

1. Have you been arrested? When? Where? Booked?
2. Since your arrest, have you spent time in custody (jail, hospitals, police station)? Where? When? How long?
3. What is the name of your lawyer at this time?
4. Have you had any other lawyers in this case? If so, what are their names?
5. How did you get your lawyer?
6. If you have no lawyer, will you get one, and how?

As a further example, Major Class II, Category 1 (Capacity to cooperate and collaborate with counsel) includes the following questions:

1. Are there difficulties in making contact with your lawyer? What? How?
2. Are you (will you be) able to get along with your lawyer?
3. Is there anything about your lawyer that makes it hard (impossible) for you to work with him?
4. Do you feel your lawyer is trying (will try) to help you?
5. Will your lawyer try his best in your case to be fair?
6. Do you (will you) trust your lawyer in this case?
7. Will you work with him in your case?
8. Would your lawyer work against you in this case? Why?
9. Is there anything you thought your lawyer could do to help your case, but you have not asked him to do? What? Why?
10. Is your lawyer charging you? How much? Payment style? Who pays? How?
11. If you want him to, must your lawyer do what you tell him to do in your case?

The questions were designed to generally, but not completely, cover the specific legal categories and to allow clinicians the freedom to modify, alter, or adjust the language and style of each question to suit the particular needs and capacities of individual defendants. Experience has shown that these questions can easily be simplified so that they are understood by defendants who are mildly mentally retarded, developmentally disabled, or suffering from other serious mental or physical defects. Worksheets were developed so that the clinician can record all of the defendant's verbal responses to each question. If a defendant's response is unclear to the clinician, follow-up or additional questions may be asked, in order to determine more clearly the defendant's knowledge or capacity relating to any question or category.

Considering the needs and desires of the typical clinician, working under time pressures in competency evaluations, a simple scaling procedure was devised for the LAW-COMP. The purpose of this procedure was to aid clinicians in clarifying their judgments under each of the 15 categories. The defendant's responses to each question are rated on a four-point scale: +2 (Good), +1 (Adequate), 0 (Lack of Knowledge), and -1 (Inadequate). These scores are then totaled to yield a subtotal average for each of the 15 categories. Finally, a total score is obtained for the two major classes, ranging from -5 to +10 for the Factual Criteria Class of questions and from -8 to +16 for the Inferential Criteria Class of questions. These scores were not designed to be absolute, but rather to serve as an additional aid to the clinician in developing a judgment of a defendant's competency.

REPORT WRITING

When the clinician has completed his or her assessment of the defendant's competency to stand trial, the LAW-COMP has several distinct advantages as an aid in report writing. First, the clinician may simply report his or her judgment of the defendant's present mental competency on each of the 15 categories, using the adjectives from the LAW-COMP scales: "Good," "Adequate," "Lack of Knowledge," or "Inadequate." Of course, other adjectives, such as "Grossly Inadequate," "Barely or Minimally Adequate," "Excellent," "Outstanding," and so on, may be used for finer distinctions. Additionally, the clinician may include the actual LAW-COMP subcategory and total scores in the written report.

Experience has demonstrated that courts are particularly impressed with direct quotations of a defendant's actual responses to questions, particularly if the responses are poor, bizarre, or inappropriate. When using the LAW-COMP questions, the clinician has the option of including in the report what appears to be the most appropriate mix of legal criteria, scores, and quotations under each of the 15 categories.

Reports based upon the LAW-COMP format will be thorough and detailed, will cover the entire spectrum of present mental competency criteria, and will be precisely legalistic in the final overall judgment of competency. Moreover, the clinician's legal data base and logical inferences will be clear to the report reader. Further, should clinicians be called to court to defend their reports, they will have at their fingertips, recorded on worksheets, the defendant's actual responses to each of the questions, as well as the scoring of those responses. This type of precise, organized, and legally appropriate information makes for excellent court readiness and defense of the clinician's judgment under cross-examination.

In the past, competency to stand trial reports written by mental health professionals were frequently only two or three pages long. They typically touched on identifying information, had a page of summarized life history, a paragraph or two of mental status information, and perhaps a line indicating a diagnostic impression. Seldom was there a reasonable data base or any connecting links of logical reasoning between the data and the clinician's judgment of a defendant's competency. A competency report utilizing the LAW-PSI and LAW-COMP guidelines will provide an extensive data base and will demonstrate the logical connection between data and ultimate conclusion. For published examples of such reports, see Lawrence (1982).

Comprehensive competency reports should first include a complete description of the clinician's data base and assessment procedures. This would include the date, length, and description of all documents reviewed, the name of each person interviewed, whether by phone or in person, and the number of minutes of each interview. The number and length of interviews with the defendant should also be recorded here, along with any psychological tests administered, including the LAW-PSI and LAW-COMP, and any other assessment procedures utilized. The report should include at least a page of precise mental status examination findings, approximately seven pages of life history, a page describing the defendant's cognitive and intellectual functioning, a page or two of major psychological symptoms and/or disorders, and possibly a page of personality characteristics along with a complete *DSM-III* diagnosis. The LAW-COMP findings are typically a page in length, including the clinician's judgment of the defendant's present mental competency to stand trial. Last, some clinicians may wish to make recommendations as to possible alternative dispositions in the case, sometimes with probability statements for each alternative.

Some might well judge such reports idealistic and impractical, and assume that the time required for such evaluations would be prohibitive. However, with a little practice, all of the above-described assessment procedures can be completed in less than half a day. With the LAW-PSI and LAW-COMP guidelines, competency interviews can be completed in a 2-hour period with dictation of a 10-page report completed within an hour. Although these procedures and guidelines are critical to a comprehensive report and readiness for court testimony, the reliability and accuracy of the final judgment remains highly dependent upon the education, training, experience, and maturity of the individual forensic mental health professional.

Stephen Lawrence, Ph.D., M.P.A., is a Diplomate of the American Boards of Forensic, Family, Psychotherapy, and Professional (Clinical) Psychology, and a member of the editorial board of the *American Journal of Forensic Psychology.* Dr. Lawrence, who has been in independent practice since 1964, is the author of the *Lawrence Psychological Forensic Examination* (LAW-PSI) and *LAW-PSI Reports.* He is also a Certified Polygraph Examiner.

RESOURCES

American Psychiatric Association. (1980). *Diagnostic and Statistical Manual of Mental Disorders* (3rd ed.). Washington, DC: Author.

Anastasi, A. (1976). *Psychological Testing.* New York: Macmillan.

Bloom, B. S., Englehart, M. D., Furst, E. J., Hill, W. H., & Krathwohl, D. R. (1956). *Taxonomy of Educational Objectives: The Classification of Educational Goals: Handbook 1: Cognitive Domain.* New York: Longman.

Bukatman, B. A., Foy, J. L., & DeGrazia, E. (1971). What is competency to stand trial? *American Journal of Psychiatry, 127,* 1225-1229.

Comment. (1967). Incompetency to stand trial. *Harvard Law Review, 81,* 454-473.

Cooke, G., Johnston, H., & Pogany, E. (1973). Factors affecting referral to determine competency to stand trial. *American Journal of Psychiatry, 130,* 870-875.

Cronbach, L. J., & Meehl, P. E. (1955). Construct validity in psychological tests. *Psychological Bulletin, 52,* 281-302.

Dusky v. United States, 362 U.S. 402 (1960).

Ebel, R. L. (1972). *Measuring Educational Achievement.* Englewood Cliffs, NJ: Prentice-Hall.

Eizenstat, S. E. (1968). Mental competency to stand trial. *Harvard Civil Rights and Civil Liberties Review, 4,* 379-413.

Ennis, J. B. (1972). *Prisoners of Psychiatry: Mental Patients, Psychiatrists and the Law.* New York: Harcourt Brace Jovanovich.

Fersch, E. (1979). *Law, Psychology and the Courts: Rethinking Treatment of the Young and the Disturbed.* Springfield, IL: Charles C. Thomas.

Fersch, E. (1980). *Psychology and Psychiatry in Courts and Corrections.* New York: John Wiley & Sons.

Grisso, T. (1980). Juveniles' capacity to waive *Miranda* rights: An empirical analysis. *California Law Review, 68,* 1134-1166.

Group for the Advancement of Psychiatry. (1974). Misuse of psychiatry in the criminal courts: Competency to stand trial. *Reports and Symposiums, 8,* 853-921.

Hess, J. H., Jr., & Thomas, H. E. (1963). Incompetency to stand trial: Procedures, results and problems. *American Journal of Psychiatry, 119*, 713-720.

Jackson v. Indiana, 406 U.S. 715 (1972).

Janis, N. R. (1974). Incompetency commitment: The need for procedural safeguards and a proposed statutory scheme. *Catholic University Law Review, 23*, 720-768.

Kaufman, H. (1972). Evaluating competency: Are constitutional deprivations necessary? *The American Criminal Law Review, 10*, 465-504.

Lawrence, S. (1978a). *The Lawrence Present Mental Competency Test.* San Bernardino, CA: Author.

Lawrence, S. (1978b). *The Lawrence Psychological Forensic Examination.* San Bernardino, CA: Author.

Lawrence, S. (1982). *The LAW-PSI Forensic Reports.* San Bernardino, CA: Author.

Leifer, R. (1963). The competence of the psychiatrist to assist in the determination of incompetency: A skeptical inquiry into the courtroom functions of psychiatrists. *Syracuse Law Review, 14*, 564-575.

Lilienfeld, A. M., & Lilienfeld, D. E. (1980). *Foundations of Epidemiology.* New York: Oxford University Press.

Lipsitt, P. D., Lelos, D., & McGarry, A. L. (1971). Competency for trial: A screening instrument. *American Journal of Psychiatry, 128*, 105-109.

Matthews, A. R. (1970). *Mental Disability and the Criminal Law.* Chicago: American Bar Foundation.

McGarry, A. L. (1965). Competence for trial and due process via the state hospital. *American Journal of Psychiatry, 122*, 623-630.

McGarry, A. L. (1969). Demonstration and research in competency for trial and mental illness: Review and preview. *Boston University Law Review, 49*, 46-61.

McGarry, A. L. (1971). The fate of psychotic offenders returned for trial. *American Journal of Psychiatry, 127*, 1181-1184.

McGarry, A. L. (1973). *Competency to Stand Trial and Mental Illness* (DHEW Publication No. ADM 74-103). Washington, DC: U. S. Government Printing Office.

Morris, N., & Hawkins, G. (1970). *The Honest Politician's Guide to Crime Control.* Chicago: University of Chicago Press.

Morse, S. J. (1978). Law and mental health professionals: The limits of expertise. *Professional Psychology, 9*, 389-399.

Nunnally, J. C. (1967). *Psychometric Theory.* New York: McGraw-Hill.

Pollack, M. K. (1973). An end to competency to stand trial. *Santa Clara Lawyer, 13*, 560-578.

Pollack, S. (1970). *Manual on Competency to Stand Trial.* Los Angeles: University of Southern California.

Ray, I. (1874). *A Treatise on Mental Disease.* New York: Appleton & Co.

Robey, A. (1965). Criteria for competency to stand trial: A checklist for psychiatrists. *American Journal of Psychiatry, 122*, 616-622.

Roesch, R. (1978). Competency to stand trial and court outcome. *Criminal Justice Review, 3*, 45-56.

Roesch, R. (1979). Determining competency to stand trial: An examination of evaluation procedures in an institutional setting. *Journal of Consulting and Clinical Psychology, 47*, 542-550. Rulon, P. J. (1939). A simplified procedure for determining the reliability of a test by split-halves. *Harvard Educational Review, 9*, 99-103.

Scheidemandel, P. L., & Kanno, C. K. (1969). *The Mentally Ill Offender: A Survey of Treatment Programs.* Washington, DC: American Psychiatric Association.

Schwitzgebel, R. L., & Schwitzgebel, R. K. (1980). *Law and Psychological Practice.* New York: John Wiley & Sons.

Sheffield, L. L. (1981). *Development of a Scale to Assess Competency to Stand Trial.* Unpublished doctoral dissertation, California Graduate Institute, San Francisco, CA.

Stanley, J. C. (1951). A simplified method for estimating the split-half reliability coefficient of a test. *Harvard Educational Review, 21*, 221-224.

Steadman, H. J., & Braff, J. (1974). Effects of incompetency determination on subsequent criminal processing: Implications for due process. *Catholic University Law Review, 23*, 754-768.

Stone, A. A. (1975). *Mental Health and Law: A System in Transition* (DHEW Publication No. ADM 75-176). Washington, DC: U. S. Government Printing Office.

Szasz, T. S. (1963). *Law, Liberty and Psychiatry*. New York: Collier Macmillan.

Szasz, T. S. (1965). *Psychiatric Justice*. New York: Macmillan.

Vann, C. R. (1965). Pretrial determination and judicial decision making: An analysis of the use of psychiatric information in the administration of criminal justice. *University of Detroit Law Journal, 43*, 13-33.

Walker, N. (1968). *Crime and Insanity in England* (Vol. 1). Edinburgh: Edinburgh University Press.

INSANITY AND THE ASSESSMENT OF CRIMINAL RESPONSIBILITY

David L. Shapiro

Few, if any, recent legal decisions have generated as much controversy as the jury's verdict in the trial of John Hinckley, who was accused of attempting to murder the President. Hinckley, of course, was found not guilty by reason of insanity, a verdict many considered inappropriate.

In the wake of the Hinckley verdict, many states undertook efforts to modify or abolish the insanity defense. Congress held hearings on a proposal to alter federal law dealing with this defense, the very law under which Hinckley was tried and found innocent. But the issues raised by this most highly publicized case are by no means new. Indeed the defense of insanity has been the subject of considerable debate for well over a hundred years.

This chapter will briefly examine the historical evolution of the insanity defense in the Anglo-American legal system and the controversy this defense has generated. The chapter will then move on to consider in greater detail some of the practical considerations psychologists and psychiatrists must take into account in examining defendants who assert the insanity defense, developing a comprehensive forensic report, testifying in court, and withstanding sometimes blistering cross-examination.

HISTORICAL BACKGROUND

TESTS OF INSANITY

The first major "test" or legal definition of insanity, and one which is still in effect in many jurisdictions, was developed in *Daniel M'Naughten's Case* (1843). M'Naughten had developed a delusional system concerning the government of Queen Victoria. While laboring under this delusional system, M'Naughten shot and killed Sir Robert Peel's private secretary, whom M'Naughten had mistaken for Peel himself. At M'Naughten's murder trial, four psychiatrists testified for the defense and M'Naughten was found not guilty by reason of insanity. In the aftermath of M'Naughten's trial, the British legal system developed new and more restrictive rules of criminal responsibility, the so-called *M'Naughten* or "right-wrong" test.

The *M'Naughten* test spoke of individuals who were so mentally ill that they did not know the nature and quality of their criminal acts, that is, people who really did not know what they were doing. An example was given of an individual who strangled someone else, thinking that he was squeezing a lemon rather than committing an act of criminal violence. Such an individual did not, in the logic of this test, "appreciate the nature and quality of the act."

The second and more well known part of the *M'Naughten* test indicates that even if the individual knew the nature and quality of the act, he or she might be excused from criminal responsibility if, by virtue of mental illness, he or she did not know that the act was wrong.

It is striking that the *M'Naughten* test has survived the test of time but has come into modern-day thinking as the right-wrong test, with many forgetting that there was indeed another aspect to it, namely that part of the test dealing with the nature and quality of the act. In recent years, the *M'Naughten* test has come under severe criticism, primarily from mental health professionals who regard it as an exclusively cognitive test which deals only with knowledge of right and wrong and fails to acknowledge the psychological complexity of human beings. Yet when one considers that initial part of the test which speaks of appreciating the nature and quality of the act, there is ample reason to view the *M'Naughten* test as encompassing far more than mere cognitive capacity.

Despite such criticism, the *M'Naughten* test has survived and remains in use to this very day in a number of jurisdictions. Over the course of time, however, the M'Naughten test has been challenged, supplemented, and even replaced in some jurisdictions by other tests of criminal responsibility which will be discussed below.

The second major development in thinking regarding criminal responsibility, and the first significant judicial response to criticism of the *M'Naughten* test, emerged in the late 1800s in the form of the so-called "irresistible impulse" test (see, e.g., *Parsons v. State*, 1887). The question to be answered under this test was whether the defendant had the ability to control his or her behavior. The irresistible impulse standard was never used as the sole test of insanity, but rather was used in conjunction with the *M'Naughten* test. Most frequently, when the irresistible impulse test was added, the test for criminal responsibility became an either/or situation. That is, a defendant would be exculpated if (a) he or she could not understand the nature and quality of the act; (b) he or she did not know that the act was wrong; or (c) he or she was irresistibly impelled to commit the act.

As might have been anticipated, of course, the addition of this test generated great controversy over how irresistible impulse should be defined. What, for instance, would be the difference between an irresistible impulse and an unresisted impulse? And at what point does one draw the line between a person's *choosing* not to exert control and being totally unable to exert control?

Some states attempted to cope with this vagueness by developing operational definitions of irresistible impulse. The State of Michigan, for example, developed what might be called "the policeman at the elbow test." A criminal act under this test would be deemed irresistible if the impulse was so overwhelming that even the presence of a law enforcement officer would not have been sufficient to deter the defendant.

Despite the modifications offered by the irresistible

impulse test, dissatisfaction with the *M'Naughten* test continued. This dissatisfaction, coupled with the criticisms leveled by mental health professionals who felt that the *M'Naughten* test overemphasized cognitive factors, led to the third major development in this area of the law: the limited and brief acceptance of the so-called "product test." This test was advanced by Judge David Bazelon of the United States Court of Appeals for the Washington, D. C. Circuit in *Durham v. United States* (1954). The *Durham* rule or product test held that an accused was not criminally responsible if his or her criminal activity was the product of a mental disease or defect. This test was intended, in Judge Bazelon's words, "to throw open the windows of the [insanity] defense and ventilate a musty doctrine with all of the information acquired during a century's study of the intricacies of human behavior" (*United States v. Brawner*, 1984, p. 1010).

The *Durham* rule, however, was not without its own set of problems. There were two major stumbling blocks. First, the term product was excessively vague. Fanciful manipulation of psychodynamic theories of personality could (and often did) result in a belief that virtually anything caused anything. The second, and perhaps more troubling aspect of the *Durham* rule was that the term "mental disease or defect" was never actually defined. Thus, mental health professionals and the courts were left with the task of defining this term on a case-by-case basis.

This latter problem was addressed to some extent in *McDonald v. United States* (1962). In that case, Judge Bazelon's Court attempted to provide a legal definition of mental disease and defect. A mental disease or defect, the Court held, was "any abnormal condition of the mind which substantially affects mental and emotional processes or substantially impairs behavioral controls" (p. 851). In so defining mental disease or defect, the Court did narrow somewhat the scope of the *Durham* rule since it made clear that not every diagnosable condition could result in a defendant's exculpation. The *McDonald* decision did not, however, address the definition of product.

Even to this day, in jurisdictions utilizing some variant of the product test, one hears judges offering definitions of product which range from very narrow to exceedingly broad. Some judges instruct jurors to construe the product test as a "but for" test—that is, to ask: Had it not been for the mental illness, would the defendant have committed the offense at all? Jury instructions from other judges, however, speak of product in a very broad sense, thus conveying the notion that jurors should consider virtually anything in the defendant's history which might relate to the criminal behavior at issue.

Ultimately, the *Durham* rule or product test was laid to rest by the very Court which created it. Recognizing that *Durham* had led to "trial by label"— that is, the indiscriminate use of conclusory labels by mental health professionals, who testified that various criminal activities were the product of various mental illnesses but failed adequately to define the relationship between the mental illness and the crime—the D. C. Circuit Court of Appeals in 1972 rejected the product test (*United States v. Brawner*, 1972). In so doing, the Court decided that future insanity pleas in its jurisdiction should be adjudicated on the basis of the test formulated by the American Law Institute as part of its Model Penal Code.

The Model Penal Code test, the last widely accepted reformulation in this area of the law, indicates that an individual should not be held criminally responsible if, by reason of mental disease or defect, he or she lacked substantial capacity to appreciate the wrongfulness of his or her conduct or lacked substantial capacity to conform his or her behavior to the requirements of the law. By its further terms, this test specifically excludes from its purview those diseases or defects whose only manifestation is repeated criminal conduct or otherwise antisocial behavior. In other words, this test would virtually eliminate use of the insanity defense by those diagnosed as antisocial, psychopathic, or sociopathic.

DIMINISHED CAPACITY

The defendant who invokes the insanity defense will be found either guilty of the crime charged or not guilty by reason of insanity. One relatively recent approach which offers an alternative to this all or nothing aspect of the insanity defense is the concept of diminished capacity or diminished responsibility. Diminished capacity or diminished responsibility laws have been adopted in a number of jurisdictions and range from extremely conservative to rather radical ways of dealing with the issue of criminal responsibility.

The more common and most conservative approach is typified by laws which tie the concept of diminished capacity directly to the question of specific intent. General intent is common to all crimes (except for those few strict liability offenses) and refers simply to the intent to do that which the law forbids. Specific intent, on the other hand, applies to a limited class of crimes thought to require a higher level of cognitive involvement, that is, "the intent to accomplish the precise act which the law prohibits" (Black, 1979, p. 727). In jurisdictions adhering to this conservative approach, the question is whether, at the time of the criminal act, the defendant's mental condition impaired or diminished his or her capacity to form the requisite specific intent.

For example, a defendant who killed someone may have been suffering from some mental condition which interfered with his or her capacity for premeditation or malice aforethought of the sort required for first degree murder. In such a case, the defendant's mental condition would lead not to an acquittal but rather to a finding of diminished capacity and reduction of the charge from first degree murder to second degree murder or perhaps manslaughter, lesser offenses which do not require proof of premeditation or malice aforethought.

A second, somewhat more liberal formulation of the diminished capacity concept admits for the jury's consideration a vast amount of data regarding the defendant's background, psychological functioning, and personal characteristics—virtually any evidence which bears directly on questions of intent, impulse control, or understanding of the wrongfulness of the criminal acts charged. A third and even more radical approach, rarely utilized in practice, would allow the jury to consider the defendant's entire life history in determining whether there is reason to mitigate the charges on the basis of diminished capacity or diminished responsibility.

THE MOVE TO ABOLISH THE INSANITY DEFENSE

A growing school of thought regards the insanity defense as a totally unworkable concept that should be abolished. Some states, as noted above, have begun to utilize the concept of diminished capacity, but generally as a supplement to rather than a replacement for the insanity defense. Other states, however, have adopted a concept known as "guilty but mentally ill." In these jurisdictions, the defendant is tried on the facts of the case and is either acquitted or convicted, regardless of his or her mental condition. If the defendant is convicted, a separate hearing is then held regarding the defendant's mental condition. If, at that time, the defendant is judged to be in need of treatment, he or she may then be committed to a mental institution, where time spent will be credited toward the defendant's prison sentence.

The State of Idaho, for example, recently revised its law regarding the insanity defense. Kenneth McClure (1982), Deputy Attorney General of Idaho, has described the new statute as follows:

> [Subsection] (a) provides that insanity is not a defense to a criminal charge. [Subsection] (b) provides that if someone is convicted and suffers from a mental condition which requires treatment that person shall be committed to the Board of Corrections (or if a misdemeanor, to the county or city jail or, if appropriate, to the Department of Health and Welfare). This subsection also provides that if treatment is ordered and successfully completed before the expiration of [the defendant's sentence] the defendant must serve the remainder of the sentence subject to the normal rules of commutation. [Subsection] (c) underscores the fact that evidence concerning issues of intent and culpable state of mind shall be admissible at trial. If a person cannot [form] the intent or culpable state of mind he cannot be convicted of a crime and will be acquitted. Of course, if the person is acquitted, involuntary civil commitment proceedings can be brought against him and he

will be involuntarily committed if he is mentally
ill and dangerous. (pp. 1-2).

AN ALTERNATIVE TO ABOLITION:
THE "BONNIE" TEST

Even those who reject abolition of the insanity
defense on moral grounds recognize that the defense is
subject to significant abuse and have argued that it
should be narrowed. Bonnie (1983), for example, has
proposed a model statute which would provide that a
defendant be relieved of criminal responsibility "if he
proves, by the greater weight of the evidence, that, as a
result of mental disease or mental retardation, he was
unable to appreciate the wrongfulness of his conduct at
the time of the offense" (p. 197).

This formulation would not only shift the burden of
proof to the defendant but would also eliminate the need
for speculation regarding whether or not the defendant
had the capacity to control his behavior or to resist the
criminal impulse. Such a proposal is, of course, not
without critics of its own, and has been adopted in only
one American jurisdiction (see *United States v. Lyons*,
1984). Yet this formulation has been endorsed by a task
force of the American Psychiatric Association and is
likely to have significant impact upon future efforts to
modify the insanity defense.

THE FORENSIC EVALUATION: ISSUES
AND TECHNIQUES IN RECONSTRUCTION

One of the primary arguments for abolition of the
insanity defense is that it is exceedingly difficult, if not
impossible, to determine accurately what the defendant's
mental state was at the time of the alleged criminal act(s).
There is, of course, some merit to this argument—although
it should be observed that most criminal trials require the
fact finder (judge or jury) to make at least some
inference regarding the mental state of the defendant
(e.g., intent) at the time of the offense. People's
perceptions of past events can and do change with the
passage of time and there is often a tendency, consciously

or unconsciously, to distort what one's experience was at the time of a criminal offense. Despite the cogency of this argument, however, it seems unlikely that there will be any wholesale abandonment of the insanity defense in the foreseeable future. Nor is it likely that psychologists and psychiatrists will soon cease to play a significant role in the reconstruction of the mental states of defendants who assert the insanity defense. Thus, it is important to consider some of the more significant practical issues which arise when the forensic expert attempts such a reconstruction.

DETERMINING WHAT HAPPENED

Since a major aspect of the mental health professional's role in insanity cases is the reconstruction of the defendant's mental state at the time of the alleged crime, it should be obvious that the forensic expert must acquire a fairly complete understanding of the events involved in the crime and the defendant's behavior at the time.

Interviews with the defendant, of course, provide one source of such information. But the conscientious expert should also consult all available secondary sources in attempting to ascertain what went on at the time of the offense. It should be a rule of thumb, for example, never to prepare a report without first reviewing a complete police report of the offense. Wherever possible, the expert should also interview witnesses to the offense as well as family members, friends, employers, teachers, and so forth—anyone who can describe what transpired and/or what the defendant's functioning was like at or around the time of the offense. Naturally, some practical difficulties may arise in terms of what sorts of data are discoverable, especially in an adversary system where the expert has been retained by one side or the other (i.e., prosecution or defense). Nevertheless, a conscientious effort should be made to obtain as much of this information as possible. One of the author's recent cases illustrates this point:

> The defendant was admitted to the hospital in an acutely psychotic state and required massive

doses of psychotropic medication to sedate him. He had been in jail for approximately two months following the alleged offense. Given this lapse of time between offense and evaluation, it could not be assumed that since he was psychotic at the time of admission he must have been so at the time of the offense. In point of fact, interviews with several government witnesses established that the defendant had manifested no signs of psychosis at the time of the offense, but apparently had suffered an acute psychotic episode while in jail following his arrest. In other words, the defendant had decompensated during the two-month period in jail and was, by any legal test, responsible for his behavior at the time of the offense.

In addition to interviewing the defendant, witnesses, and significant others and reviewing police reports of the offense, the expert will often find it helpful to examine any records kept (even anecdotal entries) while the defendant was incarcerated or hospitalized after the offense. Such records frequently provide valuable clues as to the defendant's behavior and psychological functioning at the time of the offense, and almost always offer at least some base line against which observations made upon evaluation may be compared.

EVALUATING THE CONSISTENCY OF BEHAVIOR AND FUNCTIONING

Clearly, in every criminal responsibility evaluation, there is a need to determine whether the defendant's behavior and psychological functioning at the time of evaluation is consistent with that present at the time of the offense. Such a determination is often complicated not only by the passage of time between offense and evaluation but, often more acutely, by the fact that the defendant has been in jail between the time of the offense and that of the evaluation. It is important to note that jails and other correctional facilities are stressful environments and that a defendant may appear acutely psychotic while in such settings but demonstrate rapid and dramatic improvement once released or transferred to a hospital setting for evaluation. In all cases in which the defendant has come to the evaluation from jail, the expert needs to evaluate the defendant's history carefully (particularly with regard to the presence or absence of psychosis in the past) in order to determine whether what is observed upon examination is an acute situational reaction to jail conditions (e.g., sensory deprivation, jail house homosexuality, etc.) or rather a reflection of some more enduring pathology which may have been present at the time of the offense.

The expert should not fall into the trap of assuming that behavior seen at the time of the evaluation is the same as that which occurred at the time of the offense. What is observed upon examination may well be post-arrest behavior due to some sort of deterioration or decompensation precipitated by the arrest, itself, or conditions of incarceration. On the other hand, the defendant may have been psychotic at the time of the offense and yet appear psychically intact at the time of evaluation as a result of restitutive processes triggered by the defendant's release from jail. Thus, wherever possible, the expert should examine jail records and interview jail staff regarding the defendant's behavior and functioning while incarcerated, and then compare that information with reports of the police, witnesses, significant others, and the defendant.

A related issue concerns whether or not the behavior at the time of the offense is consistent with the behavior typical of the defendant's mental condition. Consider, for example, the following case:

> The defendant had been charged with assault with intent to kill and a bank robbery committed several days after the assault. The first psychologist who examined the defendant, some nine months after the offenses, found him to be overtly psychotic. This psychologist did not interview any witnesses. He simply reasoned that, since psychosis represents a breakdown in an individual's ability to control impulses and exert appropriate judgment, the two crimes must have been causally related to the defendant's psychosis.

A second psychologist examined the defendant and also concluded that the defendant was overtly psychotic. This psychologist, however, then proceeded to interview many witnesses to the defendant's behavior around the time of the offense and also took the time to review the defendant's previous hospital records.

The defendant's mother indicated that her son's psychotic episodes were characterized by withdrawal, seclusiveness, and a sense of preoccupation and fearfulness, but were never characterized by any aggressive behavior. The victim of the assault, a retired police officer with experience transporting psychotic individuals to the local state hospital, indicated that at the time of the offense the defendant appeared angry but was not manifesting any signs of psychosis.

Hospital records revealed that the defendant's psychotic episodes had been characterized by confusion and inappropriate sexual activity, but, again, no aggressive or hostile behavior consistent with assault was ever documented. These records further indicated that since the time of his arrest, the defendant had been shuttled among some six different hospitals and correctional facilities, had suffered significant deterioration, and had been diagnosed as a catatonic schizophrenic.

Based upon the above data, the second psychologist concluded that the defendant's behavior at the time of the offense was not consistent with, nor causally related to, the defendant's psychotic symptomatology.

This case also highlights the need for careful investigation in forensic evaluations to determine whether or not the behavior observed by the examiner is consistent with the defendant's behavior at the time of the offense. In this case, since the defendant had been hospitalized and records were available, it was also noteworthy that none of the symptoms manifested in the past were consistent with the defendant's criminal behavior. This case also points out the obvious dangers of inferring backward in time solely from current clinical symptoms.

EVALUATING DELUSIONAL SYSTEMS

As noted above, the expert cannot assume that behavior observed at the time of evaluation is consistent with behavior at the time of the offense. On occasion, a defendant's behavior may be related to several delusional systems, one (or more) of them dominant at the time of the offense, and another (or others) present only at the time of evaluation. The significance and evaluation of varying delusional systems is illustrated by a case from the author's recent experience:

> The defendant had committed a murder but was not apprehended until six years later. When admitted to the hospital for evaluation, following his arrest, he was acutely psychotic, bizarre, and delusional, expressing grandiose ideas about having developed a "hydrocompression machine" capable of growing vast quantities of marijuana. The delusional system also focused upon various underworld figures who wanted the defendant's "machine." The defendant indicated that the man he killed had been a "hit man" for the underworld.

This case illustrates the difficulty in immediately leaping to a conclusion about the relevance of a contemporary delusional system to a defendant's thinking at the time of the offense. The defendant's history revealed that he had never expressed these delusional beliefs to anyone at the time of the offense, and that the current talk about "hydrocompression machines" and underworld conspiracies was a recent development. It appeared that the defendant had committed the offense and then reconstructed his motivations in a psychotic manner.

The critical task of the examiner was to determine when this delusional thinking began, when the defendant had begun to deteriorate, and what, if any, kind of disorder had been manifest at the time of the offense or prior to the offense. Interviews with his wife revealed that the defendant had indeed been delusional at the time of the offense but had been suffering from a completely different delusional system. He had seen a "down and out" alcoholic on the street, stated "Here comes my father, I'm going to get him before he gets me," and then shot the man several times. Further exploration of the defendant's history revealed that his father had indeed been an alcoholic and had frequently abused the defendant, both verbally and physically. Ultimately it appeared that many of the decedent's actions and behavior patterns had unconsciously reminded the defendant of his father.

EVALUATING PHYSICAL EVIDENCE

Very frequently, one of the most discomforting aspects of forensic work is the need to consider carefully the physical evidence related to the offense. The expert, especially the novice, often feels that his or her work should take place in a more rarefied atmosphere than that in which a police investigation is conducted. However, in many cases effective forensic assessment requires a careful evaluation of the physical evidence, and assessment of its relationship to the defendant's claimed mental state, before any opinion can be rendered. This point is illustrated by the following case in which the author was involved several years ago.

The defendant, who had a history of epileptic seizures and chronic alcoholism, had been charged with murder. The defendant had been in another man's apartment and, while there, had stabbed the other man a number of times. The defense claimed that the defendant had acted while in the throes of some form of seizure activity precipitated by alcohol abuse. According to the defense, the defendant had either lost control and stabbed the victim during a temporal lobe seizure or, alternatively, had taken the victim's life in an episode of post-ictal violence (i.e., in the phase immediately following the seizure).

It has been observed that if one tries to move patients too rapidly before they emerge from the stuporous state following seizure activity, they may explode into rather violent and aggressive behavior. The defense sought to establish this kind of response as the grounds for a lack of criminal responsibility. During a previous hospitalization, when the staff had tried to move the defendant too soon after a seizure, he had indeed gone "absolutely wild." Hospital records indicated that he had demonstrated unusual strength, had pushed doctors aside, had held nurses at bay, and had thrown chairs and waste baskets around the hospital room.

The physical evidence in this case included the pattern of stab wounds on the victim's body and the trail of blood found in the victim's apartment. The pattern of wounds indicated that the stabbing was not at all the wild, random, purposeless thrashing movement that might have been expected had the defendant been experiencing a temporal lobe seizure at the time. Moreover, there was clear physical evidence that the defendant had chased his victim from room to room.

Another striking aspect of this particular case was that the police report contained a rather coherent statement made by the defendant to the police very shortly after the stabbing. Had the defendant indeed been in a stuporous state following a seizure, it is quite unlikely that he would have been capable of making such a statement. This observation, combined with evaluation of the physical evidence, and analyzed in light of clinical knowledge regarding seizure disorders, led to the expert opinion that the defendant had not experienced a seizure at the time of the murder. This was, again, one of those cases in which there is a documented history of a clinical disorder but no apparent relationship between the disorder and the offense. It appeared that the defendant's excessive consumption of alcohol, rather than any seizure activity, may have been the precipitant of the stabbing.

EVALUATING THE ROLE OF DRUGS AND ALCOHOL

There is a great temptation, when dealing with a defendant who appears to have a long alcohol history and claims to have been drinking heavily at the time of the offense, to attribute the offense merely to the fact that the defendant was intoxicated. Here again, the clinical examination and psychiatric history should be supplemented by careful interview of witnesses and others who know the defendant. In a recent case, for example, the defendant professed amnesia for the offense, claiming to have been drunk at the time. An interview with his sister, however, revealed that the defendant had stopped drinking 3 or 4 days prior to the offense and had been experiencing symptoms consistent with delirium tremens at the time of the offense.

When the mental health expert encounters an alcohol-related crime, he or she should always attempt to obtain data from secondary sources which can either substantiate or contradict the defendant's own recognition and memory of what happened, particularly since confabulation regarding time sequences is common in an alcoholic's reconstruction of past events. Furthermore, the expert needs to ascertain how much alcohol was consumed and when it was imbibed in relationship to the offense.

A related issue deals with the concept of drug-induced psychosis, a diagnosis becoming more and more prevalent due to the current proliferation of powerful hallucinogenic drugs such as PCP. Current law in most states does not allow for an insanity defense based solely on evidence of a psychosis induced by drugs. Rather it must be demonstrated that there was at least a potential for psychosis, some underlying mental disease or defect, that was activated or exacerbated by the drug. Some case law even requires proof of an illness which manifests itself after the drug is out of the defendant's system.

When a mental health expert conducts a forensic evaluation in any case in which a drug-induced psychosis is suspected, he or she must first wait for the acute psychotic symptoms to clear and then perform a careful clinical evaluation (including neurological work up and a complete battery of psychological and neuropsychological tests) in order to determine whether or not there was an underlying mental disease or defect which may have interacted with the drug.

EVALUATING NEUROLOGICAL DYSFUNCTION

The relationship of neurological dysfunction to various forms of violent behavior and other criminal conduct is currently the subject of heated debate. A growing body of literature suggests that violent behavior, especially when it is episodic, explosive, and out of all proportion to provocation, may be a manifestation of what is described as the episodic dyscontrol syndrome. On the other hand, many attempts to link maladaptive antisocial behaviors to various forms of brain dysfunction have been sharply criticized by neurologists and other neuroscientists. In order legitimately to utilize neurological and/or neuropsychological input as the basis for an insanity defense, the physical and other evidence of the crime must be consistent with the sort of syndrome just described, that is, the criminal act must have been episodic, explosive, and out of all proportion to provocation. In other words, if the violent behavior is a chronic way of life or character style, it would not be appropriate to utilize such input as the basis for a defense of insanity. The same would also be true, of course, if the violent behavior had been an expected reaction to provocation. In that case, however, the defendant might have a legal defense other than insanity.

Despite these limitations, however, mental health experts and attorneys all too often attempt to interject the concept of brain damage into a defense against charges based upon criminal activity which is not episodic or explosive but rather well planned, carefully executed, and apparently motivated by a desire for profit. For example, a recent case involved a brain damaged individual, suffering from epilepsy, who robbed a fast-food restaurant. The defense expert attributed the defendant's behavior to a "complex partial seizure." This expert noted that the defendant's injury was in the left temporal area of the brain, an area thought to be responsible for judgment, and that the defendant had shown "poor judgment" by attempting an armed robbery in broad daylight. In this case it would appear that the expert had inappropriately attempted to explain the defendant's criminal behavior in terms of his illness, rather than merely stating that while the defendant did suffer from some central nervous system impairment, such impairment did not provide an explanation consistent with the defendant's criminal activity.

DIFFERENTIATING PSYCHOTIC AND SOCIOPATHIC MOTIVATION

Another common problem in the forensic assessment relates to the defendant who appears to have been suffering from a psychosis but also appears to have had other motivations, perhaps sociopathic in nature, at the time of the offense. In performing the evaluation, the examiner may see both aspects of the diagnostic picture and thus be placed in the position of having to tease out their relative contributions to the offense charged. Was the crime related more to the sociopathic features or more to the psychotic features?

This problem frequently occurs when a defendant has had psychotic episodes but, when in remission, appears to have a sociopathic life style. The problem, of course, is to determine what the defendant was like at the time of the offense. Simply because the defendant looks more sociopathic at the time of evaluation does not necessarily mean that sociopathic features were dominant at the time of the offense. Nor does a present psychotic condition mean that the defendant was laboring under a psychosis at the time of the offense. The defendant may well have been in remission from the psychosis at the time of the offense and acting in a more calculating and profit-oriented sociopathic manner. The expert needs always to ask which appears to have been the more dominant feature at the time of the offense. And here, again, reference must often be made not only to clinical data but also to evidence obtained from secondary sources (e.g., police reports, witness interviews, etc.).

EVALUATING A DEFENDANT'S REFUSAL TO ASSERT A VALID INSANITY DEFENSE

Not infrequently, a defendant may refuse to assert what appears to be a valid defense of insanity. In recent years, the courts have shown an increasing sensitivity to this issue and have generally required that a hearing be held to determine whether the defendant's position has a rational or irrational basis (see, e.g., *Frendak v. United States*, 1979). In such cases, the expert may well wonder what dimensions need to be considered in evaluating this question.

In some cases, the irrationality of the defendant's thinking on this issue may be readily apparent. Consider, for example, cases in which the defendants, who are clearly disturbed, contend that they are not mentally ill and that the entire attempt to discuss the insanity defense is a conspiracy against them. On the other hand, there may be cases in which the defendant's position appears to have a clearly rational basis. The defendant may, for example, be aware that commitment following an insanity acquittal will be indefinite (as opposed to the definite term he or she would receive if convicted) and/or be concerned with the realistic likelihood of being stigmatized for life as mentally ill if found not guilty by reason of insanity.

Merely because the defendant is mentally ill does not mean that his or her reason for rejecting an insanity defense is grounded in the mental illness. In conducting the forensic evaluation, the expert needs to keep in mind that even an acutely psychotic defendant may have valid and rational reasons for refusing to plead not guilty by reason of insanity. Ordinarily, the question, as posed by the court, is whether the defendant can intelligently and rationally waive the defense of insanity.

FORENSIC TESTIMONY: STRATEGIES FOR THE EFFECTIVE PRESENTATION OF THE EVALUATION

Even the most careful and exacting forensic evaluation may prove to be an unmitigated disaster in court unless it is effectively presented. Thus it is essential to consider not only how to conduct such an evaluation, but also the means for assuring that the evaluation will be given proper weight by the trier-of-fact, that is, judge or jury.

PREPARATION BY EXPERT AND ATTORNEY

The first and most essential aspect of effective presentation is *preparation* by both the attorney and the forensic expert. Both attorney and expert must anticipate and discuss in advance of trial any challenges likely to be raised to the expert's opinion. They must make a frank assessment of the weakest aspects of the evaluation and opinion. Furthermore, they need to plan to deal with any weaknesses during the direct examination of the expert, rather than allowing them to be exposed for the first time on cross-examination. One of the author's recent cases provides a good example of this sort of preparation:

> The insanity defense was raised on the basis of evidence that the defendant had suffered from an acute psychotic episode. While hospitalized for evaluation, however, the defendant manifested virtually no evidence of disturbed behavior. Thus it was anticipated that the prosecutor would raise at trial the question of how the forensic expert could state that the defendant was so disturbed at the time of the offense when there was no evidence of disturbed behavior at the time of evaluation.

> Having anticipated such potentially damaging cross-examination, the attorney and the expert decided to deal with this discrepancy in the course of the attorney's direct examination of the expert at trial. Thus, on direct examination, the expert testified that a person could experience an acute psychotic episode, that the psychosis could go into substantial remission, and that following such an episode there might well be few residual signs of psychosis in the person's day-to-day behavior.

> In this case, the residual signs of psychosis were very clear in the defendant's psychological test results though not in his everyday behavior in the hospital. On direct examination, the expert further indicated that often one must look for more subtle indications of the disorder and cannot merely rely upon behavioral observations.

The attorney's questions to the expert on direct examination were aimed at highlighting the distinction between the day-to-day behavioral observations of the defendant on the ward and the indices of psychosis found in the psychological testing. By covering this material on direct examination, the attorney was able to defuse much of the impact of aggressive cross-examination on this critical point.

While appropriate preparation in most cases requires fairly extensive consultation between attorney and expert, it should be observed that such consultation, itself, may provide ammunition for an attack on the expert's credibility. On cross-examination, for example, the opposing lawyer may raise such consultation with the implication that the expert's opinion was somehow altered as a result of his or her discussions with the attorney. The expert can avoid problems of this sort by engaging in extended consultation with the attorney only once the expert's opinion has been established and recorded. Then if the issue is raised on cross-examination, the expert can indicate that he or she reached an opinion on a certain date and communicated that opinion to the attorney on some subsequent date, thereby defusing any inference that the attorney influenced the opinion. As a practical matter, of course, the examiner must, in every case, record the date the opinion was reached, the date of the report, and the date of consultation with the attorney.

RESPONDING TO ATTACKS ON PSYCHOLOGICAL TESTING

A complete criminal responsibility evaluation ordinarily involves psychological testing, and often the expert will rely upon the results of such testing in his or her testimony. Since few attorneys are well versed in the intricacies of psychological testing and many regard such testing with disdain if not scorn, the expert whose testimony relies to any extent upon psychological testing must be prepared to respond effectively to attacks upon this well-established but often misunderstood method for gathering clinical data.

Attorneys will often ask on cross-examination questions such as, "Isn't it true that the test you gave [relied upon] is invalid?" When such questions are asked, the expert may well respond that he or she is unable to answer since the attorney has not specified whether he or she is asking about predictive validity, construct validity, or face validity. The expert should, of course, be prepared to address all of these forms of validity, should the attorney choose to pursue the matter further, but such a response is often sufficient to put an end to the inquiry.

Another common line of attack to be anticipated is that of confronting the expert with data derived from various studies of psychological testing. Obviously the expert will need to be fully versed in the research literature regarding the specific test(s) upon which he or she has relied. But generally the expert can simply respond that the studies cited relied upon research rather than clinical methodologies. Research methodology, it may be explained, often takes one isolated variable from a test protocol and attempts to use that variable to predict another isolated variable (e.g., using the number of color responses in a Rorschach protocol as a predictor of future violent behavior). This, of course, is not the nature of the clinical examination, where a wide variety of observations, tests, and impressions go into forming a particular opinion.

Another way of handling the above line of attack, particularly when dealing with a more sophisticated judge or jury, is to draw specific parallels between test responses (and the expert's interpretation of them) and the actual behavior of the defendant at the time of the offense. It goes without saying, of course, that in following such an approach the psychologist must have administered the tests, analyzed them, and drawn inferences from them in a "blind" fashion (i.e., without having the details of the criminal offense in mind). Consider, for example, the use of this technique in the following case:

A defendant's responses to a series of projective techniques were basically intact with notable exceptions surrounding his perception of older men, authority figures, and "father figures."

When presented with test stimuli evoking such images, the defendant's thought processes became loose and illogical and his reality testing seemed grossly impaired.

The defendant's history revealed that his mother had been murdered several years earlier and that the defendant suspected that his father had been involved. The defendant, it was learned, had been charged with shooting a total stranger, an individual who closely resembled his father in terms of height, weight and body build. Moreover, the shooting had occurred during the early hours of the morning in a setting virtually identical to his father's place of business.

The parallels between the inferences drawn from the psychological testing and the facts of the offense were striking and led to the opinion that the defendant had misperceived his victim as his father, and had become acutely psychotic at the time of the shooting.

DEALING WITH HEAVILY LOADED WORDS

The expert witness must constantly be aware of and alert to the use of certain words which are heavily loaded in terms of their legal implications. Examples of such words are *"planning"* and *"knowing."* In legal parlance the word knowing is clearly related to the concepts of intent and premeditation, both of which are significant in the insanity defense. In cross-examining a defense expert, the prosecutor may, for example, point to the amount of planning that appears to have gone into the offense, thus attempting to rebut testimony that the defendant was mentally ill. But, of course, as the expert may point out, planning does not necessarily contraindicate the presence of serious mental illness.

In many cases, some of the most involved criminal activity may be based upon careful plotting, systematic planning which is itself rooted in some elaborate delusional system. *Daniel M'Naughten's Case* (1843) provides an excellent historical example. M'Naughten, it will be recalled, suffered from delusions regarding the Queen's government, psychotic thinking which ultimately led him to shoot and kill a government secretary. While M'Naughten ended up shooting the wrong man, there is little question that he had carefully planned the shooting over an extended period of time.

In a similar fashion, the words *know clearly* has major implications in the insanity defense and may be used in cross-examination to discredit or undermine the unwary expert's opinion that the defendant was mentally ill at the time of the defense. The implication, in such instances, is generally that the defendant knew what he or she was doing and/or knew that it was wrong. In response, the expert should point out that the word know (or knew, knowing, knowingly, knowledgeable, etc.) may be used in a variety of ways, with a variety of meanings, often depending upon the context. The expert might also point out, where appropriate, that while an individual may cognitively know what he or she is doing or that the act is wrong, he or she may nevertheless lack an emotional understanding or appreciation of the act or its wrongfulness.

OTHER PRACTICAL CONSIDERATIONS

As a practical matter, the expert must also bear in mind the actual impact a particular crime (or series of crimes) is likely to have upon the jury and the difficulty the expert may have in presenting credible evidence of insanity in light of that impact. While it is not the function of the expert to try to influence legal proceedings, there are circumstances in which it may be appropriate for the expert to discuss with the attorney the possibility of foregoing an insanity defense and, instead, using the expert's testimony in support of another defense (e.g., diminished capacity) or at sentencing following a plea of guilty. The ultimate decision, of course, will lie with the defendant in consultation with the attorney. It is worth noting in this regard, however, that, for obvious reasons, few attorneys will call to the witness stand a reluctant forensic expert.

This particular issue is most likely to arise in cases involving an especially heinous crime in which the defendant may have been delusional or psychotic at the time of the offense, but shows no evidence of delusional thinking or psychosis upon evaluation or at the time of trial. An insanity defense may still be effective, depending upon the evidence and the extent to which the defense expert's testimony is convincing. But both the attorney and the expert should evaluate how jurors are likely to respond to testimony that suggests insanity at the time of the offense, when their own observations of the defendant in court reveal no indication whatsoever of a mental disorder. In such cases, the expert's testimony may well be significantly outweighed by the jurors' own visceral reaction to the crime and the defendant.

One final practical consideration worth mentioning relates to the attorney's attack on opposing expert witnesses. While most experienced trial lawyers are aware of this problem, forensic experts would do well to warn the attorney who has retained them to testify not to launch too harsh an attack on opposing experts. Specifically, it should be noted that if the attorney goes too far in attempting to discredit opposing witnesses' scientific credibility, the impression created may carry over to those experts called by the attorney in support of his or her own case. The result, of course, may be that the trier-of-fact ultimately gives no credence to the testimony of any of the experts.

Where a battle of the experts is anticipated in an insanity case, the forensic expert may be most helpful by encouraging the attorney to restrict his or her attack on opposing experts to actual substantive weaknesses in their testimony, rather than broadly attempting to discredit the scientific basis for their testimony.

THE COMPREHENSIVE FORENSIC REPORT: A RECOMMENDED FORMAT

In addition to the above-described attacks which the forensic expert may expect upon cross-examination, there is almost always at least some effort made to highlight inadequacies in the expert's evaluation and report. Much of the sting engendered by such efforts may be alleviated by conducting a comprehensive evaluation and offering a detailed report of that evaluation in accord with the following format.

The forensic report should begin with a statement of the specific assessment procedures utilized (including but not limited to clinical interviews and psychological tests). If other professionals (e.g., social work, medical, psychological, or psychiatric consultants) have been involved in the assessment, their names, professional status, and contributions should be specified.

This statement should be followed by a detailed description of the facts of the case. This description should include: (a) the official (i.e., government) version of the offense; (b) the official allegations regarding the defendant's role in the offense; (c) the formal charges lodged by the government against the defendant; (d) any corroborating or conflicting accounts of the offense or the defendant's role in the offense given by witnesses; and (e) any *independent* information (i.e., information from sources other than the defendant) regarding the defendant's behavior and functioning before, during, and after the offense. In developing this statement of facts, the expert should carefully specify the source of each piece of data mentioned, that is, whether it came from police reports, the indictment, defense counsel, probation, jail, or parole records, medical or psychiatric records, or from interviews with witnesses, family, friends, employers, teachers, or others in the defendant's environment around the time of the offense. If the expert has failed to gain access to data necessary to a complete understanding of the facts of the case, the nature of such data and the reason it was not obtained (e.g., refusal of the prosecutor to release a police report or refusal of the defendant to consent to release of medical records) should be noted here as well.

Next the report should relate the defendant's version of the offense, compare that with the official version, note and explore any inconsistencies between these versions, and indicate whether any apparent distortions on the defendant's part are consistent with some particular mental disorder (e.g., the sort of confabulation common in organic amnesic syndrome).

This aspect of the report should be followed by the results of a complete mental status evaluation, accompanied by a detailed history including statements regarding the defendant's: (a) family background; (b) physical and psychosocial development; (c) sexual and marital patterns; (d) educational and vocational experience; (e) military record; (f) psychiatric history; (g) relevant medical and surgical history; (h) use of drugs and alcohol; and (i) criminal record (both juvenile and adult). In detailing the defendant's criminal record, if any, reference should be made not only to the defendant's own report, but also to independent sources such as parole and probation records. Wherever possible, a psychiatric history of members of the defendant's immediate family should also be obtained and reported.

Next the report should deal with the psychological tests administered to the defendant. Ideally a comprehensive test battery (including both objective and projective measures) will have been utilized. In addition to the commonly administered intellectual and personality measures, such a battery should include some instrument(s) to assess, if only in a screening capacity, the possibility of central nervous system impairment. Of course, in cases presenting evidence of unprovoked violence, violent overreaction and/or a history of neurological dysfunction, a broad range of neuropsychological measures may be indicated. Finally, the comprehensive battery should also include assessment of the possibility of malingering (e.g., through use of the validity scales of the Minnesota Multiphasic Personality Inventory).

In describing the results of psychological testing, the examiner should include not only the findings of the tests, but also the defendant's test-taking attitude, the defendant's ability to concentrate on the test materials, and any other behavioral observations relative to the manner in which the tests were completed. In assessing the results of the psychological tests, the examiner should bear in mind and honestly disclose any reservations he or she has regarding their validity or reliability (e.g., any indication of deception by the defendant) and the implications that such reservations may have for the rest of the assessment. Moreover, the examiner needs to be exceedingly careful about the inferences drawn from the testing, remaining relatively close to the data at hand and avoiding unwarranted inferences or broad, sweeping generalizations.

The final aspect of the report, of course, will be some statement of the examiner's overall clinical findings. Such findings should be presented with a minimum of professional jargon and should be appropriately qualified (e.g., the examiner might refer to the difficulty involved in retrospective evaluations as well as any other factors, such as a lack of cooperation from the defendant or limited access to significant data, which may have hindered the evaluation). All conclusions should be adequately explained and supported by reference to specific data. Conclusions as to the ultimate issue of criminal responsibility should be left to the trier-of-fact.

David L. Shapiro, Ph.D., Diplomate of the American Board of Forensic Psychology, is a psychologist in independent practice in Washington, DC and Baltimore, MD. He is the author of the recently published book, *Psychological Evaluation and Expert Testimony: A Practical Guide to Forensic Work* (Van Nostrand Reinhold, 1983).

RESOURCES

Black, H. C. (1979). *Black's Law Dictionary* (rev. 5th ed.). St. Paul: West.

Bonnie, R. J. (1983). The moral basis of the insanity defense. *American Bar Association Journal, 69,* 194-197.

Durham v. United States, 214 F.2d 862 (D.C. Cir. 1954).

Frendak v. United States, 408 A.2d 364 (D.C. 1979).

McClure, K. R. (1982, February 24). Memorandum to Hon. Roger Fairchild, Senator, State of Idaho.

McDonald v. United States, 312 F.2d 847 (D.C. Cir. 1962).

M'Naughten's Case, 8 Eng. Rep. 718 (1843).

Parsons v. State, 81 Ala. 577, 2 So. 854 (1887).

United States v. Brawner, 471 F.2d 969 (D.C. Cir. 1972).

United States v. Lyons, 731 F.2d 243 (D.C. Cir. 1984).

SENTENCING GUIDELINES: CONSTRUCTION AND UTILIZATION*

Jolene Galegher and John S. Carroll

For most of the 20th century, sentencing practice has been based on the assumption that every case is unique and that sentences should, therefore, be determined by the individual needs and characteristics of the offender. The position of a judge under this "rehabilitative ideal" is analogous to that of a physician who must diagnose and treat the patient. In order to provide this individualized treatment, judges must have a range of sentencing options available and the authority to select the most appropriate alternative for each offender. In the past, the authority to make decisions on a discretionary basis has been insured by the enactment of indeterminate sentencing laws. These laws provide abstract principles to guide judicial decision making and provide broad limits on the range of acceptable sentences. For instance, there have been a number of attempts to provide judges with descriptions of what they should seek to achieve with sentences and what case factors they should consider (e.g., Model Penal Code, 1962) and most sentencing codes specify several degrees of misdemeanors and felonies with

*Preparation of this chapter was supported by Grant MH32855 from the National Institute of Mental Health. Portions of this chapter were adapted from "Voluntary Sentencing Guidelines: Prescription for Justice or Patent Medicine?" by J. Galegher and J. S. Carroll, 1983, *Law and Human Behavior, 7*, pp. 361-400.

maximum sentences graded by the seriousness of the offense. Within this general framework, however, judges have had considerable freedom to impose whatever sentence seems most appropriate to them.

In the past decade, we have witnessed a growing tide of criticism directed at these discretionary sentencing policies and practices. Several researchers have surveyed criminal justice rehabilitation programs and have failed to find evidence for the effectiveness of such rehabilitative efforts (Bailey, 1966; Greenberg, 1977; Lipton, Martinson, & Wilks, 1975). In addition to the argument that individualized sentencing practices have failed to produce the promised rehabilitation of offenders, some critics have charged that the existence of judicial discretion has led to unwarranted disparity in sentencing. In a book whose influence stemmed partly from the fact that it was written by a federal judge, Frankel (1973) charged that different judges assign different sentences to similarly situated offenders. His observations are supported by the results of numerous empirical investigations (Diamond & Zeisel, 1975; Forst & Wellford, 1981; Green, 1961; Hogarth, 1971; Hood, 1972; Partridge & Eldridge, 1974). In a study on Canadian magistrates, Hogarth (1971) concluded that "one can explain more about sentencing by knowing a few things about the judge than by knowing a great deal about the case" (p. 350).

Indeterminate sentencing laws and individualized sentencing practices have also been criticized on philosophical grounds. In *Struggle for Justice*, the American Friends Service Committee (1971) argued that sentencing policies based on the idea of rehabilitation are intrusive and discriminatory, resulting in the repression of political and social minorities. The Committee contended that rehabilitative programs were, in fact, cultural indoctrination efforts on the part of dominant groups within the society. They and other authors (The Twentieth Century Fund, 1976; von Hirsch, 1976) proposed that criminal sentences be based upon the principle of "just deserts," meaning that the severity of sanctions should be determined by the severity of the offense rather than the characteristics of the offender.

This widespread and multifaceted dissatisfaction with the exercise of judicial discretion has resulted in a range of reforms including bans on plea bargaining, collegial review of sentences by sentencing councils, the adoption of mandatory minimum prison terms, abolition of parole, provision for appellate review of sentences, legislatively-mandated sentencing guidelines or determinate sentencing laws, and voluntary sentencing guidelines (Blumstein, Cohen, Martin, & Tonry, 1983). Of these methods, sentencing guidelines seem to have become the most popular approach to sentencing reform. Sparks, Stecher, Albanese, and Shelly (1982) report that guidelines have been implemented on a state-wide basis in four states and Sparks (1981) noted that guidelines are being developed or at least considered in several other jurisdictions. The interest in guidelines appears to stem from the fact that they offer a means of reducing disparity and establishing a consistent rationale for a decision, without totally eliminating judicial discretion.

In this chapter, we will describe the guidelines approach, major types of guidelines and their advantages and disadvantages, the impact of guidelines on interrelated components of the criminal justice system, and some caveats for using guidelines and avoiding their misuse. Our intent is to provide an overview of the issues involved in the construction and implementation of sentencing guidelines that will be useful to attorneys, members of the judiciary, court administrators, legislators, and others who may be interested in this approach to sentencing reform. Readers who desire more detailed descriptions of the guidelines projects we discuss or more thorough examination of the statistical and social aspects of these projects should consult the sources to which we refer in our presentation.

THE GUIDELINES
APPROACH TO SENTENCING REFORM

Essentially, guidelines are decision aids which specify the factors to be considered in a decision and link these factors to a range of recommended options. For example, sentencing guidelines could specify how elements of the *crime* (e.g., crime type, injury to victim), *criminal record* (e.g., number of prior felony convictions), and *offender characteristics* (e.g., age, drug use) should be combined to produce a presumptive sentence or sentence range. Tables 1 and 2 (pp. 99, 100), which are adapted from a set of sentencing guidelines implemented in Denver, Colorado (Kress, 1980), provide a general illustration of how this system works. Using a worksheet such as the one shown in Table 1, the decision maker calculates offender and offense scores. The number of points to be assigned for various levels of each factor is specified in a manual prepared for use with the guidelines. After calculating the scores, the decision maker refers to a matrix such as the one shown in Table 2. This matrix specifies a range of sentences recommended for each combination of offender and offense scores.

As noted above, guidelines have spread rapidly because they offer an apparent balance of useful characteristics. Because the sentence is chosen from within a narrow range, as shown in Table 2, guidelines reduce (unwanted) disparity. However, the guidelines also retain (desired) discretion in two forms. First, because the guidelines specify ranges instead of points, the judge has the opportunity to adjust sentences within that range in response to the subtleties of specific cases. Second, in most cases, judges retain the authority to override the guidelines as deemed necessary. For example, under the guidelines shown here, the judge may go outside the guidelines and assign any legal sentence as long as a written justification is provided. Thus, according to the developers of the guidelines used by the U. S. Parole Commission (formerly the U. S. Board of Parole), guidelines of this type offer a means to "structure and control discretion—thus strengthening equity (fairness)—without eliminating it" (Gottfredson, Hoffman, Sigler, & Wilkins, 1975, p. 41).

In addition, guidelines are an explicit statement of policy that can be discussed, communicated to offenders and the public, and changed as appropriate. Thus, the basis of decisions is made clear and subject to scrutiny from both inside and outside the criminal justice system. This makes possible more informed discussions regarding

TABLE 1: GUIDELINE SENTENCE WORKSHEET

Offender_____ Docket Number_____

Judge_____ Date_____

Offense(s) Convicted of: _____

_____

_____

_____

OFFENSE CLASS (MOST SERIOUS OFFENSE)

A. Intra-Class Rank _____ +

B. Seriousness Modifier _____ +
   0 = No injury 0 = No weapon 0 = No sale of drugs
   1 = Injury   1 = Weapon   1 = Sale of drugs
   2 = Death

C. Victim Modifier (Crime Against Person) _____ =
    0 = Unknown victim
    −1 = Known victim

> OFFENSE SCORE

OFFENDER SCORE

A. Current Legal Status _____ +
   0 = Not on probation / parole, escape
   1 = On probation / parole, escape

B. Prior Juvenile Convictions _____ +
   0 = No convictions
   1 = 1-3 convictions
   2 = 4 or more convictions

C. Prior Adult Misdemeanor Convictions _____ +
   0 = No convictions
   1 = 1-3 convictions
   2 = 4 or more convictions

D. Prior Adult Felony Convictions _____ +
   0 = No convictions
   1 = 1 conviction
   3 = 2 or more convictions

E. Prior Adult Probation / Parole Revocations _____ +
   0 = None
   2 = 1 or more revocations

F. Prior Adult Incarcerations (Over 30 Days) _____ =
   0 = None
   1 = 1 incarceration
   3 = 2 or more incarcerations

> OFFENDER SCORE

Guideline Sentence_____

Actual Sentence_____

Reasons (if actual sentence does not fall within guideline range):

_____

Note. From *Prescription for Justice* (p. 258) by J.M. Kress, 1980, Cambridge, MA: Ballinger Publishing Company. Copyright © 1980 by Ballinger Publishing Company. Reprinted by permission.

TABLE 2: SENTENCE RECOMMENDATION MATRIX FOR CLASS THREE FELONIES (DENVER GUILDELINES)

OFFENSE SCORE	Offender Score						
	0-1	2	3	4	5-8	9-10	11-13
4-5	5-7 yrs. minimum 8-10 yrs. maximum	7-9 yrs. minimum 12-15 yrs. maximum	10-12 yrs. minimum 15-20 yrs. maximum	12-15 yrs. minimum 15-20 yrs. maximum	12-15 yrs. minimum 15-20 yrs. maximum	17-22 yrs. minimum 35-40 yrs. maximum	17-22 yrs. minimum 35-40 yrs. maximum
3	OUT	7-9 yrs. minimum 12-15 yrs. maximum	7-9 yrs. minimum 12-15 yrs. maximum	7-9 yrs. minimum 12-15 yrs. maximum	8-10 yrs. minimum 15-20 yrs. maximum	17-22 yrs. minimum 35-40 yrs. maximum	17-22 yrs. minimum 35-40 yrs. maximum
2	OUT	5-7 yrs. minimum 12-15 yrs. maximum	5-7 yrs. minimum 12-15 yrs. maximum	5-7 yrs. minimum 12-15 yrs. maximum	8-10 yrs. minimum 12-15 yrs. maximum	17-22 yrs. minimum 35-40 yrs. maximum	17-22 yrs. minimum 35-40 yrs. maximum
1	OUT	OUT	OUT	5-7 yrs. minimum 12-15 yrs. maximum	5-7 yrs. minimum 12-15 yrs. maximum	8-10 yrs. minimum 12-15 yrs. maximum	8-10 yrs. minimum 15-20 yrs. maximum

Note. From *Prescription for Justice* (p. 270) by J.M. Kress, 1980, Cambridge, MA: Ballinger Publishing Company. Copyright © 1980 by Ballinger Publishing Company. Reprinted by permission.

future policy developments and establishes a basis for accountability.

The guidelines approach includes two components: the guidelines themselves and a guidelines process that establishes how the guidelines are to be constructed and changed as warranted in the future. The guidelines themselves are, of course, the set of rules to be used for making a decision. Various versions of guidelines may differ on issues such as the number of factors to be considered in calculating offender and offense scores and the range of sentence recommendations contained in the guidelines matrices. The reader is referred to Sparks et al. (1982) for a discussion of issues related to the structure of the guidelines themselves. This chapter is primarily concerned with conceptual issues in the guidelines process. The guidelines process is a higher order set of procedures for making, implementing, and changing the rules. In general, the relationship between the guidelines and the guidelines process is analogous to that between the laws as currently in force and the legislative and appellate processes that create and change the laws (cf. Sales, 1983).

In terms of the *development* of guidelines, the process must involve some decision as to what the guidelines are intended to achieve. In general, guidelines may be distinguished on the basis of whether they were designed simply to standardize sentencing practice within a particular court or to reflect specific sentencing policies. In terms of *implementation*, the guidelines process must involve a strategy or set of procedures for introducing guidelines into the criminal justice system and eliciting compliance from justice system decision makers. Implementation strategies may vary on issues such as whether constraints on judicial discretion are legally binding and the nature of the procedures established to monitor compliance.

In order to provide for *evaluation* and *revision*, the guidelines process ordinarily requires a comparison between specific decisions and the decision recommended or specified by the guidelines. The results of these comparisons may be used to modify the guidelines by altering the factors, combination rules, or ranges of sentencing options. They may also be used to exhort decision makers to comply with the guidelines more consistently, or to reward or punish them as a function of their compliance. Thus, the complete guidelines process involves a cycle of policy generation, policy implementation, and policy evaluation.

We will discuss the development and implementation of guidelines in separate sections. However, since the evaluation of guidelines involves both the question of compliance (i.e., Are the guidelines being used correctly and consistently?) and the question of effectiveness (i.e., Do they produce the desired results?) our discussion of guidelines evaluation will be integrated into both sections.

THE GUIDELINES PROCESS

DESCRIPTION AND PRESCRIPTION IN THE DEVELOPMENT OF GUIDELINES

The guidelines currently used in the criminal justice system have been constructed by using either a descriptive ("bottom-up") or a prescriptive ("top-down") strategy. *Descriptive guidelines* are developed by analyzing past decisions to identify factors that predict case dispositions. The result is a model that provides a presumptive decision for each combination of relevant case factors. These empirically-based guidelines are similar to the "bootstrapping" (Dawes, 1971) or "policy-capturing" (Slovic, Fischhoff, & Lichtenstein, 1977) approaches developed by decision researchers. The principle is that the decision maker applies his or her own model with some undesirable error or noise due to fatigue, distraction, mood, and so forth. Mathematical analyses of past decisions allow us to uncover the underlying model and encourage the decision maker to follow his or her own model more closely. By using the mathematical model of a decision policy as a bootstrap to pull the decision maker up, or more accurately, into line, disparity is reduced. In the case of guidelines in the criminal justice system, researchers have assumed that all decision makers *share* a model or policy that may be uncovered and that disparity among individuals includes undesirable error to be removed.

Prescriptive guidelines are developed by specifying the ideal rather than summarizing past decisions. Policy makers identify the goals they wish to achieve and establish priorities or combination rules for translating these goals into sentences. Prescriptive guidelines are like a penal code established on the basis of legal theory and philosophy. For example, policy makers could decide that guidelines should embody a "modified just deserts" model of sentences graded according to crime seriousness and extent of prior criminal record. The guidelines would include seriousness and criminal record categories, with sentences recommended for each combination of crime and record. In a purely prescriptive system, these guidelines are arrived at by thoughtful discussions among authorized policy makers.

In this section we will discuss three examples of decision guidelines, developed for use within the criminal justice system, that have attracted national attention. Each of these three sets of guidelines represents a different mode of dealing with the prescription versus description issue. In discussing them, we will attempt to point out the differences among them and the advantages and disadvantages of each of these strategies. Although our focus is on *sentencing* guidelines, we will begin by discussing a set of guidelines developed for use in *parole* decisions because of their historical importance and because they represent a unique combination of descriptive and prescriptive approaches to guidelines development.

Parole Guidelines. The modern guidelines approach began with the landmark work of Gottfredson, Wilkins, and their colleagues with the U. S. Parole Commission in the early 1970s. Wilkins (1981) explains that the discussions that led to the parole project were initiated by the Chairman of the U. S. Parole Commission following a chance encounter with the researchers at a professional meeting.

The guidelines project began by asking parole board members to evaluate offenders on four criteria listed in the Model Penal Code (1962) as primary reasons for denial of parole: offense severity, participation in programs, institutional discipline, and certainty of favorable parole outcome. Thirty percent of all Youth Corrections Act cases during a 7-month period were rated on these four case factors. Recommendations for release or denial of parole and recommendations for time to serve before the next parole review were related to judgments on these four factors. The results showed that parole decisions at the initial hearing were related to offense severity and prognosis for success on parole, but not to the remaining factors. At later hearings for those initially denied parole, institutional discipline was strongly related to decisions.

The second step in the guidelines process was to establish objective indicators of the two factors related to initial parole decisions: severity and prognosis (risk). An objective indication of offense severity was developed by relating offense types to median time served by offenders paroled in the preceding 2 years. Offense ratings with similar median time served were combined to produce six severity categories. An objective indication of risk was constructed by relating characteristics of the case to known post-release outcomes of a sample of cases. The result was an actuarial prediction device called a Salient Factor Score placing cases into four risk categories. Table 3 (p. 105) presents the original device (Gottfredson, Wilkins, & Hoffman, 1978, p. 17).

The guidelines could then be constructed from these objective indicators of severity and risk. The median time served for each severity/risk combination was determined (separately for youth and adult cases) on a large sample of parole decisions. Some "smoothing" of the medians was made by visual inspection to increase consistency. Ranges around each median were then set by discussion with board members and hearing examiners. Table 4 (p. 106) presents the original parole guidelines (Gottfredson et al., 1978, p. 20-21).

These guidelines have been referred to as *descriptive* guidelines, although the developers acknowledge that they are intended to *prescribe* appropriate parole recommendations for particular cases. However, the use of the term descriptive, is justified in that the guidelines construction process was based on an analysis that described the major dimensions considered in parole decisions, and the median time served was derived from

TABLE 3: ORIGINAL SALIENT FACTOR SCORE

Salient Factors (please check each correct statement):

_____ A. Commitment offense did not involve auto theft.

_____ B. Subject had one or more codefendants (whether brought to trial with subject or not).

_____ C. Subject has no prior (adult or juvenile) incarcerations.

_____ D. Subject has no prior (adult or juvenile) sentences (i.e., probation, fine, suspended sentence).

_____ E. Subject has not served more than 18 consecutive months during any prior incarceration (adult or juvenile).

_____ F. Subject has completed the 12th grade or received G.E.D.

_____ G. Subject has never had probation or parole revoked (or been committed for a new offense while on probation or parole).

_____ H. Subject was 18 years old or older at first conviction (adult or juvenile).

_____ I. Subject was 18 years old or older at first commitment (adult or juvenile).

_____ J. Subject was employed, or full-time student, for a total of at least 6 months during the last 2 years in the community.

_____ K. Subject plans to reside with spouse and / or children after release.

_____ Total number of correct statements = favorable factors = score

TABLE 4: GUIDELINES FOR DECISION MAKING (ADULT CASES): AVERAGE TOTAL TIME SERVED BEFORE RELEASE (INCLUDING JAIL TIME)

Offense Characteristics (Seriousness)	Offender Characteristics — Salient (Favorable) Factor Score (Probability of Favorable Parole Outcome)			
Severity	(9-11) Very High	(6-8) High	(4-5) Fair	(0-3) Low
Category A: Low Severity Offenses				
Minor theft; walkaway; immigration law violations; alcohol law violations	6-10 months	8-12 months	10-14 months	12-16 months
Category B: Low/Moderate Severity Offenses				
Possess marijuana; possess heavy narcotics, less than or equal to $50; theft, unplanned; forgery or counterfeiting, less than $500; burglary, daytime	8-12 months	12-16 months	16-20 months	20-25 months
Category C: Moderate Severity Offenses				
Vehicle theft; forgery or counterfeiting, greater than $500; sale of marijuana; planned theft; possess heavy narcotics, greater than $50; escape; Mann Act — no force; Selective Service	12-16 months	16-20 months	20-24 months	24-30 months
Category D: High Severity Offenses				
Sell heavy narcotics; burglary, weapon or nighttime; violence, "spur of the moment"; sexual act, force	16-20 months	20-26 months	26-32 months	32-38 months
Category E: Very High Severity Offenses				
Armed robbery; criminal act — weapon; sexual act, force, injury; assault, serious bodily harm; Mann Act — force	26-36 months	36-45 months	45-55 months	55-65 months
Category F: Highest Severity Offenses				
Willful homicide; kidnapping; armed robbery, weapon fired or serious injury	Information not available owing to limited number of cases			

Notes:

1. If an offense behavior can be classified under more than one category, the most serious applicable category is to be used. If an offense behavior involved multiple separate offenses, the seriousness level may be increased.

2. If an offense is not listed, the proper category may be obtained by comparing the seriousness of the offense with those of similar offenses listed.

3. If a continuance is to be recommended, subtract 30 days (1 month) to allow for release division.

past sentences. These guidelines were first implemented in a pilot project in 1972 and, since that time, have become a regular part of the Parole Commission's decision procedures.

Successful construction and implementation of parole guidelines prompted the developers to consider extension of their approach to the domain of sentencing decisions. However, as will be seen below, confusion over what these descriptive guidelines actually described made early sentencing guidelines less successful than their predecessors in the parole context.

Early Sentencing Guidelines. Beginning in mid-1974, a set of feasibility studies were carried out in Denver and the district courts of Vermont to determine whether the guidelines approach could be used with sentencing decisions in those jurisdictions (Wilkins, Kress, Gottfredson, Calpin, & Gelman, 1978). Later, under the direction of Jack Kress (Kress, 1980), guidelines were constructed using a strategy that involved specifying several models that "predicted" prior case dispositions, and using these models as a basis for decisions about factors to be included in sentencing guidelines. Separate sets of guidelines were constructed for criminal courts in Denver, Chicago, Newark, and Phoenix. Kress and his colleagues also provided technical advice and assistance in the construction of a similar set of guidelines in Philadelphia.

In each jurisdiction, data regarding the offender's personal and criminal history, the nature of the present offense, case processing factors (such as bail status at the time of conviction), and length and type of sentence were coded from case records. Using this archival data, a series of analyses was conducted in order to identify combinations of variables that accounted for substantial portions of variance in the prediction of sentences. These combinations of variables were then used as a basis for constructing models of sentencing guidelines.

Several different versions of guidelines were developed in each jurisdiction by partitioning cases in different ways or by including or excluding controversial variables such as juvenile record. These models were then presented to members of the judiciary as alternative ways of representing the basic policy discovered through statistical analysis; the judges used them as a basis for making decisions about the particular offender and offense variables to be included in the final form of the guidelines. According to Kress (1980), this procedure allowed both judges and researchers to participate in the guidelines development process with decisions being made on the basis of judicial preferences informed by the recommendations of the researchers.

In general, the guidelines eventually developed in each of the jurisdictions were similar to those shown in Tables 1 and 2. They include two major dimensions—criminal history and crime seriousness—and were presented to the judges in the form of a set of matrices or grids with one of these dimensions on each axis. In order to determine the appropriate sentence in a particular case, the judge examines the matrix for the point of intersection between offender and offense scores. Thus, the procedures followed by Kress and his colleagues appear to be similar to those used in the development of the earlier parole guidelines. However, because of subtle differences in the methodologies employed by the two sets of researchers, the two projects produced guidelines fundamentally different in their descriptive bases.

The parole guidelines developers began by asking board members to evaluate offenders on abstract dimensions that reflected major issues or normative goals in parole decision making. That is, an offender's rating on likelihood of a favorable parole outcome, for instance, may be interpreted as an indicator of the likelihood of achieving a particular decision goal—in this case, success on parole. Thus, by examining the relationship between ratings on these variables and parole decisions, the developers of the parole guidelines were, in fact, measuring the relative importance of these normative goals and concerns. When understood this way, this analysis indicated that parole decision makers were primarily concerned with insuring that offenders are punished in proportion to the seriousness of their offenses and with protecting the community from offenders who are unlikely to perform favorably on parole. It should be clear, then, that these descriptive guidelines were not composed of specific case facts that decision makers considered during formulation of their recommendations.

Rather, this analysis identified (described) the issues or goals of concern to the decision makers.

Adopting a similar approach in the sentencing context would have meant asking judges to rate offenders on abstract variables such as dangerousness and amenability to rehabilitation as well as seriousness of offense, and then attempting to objectify the subjective variables that were the strongest predictors of sentencing decisions. It appears that the sentencing guidelines developers intended to parallel the methodology of the parole guidelines project, but that the parallel was not exact. In their feasibility studies (Wilkins et al., 1978), sentencing guidelines developers asked judges to rate offenders on three dimensions—perceived public disapprobation of the offense, perceived public disapprobation of the offender's criminal record, and probability of recidivism—that might reasonably be construed as relevant to various normative sentencing goals. However, their attempts to obtain more objective measures of these dimensions did not follow the approach used in the parole situation. For instance, despite the fact that rated probability of recidivism was identified as the strongest subjective predictor of sentencing decisions in Denver, the developers did not identify variables that predicted *actual* recidivism. Instead, a number of criminal history variables that correlated with sentence severity were used as a basis for calculating the score on the offender dimension of the guidelines. Although these variables probably predict recidivism, the guidelines developers did not obtain direct evidence to that effect.

Following the feasibility studies, the sentencing guidelines researchers apparently dropped the idea of obtaining subjective ratings of offender and offense characteristics. Instead, they bypassed the step of empirically assessing the dimensions that influence judicial decisions and proceeded directly to an assessment of the relationship between case factors and decision outcomes. The result of this tactic was that the factors identified as predictors of sentences in this research were, of course, specific case facts that could only be summarized in terms of kinds of information, that is, information about the offense, social stability, or criminal history. Consequently, the dimensions used in the construction of the sentencing guidelines were conceptually quite different from those that formed the basis of the parole guidelines. In the former case they can only be conceptualized as "kinds of information that are related to sentencing decisions," whereas in the latter case they can be understood as "issues that are important in parole decisions." Another way of expressing this difference is that the sentencing guidelines were organized on the basis of *input* to the decision process but the parole guidelines were organized on the basis of desired decision *outcomes* (Rich, Sutton, Clear, & Saks, 1982).

The methodological differences in the construction of these two sets of guidelines are important for three reasons. First, the fact that the parole guidelines were constructed on the basis of issues that had been empirically identified as important to parole decision makers meant that the completed guidelines were compatible with decision makers' goals and values. Second, construction of the guidelines on the basis of issues rather than case facts meant that the guidelines serve as a clear statement of public policy about the goals of the parole board. The offense severity dimension reflects an intention to assign more severe penalties to more serious crimes and the parole prognosis dimension reflects an intention to provide more extended protection of the public from offenders who appear to be likely to commit future crimes. Third, and perhaps most important, the difference in the way the two sets of guidelines are constructed means that there is a difference in the way that their impact can be evaluated.

In order to understand this difference, it is useful to consider what it means for these guidelines to work. The fact that the dimensions used in the construction of the parole guidelines embodied normative decision goals means that there are external criteria against which the correctness of the decisions can be measured. This is most apparent in the case of the parole prognosis dimension. Because probability of recidivism is used as a basis for parole release decisions and because recidivism is a measurable outcome, one can observe whether the predicted outcomes do occur. The Parole Commission has, in fact, carried out subsequent studies to determine whether the Salient Factor Score has retained its validity as a predictor of parole success (Hoffman, 1982a, 1982b; Hoffman & Beck, 1976, 1980; Hoffman & Stone-Meierhoefer, 1979; Hoffman, Stone-Meierhoefer, & Beck, 1978). On the basis of these studies, the guidelines have since been modified by the Parole Commissioners in accordance with the principles of self-correction which were part of the original guidelines model (Gottfredson et al., 1978). Thus, over time, there is the potential for the scale to become an increasingly accurate predictor of success on parole.

However, it is not imperative that the normative dimensions used in the construction of guidelines involve the prediction of subsequent events or outcomes. All that is necessary is the specification of some criterion or principle to be used as a basis for decisions. One can then observe whether decisions were, indeed, based on the designated criteria, and, if not, make the proper adjustments in decision practices and/or examine instances of noncompliance to determine whether the departure seems justified, is a result of ambiguity in the policy statement, or is a true error.

In discussing evaluation of the sentencing guidelines, Kress (1980), proposed the creation of a forum for examining departures from the guidelines in order to discern whether they represent some substantive disagreement with the guidelines that should be considered in the development of future versions. But in the absence of some prescriptive basis for the guidelines, it seems that it would be impossible to know which departures were because of extraordinary circumstances, which were because of substantive disagreements or ambiguities, and which were unjustified errors. Thus, failure to specify a normative decision criterion means that observation of compliance rates would not yield information that can be used to inform or adjust decision practices; nor would the examination of departures lead to the identification of gaps or ambiguities in decision policy. Under these circumstances, the idea of using information about decision practices after guidelines are implemented as feedback to improve subsequent versions of the guidelines ultimately reduces to making the guidelines more like "whatever is being done."

Thus, there is a clear difference in the potential benefit or advantage that the two sets of guidelines provide. The sentencing guidelines offer only the possibility of making more consistent, or equitable, decisions, whereas the parole guidelines offer the possibility of obtaining feedback regarding the attainment of normative decision goals in addition to enhancing equity in decision making.

From our present vantage point, it may seem obvious that, in order to serve as an instrument for the expression and enactment of policy, decision guidelines must be constructed on the basis of what that policy is intended to achieve. However, as the preceding discussion indicated, it did not seem so obvious to the developers of either of these sets of guidelines. Normative decision goals were included in the parole guidelines almost by accident and were excluded completely from the sentencing guidelines constructed by Kress and his colleagues. However, the lessons derived from these early experiences led to the decision to proceed on an explicitly prescriptive basis in the most recent, and most successful, effort to regulate judicial discretion through sentencing guidelines.

The Minnesota Sentencing Guidelines. The discussion above has focused on the necessity to specify normative decision goals in the construction of decision guidelines. Most philosophical treatments of sentencing specify five potential ideals or goals of this type (cf. Diamond & Herhold, 1981). They include retribution or "just deserts," incapacitation, rehabilitation, and general and specific deterrence. In addition, sentencing decisions may be based on concern for the achievement of functional goals such as assigning sentences compatible with the rehabilitative, supervisory, or incarcerative resources of the criminal justice system. Recently, guidelines incorporating both of these kinds of policy goals were constructed and implemented on a state-wide basis in Minnesota.

The construction of the Minnesota guidelines was based on a concern for keeping the prison population at a constant level and, within this stipulation, decisions about the distribution of punishments for various classes of offenders were made on the basis of a "modified just deserts" policy (Minnesota Sentencing Guidelines Commission, 1982). This means that sentence severity is determined primarily by offense severity with less emphasis given to criminal history. The choice of the just deserts model as the normative basis for sentencing is appealing on practical grounds because the only requirement is some way of ranking offenses on the basis of severity. Although there is no doubt that this is a difficult process and that there are also difficulties associated with linking offenses to penalties, it seems clear that these determinations are less complicated than the range of measurement issues associated with utilitarian sentencing philosophies (i.e., predicting dangerousness or other recidivism, specifying the deterrent effect of particular sanctions for particular classes of offenders, evaluating amenability to rehabilitation efforts or determining the cost of imprisonment). Thus, the primary empirical issue in the construction of the Minnesota guidelines was the accuracy of the projections made to predict demand for incarceration.

However, this comment should not be taken to mean that we advocate the just deserts principle as the basis for sentencing or that it is impossible to create guidelines on any other grounds. Indeed, some authors (Forst & Wellford, 1981) have begun to specify the measurement problems that would need to be considered to develop guidelines based on other principles and have also suggested the development of hybrid sentencing guidelines based on different principles for different classes of offenders. And, as noted above, Sparks et al. (1982) have described methods that can be used to analyze the appropriateness of a proposed set of guidelines in light of particular policy preferences.

As we have argued above, the benefit of clearly stated normative and/or functional goals for sentencing is that they make possible an intelligent assessment of the effectiveness of the specified sentencing practices in the achievement of those goals. For instance, in Minnesota the guidelines specify a general policy, presumptive sentences intended to reflect that policy, and fairly specific conditions that indicate when imposition of a sentence other than the presumptive sentence would be a more appropriate means of carrying out the general policy. This combination of criteria makes it possible to evaluate decisions that involve departures from the guidelines in order to determine whether they were warranted and, if necessary, to formulate more detailed rules governing departures. If sentencing guidelines do not embody such criteria, no meaningful evaluation (i.e., evaluation that makes it possible to improve practice) is possible.

More generally, we believe that the construction of sentencing guidelines on normative grounds could have salutary effects on the criminal justice system as a whole. This speculation is based on the interrelationship between the attributes of a comprehensive sentencing policy. If sentencing goals are clearly stated, along with rules for equitable distribution of the penalties or treatments believed to produce those goals, the availability of goal-relevant effectiveness data would eventually create pressure to adopt achievable goals or to provide resources that are adequate to achieve the goals that are preferred.

In sum, although it may be difficult, it is possible to create guidelines that are compatible with whatever sentencing goals are preferred. Further, the possibility of assuring equity in sentencing and the promise of obtaining information relevant to the achievement of goals means that guidelines of this type represent a substantial advance in sentencing practice.

However, even the most sensibly constructed guidelines will not be useful as a policy instrument unless they are successfully implemented. Rich et al. (1982) have shown that sentencing practices were not materially affected by the voluntary sentencing guidelines developed by Kress (1980) and his colleagues. Although the goal of the project was to make sentences consistent with the description of past sentencing practice embodied in the guidelines, impact analyses by Rich et al. (1982) indicate that, in general, sentences were no more consistent with what the guidelines would recommend after they were introduced than they were before. However, the authors were not surprised by this finding because their interviews with court personnel indicated that the guidelines were never effectively implemented. In the following section we will discuss the nature of the sentencing system in order to develop an appreciation of the problems involved in the implementation of sentencing guidelines and will use the two sets of sentencing guidelines we have discussed above as examples of relatively successful and unsuccessful strategies for overcoming obstacles to successful implementation.

GUIDELINES IMPLEMENTATION

In order to understand the issues associated with the implementation of sentencing guidelines, it is useful to conceive of the criminal courts as an organization with certain structural features. These features include a high degree of *complexity* and a low degree of *centralization*. *Complexity* is a multifaceted concept, referring to the number of occupational specialties within an organization, the level of professionalization, and the potential for differentiation in task structure. *Centralization* refers to whether the organization has a well-defined, hierarchical authority structure.

We regard the courts as a complex and decentralized organization for several reasons. The courts are complex because the main actors, judges and attorneys, are all high-status professionals, accustomed to a high level of autonomy in their work, whose roles within the courts differ. Sentence determinations are largely a product of negotiations among members of these various occupational specialties, who operate as a work group organized by courtroom (Eisenstein & Jacob, 1977). These work groups operate relatively autonomously; negotiations among members of the work group are ordinarily carried out in private, and the resulting decisions are only sometimes subject to appellate review. Thus, the courts are also decentralized. The implications of these structural features for the attainment of functional goals (such as achieving a satisfactory rate of case dispositions and obtaining opportunities for the expression of expertise and power) and the effects of decision guidelines on efforts to attain those goals are very important.

First, consider the impact of sentencing guidelines on the achievement of case dispositions. In a detailed critique of the Kress (1980) guidelines, Rich et al. (1982)

argue that guidelines are inherently problematic as an approach to sentencing reform because this method of constraining judicial discretion fails to consider the reality of plea bargaining as a means of maintaining a satisfactory level of dispositions in the courts. In the usual case, the offender can be persuaded to waive his or her right to a trial and the possibility of being acquitted in return for the promise of a lighter sentence than would be imposed if he or she went to trial and were found guilty. Since jury trials are expensive and time consuming, this practice saves the court time and money. As all observers of the criminal justice system know, plea bargaining is a frequent and widespread phenomenon. In some courts, 90% or more of convictions are obtained by guilty plea. In general, the problem associated with introducing guidelines in situations like these is that to the extent guidelines render sentences more predictable, offenders have no incentive to forego a jury trial. If the outcome will be the same regardless of whether one pleads guilty or is convicted after trial, one might as well go to trial and hope for a sympathetic jury or an incompetent prosecutor.

Description of sentencing practices in Philadelphia as noted in Rich et al. (1982) provides a striking example of the importance of the threat of harsher punishment in holding down the trial rate. In the Philadelphia Court of Common Pleas, guilty pleas are "encouraged" by the practice of assigning jury trial cases to judges known to give especially severe sentences. Indeed, the authors present evidence indicating that offenders sentenced by these judges receive prison sentences that are, on the average, 10 years longer than those assigned to offenders who pleaded guilty or were convicted at a bench trial. According to Rich et al. (1982), it is general knowledge within the Philadelphia court system that, whatever other judges in that court did with the sentencing guidelines, those who handled jury trials ignored them. In fact, one Philadelphia judge stated openly that, "Sentence disparity is used as a tool to dispose of cases" (Rich et al., 1982, p. 181).

However, in the more typical case, guilty pleas are encouraged by offers of lower sentences (sentence bargaining) or reduced charges (charge bargaining), rather than through the manipulation of case assignments as in Philadelphia. In situations like these attaining a satisfactory rate of case dispositions is a relatively complicated matter. It requires agreement among several individuals who have competing interests. They must achieve a fairly delicate balance between their need to settle cases and their desire to obtain favorable outcomes. Thus, discretion on the part of all actors is an essential element in the bargaining process. If there is no room for discretion the capacity to make offers that will facilitate case disposition is eliminated.

In general, there are two problems associated with introducing sentencing guidelines in this kind of situation. First, because the opportunity for obtaining a reduced sentence on a particular charge is more limited, the likelihood of turning to charge bargaining as a means of achieving a satisfactory level of case processing increases. Second, because the sentence associated with a particular charge is more clearly specified, the power to set charges is, effectively, the power to determine sentences. In most jurisdictions, charges are determined by the prosecutor. Consequently, in addition to the potential of increasing the demand for jury trials to an economically unacceptable level, sentencing guidelines carry with them the potential for simply shifting discretion in sentencing decisions from the judge to the prosecutor rather than minimizing overall discretion (Alschuler, 1978).

In addition to these procedural difficulties, guidelines trigger the repugnance felt by many professionals for any form of standardization. In commenting on implementation problems in human service delivery systems, Rossi (1978) has observed that,

It is of the essence of a professional occupation that incumbents function with minimal supervision, the assumption being that professionals need little supervision because their training fits them to make appropriate discretionary decisions about the content, pacing and outcome of their work. (p. 585)

Diamond (1981) notes that, "Sentencing provides one of the clearest examples of a legal decision able to absorb legal reform with an apparent minimum of reverberation..." (p. 151), and provides interesting accounts of how these accommodations are accomplished. It is likely that professional workers' reluctance to relinquish the capacity to do what they think is right in a particular situation is part of the explanation for these adaptive processes. In general, then, consideration of the structural characteristics of the courts suggests that there are likely to be significant problems associated with the implementation of sentencing guidelines.

Overcoming this latter problem, the reluctance of organizational authorities, appears to depend on the nature of the implementation strategy adopted. The early sentencing guidelines (Kress, 1980) were implemented on a *voluntary* basis. Because the guidelines did not have the force of law or administrative authority, there were no sanctions attached to imposing a sentence outside the range recommended by the guidelines or failing to specify a reason for doing so. Furthermore, it does not appear that there was a high degree of interest among or participation by judges in the decision to adopt these guidelines. In fact, Rich et al. (1982) have pointed out that some judges do not appear to have understood the purposes of the guidelines or how to use them (see Galegher & Carroll, 1983 and Rich et al., 1982 for a more detailed discussion of these issues). The failure to elicit support for the guidelines and involvement in their development and implementation almost certainly contributed to their demise. Indeed, common sense would seem to dictate that, where the success of a planned change effort depends on voluntary compliance with new procedures, it is essential to elicit broad support at an early stage of the process.

In the Minnesota guidelines process, these issues were handled more successfully. The most obvious difference between the Minnesota guidelines and those developed by Kress (1980) and his colleagues is that the Minnesota guidelines were *legislatively imposed* rather than voluntarily adopted. The legislature provided for the establishment of a commission made up of private citizens and individuals from various criminal justice interest groups, charged with the responsibility of preparing a proposed set of guidelines for the legislature's approval.

The fact that the guidelines were legislatively imposed meant that they could not simply be ignored by system actors inclined to resist change. Representatives from the judiciary and the prosecution and defense bars, along with criminal justice system administrators and citizens participated in the development of the Minnesota guidelines. Hence the interests of these groups were considered and individual representatives could serve as guidelines interpreters and advocates within their professional groups. In general then, this combination of authority and participation in the development process by members of the affected groups was an appropriate strategy for introducing an innovation like sentencing guidelines in a complex, decentralized organization like the courts. The inappropriateness of a voluntary strategy, involving only judges, is indicated not only by its ineffectiveness, but by the fact that a guidelines system instituted without legislative approval can, very easily, be rendered totally obsolete by legislature alterations in sentencing laws. In fact, this is precisely what occurred in several of the jurisdictions involved in the voluntary guidelines project, even before an initial evaluation was possible (Rich et al., 1982).

In addition to providing an authority structure appropriate for the organization and the nature of the task during the development phase, the establishment of an administrative agency meant that there was an organizational unit responsible for overseeing the implementation process. The reports cited above, as well as Sparks et al. (1982), indicate that these activities were characterized by a high level of professionalism and meticulous attention to detail. This list of implementation activities carried out by the Minnesota Sentencing Guidelines Commission and reported in Blumstein et al. (1983) demonstrates the range of procedural issues that must be considered. The Commission:

—Prepared commentary included in training materials on the guidelines to clarify the commission's intent, relevant statutory provisions, and applicable rules of criminal procedure to aid court personnel.

—Worked with the corrections department to supplement the statewide criminal records information system to ensure the availability of necessary data.

—In conjunction with the Minnesota Corrections Association, devised a new presentence investigation form that includes information necessary for the calculation of the guidelines sentences.

—Recommended several legislative changes necessary to facilitate transition to the new system.

—Conducted extensive training sessions for all judges, prosecutors, probation personnel, and defense attorneys to familiarize them with the guidelines. (p. 176-177)

The Commission's staff also has responsibility for monitoring compliance with the guidelines and evaluating their impact. Again, this activity seems to have been very carefully executed. In particular, the Commission staff reviewed each incoming sentencing worksheet and contacted probation officers to clarify and correct errors prior to sentencing for a period of *2 years* after the guidelines became effective (Minnesota Sentencing Guidelines Commission, p. 15). This practice resulted in a decline in error rates from over 50% to 3-5% eighteen months after implementation. Similarly, the staff's ongoing evaluation activities have examined the effects of the guidelines not only on sentencing practices, but also on other aspects of the operation of the criminal justice system. Early indications are that the guidelines developed by the Commission and its staff have substantially increased uniformity and proportionality in felony sentencing in Minnesota (Minnesota Sentencing Guidelines Commission, 1982). Although important problems remain (Blumstein et al., 1983; Minnesota Sentencing Guidelines Commission, 1982), at least some of them seem to be manageable within the present legal and administrative framework.

This brief review of the Minnesota guidelines project indicates that if guidelines are constructed on the basis of preferred normative and/or functional goals and the development and implementation processes are carried out with adequate concern for administrative procedure within an appropriate authority structure, they can help to produce meaningful sentencing reform. However, it is important to note two important caveats regarding this hopeful conclusion. First, a detailed report (Martin, 1983) comparing the development of state-wide sentencing guidelines in Minnesota and Pennsylvania points out that the establishment of a commission authorized to develop sentencing guidelines under the auspices of the state legislature is not, by itself, a procedural panacea. Although Pennsylvania created a similar commission, differences in the political culture of these two states, differences in task definition, and differences in the personalities and views of Commission members meant that the development process and the guidelines eventually created were quite different. The Pennsylvania guidelines are *advisory* rather than presumptive and sentence recommendations consist of relatively broad, rather than narrow, ranges. Martin (1983) concludes that the Pennsylvania guidelines serve symbolic political ends by affirming the desirability of statewide sentencing policy and providing a common reference point for judges but are likely to have little real effect on discretion or sentencing outcomes.

Future efforts to develop and implement sentencing guidelines along the lines of the Minnesota project will help determine whether the early positive outcomes obtained there can be achieved in other locations or whether the Minnesota experience represents a particularly auspicious combination of political culture, task structure, skillful leadership, and professional expertise impossible to replicate (Cook, 1981). At this point, the lessons available from careful study of experience with state-wide guidelines in Minnesota, Pennsylvania, and also New Jersey and Massachusetts (see Sparks et al., 1982 for a preliminary analysis) seem to indicate that the commission model has important advantages and could be viable in many locations if careful consideration were given to various features of the organization's environment.

The second, and more important, caveat involves the inherent limitations of guidelines as a mechanism for sentencing reform. As Rich et al. (1982) warn,

> Merely giving sentencing guidelines the force and effect of law will not, however, obviate the difficulties caused by the interdependence of judges, prosecutors and defense attorneys. The need to induce guilty pleas will continue to create pressure to charge bargain. (p. 207)

In other words, even sensible, well-constructed, carefully implemented guidelines do not eliminate the possibility of shifting discretion in sentencing decisions from judges to prosecutors (Alschuler, 1978).

Although detailed studies of plea negotiation practices are now being carried out to determine the extent and form of charge bargaining and its overall impact on sentencing practices in Minnesota (Minnesota Sentencing Guidelines Commission, 1982), early analyses indicate some evidence of shifting discretion there (Blumstein et al., 1983). Rich et al. (1982) contend that dealing with this dilemma will eventually require including method of conviction in sentencing guidelines and, thus, preventing prosecutorial abuse of charging discretion while providing explicit notice to defendants regarding the cost of going to trial. The legal questions surrounding this idea are beyond our expertise, but we want to point out that the Minnesota Commission's research activities again demonstrate the advantage of having an organizational unit charged with monitoring sentencing practices. If their research identified charge bargaining practices that distorted the intent of the overall sentencing policy, presumably they would be in a strong position to recommend changes in the guidelines or restrictions on charge bargaining activities.

SUMMARY: PROMISES AND PITFALLS

The guidelines approach has captured attention in the past decade as a way to reduce disparity and make policy explicit without eliminating discretion to deal with individual cases. Notable successes have occurred, but widespread imitation has produced notable failures as well (Galegher & Carroll, 1983; Rich et al., 1982; Sparks et al., 1982). This chapter has attempted to capture the conceptual framework of guidelines so that potential imitators or critics will understand the process of guidelines development and implementation.

To be effective, guidelines must be predicated on an understanding of the way decisions are made and their impact on other elements of the criminal justice system. Guidelines must incorporate a clear and consensual statement of policy goals. Implementation requires a felt need for involvement and support from key decision makers, representation of constituencies on commissions, and administrative procedures to monitor compliance that have some informal or formal authority. Steps must be taken throughout the process to motivate and educate key personnel to avoid errors, misuse, and circumvention of the system.

It seems that we have entered a new era of criminal justice policy making. No longer is policy set implicitly by individual whim or legislative vagary. Instead, policy makers are recognizing the value of an explicit public policy backed by careful research rather than mere ideology. The role of the researcher as partner with the decision maker in the criminal justice system is emerging as the new rigor of the 1980s.

Jolene Galegher, Ph.D., a social psychologist, is a Post-Doctoral Fellow in the Department of Psychology at the University of Illinois at Urbana-Champaign. Previously a research associate at Loyola University of Chicago, Dr. Galegher's research interests include individual and organizational factors affecting legal decision making.

John S. Carroll, Ph.D., a social psychologist, is an Associate Professor of Organizational Studies at the Sloan School of Management of the Massachusetts Institute of Technology. Until recently, Dr. Carroll was on the psychology faculty at Loyola University of Chicago. His research interests and publications are in the areas of decision making, cognitive social psychology, and law and psychology.

RESOURCES

Alschuler, A. W. (1978). Sentencing reform and prosecutorial power: A critique of recent proposals for "fixed" and "presumptive" sentencing. *University of Pennsylvania Law Review, 126*, 550-577.

American Friends Service Committee. (1971). *Struggle for Justice: A Report on Crime and Punishment in America.* New York: Hill and Wang.

Bailey, W. C. (1966). Correctional outcome: An evaluation of 100 reports. *Journal of Criminal Law and Criminology, 57*, 153-171.

Blumstein, W., Cohen, J., Martin, S. E., & Tonry, M. (Eds.). (1983). *Research on Sentencing: The Search for Reform.* Washington, DC: National Academy of Sciences.

Cook, T. D. (1981). Dilemmas in evaluation of social programs. In M. B. Brewer & B. F. Collins (Eds.), *Scientific Inquiry and the Social Sciences* (pp. 257-286). San Francisco: Jossey-Bass.

Dawes, R. M. (1971). A case study of graduate admissions: Application of three principles of human decision making. *American Psychologist, 26*, 180-188.

Diamond, S. S. (1981). Detecting legal change and its impact. (1981). In L. Bickman (Ed.), *Applied Social Psychology Annual* (Vol. 2, pp. 139-164). Beverly Hills: Sage Publications.

Diamond, S. S., & Herhold, C. J. (1981). Understanding criminal sentencing: Views from law and social psychology. In G. M. Stephenson & J. M. Davis (Eds.), *Progress in Applied Social Psychology* (Vol. 1, pp. 67-102). London: John Wiley & Sons, Ltd.

Diamond, S. S., & Zeisel, H. (1975). Sentencing councils: A study of sentencing disparity and its reduction. *University of Chicago Law Review, 43*, 109-149.

Eisenstein, J., & Jacob, H. (1977). *Felony Justice: An Organizational Analysis of the Criminal Courts.* Boston: Little, Brown & Co.

Forst, B., & Wellford, C. (1981). Punishment and sentencing: Developing sentencing guidelines empirically from principles of punishment. *Hofstra Law Review, 9*, 799-837.

Frankel, M. E. (1973). *Criminal Sentences: Law Without Order.* New York: Hill and Wang.

Galegher, J., & Carroll, J. S. (1983). Voluntary sentencing guidelines: Prescription for justice or patent medicine? *Law and Human Behavior, 7*, 361-400.

Gottfredson, D. M., Hoffman, P. B., Sigler, M. H., & Wilkins, L. T. (1975). Making paroling policy explicit. *Crime and Delinquency, 21*, 34-44.

Gottfredson, D. M., Wilkins, L. T., & Hoffman, P. B. (1978). *Guidelines for Parole and Sentencing.* Lexington, MA: Lexington Books.

Green, E. (1961). *Judicial Attitudes in Sentencing.* London: Macmillan.

Greenberg, D. (1977). The correctional effects of corrections. In D. Greenberg (Ed.), *Corrections & Punishment* (pp. 111-148). Beverly Hills: Sage.

Hoffman, P. B. (1982a). *Screening for Risk: A Revised Salient Factor Score (SFS 81)* (Report 31). U. S. Parole Commission.

Hoffman, P. B. (1982b). Females, recidivism and the Salient Factor Score: A note. *Criminal Justice and Behavior, 9*, 121-125.

Hoffman, P. B., & Beck, J. L. (1976). Salient Factor Score validation: A 1972 release cohort. *Journal of Criminal Justice, 4*, 69-76.

Hoffman, P. B., & Beck, J. L. (1980). Revalidating the Salient Factor Score: A research note. *Journal of Criminal Justice, 8*, 185-188.

Hoffman, P. B., & Stone-Meierhoefer, B. (1979). Post-release arrest experiences of federal prisoners: A six-year follow-up. *Journal of Criminal Justice, 7*, 193-216.

Hoffman, P. B., Stone-Meierhoefer, B., & Beck, J. L. (1978). Salient Factor Score and releasee behavior: Three validation samples. *Law and Human Behavior, 2*, 47-63.

Hogarth, J. (1971). *Sentencing as a Human Process.* Toronto: University of Toronto Press.

Hood, R. (1972). *Sentencing the Motoring Offender—A Study of Magistrates' Views and Practices.* London: Heinemann.

Kress, J. M. (1980). *Prescription for Justice: The Theory and Practice of Sentencing Guidelines.* Cambridge, MA: Ballinger Publishing Company.

Lipton, D., Martinson, R., & Wilks, J. (1975). *The Effectiveness of Correctional Treatment.* New York: Praeger.

Martin, S. E. (1983). Interests and politics in sentencing reform: A comparative case study of the development of sentencing guidelines in Minnesota and Pennsylvania. In W. Blumstein, J. Cohen, S. E. Martin, & M. Tonry (Eds.), *Research on Sentencing: The Search for Reform* (pp. 265-304). Washington, DC: National Academy of Sciences.

Minnesota Sentencing Guidelines Commission. (1982). *Preliminary Report on the Development and Impact of the Minnesota Sentencing Guidelines.* St. Paul, MN: Author.

Model Penal Code (Proposed Official Draft). (1962). Philadelphia: American Law Institute.

Partridge, A., & Eldridge, W. B. (1974). *Second Circuit Sentencing Study: Report to the Judges of the Second Circuit.* Washington, DC: Federal Judicial Center.

Rich, W. D., Sutton, L. P., Clear, T. R., & Saks, M. J. (1982). *Sentencing by Mathematics: An Evaluation of the Early Attempts to Develop and Implement Sentencing Guidelines.* Washington, DC: National Center for State Courts.

Rossi, P. H. (1978). Issues in the evaluation of human services delivery. *Evaluation Quarterly, 2,* 573-599.

Sales, B. D. (1983). The legal regulation of psychology: Professional and scientific interactions. In C. J. Scheier & B. L. Hammonds (Eds.), *The Master Lecture Series: Psychology and Law* (Vol. 2). Washington, DC: American Psychological Association.

Slovic, P., Fischhoff, B., & Lichtenstein, S. (1977). Behavioral decision theory. *Annual Review of Psychology, 28,* 1-39.

Sparks, R. F. (1981). *The Construction of Sentencing Guidelines: A Methodological Critique.* Presented to the Panel on Sentencing Research, Committee on Research on Law Enforcement and the Administration of Justice, National Academy of Sciences, Woods Hole, MA.

Sparks, R. F., Stecher, B. F., Albanese, J. S., & Shelly, P. L. (1982). *Stumbling toward Justice: Some Overlooked Research and Policy Questions about Statewide Sentencing Guidelines.* Final Report of the Evaluation of Statewide Sentencing Guidelines Project, Rutgers University, Newark, NJ.

The Twentieth Century Fund Task Force on Criminal Sentencing. (1976). *Fair and Certain Punishment.* New York: McGraw-Hill, 1976.

von Hirsch, A. (1976). *Doing Justice: The Choice of Punishments.* New York: Hill and Wang.

Wilkins, L. T. (1981). *The Principles of Guidelines for Sentencing: Methodological and Philosophical Issues in Their Development.* Washington, DC: U. S. Department of Justice.

Wilkins, L. T., Kress, J. M., Gottfredson, D. M., Calpin, J. C., & Gelman, A. M. (1978). *Sentencing Guidelines: Structuring Judicial Discretion—Report on the Feasibility Study.* Washington, DC: U. S. Department of Justice.

THE PSYCHOLOGIST AS CHANGE AGENT IN CORRECTIONS

Robert B. Levinson

> I view the entire concept of an inmate coming to a therapist asking to resolve an institution procedural issue in the same light as I would if an inmate approached me and asked me if I could say, for example, perform an exorcism or a cornary [sic] bypass operation. Neither of those are my job and other employees of the facility have been designated to resolve procedural issues. My feeling is that a correctional psychologist who allows himself to be put in this place needs to sit down with him or herself and do some serious soul-searching about exactly what his role in the facility would be.

The above quote is from a letter received from a psychologist employed in the Mental Health Satellite Unit at New York State's Auburn Correctional Facility. It exemplifies one end of the spectrum of attitudes regarding the role of the correctional psychologist.

"PRIVATE PRACTICE" IN PRISON

The professional training received by most psychologists prepares them best to function in a private practice mode, either in independent practice or in a medically-oriented mental health situation. In these settings, the psychologist sits in an office and works with clients; referrals are self-generated or made by other staff

129

members. Reports are written and discussed at team meetings where (combined with information gathered by other mental health disciplines) they form part of the basis upon which decisions are made. Psychologists generally feel comfortable following this model; they may become distressed when situation-generated demands do not match their own preconceived role expectations.

Prisons are strange places. In a very real sense they are quintessentially closed societies, but with a definite difference. They must provide all the services of a small city while maintaining a high degree of security for a population composed entirely of felons. No small task!

Typically, the correctional psychologist does not see a client only in an office during the "fifty-minute hour" or hour-and-a-half group session, but may encounter this individual a half dozen times during the week, occasionally providing impromptu, "corner-of-the-corridor" counseling. Moreover, in prisons, psychologists become privy to much client information from sources other than the individual involved; often such information is from sensitive sources who must remain unnamed or cannot be quoted without thereby revealing the only possible origin of the information. The psychologist may be asked to contribute knowledge which will have very substantial effects upon the client's life style. Thus, the ground rules concerning confidentiality and privileged communication change (see Brodsky, 1977). Information which pertains to potential disruption of the orderly operation of the institution becomes akin to that ruled on in the *Tarasoff* (1976) decision (i.e., it must be revealed for the protection of others).

In a corrections setting, the inappropriate private practice model should be replaced by a more productive community psychology approach, one in which the psychologist functions as a change agent (Levinson, 1973).

THE CHANGE AGENT

The role of change agent means that the correctional psychologist's client is not simply the individual offender (or the inmate group) but rather the whole prison community. The focus is too narrow when the psychologist views his or her area of functioning as limited to the therapist-client(s) relationship. Services psychologists deliver do not just happen to be in a prison, rather they are part of and affect the total climate of that facility. Psychology services play an integral role in humanizing prison environments and helping insure that prisoners are treated with dignity.

Of course, psychologists attempting to function in this broader role may not endear themselves to other players on the prison scene. Many staff members are quick to circumscribe the area in which the psychologist performs. "Stick to your testing!" may be one of the milder ways in which psychologists are informed that they are intruding on someone else's turf.

Psychology is a profession performed by highly trained individuals and requiring specially honed skills. One of the hallmarks of a profession is that it sets its own standards. The policies and procedures of the organization for which the psychologist works must be integrated with professional and ethical standards promulgated by national organizations, such as the American Psychological Association (1979), the American Correctional Association (1981), and the American Association of Correctional Psychologists (1980). Establishing operating procedures which are sensitive to demands of both corrections and psychology requires expertise in both fields by individuals trained in the profession of psychology.

If the proper role for the correctional psychologist is as a change agent, what does this entail? The remainder of this chapter will attempt to explicate the characteristics of this role, which may be subdivided into two major parts: (a) duties more directly relating to activities traditionally ascribed to psychologists; and (b) additional areas of responsibility envisioned as aspects of the change agent model. But first a little organizational philosophy.

ORGANIZATIONAL APPROACHES

Psychologists unfamiliar with correctional practices are often surprised to discover the pervasive role played by an institution's warden in the facility's daily activities and programs. The warden has ultimate authority. While responsibility may be delegated to department heads, final authority cannot. In practical terms, this means the warden can require the institution psychologist to refrain from performing certain functions and/or request that other activities be accomplished.

At first blush, this may seem an unwarranted intrusion into professional prerogatives. Not necessarily so. Almost all wardens recognize the uniqueness of the psychologist's professional skills. Further, they rely on psychology services administrators to evaluate the performance of staff psychologists. Considerable professional autonomy is permitted and national standards are recognized. But as in any complex organization, there are policies which define and legitimate the scope of activities. Going beyond such boundaries is impermissible.

ORGANIZATIONAL MODELS*

At least three approaches can be delineated regarding the structuring of psychological services within a department of corrections: direct-line, centralized, and decentralized.

In some correctional systems psychologists are hired by, and responsible to, a separate department (e.g., Mental Hygiene). They are based in a prison but have their *direct-line supervision* by an administration outside the correctional system's hierarchy. Under this arrangement, psychologists function rather independently of institutional authority; the structure assures complete professional autonomy. But it also serves to heighten destructive "treatment versus custody" conflicts and fosters the concept of the psychologist as an "outsider." Consequently, the direct-line approach lessens the likelihood that psychologists can function as effective mental health staff, let alone as change agents.

---

*This section reflects discussions with Robert J. Powitzky, Ph.D., Psychology Services Administrator, South Central Region, Federal Bureau of Prisons.

Some correctional systems have established separate institutions (more often, sections within prisons) designated for inmates with mental health problems. (Sometimes these facilities also perform a *centralized* diagnostic function for the prison system.) These institutions, almost always administered by a psychiatrist or psychologist, follow the traditional mental hospital model. Again, mental health staff are kept separate from the rest of the prison system. They deal only with the most severely disturbed prisoners and there are continual conflicts over who is (or is not) an appropriate referral and when a treated individual is ready for return to regular institutional living.

A variation on the centralized organizational model, which includes elements of the direct-line approach, is the separate facility for disturbed offenders which is not in the correctional system but part of a different department (e.g., Mental Hygiene). This arrangement introduces a variety of legal issues concerning transfers of individuals across jurisdictional lines (see, e.g., *Vitek v. Jones*, 1980) and exacerbates feelings of staff in both systems that they are being "dumped" on.

The completely *decentralized* organizational approach has staff psychologists in several (one would hope, all) of the system's prisons but is devoid of any centralized direction or support. This approach enhances the likelihood of inconsistent practices and poor coordination of services when inmates are transferred from one facility to another within the same prison system. It sometimes results in psychologists performing nonproductive, idiosyncratic functions tailored to a particular institution's overly specialized needs.

The most effective organizational approach combines elements of both the centralized and decentralized alternatives. The direct-line organization, outside the structure of the department of corrections, appears to have too many inherent coordination problems to be effective. Under a combined or tiered approach there is a central office psychology services administrator who, through policy and annual audits, provides direction and support to institution-based psychology staff. Psychology services personnel at the institutional level develop appropriate procedures to implement system-wide policy and are more directly responsible to the warden. This is an attempt to integrate administrative control (warden and correctional concerns) with professional standards (central office psychology administrator). Maintaining this balance requires constructive efforts by quality administrators at both levels and across all disciplines; it presupposes individuals who have credibility and confidence in one another's competence. Striving to reach such balance results in mutual benefits not only among staff but, equally important, between staff and inmates.

PSYCHOLOGY DUTIES

Correctional psychologists function in five general areas: assessment, treatment, training, administration, and research. Each of these areas will be detailed below. The first two areas are part of the more traditional/private practice role, while the last two are more in the change agent/community mode. Although the proportion of time spent in each component may differ, depending upon the psychologist's rank in the tiered hierarchy and the nature, size, and staffing pattern of the prison, the fully functional psychology staff member should devote some hours every week to each element of this pentad.

ASSESSMENT

Assessment responsibilities of the correctional psychologist are of two major types: routine and special. Within each of these categories, in turn, there are several variations.

Routine Evaluations: No one enjoys doing routine evaluations. But it is important that all new admissions to a prison be *screened*. Correctional staffs need to know what types of individuals are being admitted, what kind of behavior they are likely to display, how intellectually impaired or mentally disturbed they are, and so forth. Such information is a critical component of any program planning effort for the inmate and any population management strategy for the facility's administration.

The important questions here are: How can this function be competently accomplished with a minimal expenditure of scarce professional resources? What are the most cost-effective methods of interviewing, testing, and conveying obtained results to the decision makers? Answers to these questions require a determination of the purpose of testing.

The majority of offenders admitted to prison are of average intelligence, although they are probably academically retarded several grades, and they span the spectrum of emotional stability. What is needed is a way to identify those who deviate from the mode. This, then, is the purpose of routine screening: to identify those who are different, so that they can be examined more comprehensively, while providing some basic information on the others to aid staff in decision making. Group testing and interviewing along with a checklist type reporting format is generally sufficient for routine evaluations. Nontypical inmates (either intellectually or emotionally different) identified through such screening may be referred for special follow-up evaluations including more comprehensive and individualized testing.

Special Evaluations: Sources of inmate referrals for special evaluations are the courts, results from screening assessments, and individuals referred by other institutional staff. In all cases, individual testing is required and clear and comprehensive reports are expected. Psychologists should direct their procedures toward answering specific referral questions and providing any additional helpful information they may uncover. If there are no referral questions, a telephone call may elicit some and avoid wasted hours of professional time.

The *courts* refer offenders in various stages of the criminal justice process. Questions may be asked concerning a person's competency to be tried, or requests made for assistance in determining whether or not an individual was responsible for actions committed at the time of an offense. A third type of referral seeks help in establishing the offender's sentence and eventual placement. To be responsive, the correctional psychologist must be a knowledgeable, well trained clinician, aware of the legalities and rights of all the parties involved. Some specialized training, if only to help understand the "legalese," is most beneficial.

Routine screening procedures will identify the unusual inmate who warrants a more comprehensive assessment. Here, frequently, the psychologist must construct the referral question(s). Is this person really intellectually deficient, or was it just a "bad day" when the group test was administered? Was this individual "playing games" on the personality assessment test, or are those strange answers reflective of some pervasive underlying pathology? The institution needs to know so that appropriate management strategies can be prepared; the psychologist's comprehensive report should both clarify the situation and offer specific recommendations regarding realistic remedial responses.

"Hey, Doc, Joe Blank's been acting a little strange. Maybe you ought to see him!" could be the telephone call that serves as a *staff referral.* The psychologist should get more information about Blank's strange behavior and then arrange for an individual interview (and some testing, if necessary). The resulting report is placed in the inmate's file and a follow-up memo sent to the staff member who made the initial referral.

TREATMENT

Therapeutic interventions conducted in a correctional environment are in most respects performed just as they would be "on the street." While this section will focus on differences which reflect the prison setting, the interaction between therapist and inmate/client relies upon the same principles and procedures applicable in more usual circumstances. Modes of treatment available to the correctional psychologist are those generally accepted by the professional community—with one exception: Aversive techniques are not permitted. The most frequently used therapeutic approach is group therapy; individual psychotherapy is a close second.

Questions related to trust make therapy different in prisons. The fact that trust is a "two-way street" frequently goes unrecognized. Not only must the inmate/client learn to trust "a company man," but the psychologist, particularly in group therapy, has to learn to trust adjudicated felons. These issues may be even further confounded by snide remarks from an occasional staff member who sees psychotherapy with prisoners as a joke— "They're only doing it to get out of work!"

Concerns about confidentiality must be addressed explicitly at the beginning of a therapeutic relationship. The ground rules need to be discussed and, as one prison psychologist put it, "the prisoner [must be] told his psychotherapy *Miranda* rights" (Moss, personal communication, 1981). In other words, confidentiality will be respected except where there is a clear risk of serious injury to another person or a serious threat to the security of the institution.

CHANGE AGENT FUNCTIONS

The remaining three areas to be discussed are more relevant to aspects of the change agent role than the two elements described previously. While distinctions between these functions are somewhat arbitrary, they will be emphasized here for expository purposes.

TRAINING

The correctional psychologist as trainer is one of the more easily accepted departures from the traditional testing-and-treatment role. Knowledge that the psychologist has acquired is frequently seen by others as potentially helpful to them in carrying out their own assigned responsibilities. For example, line correctional staff are often quite interested in learning about cues which will help them identify potentially suicidal inmates; other personnel may welcome assistance in areas relating to the establishment of better working relationships with their colleagues or supervisees.

In general, there are three situations in which the prison psychologist can most profitably function as a trainer: with staff, with other psychologists and trainees, and with inmates.

Staff Training: This type of training can occur either formally or informally. When psychologists make themselves available at institution-sponsored functions or at slack times (such as before or after work hours or during lunch or dinner breaks) there are many opportunities to convey an impression about psychology which can change negative stereotypes. More formal sessions are held in the institution's training area; workers are required to attend as part of the system's in-service training. Frequently, these are of a "how to" nature (e.g., how to screen incoming inmates for signs of mental disturbance; how to recognize signs of stress in a supervisee and what to do about it; how to deal with inmates who are psychotic, mentally retarded, epileptic, suicidal, etc.; how to counsel inmates; and so on).

Interacting as a trainer with other correctional staff often results in the psychologist hearing about workplace procedures and problems which otherwise would remain unknown. Frequently, an idea can be offered to help improve the situation. Psychology gains an increment of credibility and the prison environment may become a little less oppressive for both staff and inmates.

Training Correctional Psychologists: Although their number is increasing, there still are relatively few places where psychologists in training may obtain education and experience in a correctional setting. A limited number of universities offer graduate training in this area. For the most part, the newly hired prison psychologist has little idea as to what clinical work in prison is like. Usually it takes about a year to understand how things "really work" in a correctional institution. Meanwhile the rookie needs help. Other more experienced staff psychologists are of great assistance when they share their experiences and insights. For at least the first 6 months, the new recruit should have a veteran nearby to offer advice and encouragement.

The neophyte needs to be made aware of others' views of a newly minted doctoral degree. Unlike academia or a medically oriented setting, in a prison, the Ph.D. does not confer instant expertise. While it gets one hired, there still is a credibility-establishing period which, like every correctional worker, the new psychologist must endure. In a prison, as in other settings, book learning is not always highly correlated with the presence of common sense.

The appropriate atmosphere for prison psychologists is one in which they learn to convert knowledge into wisdom. The facility's chief psychologist can foster such a climate. Correctional psychology staffs should meet in the institution on a regular basis, biweekly at a minimum, to fill each other in as to "what's going on." Such meetings provide an opportunity for keeping up to date with the literature, sharpening clinical skills, learning about newly promulgated policies, and helping delay staff burnout by reducing stress.

Psychology practicum students, trainees, and interns provide an additional avenue for training activities. Developing relationships with a nearby college or university can result in more helping hands and bright brains participating, under supervision, in psychology services activities. Not only do the students gain, but so do staff members. Those young "bright-eyed types" have an uncanny way of asking the wrong questions which result in the dean of the psychology staff wondering: "Now, why-in-hell do we do it that way?" Once again the potential for all concerned to benefit has been heightened.

Inmate Training: This type of psychologist-inmate interaction might occur in an education setting. It differs from the more typical situation in which the learning process results in insights for the individual student. The training alluded to here may have indirect benefits for the involved prisoner, but its intent is for the inmate/student to help others.

The idea of training prisoners to help other inmates turns on the alert signal for most correctional workers. And rightly so! Unfortunately there have been all too many instances in which putting inmates in charge of other prisoners has resulted in vicious exploitation. All the war stories notwithstanding, offenders can help one another—the critical variable is staff. The selection of the inmates to be trained is neither random nor voluntary. Staff pick the prisoner/trainees (who can always opt out); staff decide who has completed the training with a sufficient degree of understanding; and staff never stop functioning in a supervisory role. In other words, as this sort of experience is envisioned, staff do not abdicate their responsibilities.

Successful examples of this type of inmate training include peer counseling (Hosford & Moss, 1975), therapeutic communities (Toch, 1980), and the use of inmate "companions" in suicide prevention programs (Bureau of Prisons, 1982). Despite the high level of caution required, there is still something to be said for the notion that those who have had the problem *and have conquered it* may be able to help those still struggling—provided there is close and continual professional instruction and supervision.

These three aspects of training, in which the correctional psychologist plays a less traditional role, have in common that the psychologist is interacting with others (staff or inmates) outside both the office and the assessment/treatment paradigm. Often, such training involves becoming concerned about nonpsychology programs which also operate in the institution. While this poses the risk of "treading ahead of the angels," it also offers the chance to help make some positive changes in the institutional environment.

ADMINISTRATION

As construed under the change agent model, administrative responsibilities for the correctional psychologist are broader than simply managing the institution's psychology services department. However, this is not intended to minimize the importance of the day-to-day activities which must be accomplished so that mental health services can be delivered. Someone had to anticipate the need, estimate the cost, write up the justification, defend against the challenges from other departments, convince the chief executive officer, monitor the allocation of funds, protect the monies when other departments ran short, prepare the requisition, track the purchasing process, and sign for the delivery before that "widget" came to rest on a shelf an arm's length away.

This broader view of the administrative function goes beyond that which has immediate relevance for psychology services. Should the psychologist be a member of the classification (program decision making) team (Levinson, 1982)? What about the disciplinary committee? Shouldn't there be a psychology member on the institution panel which interviews all prospective employees? What about serving, in rotation with other staff, as the institution duty officer? Is there a role for psychology to play in the prison's employee assistance program? (Not to do therapy with staff, but to assist in directing troubled employees to appropriate mental health resources in the community.) What about that new approach for working with learning disabled adults the staff psychologist read about in a recent journal? Is consultation with the education department warranted? Then there was the article about nutrition and behavior—should someone talk to the food service administrator?

The point seems clear: Psychological skills have ripple effects in unsuspected ponds. Psychologists read a different literature than do other correctional staff. Many studies have implications beyond the traditional concerns of psychology services. If there is not a mandate, at least it should be okay for the psychologist to talk about these ideas and consult with personnel in other prison departments. Not only will it make everybody's job more interesting but clients may benefit as well.

RESEARCH

This is also an area which has a greater scope than under the more traditional private practice concept. Rather than a luxury one wishes institutions could better afford (Bureau of Prisons, 1977), research becomes a necessity once priorities are understood. Program evaluation is the number one priority, well ahead of both applied and basic research.

What warden is not interested in learning whether Program A or Program B is better at reducing inmate management problems? Is there a department head who would not like to know which of the available options gives "the bigger bang for the buck?" Wouldn't every level of management in the facility like to know how they did this year compared with last year?

It just so happens that there may be somebody on the prison staff who knows how to come up with answers for these queries. Note that these questions are not limited to: Is the MMPI or the CPI more appropriate for testing inmates?—although that, too, may be a worthwhile project. Correctional workers would like to know: "How am I doing?" Psychology can perform a very tangible service to the total institution community by helping them discover the answer.

Also included as a major aspect of research responsibilities should be the area of program development. Bright people (among whom psychologists, as a class, are numbered) generally think up new ideas. Prisons, along with most of society's other institutions, need to be open to possibilities for making constructive changes. The tough task—"making it happen"—requires a special set of skills:

> The complex human problem is how to get organizations, institutions and individual decision-makers to develop a climate of non-defensive open-minded willingness to review their standard practices and become receptive to the change that may be required for the adoption of given promising innovative procedures or policies. (Glaser, 1973, p. 443)

CONCLUSION

To return to the opening quote, correctional psychologists should be as free as any other professional group to define their role. The critical question, as others (e.g., Monahan, 1980) have noted, is "Who is the client?"

Some will answer this question in terms of the individual inmate or the prisoner group; others will take a wider view. At the risk of unbecoming hubris, the author suggests that an important opportunity will be lost if the narrower view is adopted.

Psychologists are among the most highly trained people working in the field of corrections. If they do not push for positive reforms, who will? If not now, when?

Robert B. Levinson, Ph.D., a psychologist, is Deputy Assistant Director, Inmate Program Services, for the Federal Bureau of Prisons. Involved in correctional psychology for more than 25 years, Dr. Levinson has served on task forces of the American Medical Association, the American Association of Correctional Psychologists, and the American Bar Association. Dr. Levinson also directs his own private consulting firm.

RESOURCES

American Association of Correctional Psychologists. (1980). *Standards for Psychology Services in Adult Jails and Prisons. Criminal Justice and Behavior, 7*, 81-127.

American Correctional Association. (1981). *Standards for Adult Correctional Institutions.* College Park, MD: Author.

American Psychological Association. (1979). *Standards for Providers of Forensic Psychology Services.* Washington, DC: Author.

Brodsky, S. L. (1973). *Psychologists in the Criminal Justice System.* Urbana, IL: University of Illinois Press.

Brodsky, S. L. (1977, September 8-9). *Ethical Issues for Psychologists, in Corrections.* Report prepared for the American Psychological Association on the Role of Psychology in the Criminal Justice System.

Bureau of Prisons. (1977). Task Force and executive staff reports on the role of psychologists in federal prisons (Mimeo).

Bureau of Prisons. (1982). Program Statement 6341.1, Suicide Prevention Program (Mimeo).

Glaser, E. M. (1973). Knowledge transfer and institutional change. *Professional Psychology, 10*, 434-444.

Hosford, R. E., & Moss, C. S. (Eds.). (1975). *The Crumbling Walls.* Urbana, IL: University of Illinois Press.

Levinson, R. B. (1973). *Influencing Change from the Inside.* First Alabama Symposium on Justice and the Behavioral Sciences, University, AL.

Levinson, R. B. (1982). A clarification of classification. *Criminal Justice and Behavior, 9*, 133-142.

Monahan, J. (Ed.). (1980). *Who Is the Client?*. Washington, DC: American Psychological Association.

Tarasoff v. Regents of the University of California, 131 Cal.Rptr. 14 (1976).

Toch, H. (Ed.). (1980). *Therapeutic Communities in Corrections*. New York: Praeger.

Vitek v. Jones, 445 U.S. 488 (1980).

INTRODUCTION TO SECTION II: PSYCHOLOGY, PSYCHIATRY, AND CIVIL COMMITMENT

The power of the state to impose mental health treatment upon unwilling individuals has long troubled both legal and mental health professionals as well as philosophers, behavioral scientists, lawmakers, administrators, and members of the general public. Legal commentators have argued that enforced confinement and treatment of the "mentally ill" represents a massive and often unwarranted encroachment upon fundamental civil liberties. Many psychologists and psychiatrists have expressed grave doubts about both the ethicality and the efficacy of involuntary mental health treatment. Critics from both the legal and mental health professions have decried the inability of psychologists and psychiatrists to identify reliably those who are "mentally ill" and "dangerous" (i.e., those who meet the legal conditions for civil commitment).

Proponents of civil commitment have urged that the state has a right, if not an obligation, to protect the "mentally ill" from themselves and the public from the "mentally ill." According to this view, civil commitment and enforced treatment are justified by the state's traditional "*parens patriae*" and "police" powers.

Over the past 2 decades or so, this controversy has erupted into a lengthy and as yet unsettled course of litigation aimed at establishing the limits of the state's authority to confine and impose treatment upon those deemed "mentally ill." As a result of this litigation, mental health professionals today are confronted with a growing and rapidly changing body of law which governs civil commitment and the rights of committed patients to refuse mental health treatment.

The purpose of the three chapters in this section is to provide mental health practitioners with an overview of the issues involved in the controversy surrounding enforced treatment of the "mentally ill," an understanding of current legal doctrine regarding civil commitment and treatment refusal, and some notions about how clinicians might deal with such doctrine in the course of everyday clinical practice.

This section opens with Robert Miller's chapter on civil commitment. Dr. Miller, a clinical, forensic, and research psychiatrist, details the history of civil commitment in the United States, examines the legal and psychiatric aspects of the controversy surrounding civil commitment, explores suggested reforms and alternatives to the civil commitment process, and concludes with a discussion of future trends in law and clinical practice.

Dr. Miller's contribution is followed by Elliot Silverstein's chapter on the civil commitment of minors, a topic which raises questions of law, public policy, and clinical practice often left unexplored in more general discussions of civil commitment. Dr. Silverstein, a psychologist and attorney, begins by describing the development of due process standards in the juvenile justice system and then examines some of the costs of importing such standards into the civil commitment context. After reviewing the most recent major court decisions in this area of mental health law, Dr. Silverstein considers the implications of these rulings for clinicians, juvenile treatment facilities, and their young patients.

This section concludes with a chapter by Philip Kraft, a psychiatrist and lawyer, examining legal and clinical issues related to the right of committed patients to refuse treatment. Dr. Kraft begins by describing recent legal trends in the "right to refuse" controversy. He then explores the clinical phenomenon of the refusing patient and describes how the right to refuse has been perceived by practicing clinicians. Dr. Kraft concludes by offering what he describes as "a new clinical agenda in the right to refuse debate"—an analysis of how clinicians might best respond to the tensions and conflicts created by the recent move toward recognition of a committed patient's right to refuse treatment.

CLINICAL AND LEGAL ASPECTS OF CIVIL COMMITMENT

Robert D. Miller

Involuntary civil commitment continues to affect more people, directly or indirectly, than all of the other areas of interface between the mental health professions and the law, yet civil commitment is no longer at the forefront of that interface as it was in the 1960s and early 1970s, when landmark legal cases were being brought. There are many reasons for this shift in emphasis, and they will be discussed more fully after we have taken a look at the events leading up to that period of great change in the 1960s and 1970s.

HISTORY

Despite criticisms leveled at state mental hospitals by commentators such as Szasz (1963), ostracism and sequestration of the "mentally disordered" has been practiced as long as there have been organized societies. At times those displaying the symptoms of mental illness, especially those we now call psychotic, have been thought to be chosen by the gods and have received special deference; more frequently, they have been feared and punished. But in either case, they have been clearly treated as different and carefully kept away from the "sane" parts of society. It is only relatively recently that organized efforts have been made to normalize the lives of the mentally disordered. And it is only recently that a prevailing philosophy has arisen that such people would be better off in the mainstreams of communities rather than protected from them.

The customs and laws governing commitment in this country have their origins in English common law and traditions dating back before the 18th century, when the *parens patriae* concept (i.e., the notion of the state acting to "protect" those who could not protect themselves) arose. In fact, this custom came not out of humanitarian desires, but out of the king's interest in preventing the lands of deranged noblemen from falling into the "wrong" hands; the principle was not applied to the mentally disordered poor, who were either imprisoned along with other debtors, charged with crimes, or simply cast out of their communities (often in the dead of night) (Bromberg, 1979; Deutsch, 1949). It was not until the moral reform movements of Pinel and Isaac Ray that the mentally disordered were viewed as "sick" and the prisons and almshouses which housed them began to be called "hospitals." Since there was still no treatment available, conditions continued to be little better and sometimes even worse than those in prisons. Since the mentally disordered were thought not to feel hunger or pain, they were often deprived of food and clothing, and their cells went without heat, even in the most enlightened establishments (Bromberg, 1979; Deutsch, 1949).

In the early part of this century, a number of small private facilities were created, in the United States as well as in Europe. These institutions were administered by physicians, forerunners of what would become the profession of psychiatry. For the first time, there were incentives for physicians to *treat* patients (as they were now called) and even to release them. Indeed, a strong competition arose as to which facility could "cure" more patients. The wave of therapeutic optimism which grew out of these private facilities spread into the public sector and state hospitals proliferated in the early part of the century, frequently built in rural settings as asylums where patients could escape from the stresses of their illnesses and recuperate. But the early promise of successful treatment did not materialize. Many of the hospitals grew into self-contained cities which depended on patient labor for their existence (Bromberg, 1979; Deutsch, 1949).

During this period, all admissions were involuntary, primarily to prevent people from taking advantage of free food and shelter. Although sanctioned by common law and increasingly authorized by statutes, the effective decision making power for admissions and discharges was vested in physicians. Patients had few effective rights: They were considered to be globally incompetent on admission; they had no rights to communicate with attorneys or anyone else; and they had no legal representation. There was no mechanism for patients to request discharge except by writs of *habeas corpus*. Few patients knew about such writs, and even fewer courts accepted them.

In the late 1950s, two changes led to a reversal of the hospitalization of increasing numbers of patients for indefinite periods: (a) new and effective medications were discovered for many illnesses; and (b) the civil rights movement was extended to the mentally disordered.

CLINICAL CHANGES

Despite the enthusiasm of the early part of the century, there was little clinicians could do to affect the illnesses of most of their patients until the introduction of antipsychotic and antidepressant medications. By the 1950s, the population of hospitalized patients had grown to over 550,000, and criticisms of warehousing and patient neglect were widespread (Bachrach, 1976; Bromberg, 1979; Solomon, 1958). The initial results of newly available drug treatment were so dramatic that a new wave of optimism swept over clinicians, and predictions were made that the hospitals could be emptied (Bachrach, 1976). Old theories that patients would benefit from withdrawal from the stressful circumstances in a society for which they were not prepared were abandoned in favor of the concept of "deinstitutionalization," which held that the very *process* of hospitalization was antitherapeutic and that treatment could be more effectively pursued in the patients' home communities. Medication permitted the release of thousands of long-term patients, and the community mental health center movement was born as both a clinical and a political movement, stimulated initially by large amounts of federal and state money (Bachrach, 1976; Hersch, 1972).

LEGAL CHANGES

The wave of attention to individual liberty, which arose in the 1960s and resulted in numerous Supreme Court decisions, spread from civil rights for minorities to procedural rights for criminal defendants. The transition to interest in mental patients came through concern for the rights of mentally disordered offenders and was initially directed toward procedural issues connected with the admission process. Previously, the courts had subscribed to the position that involuntary admissions were in the best interests of patients and that the attendant loss of liberty was justified by the need for treatment (Ennis, 1972). But after the Supreme Court held that juveniles charged with offenses deserved the same due process protections afforded adult defendants because liberty was at stake (*In re Gault*, 1967), that principle was applied to the civil commitment process as well. Courts held that patients should be provided with attorneys (*Hawks v. Lazaro*, 1973; *Heryford v. Parker*, 1968; *Lessard v. Schmidt*, 1972; *Lynch v. Baxley*, 1974); should have the opportunity to challenge evidence against them in a judicial hearing, and should receive notice of hearings in time to prepare a defense (*Fhagen v. Miller*, 1972; *Lessard v. Schmidt*, 1972; *Suzuki v. Quisenberry*, 1976). Many of these issues had been raised before, but the realistic clinical possibilities of releasing patients from hospitals caused judges to consider such issues for the first time.

A number of other legal issues were also raised successfully in the late 1960s and 1970s: The *parens patriae* standard for commitment (usually stated as "mentally ill and in need of treatment") which had formed the basis for most civil commitments came under severe criticism from civil libertarians. Thomas Szasz, the best-known of the "antipsychiatrist" psychiatrists, claimed that mental illness was a myth, and, therefore, could not be used to justify depriving people of their freedom (Szasz, 1963); and American Civil Liberties Union

Director, Bruce Ennis, and other civil libertarians claimed that neither diagnosis nor treatment in psychiatry was sufficiently precise to form a basis for loss of liberty, and that psychiatrists were acting covertly as agents of social control (Ennis, 1972; Shah, 1973-1974). These advocates argued that the state should not have the power to deprive people of their liberty simply because they might benefit from treatment, and that in order to hospitalize someone involuntarily it must be demonstrated that he or she poses a danger to himself, to herself, or to others.

Few courts have directly decided whether proof of dangerousness is constitutionally required (*Suzuki v. Quisenberry*, 1976), but several courts have indirectly endorsed a dangerousness criterion for commitment (*Addington v. Texas*, 1979; *Cross v. Harris*, 1968; *Lessard v. Schmidt*, 1972; *Lynch v. Baxley*, 1974; *O'Connor v. Donaldson*, 1975). As of 1982, 35 states had made proof of dangerousness a statutory requirement for involuntary commitment.

With the shift towards a police power (i.e., public protection) basis for commitment, other elements of the criminal justice system have been added to involuntary hospitalization. For example, by analogy to the Supreme Court's *Miranda* decision (*Miranda v. Arizona*, 1966), some courts have held that prospective involuntary patients have the right to remain silent during all phases of the process, including the initial psychiatric interview, and must be advised of this right at the outset of the proceedings (*Lessard v. Schmidt*, 1972). The courts have also examined the burden of proof necessary to justify commitment. The Supreme Court (*Addington v. Texas*, 1979) rejected the argument that since commitment is a civil process intended for the benefit and not the punishment of the patient, the usual "preponderance of the evidence" (i.e., 51% certainty) standard should be sufficient. But the Court also rejected arguments that, since loss of liberty is involved, the standard should be the criminal justice "beyond a reasonable doubt" (i.e., 90%-95% certainty). Ultimately the Court decided that the standard should be "clear and convincing evidence" (i.e., about 75% certainty). Lower courts, however, have been persuaded by the loss of liberty argument and have held that all the necessary criteria for commitment must be established beyond a reasonable doubt (*Conservatorship of Roulet*, 1979; *Lessard v. Schmidt*, 1972; *Superintendent of Worcester State Hospital v. Hagberg*, 1978).

Another legal concept which has been applied to commitment is that of the "least drastic means" necessary to accomplish a legitimate state purpose, now usually referred to as the "least restrictive alternative" principle. Originally stated in a case dealing with the rights of teachers (*Shelton v. Tucker*, 1960), this concept has come to mean, *in theory*, the right to be treated in the setting which provides appropriate treatment with the fewest restrictions possible; *in practice*, it often has the covert meaning of treatment anywhere but in a state institution (Bachrach, 1980; Miller, R. D., 1982).

Perhaps the most controversial of all the legal changes affecting commitment has been the recent trend toward recognition of a qualified right to refuse at least some types of psychiatric treatment (*Rennie v. Klein*, 1979; *Rogers v. Okin*, 1979). Since this topic is the subject of Chapter 8 of this volume, it will not be dealt with here.

Each of these changes has had significant effects on the process of commitment and, therefore, on the patients who are its subjects. The actual *practical* results of these changes have often been quite different from those anticipated by their advocates, and will be examined individually in more detail.

CRITERIA FOR COMMITMENT

MENTAL DISORDER

All state statutes require that persons subject to involuntary commitment demonstrate symptoms of some type of mental disorder or defect. The definitions vary widely; many are circular, in that the type of behavior sought to be modified is deemed *prima facie* evidence of mental disorder. This situation has come under considerable criticism from libertarians, both on the grounds that it is unconstitutionally vague (Johnson, 1969; Ross, 1959; Shah, 1973-1974) and on the grounds that psychiatric diagnosis itself is too imprecise to form the basis for deprivation of liberty (Albers, Pasewark, &

Meyer, 1976; Ennis, 1972; Ennis & Litwack, 1974; Szasz, 1963).

In practice, however, trial and appellate courts have seldom challenged the adequacy of either statutory definitions or clinical evidence of mental disorder (Hiday, 1977b; Miller, R. D., Ionescu-Pioggia, & Fiddleman, 1983a) and legislators have therefore not exerted themselves to provide more specific statutory definitions or rules of evidence.

GRAVE DISABILITY

Until recently, the criteria for commitment in most states were based on a "need for treatment" alone; clinicians were given essentially total control over the decision making process. As libertarian reforms began to take effect, however, there was a shift in language toward a "gravely disabled" standard, which is currently at least a sufficient criterion in some 30 states. No longer is it enough in most states that a person may benefit from involuntary treatment; a lack of such treatment must be shown to result in serious physical debilitation in the near or immediate future in order for commitment to be applicable.

DANGEROUSNESS

With the shift away from the *parens patriae* clinical standards, commitment criteria have been expanded in all states. Dangerousness has been added as a necessary criterion for commitment in most states. As of 1982, the "in need of treatment" standard was sufficient by itself in only two states, Vermont and Virginia.

As dangerousness is not a clinical concept, clinicians have felt at a disadvantage when required to predict it (see Chapter 1 of this volume); but most have adapted to the changes by responding to required questions about future behavior in order to achieve their major objective, that of being able to help patients who are in need of treatment (Wexler, 1981). However, since the evidence which currently exists indicates that clinicians have very little expertise in predicting future dangerous behavior (see Chapter 1; Ennis & Litwack, 1974; Steadman &

Keveles, 1972; Stone, 1975a), they have come under severe criticism for trying to comply with the current standards for commitment from the same critics who were responsible for the establishment of that standard (Ennis & Litwack, 1974; Halleck, 1980; Shah, 1975).

TREATABILITY

State statutes have always stated that a major purpose of commitment is to provide treatment for those committed; otherwise, commitment would be nothing more than preventive detention, which has been held unconstitutional in all other circumstances (Dershowitz, 1973; Slovenko, 1973). However, this requirement had seldom assumed much significance in practice until recently, when litigation began to be brought in two areas. Dr. Morton Birnbaum first began to call for a *right to treatment* in 1960 (Birnbaum, 1960). Courts, however, have declined thus far to find a constitutional basis for such a right. They have held only that treatment must be provided as compensation for a committed patient's loss of liberty (*Nason v. Supt. of Bridgewater State Hospital*, 1969; *O'Connor v. Donaldson*, 1975; *Welsch v. Likins*, 1974; *Wyatt v. Stickney*, 1971) or on the basis of statutory requirements (*Rouse v. Cameron*, 1966).

Recently, there has also been a call for the inclusion of *treatability* as a criterion for commitment. Both civil libertarians and clinicians argue that commitment of persons for whom no effective treatment exists amounts to simple incarceration. Clinicians are opposed to being jailers, while libertarians are opposed to preventive detention (Halleck, 1980; Mental Health Law Project, 1977; Peele, Chodoff, & Taub, 1974; Sadoff, 1978; Stone, 1975a). The rise of the dangerousness standard is a major factor in the increased interest in treatability. The characteristics of persons being committed under this standard are significantly different from those committed under a need for treatment standard; the proportion of committed patients with antisocial and other personality disorders, for whom treatment is difficult if not impossible, has risen dramatically (Sosowsky, 1978, 1980).

Several states (e.g., Utah and Kentucky) have already modified their statutes to make explicit a requirement that committed individuals must, in fact, be treatable in the facilities to which commitment is proposed. And the American Psychiatric Association (1982) has recommended such a criterion in their recent *Guidelines for Legislation on the Psychiatric Hospitalization of Adults*. The majority of states, however, have resisted such changes, chiefly for two reasons:

1. With the growing pressure to protect the public from dangerous people, legislatures are reluctant to restrict commitment of persons perceived as both mentally ill and dangerous, especially as penal facilities are growing more and more overcrowded while most mental health facilities have experienced dramatic declines in census.

2. The provision of *effective* treatment is quite expensive; if states were required to provide such treatment in order to commit patients, the costs would be prohibitive and would lead to further discharges of patients (which would be counter to the perceived need to incarcerate more people) (Wexler, 1981). In fact, one of the plaintiffs' attorneys in the *Wyatt v. Stickney* (1971) suit openly admitted that a major goal of that suit was not to provide more treatment in state facilities, but to make it too expensive to operate the hospitals at all, thus furthering the cause of deinstitutionalization (Schwartz, 1974).

COMPETENCY TO MAKE TREATMENT DECISIONS

Prior to the late 1960s, committed patients were automatically assumed to be globally incompetent by the very fact that they were committed (Slovenko, 1973; Wexler, 1981). With the rise of interest in the civil liberties of mental patients, however, most states passed comprehensive statutes which explicitly guaranteed committed patients the civil rights of all citizens (except the right to leave the hospital). One exception, in most jurisdictions, is the right to refuse treatment (see Chapter 8). Chiefly because of the growing importance of this issue, a number of authors have urged legislatures to add incompetency to make treatment decisions as another criterion for commitment (Halleck, 1980; Mental Health Law Project, 1977; Roth, 1979; Sadoff, 1978; Scott, 1976). This policy would eliminate the complicated and time-consuming procedural problems caused by the incarceration of potentially treatable but refusing patients, and it would be in accord with the treatability criterion presented above: A competent, refusing patient is no more treatable in practice than one for whom no effective treatment exists, and most clinicians do not feel that such persons belong in hospitals if they cannot be treated. Several states (e.g., Wisconsin and Utah) have incorporated such criteria into their statutes although without careful guidelines for determining incompetency, such as those proposed by Roth (1979) or the staff of the Mental Health Law Project (1977).

Some authors have suggested extending the determination of competency or incompetency even further by utilizing formal guardianship procedures for many, if not all, patients who are currently committed, in order to avoid the charge of paternalism so frequently leveled against clinicians as well as to secure treatment for many patients who do not meet stricter commitment standards (Haller, 1979). Some states have incorporated some of such concepts into their statutes (Lamb, Sorkin, & Zusman, 1981). Other commentators have criticized this proposal as cumbersome and unnecessary (Applebaum, 1982; Gutheil, Shapiro, & St. Clair, 1980); and at least one court has gone so far as to rule that even a legally appointed guardian does not have the authority to make some important treatment decisions (*In re Roe*, 1981).

ADMISSION PROCEDURES

There are currently two major procedures by which patients are hospitalized involuntarily; for convenience they will be designated as "regular" and "emergency." Since the two procedures are similar in many respects, the regular process will be described first and then contrasted with emergency procedures.

Although there are variations from state to state, the basic mechanism for commitment begins with a statement from someone, a "petitioner," who is familiar with the prospective patient's behavior and feels that hospitalization and treatment are necessary. The petitioner may be a law enforcement officer, a public official, or a mental health professional; but more frequently he or she is a friend or relative of the patient. The statement, or "petition," is then usually presented to a judicial official (judge, magistrate, or clerk of court) who must decide whether or not the criteria for commitment are met. If they are, a custody warrant is issued, authorizing evaluation by one or more mental health professionals. If the designated evaluators also concur that the criteria are met, hospitalization is ordered.

Shortly after hospitalization, a formal hearing, usually presided over by a judge, must be held—the period varies from 3 to 10 days depending upon jurisdiction. Some states still provide for a jury trial at this stage, but most have abandoned juries, in practice if not in their statutes, and rely on judges or hearing officers. If at the hearing the patient is found still to satisfy the commitment criteria, hospitalization is usually continued. The initial period of commitment varies between 2 weeks and 6 months, and is renewable after periodic review in most states.

Emergency commitment procedures exist in some 40 states. Typically, they are intended as "a temporary measure for the speedy processing of emergency situations, with limited, short-range goals, to deal with suppression and prevention of conduct likely to create a clear and present danger to persons or property" (Brakel & Rock, 1971). In 31 of the states which use emergency commitment, public officials, particularly the police, can initiate the process; judicial authorization prior to admission is required in only 14; of the remaining 26, evaluation by a clinician prior to admission is necessary in 22. Physical danger to self or others is required in 39 of the 40 states.

Although the original intent of these procedures was to create a mechanism to permit rapid control and treatment of patients and to prevent imminent harm, in practice these provisions are often used to bypass the protections built into the regular commitment process. Studies in North Carolina, for example, demonstrated that the emergency process was overutilized by rural counties which did not have available the physicians required by statute for the regular process (Miller, R. D., & Fiddleman, 1983a). Studies of other jurisdictions have come to similar conclusions (Hiday, 1977b; Matthews, 1970).

Once patients are admitted under emergency provisions, subsequent procedures in most states are identical to those for regular commitment, although a few states have created separate tracks for the two admission procedures. The Model Statute of the American Psychiatric Association (1982) also recommends separate mechanisms.

DUE PROCESS

In all of the reforms for mental patients beginning in the 1960s, attorneys have concentrated on due process issues, such as rights to hearings, notification of hearings, standards of proof, rules of evidence, and stricter definitions of commitment criteria (Miller, R. D., 1983b).

Civil libertarians had long held that the availability of attorneys to represent patients in all phases of the commitment process was the most essential of all reforms—without attorneys, there would be no one to insure that all the other new due process rights would be observed. Although many jurisdictions had provided for legal representation of patients for a number of years, in most cases attorneys were court-appointed, had little knowledge of mental health law, and took virtually no time to prepare cases. Most adopted a "best interests" position, feeling that most of their clients would probably benefit from hospitalization and that physicians were in the best position to determine what was best for patients (Andalman & Chambers, 1974; Cohen, 1966; Johnson, 1969).

Critics pointed out that the mere *presence* of attorneys was insufficient to insure protection of patients; they felt that attorneys should act as active advocates for the patients' wishes and not attempt to pre-empt the court's or jury's prerogative to make dispositional decisions or to decide what the patient's "best interests" were (Andalman & Chambers, 1974; Cohen, 1966; Johnson, 1969; "Projects:

Civil commitment," 1967; Wexler & Scoville, 1971). Although only a few legislatures have defined explicit roles for patient attorneys, a number of courts have addressed the issue. Initially, most favored a "best interests" guardianship role (*In re Basso*, 1962; *Prochaska v. Brinegar*, 1960); but more recently the trend has shifted toward the libertarian adversarial position advocated by most legal scholars (*Anders v. California*, 1967; *Hawks v. Lazaro*, 1973; *Lessard v. Schmidt*, 1972; *In re Quesnell*, 1978).

In those jurisdictions which have provided effective adversarial representation for patients, the result has invariably been a dramatic decline in the number of patients committed (Gupta, 1971; Hiday, 1977b; Miller, R. D., & Fiddleman, 1983c; Wenger & Fletcher, 1969). These decreases were initially interpreted as further evidence of previous undue judicial deference to clinical opinions; in most reports, especially in the legal and sociological literature, they were viewed as desirable changes.

More recently, however, reports critical of this trend have appeared, most frequently in the clinical literature but also in the legal journals. The criticisms fall into several categories:

1. A number of clinicians (Abramson, 1972; Chodoff, 1976; Rachlin, 1974) and even some lawyers (Galie, 1978) continue to feel that the best interests model is more appropriate in civil commitment than the adversarial model because the motives of involuntary hospitalization are treatment and not punishment, and because the subjects are felt to *need* someone to make decisions for them by virtue of the very illnesses for which hospitalization is sought.

2. Many clinicians feel that the adversarial process itself is highly undesirable on clinical grounds. It is difficult enough to establish effective therapeutic alliances with uncooperative patients under involuntary conditions without accentuating the problem by forcing the treating physician to testify openly "against" his or her own patients (Amaya & Burlingame, 1981; Eisenberg, Barnes, & Gutheil, 1980; Miller, R. D., 1983b). It has also

been pointed out that the adversarial process is antitherapeutic for patients whose illnesses make it difficult for them to evaluate their own conditions, and who need others to provide consistent structure in their lives on a temporary basis. An adversarial attorney who listens only to the patient's overt demands for release and ignores the pleas for help which are frequently barely below the surface may reinforce the "sick" part of the patient against the efforts of the therapist to help strengthen the "healthy" part of the patient sufficiently to enable the patient to accept responsibility for his or her own treatment (Amaya & Burlingame, 1981; Eisenberg et al., 1980; Miller, R. D., & Fiddleman, 1981).

3. It appears that the balance of power in commitment has shifted from one extreme to the other; where previously physicians' opinions went virtually unchallenged, now in many jurisdictions the opposite is true. Patient attorneys concentrate on dangerousness criteria, to which clinicians are unprepared to speak authoritatively, and there are few attorneys available to oppose patient advocates (Lamb, 1981; Miller, R. D., & Fiddleman, 1981; Stone, 1979). While some jurisdictions utilize attorneys from the prosecutor's office to represent the state's position, these lawyers seldom have either the expertise, the interest, or the time to provide effective opposition to increasingly professional full-time patient attorneys (Miller, R. D., & Fiddleman, 1981).

RELEASE FROM HOSPITALIZATION

In all jurisdictions, court hearings currently determine only maximum periods of hospitalization for civilly committed patients. Treating clinicians retain the authority to release patients at any time prior to that maximum if clinical conditions permit; in fact, some states *require* discharge of patients as soon as they no longer meet all criteria for commitment. Until recently, most critics of this procedure claimed that clinicians kept patients too long; but with the deinstitutionalization of hundreds of thousands of patients and significantly shorter stays in public facilities (Hiday, 1976), hospitals are now more frequently criticized for releasing patients too soon.

These criticisms have been even more forceful in the case of forensic patients (i.e., committed after having been found not competent to stand trial or not guilty by reason of insanity). As a result, several states have changed their statutes to provide for judicial oversight over release of all forensic patients (Halpern, Rachlin, & Portnow, 1981; Miller, R. D., Ionescu-Pioggia, & Fiddleman, 1983b). Although some have seen these changes as further intrusions into clinical practice, others have welcomed the protection which they afford from responsibility for the actions of discharged patients. Several commentators have suggested that similar procedures be adopted for civilly committed patients as well, arguing that the major commitment criterion which causes concern for the public as well as for the courts is dangerousness rather than mental disorder, and that, therefore, the courts are in a better position than clinicians to make discharge decisions (Sadoff, 1978; Wexler, 1981).

Whether or not such oversight is added to civil commitment may largely depend on logistic rather than strictly legal considerations: The extra hearings required would not be a significant expense in time or money in states which currently hospitalize few involuntary patients, but might pose insuperable problems to already overburdened courts and hospital staffs in those states which continue to commit thousands of patients a year (Halleck, 1980).

ALTERNATIVES TO INPATIENT COMMITMENT

Until recently, virtually all involuntary treatment took place in hospitals, and the thrust of legal reforms was to improve hospital conditions or to eliminate commitments to inpatient facilities altogether. In recent years, a growing number of courts have incorporated the "least restrictive environment" principle into decisions affecting inpatient commitment criteria (*Lessard v. Schmidt*, 1972; *Lynch v. Baxley*, 1974; *Stamus v. Leonhardt*, 1976; *In re Susan Lynn Farrow*, 1977), but typically without inquiring too closely into whether or not appropriate less restrictive alternatives actually exist.

Several commentators have argued that mental health advocates must go beyond addressing conditions in state hospitals and work to establish requirements for adequate treatment for patients in the community (Perlin, 1980, 1982; Saphire, 1976). There have been a few lawsuits in which either the courts have held that there was a governmental obligation to provide appropriate community-based treatment or the government has acceded to a consent decree to that effect (*Brewster v. Dukakis*, 1977; *Dixon v. Weinberger*, 1975; *Wuori v. Zitnay*, 1978). However, to date, none of these suits has lead to a significant increase in the number of needed facilities. Moreover, there have also been suits by patients to *prevent* forced discharges as a result of court decisions (*In re Borgogna*, 1981; *Rone v. Fireman*, 1979).

Although virtually everyone agrees that community-based treatment can be effective for many patients who are not involuntarily hospitalized, a number of factors have prevented its provision:

1. Despite the good intentions of clinicians and libertarians alike, community resistance to "normalization" of living situations for former mental patients has been unexpectedly intense; zoning ordinances and outright violence have become frequent where attempts have been made to create clinically appropriate residential facilities (Aviram & Segal, 1973; Cramer, 1978; Talbott, 1979a) and jail censuses have risen as hospital populations have fallen (Abramson, 1972; Bonovitz & Guy, 1979; Lamb, 1982; Sosowsky, 1978, 1980; Stelovich, 1979). As Goffman (1961, p. 384) has stated, "If all the mental hospitals in a given region were closed down today, tomorrow relatives, police, and judges would raise a clamor for new ones; and these true clients of the mental

hospital would demand an institution to satisfy their needs."

2. Expenditure of public funds on the mentally disordered has never had a high priority; with the current economic situation, especially federal retrenchment from funding community mental health centers, the creation of new community services has become fiscally impossible. Despite many early estimates that community treatment would be not only more effective but less expensive than hospitalization (Murphy & Datel, 1976; Sharfstein & Nafziger, 1976; Test & Stein, 1978), this has not proven to be the case in practice (Aviram & Segal, 1973; Bachrach, 1976; Miller, R. D., 1982). Most plans originally called for funds to be transferred from hospitals to community facilities as deinstitutionalization was accomplished. However, many states have discovered that they have not been able to close their hospitals ("California Senate Report," 1974) and pressure from the courts and accreditation bodies has forced significant increases in expenditures per hospitalized patient, thus preventing funds from "following the patient" into the community.

Economic considerations have also dictated placement of patients: In Wisconsin, for instance, local communities are financially responsible for civilly committed patients while the state bears the burden for forensic patients (those found not competent to stand trial or not guilty by reason of mental disease or defect). One result of this arrangement is that local law enforcement personnel more frequently bring criminal charges against mentally disordered persons rather than initiating civil commitment proceedings. Interestingly, in Arizona, where the financial responsibilities are reversed, there is a pressure to use civil commitment instead of the criminal route (Wexler, 1981).

3. While early court decisions made it clear that economic considerations could not prevent provision of reforms required by statute or by the

constitution (*Wyatt v. Stickney*, 1971), these decisions made reforms contingent on hospitalization of patients, thus allowing states to "dump" patients on unprepared communities to avoid spending more money on hospitals. Following the conservative trend of the current Supreme Court, lower courts have become more circumspect in making rulings which require expenditure of public funds on handicapped persons of all types (*Buchholtz v. Iowa Department of Public Instruction*, 1982; *Garrity v. Gallen*, 1981; *Southeastern Community College v. Davis*, 1979).

OUTPATIENT COMMITMENT

Most of the advocates of treatment in the community have assumed that if appropriate treatment facilities were available, patients would utilize them and involuntary treatment would be unnecessary (Cohen, 1966; Dix, 1976; Johnson, 1969; Wexler, 1981). However, this has not proven to be the case. Many studies have shown that the clientele of community treatment centers includes few chronic patients and is comprised mostly of a new class of patients who formerly either did not seek treatment or received it from the private sector (Borus, 1981; Goldman, Adams, & Taube, 1983).

The libertarians had apparently assumed that patients' major resistance to involuntary hospitalization stemmed from objections to either incarceration or treatment in a hospital setting. The fact that these patients have not availed themselves of the community facilities which do exist demonstrates that many have strong resistance to *any* type of treatment, regardless of setting. Therefore, if society decides that treatment is indicated outside of a state inpatient facility, it will still have to be under involuntary conditions for many patients.

There is little in the literature concerning commitment to outpatient treatment (Bleicher, 1967). Despite one report of its successful use, based on reduced recidivism to a state hospital in one part of North Carolina (Hiday & Goodman, 1982), a more detailed follow-up study by the author in the same state (following statutory changes designed to facilitate its use) revealed that outpatient commitment was still used very infrequently in North Carolina and that clinicians at both the state hospital and community mental health centers continued to feel that it was not a particularly effective procedure (Miller, R. D., & Fiddleman, 1983b).

There is considerable resistance to forced outpatient treatment; mental health centers are increasingly staffed with clinicians other than psychiatrists (Fink & Weinstein, 1979; Pardes, Sirovatka, & Jenkins, 1979), who are traditionally less authoritarian than psychiatrists and less comfortable with any type of coerced treatment. In addition, the only really effective form of involuntary treatment for outpatients is medication; yet, a large number of patients either cannot benefit from medication, or need treatment in addition to medication which requires their cooperation. Moreover, with stricter criteria for commitment and for forced medication (*In re Roe*, 1981), it has become doubtful in many jurisdictions whether commitment to outpatient treatment can be ordered.

GENERAL HOSPITAL PSYCHIATRIC UNITS

One alternative to large state facilities is the use of psychiatric units in general hospitals. These units have increased significantly in the past decade and have been hailed as perfect solutions to the problems of institutionalization (Bachrach, 1981; Greenhill, 1979). But recent analysis has shown that the patients predominantly served by these units, similar to the situation as with outpatient centers, are not the chronic patients formerly involuntarily hospitalized in state facilities, but rather a new group of less severely ill and less indigent patients (Goldman et al., 1983). The attitudes of staff at these units is even more negative toward coerced therapy than those of mental health center staff; the preference for open units and active patient cooperation and the need for private remuneration for services rendered prevents most such units from being willing or able to serve a significant number of chronic patients (Leeman, 1980; Miller, R. D., 1981a).

FUTURE TRENDS

Despite continued calls for the abolition of involuntary commitment (Ennis & Emery, 1978; Miller, K. S., 1976; Morse, 1982; Szasz, 1982), a positive response from either the courts or the legislatures seems quite unlikely. The Supreme Court has become increasingly less willing to break new ground in the area of individual patient rights: It has declined to reach substantive decisions in several potential landmark cases (*Halderman v. Pennhurst*, 1982; *Rogers v. Okin*, 1979) and in several others has indicated an inclination to defer to clinical judgment on treatment issues (*Parham v. J. L. and J. R.*, 1979; *Youngberg v. Romeo*, 1982). Without definitive legal guidelines, the conflict between clinicians and civil libertarians seems destined to continue. Some advocates remain optimistic about the continuation of increases in patient rights (Perlin, 1982), and others see in such conflict a challenge for libertarians to continue their efforts in lower courts and state legislatures, which remain free to be more protective of patients than the Supreme Court has chosen to be (Wexler, 1981). There is evidence to support this view: In at least two cases, lower courts have stood their ground after cases were remanded to them by the Supreme Court (*Halderman v. Pennhurst*, 1982; *Lessard v. Schmidt*, 1976).

A major reason for reform efforts has been the appalling conditions at many state institutions, a point of agreement between clinicians and libertarians (Halleck, 1980). Clinicians have pointed out that many of the rulings which they consider intrusive into clinical practice have come in cases brought against clearly substandard facilities in which abuse of patients was obvious, and have argued that rulings stemming from these cases may not be appropriate or necessary in better facilities (Perr, 1981).

It is clear that, partially as a result of legal pressures, conditions have improved markedly in many state hospitals in the past decade (Heller, 1976; Roth, 1977). A recent study indicates that 172 out of 265 state hospitals, including all the facilities in 20 states, are currently accredited by the Joint Commission on Accreditation of Hospitals (National Association of State Mental Health

Program Directors, 1982). While these data show that a third of the facilities still do not meet current standards, the situation is a far cry from that which 25 years ago caused the President of the American Psychiatric Association to call the whole system "bankrupt" (Solomon, 1958).

Changes in commitment laws have not been unmixed blessings for patients, however: Despite evidence that many committed patients have felt that their involuntary treatment was necessary (Miller, R. D., 1980; Spensley, Edwards, & White, 1980; Toews, El-Guebaly, & Leckie, 1981), many libertarians continue to assume that all patients would agree with them that freedom from physical incarceration is the greatest good. Increased protection of liberty rights has resulted in denial of access to treatment for many patients whose illnesses render them unable to ask directly (Miller, R. D., 1980; Rachlin, 1975) or who are not overtly dangerous (Halleck, 1980). There have been other problems as well: The reform movement nearly led to federal regulations which would have virtually eliminated all research with mental patients; only a concerted effort by responsible researchers led to compromises which preserved necessary protections to prevent exploitation of mental patients while permitting vital investigations into the etiologies and treatment of mental illnesses to continue (National Commission for the Protection of Human Subjects of Biomedical and Behavioral Research, 1978).

Another example of a "reform" which would actually reduce available treatment for patients is the recent referendum in Berkeley, California, which outlawed electroconvulsive therapy, a controversial but often effective mode of treatment for severe depression. At the time of this writing, a district court has overturned the ordinance because of conflict with California law, but there is now a movement to change the law to conform to the views of the libertarians ("Judge overturns Berkeley," 1983). Similar abolitionist proposals concerning psychotropic medications have also appeared in the legal literature (Zander, 1977).

An unfortunate side effect of the increasing legal regulation of clinical (particularly psychiatric) practice in public facilities is an exacerbation of the flight of well-qualified professionals from those facilities into the comparative safety of private practice, thus further reducing the already insufficient number of staff (Miller, K. S., 1976; Stone, 1982). It would seem that at this point the most effective course for both clinicians and libertarians would be mutual cooperation rather than continuation of the struggle over absolutist positions on either side, a struggle which presents significant risks for patients, who have been caught in the middle for some time (Miller, R. D., 1983b; Schultz, 1980). If Wexler (1981) is correct that the important decisions in the future will be made at the level of lower courts and state legislatures, then it is important that those decision makers have effective input from both clinical and legal sources (Miller, R. D., 1981b; Perr, 1981; Victoroff, 1977). To date, courts have been strongly influenced by articles in legal journals, which generally quote only those clinicians with strong libertarian attitudes. It is important that more legally knowledgeable clinicians contribute to the legal as well as the clinical literature so that judges and legislators will have a better data base upon which to make their decisions.

Robert D. Miller, M.D., Ph.D., is Director of Forensic Training at Mendota Mental Health Institute in Madison, WI. Dr. Miller is also a clinical Associate Professor of Psychiatry and a lecturer in law at the University of Wisconsin at Madison. He has done extensive research in the areas of civil commitment and psychopharmacology and is particularly interested in the collaboration between the clinical and legal professions.

RESOURCES

Abramson, M. F. (1972). The criminalization of mentally disordered behavior. *Hospital & Community Psychiatry, 23*, 101-105.

Addington v. Texas, 441 U.S. 418 (1979).

Albers, D. A., Pasewark, R. A., & Meyer, P. A. (1976). Involuntary hospitalization and psychiatric testimony: The doctrine of immaculate perception. *Capital University Law Review, 6*, 11-33.

Amaya, M., & Burlingame, W. V. (1981). Judicial review of psychiatric admissions: The clinical impact on child and adolescent inpatients. *Journal of the American Academy of Child Psychiatry, 20*, 761-776.

American Psychiatric Association. (1982). *Guidelines for Legislation on the Psychiatric Hospitalization of Adults.* Washington, DC: Author.

Andalman, E., & Chambers, D. L. (1974). Effective counsel for persons facing civil commitment: A survey, a polemic, and a proposal. *Mississippi Law Journal, 45*, 43-91.

Anders v. California, 386 U.S. 738, 744 (1967).

Applebaum, P. S. (1982). Limitations on guardianship of the mentally disabled. *Hospital & Community Psychiatry, 33*, 183-184.

Aviram, U., & Segal, S. P. (1973). Exclusion of the mentally ill—Reflections on an old problem in a new context. *Archives of General Psychiatry, 29*, 126-131.

Bachrach, L. L. (1976). *Deinstitutionalization: An Analytical Review and Sociological Perspective* (DHEW Publication No. ADM 79-136). Washington, DC: U. S. Government Printing Office.

Bachrach, L. L. (1980). The least restrictive environment is always the best? Sociological and semantic implications. *Hospital & Community Psychiatry, 31*, 97-103.

Bachrach, L. L. (1981). The effects of deinstitutionalization on general hospital psychiatry. *Hospital & Community Psychiatry, 32*, 786-790.

In re Basso, 199 F.2d 933 (D.C. Cir. 1962).

Birnbaum, M. (1960). The right to treatment. *American Bar Association Journal, 46*, 499-505.

Bleicher, B. K. (1967). Compulsory community care for the mentally ill. *Cleveland-Marshall Law Review, 16*, 93-115.

Bonovitz, J. C., & Guy, E. B. (1979). Impact of restrictive civil commitment procedures on a prison psychiatric service. *American Journal of Psychiatry, 136*, 1045-1048.

In re Borgogna, 175 Cal. Rptr. 588 (Cal. Ct. App. 1981).

Borus, J. F. (1981). Deinstitutionalization of the chronically mentally ill. *New England Journal of Medicine, 305*, 339-342.

Brakel, S. J., & Rock, R. S. (Eds.). (1971). *The Mentally Disabled and the Law* (rev. ed.). Chicago: University of Chicago Press.

Brewster v. Dukakis, Civil Action No. 76-4423F (D. Mass. 1977).

Bromberg, W. (1979). *The Uses of Psychiatry in the Law.* Westport, CT: Quorum Books.

Buchholtz v. Iowa Department of Public Instruction, 315 N.W.2d 789 (Iowa Sup. Ct. 1982).

California senate report says state hospitals remain indispensable. (1974). *Hospital & Community Psychiatry, 25*, 489.

Chodoff, P. (1976). The case for involuntary hospitalization of the mentally ill. *American Journal of Psychiatry, 133*, 496-501.

Cohen, F. (1966). The function of the attorney and the commitment of the mentally ill. *Texas Law Review, 44*, 424-469.

Conservatorship of Roulet, 23 Cal.3d 219, 590 P.2d 1, 152 Cal. Rptr. 425 (1979).

Cramer, P. K. (1978). *Report on the Current State of Deinstitutionalization: Period of Retrenchment.* Philadelphia: Philadelphia Health and Welfare Council.

Cross v. Harris, 418 F.2d 1095 (D.C. Cir. 1968).

Crowder, J. E., & Klatte, E. W. (1980). Involuntary admission to general hospitals: Legal status is not the issue. *Hospital & Community Psychiatry, 31*, 325-327.

Dershowitz, A. M. (1973). Preventive confinement: A suggested framework for constitutional analysis. *Texas Law Review, 51*, 1277-1324.

Deutsch, A. (1949). *The Mentally Ill in America* (2nd ed.). New York: Columbia University Press.

Dix, G. E. (1976). The role of the lawyer in proceedings under the Texas Mental Health Code. *Texas Bar Journal, 39*, 982-990.

Dixon v. Weinberger, 405 F. Supp. 974 (D.D.C. 1975).

Eisenberg, G. C., Barnes, B. M., & Gutheil, T. G. (1980). Involuntary commitment and the treatment process: A clinical perspective. *Bulletin of the American Academy of Psychiatry and the Law, 8,* 44-55.

Ennis, B. J. (1972). *Prisoners of Psychiatry: Mental Patients, Psychiatrists, and the Law.* New York: Harcourt, Brace, and Jovanovich.

Ennis, B. J., & Emery, R. D. (1978). *The Rights of Mental Patients.* New York: Avon Books.

Ennis, B. J., & Litwack, T. L. (1974). Psychiatry and the presumption of expertise: Flipping coins in the courtroom. *California Law Review, 62,* 693-752.

Fhagen v. Miller, 29 N.Y.2d 348, 278 N.E.2d 615 (1972).

Fink, P. J., & Weinstein, S. P. (1979). Whatever happened to psychiatry? The deprofessionalism of community mental health centers. *American Journal of Psychiatry, 136,* 406-409.

Galie, L. P. (1978). An essay on the civil commitment lawyer: Or how I learned to hate the adversary system. *Journal of Psychiatry and Law, 6,* 71-87.

Garrity v. Gallen, 522 F. Supp. 171 (D.N.H. 1981).

In re Gault, 387 U.S. 1 (1967).

Goffman, E. (1961). *Asylums—Essays on the Social Situation of Mental Patients and Other Inmates.* Garden City, NY: Doubleday Anchor Books.

Goldman, H. H., Adams, N. H., & Taube, C. A. (1983). Deinstitutionalization: The data demythologized. *Hospital & Community Psychiatry, 34,* 129-134.

Greenhill, M. H. (1979). Psychiatric units in general hospitals: 1979. *Hospital & Community Psychiatry, 30,* 169-182.

Gupta, R. J. (1971). New York's Mental Health Information Service: An experiment in due process. *Rutgers Law Review, 25,* 405-450.

Gutheil, T. G., Shapiro, R., & St. Clair, R. L. (1980). Legal guardianship in drug refusal: An illusory solution. *American Journal of Psychiatry, 137,* 347-352.

Halderman v. Pennhurst, 673 F.2d 647 (3d Cir. 1982).

Halleck, S. L. (1980). *Law in the Practice of Psychiatry.* New York: Plenum Medical Books.

Haller, L. H. (1979). Guardianship: An alternative to "I'm sorry." *Bulletin of the American Academy of Psychiatry and the Law, 7,* 296-305.

Halpern, A. L., Rachlin, S., & Portnow, S. L. (1981). New York's Insanity Defense Reform Act of 1980: A forensic psychiatric perspective. *Albany Law Review,* *45,* 661-677.

Hawks v. Lazaro, 157 W.Va. 417, 202 S.E.2d 109 (1973).

Heller, H. W. (1976, September). *Bryce Hospital: Psychologists Changing Role after Two Court Orders.* Symposium conducted at the meeting of the American Psychological Association, Washington, DC.

Hersch, C. (1972). Social history, mental health, and community control. *American Psychologist, 27,* 749-754.

Heryford v. Parker, 396 F.2d 393 (10th Cir. 1968).

Hiday, V. A. (1976). Mental commitment legislation: Impact on length of stay. *Journal of Mental Health Administration, 6,* 4-12.

Hiday, V. A. (1977a). The role of counsel in civil commitment: Changes, effects, and determinants. *Journal of Psychiatry and Law,* Winter, 551-569.

Hiday, V. A. (1977b). Reformed commitment procedures: An empirical study in the courtroom. *Law and Society Review, 11,* 651-666.

Hiday, V. A., & Goodman, R. R. (1982). The least restrictive alternative to involuntary hospitalization, outpatient commitment: Its use and effectiveness. *Journal of Psychiatry and Law, 10,* 81-96.

Johnson, C. E. (1969). Due process in involuntary civil commitment and incompetency determinations: Where does Colorado stand? *Denver Law Journal, 46,* 516-578.

Judge overturns Berkeley ECT ban. (1983, February 4). *Psychiatric News,* p. 19.

Lamb, H. R. (1981). Securing patient's rights—responsibly. *Hospital & Community Psychiatry, 32,* 393-397.

Lamb, H. R. (1982). The mentally ill in an urban county jail. *Archives of General Psychiatry, 39,* 17-22.

Lamb, H. R., Sorkin, A. P., & Zusman, J. (1981). Legislating social control of the mentally ill in California. *American Journal of Psychiatry, 138,* 334-339.

Leeman, C. P. (1980). Involuntary admissions to general hospitals: Progress or threat. *Hospital & Community Psychiatry, 31,* 315-318.

Lessard v. Schmidt, 349 F. Supp 1078 (E.D. Wis. 1972).

Lessard v. Schmidt, 413 F. Supp. 1318 (E.D. Wis. 1976).

Lynch v. Baxley, 386 F. Supp. 378 (M.D. Ala. 1974).

Matthews, A. (1970). Observations on police policy and procedures for emergency detention of the mentally ill. *Journal of Criminal Law, Criminology, and Police Science, 61*, 283-295.

Mental Health Law Project: Legal issues in state mental health care: Proposals for change. (1977). *Mental Disability Law Reporter, 2*, 77-159.

Miller, K. S. (1976). *Managing Madness: The Case against Civil Commitment.* New York: The Free Press.

Miller, R. D. (1980). Voluntary "involuntary" commitment—The briar patch syndrome. *Bulletin of the American Academy of Psychiatry and the Law, 8*, 305-312.

Miller, R. D. (1981a). Psychiatric units in general hospitals: Elitism revisited. *Hospital & Community Psychiatry, 32*, 804-805.

Miller, R. D. (1981b). Beyond the old state hospital: New opportunities ahead. *Hospital & Community Psychiatry, 32*, 27-31.

Miller, R. D. (1982). The least restrictive environment: Hidden meanings and agendas. *Community Mental Health Journal, 18*, 46-55.

Miller, R. D. (1983a). Involuntary commitment of the mentally ill: A physician's view. *Popular Government, 48*, 31-36.

Miller, R. D. (1983b). Friction between psychiatry and law—A practical consideration. *North Carolina Journal of Mental Health, 9*, 29-34.

Miller, R. D., & Fiddleman, P. B. (1981). The adversary system in civil commitment of the mentally ill: Does it exist and does it work? *Journal of Psychiatry and Law*, Winter, 403-421.

Miller, R. D., & Fiddleman, P. B. (1983a). Emergency involuntary commitment: Misuse of a necessary process. *Hospital & Community Psychiatry, 34*, 249-254.

Miller, R. D., & Fiddleman, P. B. (1983b). Outpatient commitment: Treatment in the least restrictive environment? *Hospital & Community Psychiatry, 35*, 147-151.

Miller, R. D., & Fiddleman, P. B. (1983c). Changes in North Carolina Civil Commitment Statutes: The impact of attorneys. *Bulletin of the American Academy of Psychiatry and the Law, 11*, 43-50.

Miller, R. D., Ionescu-Pioggia, R. M., & Fiddleman, P. B. (1983a). The effect of witnesses, attorneys, and judges upon civil commitment in North Carolina—A prospective study. *Journal of Forensic Sciences, 28,* 829-838.

Miller, R. D., Ionescu-Pioggia, R. M., & Fiddleman, P. B. (1983b). Judicial oversight over release of patients committed after being found not competent to stand trial or not guilty by reason of insanity of violent crimes. *Journal of Forensic Sciences, 28,* 839-845.

Miranda v. Arizona, 384 U.S. 486 (1966).

Morse, S. J. (1982). A preference for liberty: The case against involuntary commitment of the mentally disordered. *California Law Review, 700,* 54-106.

Murphy, J. G., & Datel, W. E. (1976). A cost-benefit analysis of community versus institutional living. *Hospital & Community Psychiatry, 27,* 165-170.

Nason v. Supt. of Bridgewater State Hospital, 353 Mass. 774; 233 N.E.2d 908 (1969).

National Association of State Mental Health Program Directors. (1982). *Study* #83-413-B. Washington, DC: Author.

National Commission for the Protection of Human Subjects of Biomedical and Behavioral Research. (1978). *Research Involving Those Institutionalized or Mentally Infirm.* Washington, DC: U.S.D.H.E.W.

O'Connor v. Donaldson, 422 U.S. 563 (1975).

Pardes, H., Sirovatka, P., & Jenkins, J. W. (1979). Psychiatrists in public service—Challenge of the eighties. *Hospital & Community Psychiatry, 30,* 756-760.

Parham v. J. L. and J. R., 99 S.Ct. 2493 (1979).

Peele, R., Chodoff, P., & Taub, N. (1974). Involuntary hospitalization and treatability: Observations from the District of Columbia Experience. *Catholic University Law Review, 23,* 744-753.

Perlin, M. (1980). Rights of ex-patients in the community: The next frontier. *Bulletin of the American Academy of Psychiatry and the Law, 8,* 33-43.

Perlin, M. (1982). Psychiatric hospitalization—Some predictions for the eighties. In R. Rosner (Ed.), *Critical Issues in American Psychiatry and the Law* (pp. 239-262). Springfield: C. C. Thomas.

Perr, I. N. (1980). Legislative acts and psychiatric input: A New Jersey experience. *Bulletin of the American Academy of Psychiatry and the Law, 8,* 412-425.

Perr, I. N. (1981). Effect of the Rennie decision on private hospitalization in New Jersey: Two case reports. *American Journal of Psychiatry, 138,* 774-778.

Prochaska v. Brinegar, 251 Iowa 834, 102 N.W.2d 870 (1960).

Projects: Civil commitment of the mentally ill. (1967). *U.C.L.A. Law Review, 14,* 822-869.

In re Quesnell, 83 Wash.2d 224, 517 P.2d 568 (1978).

Rachlin, S. R. (1974). With liberty and psychosis for all. *Psychiatric Quarterly, 48,* 410-420.

Rachlin, S. R. (1975). One right too many. *Bulletin of the American Academy of Psychiatry and the Law, 3,* 99-102.

Rennie v. Klein, 462 F. Supp. 1131 (D.N.J. 1979).

Robitscher, J. (1980). *The Powers of Psychiatry.* Boston: Houghton-Mifflin.

In re Roe, 421 N.E.2d 40 (Mass. 1981).

Rogers v. Okin, 478 F. Supp. 1342 (D. Mass 1979).

Rone v. Fireman, 473 F. Supp. 92 (D. Ohio, 1979).

Ross, H. A. (1959). Commitment of the mentally ill: Problems of law and policy. *Michigan Law Review, 57,* 945-1007.

Roth, L. H. (1977). Involuntary civil commitment: The right to treatment and the right to refuse treatment. *Psychiatric Annals, 7,* 244-257.

Roth, L. H. (1979). A commitment law for patients, doctors, and lawyers. *American Journal of Psychiatry, 136,* 1121-1127.

Rouse v. Cameron, 373 F.2d 451 (D.C. Cir. 1966).

Sadoff, R. L. (1978). Indications for involuntary hospitalization: Dangerousness or mental illness? In W. E. Barton & C. J. Sanborn (Eds.), *Law and the Mental Health Professions* (pp. 297-310). New York: International Universities Press.

Saphire, R. B. (1976). The civilly-committed public mental patient and the right to aftercare. *Florida State University Law Review, 4,* 232-295.

Schultz, S. (1980). The Boston State Hospital case: Its impact on the handling of future mental health litigation. *Bulletin of the American Academy of Psychiatry and the Law, 8,* 345-351.

Schwartz, L. H. (1974). Litigating the right to treatment: Wyatt v. Stickney. *Hospital & Community Psychiatry, 25,* 460-463.

Scott, E. P. (1976, June). Viewpoint: Another look at the crossroads. *Mental Health Law Reporter,* p. 9.

Shah, S. A. (1973-1974). Some interactions of law and mental health in the handling of social deviance. *Catholic University Law Review, 23,* 674-719.

Shah, S. A. (1975). Dangerousness and civil commitment of the mentally ill: Some public policy considerations. *American Journal of Psychiatry, 132,* 501-505.

Sharfstein, S. S., & Nafziger, J. C. (1976). Community care: Costs and benefits for a chronic patient. *Hospital & Community Psychiatry, 27,* 170-173.

Shelton v. Tucker, 364 U.S. 479, 488 (1960).

Slovenko, R. (1973). *Psychiatry and Law.* Boston: Little, Brown and Company.

Solomon, H. (1958). Presidential address. *American Journal of Psychiatry, 115,* 1-9.

Sosowsky, L. (1978). Crime and violence among mental patients reconsidered in view of the new legal relationship between the state and the mentally ill. *American Journal of Psychiatry, 135,* 33-42.

Sosowsky, L. (1980). Explaining the increased arrest rate among mental patients: A cautionary note. *American Journal of Psychiatry, 137,* 1602-1605.

Southeastern Community College v. Davis, 442 U.S. 397 (1979).

Spensley, J., Edwards, D. W., & White, E. (1980). Patient satisfaction and involuntary treatment. *American Journal of Orthopsychiatry, 50,* 725-727.

Stamus v. Leonhardt, 414 F. Supp. 439 (S.D. Iowa 1976).

Steadman, H. F., Cocozza, J. J., & Melich, M. E. (1978). Explaining the increased arrest rate among mental patients: The changing clientele of state hospitals. *American Journal of Psychiatry, 135,* 816-820.

Steadman, H. F., & Keveles, C. (1972). The community adjustment and criminal activity of the Baxstrom patients, 1960-1966. *American Journal of Psychiatry, 129*, 304-310.

Stelovich, S. (1979). From the hospital to the prison: A step forward in deinstitutionalization? *Hospital & Community Psychiatry, 30*, 618-620.

Stickney, S. B. (1974). Problems in implementing the right to treatment in Alabama: The Wyatt v. Stickney case. *Hospital & Community Psychiatry, 25*, 453-460.

Stone, A. A. (1975a). *Mental Health and Law: A System in Transition* (DHEW Publication No. ADM 76-176). Washington, DC: U. S. Government Printing Office.

Stone, A. A. (1975b). Overview: The right to treatment—Comments on the law and its impact. *American Journal of Psychiatry, 132*, 1125-1134.

Stone, A. A. (1979). The myth of advocacy. *Hospital & Community Psychiatry, 30*, 819-822.

Stone, A. A. (1982). Psychiatric abuse and legal reform: Two ways to make a bad situation worse. *International Journal of Law and Psychiatry, 5*, 9-28.

Superintendent of Worcester State Hospital v. Hagberg, 374 Mass. 271, 372 N.E.2d 242 (Mass. 1978).

In re Susan Lynn Farrow, 41 N.C. App. 680, 255 S.E.2d 777 (1977).

Suzuki v. Quisenberry, 411 F. Supp. 1113 (D. Hawaii 1976).

Szasz, T. S. (1963). *Law, Liberty, and Psychiatry.* New York: Macmillan.

Szasz, T. S. (1982). The psychiatric will—A new mechanism for protecting persons against "psychosis" and psychiatry. *American Psychologist, 37*, 762-770.

Talbott, J. A. (1979a). Why psychiatrists leave the public sector. *Hospital & Community Psychiatry, 30*, 778-782.

Talbott, J. A. (1979b). Deinstitutionalization: Avoiding the disasters of the past. *Hospital & Community Psychiatry, 30*, 621-624.

Test, M. A., & Stein, L. I. (1978). Community treatment of the chronic patient: Research overview. *Schizophrenia Bulletin, 4*, 350-364.

Toews, J., El-Guebaly, N., & Leckie, A. (1981). Patients' reactions to their commitment. *Canadian Journal of Psychiatry, 26*, 251-254.

Victoroff, V. M. (1977). Collaboration between Ohio psychiatrists and the legislature to update commitment laws. *American Journal of Psychiatry, 134,* 752-755.

Welsch v. Likins, 373 F. Supp. 487 (D. Minn. 1974).

Wenger, D. L., & Fletcher, C. R. (1969). The effect of legal counsel on admissions to a state mental hospital: A confrontation of professions. *Journal of Health and Social Behavior, 10,* 66-72.

Wexler, D. B. (1981). *Mental Health Law: Major Issues.* New York: Plenum Press.

Wexler, D. B., & Scoville, S. E. (1971). The administration of psychiatric justice: Theory and practice in Arizona. *Arizona Law Review, 13,* 1-259.

Wuori v. Zitnay, 1981 *Mental Disability Law Reporter,* 192 (D. Me. 1978).

Wyatt v. Stickney, 325 F. Supp 781 (M.D. Ala. 1971).

Youngberg v. Romeo, 50 U.S.L.W. 4681 (U.S. June 18, 1982).

Zander, T. K. (1977). Prolixin decanoate: Big brother by injection. *Journal of Psychiatry and Law, 5,* 55-75.

CIVIL COMMITMENT OF MINORS: LEGAL AND CLINICAL ISSUES AFTER *PARHAM V. J. R.*

Elliot M. Silverstein

> This is not an easy case. Issues involving the family and issues concerning mental illness are among the most difficult that courts have to face, involving as they often do serious problems of policy disguised as questions of constitutional law.
>
> Justice Potter Stewart, concurring
> in *Parham v. J. R.* (1979, p. 624)

In any society, there is an inevitable tension between the need for a society to care for those in need of supervision and an individual's autonomy and freedom. Despite this tension, there is also a clear interdependence between the two since elements of both need to exist in any just society. One of the law's great tasks, therefore, is to balance the competing claims of each in order to maximize the overall benefit to society. The enormity of this task is obvious, as is the certainty of dissatisfaction with the compromises that are inevitably forged, since few people would have the same prescription for which values are paramount.

While it is an oversimplification to look at any issue exclusively in these terms, it is the author's belief that much of the controversy regarding the civil commitment of minors to mental hospitals contains inherent elements of this philosophical struggle. Different people have fundamentally different views on the primacy of each value, and their discomfort and suspicion for the other causes them to weigh less heavily or perhaps even gloss over the costs in advocating one particular course of action.

The purpose of this chapter, however, is not to attempt to balance these competing values, but to examine some of the costs of providing certain forms of due process safeguards to emotionally disturbed youngsters in order to protect their right to freedom. In exploring some of the historical and current legal developments regarding the treatment of emotionally disturbed minors, several propositions will be advanced. First, for the most part, clinicians view legal reforms as fundamentally misdirected. They feel that these proposed safeguards provide little real protection to those affected, and may prove an important obstacle to providing effective treatment. Second, the most severely disturbed and disturbing youngsters are those most likely to be adversely affected by the "protection" offered them from the mental health system. Third, there are no coruscatingly clear solutions since we are really dealing with large social problems and fundamental values that are unlikely in a pluralistic society to readily reconcile themselves.

DUE PROCESS FOR THE JUVENILE

Since proposed changes in the mental health laws for juveniles have been patterned after changes in criminal procedures in juvenile cases, it is illuminating to examine those changes first. The basic philosophy for dealing with juveniles has been very different from the standards applied to adults. Beginning in 1899, with the first juvenile court in Cook County, Illinois, the goal of the juvenile justice system was to offer the adolescent "individualized justice and treatment rather than impartial justice and punishment" (Halleck, 1967, p. 245). Therefore, instead of being dealt with as a criminal, the minor was committed for treatment in a civil proceeding. Hearings were often conducted informally and secretly in an effort to spare the juvenile embarrassing publicity. Since the goal was to insure help for the child, the standard of proof of guilt was not the same as with adults, and offenses such as truancy, talking back to one's parents, or incorrigibility could draw potentially lengthy sentences.

As a result of their supposed *parens patriae* functions (or the state's sovereign power of guardianship over persons of disability), juvenile courts were accorded substantial latitude and authority. Youngsters coming before a juvenile court judge were to be helped rather than punished, and were sent to places called "reform" or "training" schools rather than jails. The goal of such special treatment was to temper the severity of the traditional criminal justice system. Unfortunately, there was a growing suspicion that this *parens patriae* function, instead of providing wayward youths with rehabilitation, served society for the most part as an old-fashioned jailer (Kittrie, 1971). As a result, juveniles received the worst of both worlds: They were stripped of many of the due process safeguards accorded adults, and were often thrust into brutal and punitive state institutions.

Another problem endemic to the juvenile justice system was the lack of real dispositional alternatives. For example, in many states, juvenile statutes did not differentiate between neglected and delinquent children in describing a judge's dispositional alternatives (Foote, Levy, & Sander, 1966). As a result, youths with very different needs and very different backgrounds would end up in the same facilities. The system then adequately helped neither the most seriously delinquent nor the more mildly troubled. In addition, lack of a broad spectrum of services, overcrowding in existing facilities, and lack of training of those supposedly servicing the juvenile all combined to create conditions mirroring many of the problems of adult corrections.

This disparity between the theory and practice of the juvenile justice system was illustrated by the facts of the United States Supreme Court's landmark decision in *In re Gault* (1967). On June 8, 1963, 15-year-old Gerald Gault was taken into custody for allegedly making a lewd phone call to a neighbor consisting of moderately suggestive sexual questions. Gerald, who was still under a 6-month probation order for being in the company of another adolescent who had stolen a wallet from a lady's purse, was taken by police officers from his home to a detention center while his parents were at work. No notice was left for his parents of his whereabouts, and at a hearing in the juvenile court judge's chambers the next day, neither Gerald's father nor the complainant were present when the judge questioned Gerald. No transcript or recording was made of the proceedings. Gerald was released several days later with no further explanation to him or his parents. At a second hearing the following week, a referral report by probation officers was read without the presence of the complainant, and Gerald was committed to the State Industrial School "for a period of his minority [that is, until 21], unless sooner discharged by due process of law" (p. 7). Gerald could have been incarcerated for 6 years.

The Supreme Court's reversal of Gerald's conviction became a milestone in the establishment of legal rights for minors. While the opinion was limited to the adjudicatory stage of the juvenile court process, and did not consider questions raised by intake or arrests, detention or disposition, it did provide for rights in four areas: notice, counsel, privileges against self-incrimination, and confrontation of witnesses available for cross-examination.

Later cases further expanded the due process protection of minors in juvenile courts. In 1970, the Supreme Court held that the burden of proof in juvenile cases was similar to that in adult cases—"beyond a reasonable doubt" and not merely "a preponderance of the evidence" (*In re Winship*, 1970). While in *McKeiver v. Pennsylvania* (1971), the Supreme Court held that a trial by jury was not constitutionally required in the adjudicative phase of a state juvenile court delinquency proceeding, the court later held in *Breed v. Jones* (1975) that the prosecution of a juvenile as an adult in criminal court after one adjudicatory finding in juvenile court was a violation of the Double Jeopardy Clause of the Fifth Amendment. In his opinion, Chief Justice Burger acknowledged that the juvenile justice system had fallen short of the high expectations of its sponsors to ameliorate the harshness of criminal justice when applied to youthful offenders. In Burger's words:

Although the juvenile court system had its genesis in the desire to provide a distinctive procedure and setting to deal with the problems of youth, including those manifested by antisocial conduct, our decisions in recent years have recognized that there is a gap between the originally benign conception of the system and its realities. (p. 528)

These cases, then, did much to involve lawyers with juveniles in order to assure the traditional safeguards of due process. The more traditional adversary system supposedly mitigates absolute discretion by a juvenile court judge. While this development may vitiate or alleviate some ills of the existing system, it raises a fundamental issue. Kittrie (1971), himself in favor of such a change, states:

Thus, those seeking to expand the availability of legal services in the juvenile court must shoulder a dual burden: To accord the child his constitutional safeguards while guarding against a diminution of the child's sense of social responsibility, so that the child who requires treatment in his own and in society's interest is not merely turned loose to become the eventual victim of pyrrhic courtroom victories. (p. 158)

This admonition seems at least as warranted when discussing changes or potential changes in the mental health laws.

CIVIL COMMITMENT OF JUVENILES

Accompanying the significant changes in juvenile court procedures in the past two decades have been similar efforts to revise mental health law for minors. These efforts, however, have been complicated by the traditional role of parents in our society. Even if it is felt there are reasons not to force hospitalization on adults, the standards for children are not necessarily the same. Parents are often allowed to force or volunteer their children for services they may not choose for themselves. In most states, it was and still is permissible for parents or legal guardians to voluntarily admit their child into a mental hospital. Since this is possible both with or without the child's consent, the term "voluntary admission" is really a misnomer. The importance of the voluntary admission has been to circumvent the need for a court hearing or review. Since the parent is acting for and on behalf of the minor, the typical standard for a voluntary admission was thought applicable, that is, the presence of "mental illness," but not necessarily "imminent danger." Similarly, no court hearing was required.

More recently, this type of parental prerogative has come under increasing attack, with heavy emphasis placed on the loss of liberty involved in such hospitalizations. Such advocates typically see the need for the same type of due process safeguards accorded those subject to the juvenile justice system. Nevertheless, as Ellis (1974) has pointed out:

> [T]here are three justifications that could be used for forcing hospitalization on young patients who would not be subject to such commitment if they were adults. (1) Children are not old enough to make a mature judgment about whether they need treatment or not, and therefore someone else must make it for them. (2) Children are subject to the decisions made for them by their parents, and a commitment decision is within the scope of parental authority. (3) Mental disorders are much more treatable when the patient is young, and therefore there is a greater state interest in forcing treatment on mildly ill young persons than on mildly ill adults. (p. 850, n. 54)

This third reason is given even greater currency when intervention seems to be necessary to prevent graver and more ingrained problems. Furthermore, the autonomy of the family unit from external control by the state and others and the accompanying authority over the conduct of a child are deeply embedded values in our society. Family autonomy and parental control have long been central to the American concept of freedom and individuality (Bezanson, 1978). Interference, then, with a joint decision by a mental health facility and parents to commit a child runs contrary to some basic American values and departs from the privileges and responsibilities that parents customarily exercise in raising their children.

It is argued, nonetheless, that commitment to a mental hospital is so serious an act as to challenge these parental rights and prerogatives, and that the traditional check against parental excess, the screening by the admitting psychiatrists, is more theoretical than real. As Ellis (1974) states:

> Experience shows that in the most blatant cases of parental error psychiatrists do screen out admissions which are not warranted by apparent pathology in the child. In less obvious cases, however, psychiatrists may fail to perform an effective screening function. There are three reasons for this failure: (1) The performance of psychiatrists in precommitment interviews and examinations is often perfunctory and tends toward over diagnosis; (2) Psychiatrists may be insensitive to legally important commitment issues; (3) The effectiveness of the psychiatrist in the admitting process is weakened by uncertainty over whose agent he or she is in such circumstances—the parent's or the child's. (p. 864)

An additional, important criticism of the current system is that many states allow legal guardians such as social service agencies to act as a parent. This creates the possibility of collaboration or collusion between state agencies, which may seek admission of juveniles to state hospitals for reasons other than treatment. Thus, some commentators feel that the most effective and objective protection for children would be independent legal counsel. In fact, it can be argued that, given a minor's immaturity, it is even more important for a minor to be protected (Szasz, 1977).

Significantly, the United States Supreme Court in its opinions in *Parham v. J. R.* (1979) and *Secretary of Public Welfare v. Institutionalized Juveniles* (1979) clearly rejected the idea of a mandated commitment hearing, overruling two District Court decisions that had concluded that due process demanded an impartial adversarial hearing. While the two cases, one from Pennsylvania and one from Georgia, have rather dissimilar histories, they in essence raise the same due process questions. The Pennsylvania case, (*Kremens v. Bartley*, 1977) and its successor (*Institutionalized Juveniles v. Secretary of Public Welfare*, 1978), have a somewhat complex history. The original case, which was brought in the U. S. District Court for the Eastern District of Pennsylvania, was instituted on behalf of five mentally ill individuals between 15 and 18 years old who were challenging the constitutionality of a 1966 Pennsylvania statute governing voluntary admission and voluntary commitment to a state mental health institution of persons aged 18 or younger. The statute provided that a juvenile could be admitted upon a parent's application and was free to withdraw only with the consent of the parent admitting him or her.

After the commencement of the suit, the Pennsylvania Department of Public Welfare promulgated regulations which substantially increased procedural requirements with regard to minors 13 years of age or older by requiring that they be given notification of their rights, the telephone number of counsel, and the right to institute an involuntary commitment hearing. Notwithstanding those changes, the District Court later issued a decision holding those provisions violative of due process (*Bartley v. Kremens*, 1975). This decision was appealed to the U. S. Supreme Court. In July of 1976, a year after the District Court decision and after the Supreme Court had noted probable jurisdiction to hear the case, a new statute was passed that, in essence, allowed 14 year olds to be treated as adults. They were allowed to admit and discharge themselves, with parents being restricted to admitting children 13 or younger. The Supreme Court thus easily disposed of the case by claiming that all the original plaintiffs (appellees) would now be treated as adults and free to leave the hospital, obviating their demand for a hearing and other procedural protection. They and other mentally ill children over 14 years of age would now have the same freedom as adults to leave the hospital and not be forced to return without their consent. The Court declined to pass judgment on those classes unaffected by the changes in Pennsylvania law—namely, mentally ill children under 14 and mentally retarded minors under 18—and remanded the case back to the District Court.

While the Supreme Court essentially postponed deciding the role of the legal system in the commitment process of juveniles by mooting *Bartley*, a case from Georgia, *Parham v. J. R.*, was argued before the Supreme Court on December 6, 1977, and then restored to the Court's calendar for reargument on January 16, 1978. This was a suit filed for two minors alleging that they and others similarly situated had been deprived of their liberty without due process by virtue of the mental health laws of Georgia, which were similar to those in Pennsylvania in 1966 before all the subsequent Pennsylvania changes. Under the Georgia statute, a minor could be signed into a hospital by a parent or guardian if he or she showed "evidence of mental illness and [were] suitable for treatment" (*Parham v. J. R.*, 1979, p. 591). Before the minor attained the age of 18, the only discharge mechanism in addition to that provided by the hospital would be by application of the parent or guardian. The U. S. District Court stated that while this statute was in effect, children were institutionalized without a hearing or other procedural safeguards, were hospitalized without initial or periodic consideration of placement in the least restrictive environment necessary for treatment, and were not afforded a hearing at any time to determine an appropriate required time for discharge. The District Court concluded the statute was unconstitutional and ordered:

> ...the defendants to proceed as expeditiously as is reasonably possible (1) to provide necessary physical resources and personnel for whatever nonhospital facilities are deemed by them to be most appropriate for these children, and (2) to place these children in such nonhospital facilities as soon as reasonably appropriate. (p. 139)

In order to attempt to understand the reason for this remedy, it is important to note that the District Court took pains to examine the type of treatment available to troubled youngsters in Georgia at the time the suit was instituted. If a minor could not be placed in a foster home or specialized foster home, hospital confinement was the only service offered by the state. In a 1973 Study Commission Report, it was felt by both hospital personnel and the Commission that more than *half* of the hospitalized children and youth would not need hospitalization if other forms of care were available. In the more than 2 years after the Commission Report and before the undertaking of the lawsuit, the State of Georgia made no effort to establish group homes or other facilities besides hospital treatment, despite the fact that such care seemed less expensive. In such circumstances, it is not very surprising that a court would order legal redress for children who could be placed elsewhere. It is also not surprising that a court would look with disfavor on a statutory system that allows a state agency custody and thereby provides the vehicle for what amounted to consignment to a mental institution for the duration of a youth's minority. It should be noted that the District Court in *Parham* did not fashion the exact nature of due process protection needed but, drawing strong support from *In re Gault* (1967), did hold that due process included at least the right, after notice, for the juvenile to be heard before an impartial tribunal.

Before the Supreme Court ruled on the *Parham* case, the successor to *Bartley* (1975) reappeared. When *Bartley* was remanded back to the District Court in Pennsylvania, there still was the substantive issue of whether the newer Pennsylvania statutory framework was acceptable for mentally retarded minors under 18 and mentally ill minors under 14. The Pennsylvania District Court, with a strongly worded dissent by Judge Broderick, held in *Institutionalized Juveniles v. Secretary of Public Welfare* (1978), that the current statutes were unconstitutional. The majority felt that despite differences between mental retardation and mental illness, there was little difference between the two groups as far as determining procedural due process requirements. The majority stressed the potential for conflict of interest between parent and child, the risks of misdiagnosis, and the stigma of being labeled mentally retarded or mentally ill. To rectify these problems, the majority, unlike in *Parham*, ordered that very specific procedural requirements be adhered to before these minors could be committed to a mental health or mental retardation facility. These requirements included: (a) the right to notice; (b) the right to counsel; (c) hearing rights, including an opportunity to be present and to offer testimony, as well as the right to confrontation and cross-examination of adverse witnesses; (d) the right to a probable cause hearing within 72 hours; and (e) the right to a full commitment hearing within 2 weeks after the initial admission, with a finding by clear and convincing proof that institutionalization is needed.

Judge Broderick, dissenting from the majority opinion, as he did in *Bartley* (1975), reiterated his fear that the majority had prescribed an "overdose" of due process and was concerned that this might discourage parents from seeking treatment for a child suffering from a mental or emotional disorder. He also questioned the facile way the majority lumped mental retardation and mental illness together, and he could not see how the procedures mandated by the majority would mitigate or eradicate the alleged conflicts between parent and child, the risk of misdiagnosis, and the alleged stigma attached to mental illness and mental retardation.

The case was then appealed to the Supreme Court on June 19, 1978, and was set for oral argument in tandem with *Parham*. In October, 1978, the two cases were argued before the Supreme Court, and on June 20, 1979, the Supreme Court rendered its opinion. By a six to three majority in each case, the Court reversed the rulings of the District Courts by finding neither the Pennsylvania nor the Georgia statutes violative of the Fourteenth Amendment's due process clause (*Parham v. J. R.*, 1979; *Secretary of Public Welfare v. Institutionalized Juveniles*, 1979). Since the Pennsylvania case rests on the standards enunciated in *Parham*, it would seem most appropriate to concentrate on the Georgia case.

Chief Justice Burger, writing for the majority in *Parham*, felt the case essentially involved a balancing of three competing interests: the child's liberty interest, the parent's interest in the welfare and health of the child, and the state's significant interest in properly utilizing its mental health facilities. Using this balancing approach, the Court concluded:

[T]he risk of error inherent in the parental decision to have a child institutionalized for mental health care is sufficiently great that some kind of inquiry should be made by a "neutral factfinder" to determine whether the statutory requirements for admission are satisfied. That inquiry must carefully probe the child's background using all available sources, including, but not limited to, parents, schools, and other social agencies. Of course, the review must also include an interview with the child. It is necessary that the decision maker have the authority to refuse to admit any child who does not satisfy the medical standards for admission. Finally, it is necessary that the child's continuing need for commitment be periodically reviewed by a similarly independent procedure. (pp. 606-607)

The neutral factfinder need not be a lawyer or a judicial or administrative officer. "Thus, a staff physician will suffice, so long as he or she is free to evaluate independently the child's mental and emotional condition and need for treatment" (*Parham*, 1979, p. 607). In fact, it is quite clear that Burger preferred leaving commitment decisions to the judgment of physicians and was wary of judicial involvement. Burger was frankly skeptical that a law trained factfinder would be better able to ascertain when a child did or did not need to be hospitalized.

Burger's concern with the burden that would be placed on the mental health system by affording full due process protection to minors during the commitment process was evident when the Chief Justice stated:

As the scope of governmental action expands into new areas creating new controversies for judicial review, it is incumbent on courts to design procedures that protect the rights of the individual without unduly burdening the legitimate efforts of the states to deal with difficult social problems. The judicial model for factfinding for all constitutionally protected interests, regardless of their nature, can turn rational decision making into an unmanageable enterprise. (*Parham*, 1979, p. 608, n. 16)

The Court also concluded that no different procedures, either preceding or immediately after admission, need be devised for children who were wards of the state (*Parham*, 1979, pp. 618-619). With respect to such a minor's need for continuing care, it is possible that different procedures may be applicable for children committed by state appointed guardians, but the Supreme Court left this issue up to the District Court on remand (p. 619). In fact, the whole area of what procedures for review are necessary to justify continuing a child's commitment was left open since the District Court did not decide the issue and the Supreme Court thus felt no need to consider it.

Justice Brennan, writing for three justices in dissent, balanced the competing interests very differently. He rejected the argument that parents and mental health professionals should be allowed to commit children in this manner. Clearly equating hospitalization with incarceration, he wrote:

Children incarcerated in public mental institutions are constitutionally entitled to a fair opportunity to contest the legitimacy of their confinement. They are entitled to some champion who can speak on their behalf and who stands ready to oppose a wrongful commitment....The risk of erroneous commitment is simply too great unless there is some form of adversarial review. And fairness demands that children abandoned by their supposed protectors to the rigors of institutional confinement be given the help of some separate voice. (*Parham*, 1979, pp. 638-639)

Similarly, Brennan did not think that children with natural parents should be dealt with in the same manner as children who were wards of the state. He felt that, with regard to children committed by their natural parents, a hearing prior to hospitalization might deter these parents from seeking needed treatment, and, by challenging parental authority, might make the child's return to his or her family more difficult. For these reasons, Brennan felt that a hearing for such children need not be held until after admission (*Parham*, 1979, p. 633). A later hearing, Brennan wrote, by merely involving a conflict between the child's physician and advocate, was not likely to lead to family discord (p. 675). Brennan could, therefore, see no legitimate state interest suffering as a consequence of such procedure.

In contrast, Brennan felt that children committed by their guardians should be required to have hearings *before* commitment (*Parham*, 1979, p. 638). He rejected the idea that these children would be protected from unwarranted commitments just because their social workers were obligated by statute to act in their best interest. "With equal logic, it could be argued that criminal trials are unnecessary since prosecutors are not supposed to prosecute innocent persons" (p. 637). He concluded that preadmission hearings would not deter social workers from seeking psychiatric attention for their disturbed clients and saw the decisions of one group of state workers reviewed by another group of state officials as unlikely either "to traumatize the children or hinder their eventual recovery" (p. 638).

In assessing the likely impact of the Supreme Court's decisions in *Parham* (1979) and *Institutionalized Juveniles* (1979), several points are worth mentioning. First, one should note the different values the justices assigned to the balancing of children's and parent's rights and the proper utilization of states' resources. In *Parham*, Chief Justice Burger spoke of the state's "significant interest in confining the use of its costly mental health facilities to cases of genuine need" (pp. 604-605) and spoke much more positively about the facilities in Georgia than had the District Court. Justice Stewart, in a concurring opinion, wrote that it was "deeply embedded" that "[f]or centuries it has been a canon of the common law that parents speak for their minor children" (p. 621). On the other hand, Justice Brennan equated hospitalization with incarceration and spoke of children needing a "champion" for those "abandoned by their supposed protectors to the rigors of institutional confinement" (pp. 638-639).

Second, as mentioned earlier, the Court concluded that commitment decisions should be considered medical rather than legal matters. Burger wrote:

> The mode and procedure of medical diagnostic procedures is not the business of judges. What is best for a child is an individual medical decision that must be left to the judgment of physicians in each case. (*Parham*, 1979, pp. 607-608)

For this view, Burger is likely to draw more praise from the mental health than the legal community, as evidenced in the many critical legal articles appearing since the decisions (Glaessner, 1981; Mabbut, 1980; Mawdsley, 1980; Note, 1979, 1979-1980, 1980c, 1980e; Tiano, 1980).

Third, the Court felt that an untreated child's abnormal behavior may be more "stigmatizing" than "labeling" the child in need of treatment (*Parham*, 1979, pp. 600-601). This point raises the important question about how truly free someone with a serious mental disorder is without care and treatment (Miller & Fiddleman, 1982; Rachlin, 1974).

Fourth, until the Court's opinion in *Parham*, only Judge Broderick's thoughtful dissenting opinions in the lower court, in *Bartley v. Kremens* (1975) and *Institutionalized Juveniles v. Secretary of Public Welfare* (1978), had focused on the fundamental issue of whether substantial intervention by the legal system into the civil commitment process would actually do anything to protect the affected juveniles or would merely create other problems.

Finally, while the Supreme Court's holding is likely to be hailed by many mental health professionals as clinically mandated, it will not, by itself, necessitate any changes in current laws with regard to hearing (Silverstein, 1980b). While states are not required to hold legal hearings, they are free to do so if they choose. Therefore, neither states currently holding hearings nor those that do not are required to change their laws. While the Supreme Court's decision is likely to slow the impetus toward imposition of adversary hearings, it is unlikely to end all efforts toward increasing legal involvement in the treatment process. The Court's opinion paves the way for those opposed to the Court's ruling to challenge the later course of hospitalization, including the review procedures used to justify continuing commitment, especially when a less restrictive alternative is arguably a possibility. Furthermore, both the majority and dissenting opinions leave open the question of whether different standards should apply, at least after the onset of hospitalization for children not committed by their natural parents. Unfortunately, from a clinical standpoint, such scrutiny at the later stages of treatment may prove more inherently deleterious than a hearing either immediately before or after admission.

CLINICAL CONCERNS

This section will attempt to present, from a clinical vantage point, some concerns about the real effectiveness or cost of the due process safeguards advocated for minors. One obvious cost is economic; the time and energy that mental health professionals spend on legal matters is then unavailable for direct care and therapy. Another economic consideration is the cost of the entire judicial procedure. For example, in an adult case, *Addington v. Texas* (1979), the jury trial to commit Addington lasted over 6 days, even though Addington did not dispute the state's evidence which showed that he suffered from serious delusions, that he often had threatened to injure both of his parents and others, that he had been involved in several assaultive episodes while hospitalized, and that he had caused substantial property damage both at his own apartment and at his parent's home (pp. 420-421). In addition, there was undisputed expert testimony that the appellant "required hospitalization in a closed area to treat his condition because in the past he had refused to attend outpatient treatment programs and had escaped several times from mental hospitals" (p. 421).

A second less easily demonstrated cost is the deleterious effect many clinicians believe that due process procedures have on treatment. Since the Supreme Court's opinion in *Parham* left open the issue of what form of later review will be sufficient to justify continuing commitment, it will be important to assess the possible impact of a judicial review at every stage of hospitalization. After all, even if a youth is rightfully admitted to a hospital, some will argue that the loss of liberty, stigma of long hospitalization, and the need for the least restrictive alternative would still leave an important post-admission role for the legal system.

While post-admission review may be heartening to some, it is an unappealing and disturbing prospect for most clinicians working with minors. These professionals view work with children or adolescents and their families as difficult enough under the best of circumstances without the intrusion of lay persons attempting to evaluate programs and procedures in which they have little or no training. Civil libertarians and mental health lawyers counter this argument by challenging the assumption that commitment decisions are really medical questions. They suggest instead that the hard moral questions raised by mental disorder should not be avoided by relying upon mental health expertise and allowing essentially social, moral, and legal questions to be "medicalized" (Morse, 1978, p. 542).

At bottom, then, the real issue may be one of control or territoriality. Unfortunately, it is just this struggle and tension surrounding control of the mental health system that may be harmful to treatment. Clinicians argue that, regardless of the merits of concerns over legal safeguards, the types of procedures advocated to monitor the system do little to correct real problems. As Stone (1979) comments:

> Legal advocates for the mentally ill have not been willing to consider seriously the needs of the mentally ill and to formulate those needs as legal rights. Instead they have done the reverse. They have treated rights as if they constituted the needs of the mentally ill. (p. 820)

Nevertheless, before examining from a clinical perspective the nature of the problems created by legal intervention, several caveats are in order. Describing treatment succinctly is no easy task. There is hardly unanimity in the field, and many "clinical truths" are difficult to demonstrate with the same sort of scientific evidence possible in other fields. What is perhaps most frustrating to legal analysts is that much of clinical work proceeds under the assumption that often people neither say what they mean, nor mean what they say. As a result, clinicians will often tend to discount what an individual may claim. Instead, most look carefully for more subtle forms of communication such as what the person avoids, the nuances of what the individual says, the individual's body language, and the next topic or type of behavior following the discussion of a subject. This creates a possible credibility gap, as a clinician may describe a person as truly wanting to remain in the hospital, at the same time the person is vigorously asking a legal representative to seek discharge.

With this in mind, the author takes responsibility for the clinical analysis, acknowledging that other interpretations of the events are possible. The analysis is based upon the author's experience in North Carolina with both a long-term intensive treatment program and a short-term crisis and diagnostic unit for adolescents, as well as discussions with other clinicians similarly situated (Amaya & Burlingame, 1978). In North Carolina, there is an initial hearing within 10 days of hospitalization and mandated periodic court reviews thereafter. At each hearing it is necessary to prove by clear and convincing evidence that the minor is both mentally ill and in need of further treatment (Silverstein, 1980b). In addition, it is also important to note that this analysis will not address the problems of the mentally retarded. This is not to say that mental retardation and mental illness are mutually exclusive but to emphasize the important clinical difference between the two groups.

In examining from a clinical vantage point the nature of the problems created by legal intervention, it will be helpful first to present a clinical view of the children and adolescents who end up in residential treatment and the effect of the legal process on them. While many types of adolescent problems are felt to require hospitalization, the focus of the following analysis will center on the problems associated with youngsters who act out their problems. These youngsters, by the nature of the difficulties they present to the community, draw the most obvious attention to themselves. They may also pose the most difficult management and treatment problems once institutionalized and seem to be the ones most affected by the judicial process.

Such youngsters often deal with their world by developing both maladaptive means of fleeing from the unpredictable nature of their upbringing and a distrust of the value of talking rather than acting. In addition, the avoidance of feelings becomes a major *modus operandi* for such teenagers, as the years only increase the variety of ways in which they can use action to deal with anxiety and frustration or any dysphoric feelings. They seek solutions to problems in quick or magical ways, solutions that are usually unplanned and often detrimental to themselves or others. The emphasis is always on external change, because in the past internal change has been too difficult or frightening and has often led to a series of failed endeavors which have further alienated the youth from society and, ultimately, from his or her own feelings.

While entrance into the mental health system varies, it rarely is embraced openly as a panacea. Many families have, or feel they have, something to be ashamed of and would prefer to have their problems remain private. In addition, while the youth's repetitive problems may be uncomfortable for the family, they are at least uncomfortable in a familiar way. The prospect of treatment introduces the possibility of change in an unknown manner and is, therefore, somewhat frightening. As a result, while to objective observers these families may appear chaotic or fragmented, often as a result of divorce or separation, they tend to show a remarkable tendency to unite in confronting an outsider who threatens to change the family dynamics. In addition, in the subculture of many of the families involved, the identification of the teenager as "mentally ill" is a stigma to the whole family. Moreover, entrance into the system is usually through the juvenile court system, low fee clinics, community mental health centers, or state institutions. The state institutions are often large, multiserviced, and perhaps substandard, and are often joked about in the local community as the last place anyone would willingly want to be, or send a relative. The decision to seek hospitalization, therefore, is often an excruciatingly painful process. Some families are never able to see any merit in this type of solution, and as a result the teenager usually only surfaces as a referral from a social service agency or a juvenile court after custody has been removed from the parents or extended family.

The teenager is also likely to be uncertain about the need for hospitalization and treatment. Even individuals who enter therapy voluntarily are ambivalent about the process, so it is only reasonable to expect a disturbed teenager to be at least as wary or ambivalent. In fact, the nature and extent of ambivalence or conflict is an essential clinical diagnostic and therapeutic issue. An immediate clinical concern is not only whether someone needs intervention, but whether he or she is treatable. Many teenagers grow up in homes with the dynamics described earlier, but few enter mental hospitals. Some seem to do reasonably well for themselves, others seem to be more delinquent, and others are felt to be more mentally ill. The vicissitudes of normal teenage development often preclude the ready identification of certain actions as *per se* indications of mental illness. Therefore, careful consideration of all the factors leading to the alarming actions, a detailed social history, including school adjustment, and psychological and psychiatric evaluations, are all important in assessing an adolescent's needs and likelihood to benefit from certain interventions. While these considerations are obviously important in assessing a minor's needs in other legal settings, such as a juvenile court, clinicians argue that they are better able, by virtue of their training and experience, to sift through the data and reach conclusions on issues surrounding emotional care or hospitalization.

When a teenager is at a point where hospitalization is recommended, there is, no matter what his or her surface reaction to hospitalization, a more subtle testing of the new environment—what are the expectations, what are the limits, what are the consequences, how do the staff respond, and how are the personal interactions different from those to which the youth has become accustomed (Planavsky, Ritchie, & Silverstein, 1978, p. 4). For many teenagers, the hospital is perceived merely as another place to fail. By definition, when hospitalization occurs there has been a rift or separation in the family. Many adolescents have never experienced what it is like to work through any problem within a system. Often any desire on the part of the child to succeed, or even to entertain hopes for the future, has been layered over by failure, self-doubt, and actions leading to guilt and/or pain to others. One key element of successful hospitalization, therefore, is to establish or reconstruct a sense of being able to succeed within a system and thus reduce the need to flee from others.

Unfortunately, the legal system's monitoring of the mental health system, and the implicit distrust this conveys, fits into the teenager's maladaptive pattern. At the point of hospitalization, many adults have already repeatedly failed the youth in their actions and have been unable to control the youth's actions. One of the implicit promises the treatment team offers is to control the behavior of the adolescent if he or she cannot. The legal system's involvement immediately undermines this promise. On some level the adolescent must realize that it is a great deal easier to attempt to manipulate a lawyer or judge than to work toward internal change. The legal process, especially an adversary court hearing, is often a recapitulation of the same events that occurred earlier, in that it causes discord, confusion, and arguments among adults, with the possibility that someone eventually may relent. Even if the court finally does give the youth a strong and therapeutic message, it cannot seriously be argued that hearing a painful rehash of one's failures and problems aired in an adversarial setting is beneficial. Furthermore, if the therapist and members of the treatment team are forced by the youth's actions to testify against him or her, the youth's belief that the hospital can be a safe place is further eroded. In fact, Justice Brennan in his dissent in *Parham* seemed to encourage this type of confrontation between treatment staff and youth, claiming that a "hearing itself [would be] unlikely so to traumatize parent and child as to make the child's eventual return to family impracticable" (p. 635). Brennan never addressed what the hearing would do to relationships between the youth and the hospital staff.

Legal intervention creates other problems as well. For example, one of the immediate issues arising in the treatment of acting-out adolescents is whether the treatment facility is strong enough to provide the protection so obviously lacking in the past. The presence of court procedures can do much to erode the hospital's therapeutic effectiveness in this regard. The existence of procedures that allow the teenagers capriciously to set in motion the mechanism for discharge must on some level be very threatening. The teenager can often do that anyway by violent or destructive acts that may indicate that hospitalization is not the proper course of action. The teenager is, however, clearly violating a taboo in such cases and will often face criminal sanctions as a result. With a courtroom fight, however, the teenager is pursuing legitimate means and may only be mirroring the distrust for the hospital that the legal procedures imply. As such, these procedures may serve to foster in the teenager negative feelings about the treatment process, thus making trust that much more difficult to achieve.

While the potential damage to treatment by legal procedures is immediately present, it is a far greater problem in later hearings. The first court hearing will relate to past events and whether they make sense in the context of how the adolescent appears at the onset of hospitalization. While clinicians may view such legal scrutiny as antithetical to the treatment process, an initial hearing may be just one more obstacle in the initial stage of treatment. Greater clinical concerns, however, arise over the monitoring of the entire treatment process. A certain vulnerability is created as treatment progresses and the adolescent starts to contain the sort of symptoms that led to hospitalization. The symptoms that had previously "defined" the teenager may have diminished, but there will not have been enough time for the establishment of any more permanent identity. The temptation to use the court hearing as a test of whether the old magical solutions to problems will work and whether the hospital is strong enough to vouchsafe treatment is often irresistible.

Even later in treatment, when it is felt that the teenager has internalized a new set of values, the spectre of the legal hearing creates problems. If the teenager is functioning better and appears rather normal, it is often not clear to someone outside the treatment setting why the hospital is still insisting the teenager needs further treatment. In fact, the teenager may need the treatment program at this stage more than ever to move realistically toward autonomy and to solidify the gains made. The teenager, with a backdrop of legal skirmishes, may feel peculiar admitting now to being mentally ill, especially since he or she feels better than ever. Furthermore, the adolescent may also be covertly supported in seeking discharge by parents who in some ways fear too much change and who prefer to hope the work is over before all the old painful interactions are rekindled in therapy. Thus, the adolescent may again be tempted to see whether someone outside of his or her daily experience can pronounce treatment finished.

These later hearings place everyone in the process in a peculiar position. As time passes, it is more difficult to convey an accurate picture of the teenager's functioning. Much evidence of past and present disturbance is, if all goes well, being channeled into therapy instead of into action. Whatever the merits of an initial court review, the treatment team by now should know far more about the adolescent than the judge is ever likely to discover, especially in an adversary hearing within a courtroom. For a judge, who is so far removed from the daily existence of the teenager, to review a teenager's progress under these circumstances and have the authority to override the treatment team's recommendations must send a mixed message to the teenager about the importance of working with the treatment team.

The artificiality of this process may explain two phenomena that are frequently observed around the time of court hearings: (a) acting out; and (b) claims of abuse. First, acting out or regressions during the court hearing often reappear, and may guarantee continued hospitalization. Clinicians view this tendency as a lamentable outgrowth of creating a system that ignores clinical reality. Taking seriously a teenager's demand or request to leave the hospital may be frightening enough to force the teenager to prove in action what words cannot. Second, often teenagers will complain during court hearings about abuse of "rights." Since this is a very

serious legal concern, lawyers are apt to give these claims
a great deal of credence. Clinicians, on the other hand,
are more likely to view these complaints as symbolic. The
adolescents may indeed be feeling abused, but by (a) the
legal system's ignorance of their ambivalent desire to stay
in the hospital; (b) their own inability not to become
involved in the process; and (c) the treatment team's
inability to protect the teenagers from themselves.
Usually, the treatment team will bear the brunt of the
adolescents' anger, since the lack of ultimate protection is
a painful repetition of what transpired throughout so
much of their lives. The inevitable cleanup by the
treatment team of the fallout from court hearings may
explain much of the resentment felt toward the legal
system.

In essence, then, clinicians are likely to see their jobs
made needlessly more complicated by the legal system.
Since the system offers one more avenue of escape from
the internal changes necessary for those adolescents to
have a chance of succeeding in society, it does a great
disservice to those it is designed to protect. By
questioning and challenging the authority and wisdom of
the recommended treatment, the system endangers the
legitimacy of the teenager working with the treatment
team. The teenager's investment must partly reside
outside of treatment, focused instead on what a judge
may do or think. The court hearings, if they operate in a
true adversary fashion, are hardly benign affairs and are
considered by clinicians to be a cruel charade. Instead of
protecting the adolescent, the legal system serves as one
more institution insensitive to the adolescent's actual
needs, and provides one more set of adults to be used and
manipulated.

WHO TRULY BENEFITS?

The desire for formal due process safeguards before
civilly committing minors and the concomitant willingness
to challenge the traditional notion of parental autonomy
appears to spring from two often cited criticisms of the
mental health system. First, involuntary treatment runs
counter to fundamental values in our society (Morse,

1982), and the mental health field undermines its credibility by its participation (Leifer, 1969; Szasz, 1982). In addition, one of the traditional rationales for civil commitment has been to relieve society and families of caring for people who are bothersome or eccentric. Stone (1975) labels this a "convenience function" and states:

> Its implementation all too obviously calls for a macrosocietal policy judgment of a type which a free society is unwilling to confront in an open forum. It is, therefore, a typical instance of the clandestine decision making role of mental health practitioners which allows society to do what it does not want to admit to doing, i.e., confining unwanted persons cheaply. (p. 45)

The plight of the mentally retarded in many jurisdictions provides a striking example of this process. For a description of the problems in different states' facilities, see the following cases—*Halderman v. Pennhurst* (1979), (Pennsylvania), *New York State Association for Retarded Children, Inc. v. Rockefeller* (1973), (New York), and *Wyatt v. Aderholt* (1974), (Alabama).

Second, mental health professionals, under the guise of treatment, have allowed and perhaps even fostered execrable conditions in their institutions. It is not easy to defend involuntarily committing someone to an institution to receive inadequate treatment, and it is hardly persuasive merely to assert that this is for the benefit of the individual. Since the promise of treatment has been an empty one for many who have been civilly committed, hospitalization has borne more of a resemblance to incarceration than treatment for a mental disorder. In such circumstances, a jaundiced view of the mental health field is somewhat appropriate, and the judicial trend toward providing procedural safeguards paralleling those of the criminal justice system is certainly understandable.

However, identifying a problem is one thing, but it is quite another to impose on the mental health system a method of reform derived from another context. If the purpose is to protect rights deemed to be so fundamental in a free society that their preservation outweighs any detriments to treatment, then this is a clear moral and legal policy decision and should be recognized as such. If, on the other hand, due process procedures that impose adversarial hearings on the mental health system are designed to protect individuals from shoddy and inadequate treatment, it is important to examine both the nature and effectiveness of this "protection." As discussed, there *is* a cost to due process procedures which may inadvertently result in reducing the effectiveness of the therapeutic enterprise by imposing on the mental health system a cadre of lawyers who can do little to remedy underlying problems.

The preceding analysis focused both on the legal perception of the needs of adolescents facing hospitalization and the clinical concerns about the detrimental effects of legal intervention on treatment. This harm to treatment is predicated on the assumption that there is actually treatment taking place. In many large state institutions, however, it was clear that hospitalization was hardly synonomous with treatment. State legislatures afforded clinicians a large latitude in treating the mentally ill, but not the financial resources necessary to deliver these services to society. Thus, both legislatures and those charged with providing mental health care helped perpetuate a system of inadequate mental health treatment. In Alabama, for instance, the amount spent for someone institutionalized was so low that it was apparent that adequate and humane treatment was not possible (*Wyatt v. Stickney*, 1972). In the case of minors, as mentioned earlier, the District Court in the *Parham* case raised the question of the sufficiency of treatment in Georgia. Georgia's failure to provide a spectrum of services to troubled minors would seem to indicate that even those services provided were suspect. Certainly, the few varieties of treatment settings operating within the state would significantly affect the dispositional alternatives for clinicians, thereby resulting in longer hospitalizations.

Although problems admittedly exist in the mental health system, judicial intervention which increasingly involves lawyers and judges at all stages of the treatment process presents other problems. Making entry into the hospital more difficult and perhaps releasing more individuals sooner does not squarely address the problem of making conditions satisfactory for those individuals who actually end up in the hospital. The legal system, by ignoring or glossing over these claims, gives credence to clinicians who feel that lawyers are insensitive or misguided about the real needs of the mentally ill (Miller & Fiddleman, 1982, pp. 1021-1023). There seems to be an assumption by some that lawyers, who are untrained in clinical matters, are well suited to balance all the competing interests. If the paramount interest involved is one of a preference for liberty (Morse, 1982), certainly the legal system should be the ultimate arbitrator. On the other hand, if the decisions of the courts are being influenced to a large degree by a concern with obvious substandard treatment, does it not make more sense to address this openly rather than provide for lawyers and hearings that merely restrict access to the system? If the legislatures do not concomitantly upgrade services, the same substandard conditions will be perpetuated, albeit with fewer people. The treatment of minors, therefore, may be hurt not only by legal reforms which create a monitoring process inherently detrimental to the treatment process, but also by the societal illusion that the courts are helping to alleviate the problem.

Ironically, but perhaps painfully predictably, the brunt of the suffering may be borne by those teenagers with the fewest emotional resources. The adolescents who seem to least misconstrue the court process are those individuals with solid parental backing, parental understanding of the need for treatment, and parental comprehension of the legal system (Planavsky et al., 1978). In contrast, those teenagers who enter the hospital through agency placements and who have no real family to return to are most prey to the harmful side effects of the court process. Even successful hospitalization must inevitably result in one more loss for them, since they most often can neither realistically return home nor stay in the hospital forever. It is just this group of severely disturbed and disturbing youngsters that legal reformers are likely to be most vigilant in protecting from the mental health system. The reason for this is obvious when viewed in an historical perspective. Since this group of youngsters is most likely to come under the purview of a social service agency, the opportunity to

place such youths in a mental hospital may be an
expedient way for a caseworker to lighten his or her case
load, especially of the troublesome and often thankless
involvement with children who are difficult to place.
The District Court in *Parham* explicitly expressed this
concern. The general reluctance to interfere with family
autonomy and parental control over children is removed
when custody or guardianship is entrusted to others. In
such cases, it would be more appropriate to question
whether a close, sensitive, and individualized
determination of a minor's needs had truly been made
(Bezanson, 1978, p. 578). In fact, there is even some
support for different standards by the American
Psychiatric Association and other mental health
professionals (Watson, 1980).

Unfortunately, these youngsters are most likely to
rely on societal institutions to make appropriate decisions
for them and will be the most likely to suffer when
friction between the institutions occurs. Since the youths
are not able to find support and guidance within their
own families, they are left with whatever inner resources
they have and whatever societal auspices are extended
them. If their own inner resources have been damaged by
their past experiences, as is likely, their capacity to risk
truly investing in others may have diminished
substantially by the time they reach the mental health
system and hospitalization is recommended. Often these
youngsters are considered marginal treatment cases at best
and simply cannot weather the detrimental effects of due
process procedures on their treatment. No matter what
the outcome of the actual court hearings, the youths may
have dissipated more energy than they can afford on
these internecine battles. In fact, if treatment goes poorly
enough, it may be quite easy to keep these youths in the
hospital, but for what real purpose?

The plight of these adolescents is symptomatic of the
problems with the interface between the legal and mental
health systems. Clinicians see the slim chances of these
youngsters evaporate with meaningless and destructive
legal procedures. The legal system sees one more example
of the failure of the mental health system to provide
adequate treatment. This increases the push for
additional monitoring, which in turn leaves the clinicians

feeling that the true treatment is even less possible to provide. Both blame the other side, while the disturbed teenagers remain caught in the middle of a dispute in which they have much at stake, but little real input.

Except for those unalterably opposed to civil commitment, there are no easy solutions. As long as society continues to permit civil commitment of juveniles, it makes no sense to undermine the control of those professionals then charged with the responsibility to make the system work. Increasing the onerousness of the task will not improve care, but contribute to the increasing deprofessionalization of care to those treated (Stone, 1983). Those who insist on the importance of adversary hearings may be attempting to commit the judicial system to a course of action that masks underlying problems with a facade of procedural rather than substantive reforms.

The real thrust of legal reform should be directed at legislatures that are unwilling to expend the resources necessary to implement and continue adequate treatment programs. Mental health professionals, in turn, must become more legally and politically sophisticated in order to voice and advocate their concerns effectively (Stone, 1979). In addition, mental health professionals must carefully evaluate and attempt to treat only those with whom they feel they have a reasonable chance of success. Mental health professionals must resist the inevitable societal pressure to use the basically humane and just concept of *parens patriae* as a means of mere social control. This means working toward a true right to treatment for those served by setting up humane treatment programs in decent treatment facilities, as well as working to create a spectrum of services outside of hospitals so that residential treatment will be utilized only when absolutely necessary. These steps by both sides would add moral force to the societal decision to provide such services to troubled teenagers, especially when they are ambivalent or unwilling participants.

Elliot M. Silverstein, J.D., Ph.D., a psychologist and attorney, is Co-Director of Psychological Services and Legal Consultant for Child Psychiatry at the Dorothea Dix Hospital in Raleigh, NC. Dr. Silverstein, a graduate of Harvard Law School, received his Ph.D. in clinical psychology from the University of North Carolina. He has supervised psychological testing for the Wake County Juvenile Court and the State Forensic Diagnostic Unit and has written for both legal and mental health journals. The present chapter is an update of an earlier article, "Civil Commitment of Minors: Due and Undue Process," published in 1980 in the *University of North Carolina Law Review* (Silverstein, 1980a).

RESOURCES

Addington v. Texas, 441 U.S. 418 (1979).

Amaya, M., & Burlingame, W. (1978, September 15). *Judicial Review of Voluntary Admissions: The Clinical Impact on Child and Adolescent Inpatients.* Paper presented at Children's Psychiatric Institute Symposium, Raleigh, NC.

Bartley v. Kremens, 402 F. Supp. 1039 (E.D. Pa. 1975).

Bezanson, R. P. (1978). Toward revision of Iowa's commitment laws: Thoughts on the limits of effective governmental intervention. *Iowa Law Review, 630,* 561-607.

Breed v. Jones, 421 U.S. 519 (1975).

Cohen, F. (1966). The function of the attorney and the commitment of the mentally ill. *Texas Law Review, 44,* 424-459.

Comment. (1979). Postadmission due process for mentally ill and mentally retarded children after Parham v. J. R. and Secretary of Public Welfare v. Institutionalized Juveniles. *Catholic University Law Review, 29,* 129-157.

Comment. (1979-1980). Constitutional law—due process—civil commitment of children by parents—Parham v. J. R. *New York Law School Law Review, 25,* 1001-1025.

Ellis, J. W. (1974). Volunteering children: Parental commitment of minors to mental institutions. *California Law Review, 62*, 840-916.

Foote, C., Levy, R. F., & Sander, F. E. A. (Eds.). (1966). *Cases and Materials on Family Law.* Boston: Little, Brown.

Foucault, M. (1965). *Madness and Civilization.* New York: Vintage Books.

Garvey, J. (1979-1980).. Children and the idea of liberty: A comment on the civil commitment cases. *Kentucky Law Journal, 68*, 809-843.

In re Gault, 387 U.S. 1 (1967).

Glaessner, P. (1981). Due process in the "voluntary" civil commitment of juvenile wards. *Journal of Legal Medicine, 2*, 169-192.

Halderman v. Pennhurst State School & Hospital, 446 F. Supp. 1295 (E.D. Pa. 1977), *modified* 612 F.2d 84 (3rd Cir. 1979).

Halleck, S. L. (1967). *Psychiatry and the Dilemmas of Crime.* New York: Harper & Row.

Harris, L. (1979-1980). Children's waiver of Miranda rights and the Supreme Court's decision in Parham, Bellotti and Fare. *New Mexico Law Review, 10*, 379-412.

Institutionalized Juveniles v. Secretary of Public Welfare, 459 F. Supp. 30 (E.D. Pa. 1978).

J. L. v. Parham, 412 F. Supp. 112 (M.D. Ga. 1976).

Kittrie, N. N. (1971). *The Right to be Different.* Baltimore: John Hopkins University Press.

Kremens v. Bartley, 431 U.S. 119 (1977).

Lachs, S. (1982). Placing minors in California mental hospitals. *Whittier Law Review, 4*, 57-75.

Lamb, H. R. (1981). Securing patient's rights responsibly. *Hospital & Community Psychiatry, 32*, 393-397.

Leifer, R. (1969). *In the Name of Mental Health: Social Functions of Psychiatry.* New York: Science House.

Mabbut, F. (1980). Juveniles, mental hospital commitment and civil rights: The case of Parham v. J. R. *Journal of Family Law, 19*, 27-64.

Masterson, J. F. (1972). *Treatment of the Borderline Adolescent: A Developmental Approach.* New York: Wiley-Interscience.

Mawdsley, R. (1980). Admission of minors to mental health facilities. *Illinois Bar Journal, 69,* 40-44.

McKeiver v. Pennsylvania, 403 U.S. 528 (1971).

Meehl, P. E. (1971). Law and the fireside inductions: Some reflections of a clinical psychologist. *Journal of Social Issues, 27,* 65-100.

Miller, R., & Fiddleman, P. (1982). Involuntary civil commitment in North Carolina: The result of the 1979 statutory changes. *North Carolina Law Review, 60,* 985-1026.

Morse, S. J. (1978). Crazy behavior, morals, and science: An analysis of mental health law. *Southern California Law Review, 51,* 527-654.

Morse, S. J. (1982). A preference for liberty: The case against involuntary commitment of the mentally disordered. *California Law Review, 70,* 54-106.

New York State Association for Retarded Children, Inc. v. Rockefeller, 357 F. Supp. 752 (E.D. N.Y. 1973).

Note. (1976-1977). Constitutional law—Fourteenth Amendment—Due process— Deprivation of children's rights—Civil commitment. *Duquesne Law Review, 15,* 337-347.

Note. (1978). The mental hospitalization of children and the limits of parental authority. *Yale Law Journal, 88,* 186-216.

Note. (1979). The Supreme Court, 1978 Term B, due process and confinement of minors in mental hospitals. *Harvard Law Review, 98,* 89-99.

Note. (1979-1980). Constitutional law—Due process—Minor child may be "voluntarily" committed to mental institution by precommitment approved by a staff psychiatrist, provided that the child's condition is then periodically reviewed. *Villanova Law Review, 25,* 537-550.

Note. (1980a). Constitutional collision course: Family autonomy and the rights of minors in voluntary commitment proceedings. *Louisiana Law Review, 40,* 987-997.

Note. (1980b). Constitutional law—Due process does not require an adversary hearing prior to commitment of children to mental hospitals by their parent or guardian, Parham v. J. R., 99 S.Ct. 2493 (1971). *Santa Clara Law Review, 20,* 269-275.

Note. (1980c). Constitutional law–Fourteenth Amendment–Due process–Civil commitment–Mentally ill and retarded juveniles–Secretary of Public Welfare v. Institutionalized Juveniles, 442 U.S. 640 (1979). *Duquesne Law Review, 18*, 969-982.

Note. (1980d). Due process rights of minors and parental authority in civil commitment cases. *Mercer Law Review, 31*, 617-625.

Note. (1980e). Institutionalization of juveniles: What process is due? *Nebraska Law Review, 59*, 190-213.

O'Connor v. Donaldson, 422 U.S. 563 (1975).

Parham v. J. R., 42 U.S. 584 (1979).

Planavsky, G., Ritchie, V., & Silverstein, E. (1978). Intensive residential treatment for adolescents in North Carolina and the present legal system: A review and proposed changes. *North Carolina Journal of Mental Health, 8*(9), 1-15.

Rachlin, S. (1974). With liberty and psychosis for all. *Psychiatric Quarterly, 48*, 410-420.

Robitscher, J. (1979). The commitment of minors: Problems of civil liberties. In S. Fernstein & P. Giovacchini (Eds.), *Adolescent Psychiatry: Development & Clinical Studies* (Vol. VII, pp. 457-465). Chicago: University of Chicago Press.

Schultz, S. (1982). The Boston State Hospital case: A conflict of civil liberties and true liberalism. *American Journal of Psychiatry, 139*, 183-188.

Secretary of Public Welfare v. Institutionalized Juveniles, 442 U.S. 640 (1979).

Silverstein, E. (1980a). Civil commitment of minors: Due and undue process. *University of North Carolina Law Review, 58*, 1133-1159.

Silverstein, E. (1980b). Civil commitment of minors in North Carolina: The case for change. *North Carolina Journal of Mental Health, 9*, 1-7.

Slovenko, R. (1977). Criminal justice procedures in civil commitment. *Wayne Law Review, 24*, 1-44.

Stone, A. (1975). *Mental Health and Law: A System in Transition.* Rockville, MD: National Institute of Mental Health.

Stone, A. (1979). The myth of advocacy. *Hospital & Community Psychiatry, 30*, 819-822.

Stone, A. (1983, June 10). *New Challenges for Law and Psychiatry in the 1980's.* Paper presented at Recent Developments in Health Law, American Society of Law and Medicine, Chicago, IL.

Szasz, T. (1963). *Law, Liberty and Psychiatry.* New York: Macmillan Co.

Szasz, T. (1977). The child as involuntary mental patient: The threat of child therapy to the child's dignity, privacy, and self-esteem. *San Diego Law Review, 14,* 1005-1027.

Szasz, T. (1982). The psychiatrist as moral agent. *Whittier Law Review, 4,* 77-85.

Talbott, J. (1979). Why psychiatrists leave the public sector. *Hospital & Community Psychiatry, 30,* 778-782.

Tiano, L. (1980). Parham v. J. R.: "Voluntary commitment of minors to the mental institution." *American Journal of Law and Medicine, 6,* 125-449.

Watson, A. (1980). Children, families, and courts: Before the best interests of the child and Parham v. J. R. *Virginia Law Review, 66,* 653-679.

In re Winship, 397 U.S. 358 (1970).

Wyatt v. Stickney, 344 F. Supp. 387 (M.D. Ala. 1972), *modified sub. nom.*; Wyatt v. Aderholt, 503 F.2d 1305 (5th Cir. 1974).

THE RIGHT TO REFUSE PSYCHIATRIC TREATMENT: PROFESSIONAL SELF-ESTEEM AND HOPELESSNESS

Philip B. Kraft

The mere mention of the right of the mentally ill patient to refuse treatment excites the sensibilities of numerous and diverse interest groups. Physicians, lawyers, civil libertarians, mental patients (past and present), and their families rise severally or in coalition to support or reject what they perceive to be the definition of such a right and the extent of its implications. The right to refuse treatment sets into motion endless reverberations which threaten to upset the precarious balances society is ever attempting to achieve among eternally plaguing dichotomies: state v. individual; autonomy v. control; rights v. needs; dignity v. repression; paternalism v. self-determination; the powerless v. the powerful; and perhaps even state power v. "self-expression." More concretely, the right to refuse treatment pits patient against doctor, expert against layman, clinician against lawyer.

The literature in the area is voluminous and often adversarial in nature. The major arenas of controversy relate not to whether such a right should exist but rather to the circumstances under which it may be exercised, the conditions upon which it may be overridden, and the procedures which ought be established to safeguard it.

Surprisingly, despite the continuing controversy as to these "subsidiary" issues, there are strands of agreement among most commentators. Most, for example, see that patients committed to underfunded, public institutions stand to gain (or lose) the most by having their right to refuse buttressed by the availability of strong legal remedies. Most commentators agree that certain forms of treatment are sufficiently safe and effective to warrant special status when the question of nonconsensual treatment arises. All, at this late date, agree that some form of a right to refuse is desirable.

What is so disturbing, then, is not the controversy but the extent of agreement among most parties concerned. Put right side up, the question presents itself quite simply: If there are so many important threads of agreement, why is there so much argumentation? Unfortunately, the answer may lie in an insidious, seldom recognized complicity between law and psychiatry which diverts lawyers, mental health practitioners, and the people they serve from the more fundamental and difficult issue of how best to serve a population which, despite the professed interests of the interest groups, remains shunned and disenfranchised. The right to refuse controversy may well be a Chinese puzzle box at the heart of which lies hopelessness and despair at the prospect of ever being able adequately to treat the severely mentally disturbed in the absence of sufficient resources.

The first part of this chapter reviews the major trends in legal thought which have fed the right to refuse controversy. The second part examines the clinical phenomenon of the refusing patient. The third part addresses the question of how the right to refuse has been perceived by the clinical community and examines the process of that perception. The last part returns to the notion of the Chinese puzzle box and suggests how the helping professional may participate in easing the struggle, heralded by recent legal decisions, which lies ahead.

LEGAL TRENDS IN THE
RIGHT TO REFUSE CONTROVERSY

A right to refuse treatment was recognized at common law long before the recent spate of right to refuse litigation (Stone, 1981). At common law, the physician who imposed a treatment upon a nonconsenting patient could be sued in tort, after the fact, for a battery, an "offensive touching." The physician's liability was negated where the patient had given an "informed consent" to the allegedly nonconsensual treatment and courts have struggled for many years to fine tune the definition of informed consent. Questions of how much information is sufficient for a truly *informed* consent, how the consent must be manifested, and what duty the physician must assume in obtaining consent continue to be hotly contested. The last question remains particularly relevant in that the more extensive the physician's duty to provide the context for the giving of an informed consent, the easier it is to charge him or her with negligence in the performance of that duty.

The mental patient has held a peculiar position, however, within the common law framework of the right to refuse. Pitted against the right of the mentally disturbed person to refuse are two potent state interests in the face of which that right often may be restricted (*Rogers v. Okin*, 1980). First is the state's "police power" which dictates that in the event of imminent danger to the community, in the person of the violent patient, for example, common law rights are to be "modified." The assaultive individual, then, who has been committed to a psychiatric facility may see his or her common law right to refuse the intramuscular administration of major tranquilizers wither away before the state's corresponding right or duty, in fact, to assure the safety of its citizens.

Second, the mental patient is the member of a class which has long been entitled to the ministrations of the state in its role as parent. The *parens patriae* power of the state allows it to intervene on the behalf of the incompetent, the retarded, and the infant in order to assure interests which those groups presumably would be unable to assert without the assistance of the sovereign (Michels, 1981; *Rogers v. Okin*, 1980). As the very sound of the term suggests, *parens patriae* is the embodiment of state paternalism. The judgment of those better equipped to know and understand is to be substituted for that of those whose decision making capacities are impaired or undeveloped. *Parens patriae* implies care, charity, and benignity.

The leitmotif running throughout these provinces of the common law is, of course, the notion of competence. An informed consent is premised upon the competence of the consenter. *Parens patriae* may be invoked most easily in the case of an incompetent patient. But while competence is omnipresent in contemporary discussions of the right to refuse, it hovers elusively beyond precise definition (Appelbaum, 1983; Byrne, 1981).

An extended discussion of the competence issue lies beyond the scope of this chapter, but some of its highlights may be pointed out. Generally, recent considerations of competence have subsumed three complex problems: (a) How is the concept of competence to be infused with meaning? (b) What procedures should structure the determination of competence? (c) Who is to preside over these determinations?

The first problem, that of meaning, commences with the proposition that competence is susceptible to clear definition: That it is possible to draw the so-called bright line between competent and incompetent. It has been suggested that this proposition is *a priori* shaky at best (Freedman, 1981). Assuming, *arguendo*, that the bright line is apt, how then does one delineate that boundary? Well-considered criteria have certainly been offered (Stone, 1979), but even they fail to resolve persistent, nagging, and paradoxical concerns.

One such concern is that strict application of competence criteria will allow a certain subgroup of patients, particularly those with paranoid illnesses, to escape the benefits of a treatment which could relieve their undoubted suffering. The other concern is that any standard of competence will allow clinicians to overcome a patient's will on the grounds that that patient's reasons for refusing treatment are somehow inadequate. For, in the end, any determination of competence reduces to the question of whether the patient's ratiocination (barring religious convictions) is somehow "good enough."

In any dialogue dealing with the right to refuse psychiatric treatment, professionals who fought long and hard to convince a skeptical public that mental illness did not necessarily subtend an incapacity to drive a car or manage funds (Stone, 1981), find themselves between a rock and a hard place: between a wish to serve the disturbed adequately and an abhorrence at bending anyone to their will. It is this very squaring off of values which has for so long seemed to lie at the core of the right to refuse controversy (Byrne, 1981; Michels, 1981; Reiser, 1980).

The second problem, that of procedures, overlaps significantly with the problem of meaning. Consider, for example, the decision, as to whether civil commitment should carry with it a presumption of incompetence to refuse treatment. In *form*, at least, this appears to be a question of procedure. But in *substance*, the answer depends upon one's willingness to believe that the patient who has behaved in such a manner as to justify the exercise of the state's police power via civil commitment is *de facto* incompetent.

In the absence of a presumption of incompetence at the time of commitment, some jurisdictions require an independent determination of competence at that point during hospitalization at which the patient refuses treatment. Even then, states vary in their approaches to the question of how long a determination of incompetence to refuse remains valid. Should the patient have access to an appeal? May guardianship be utilized by the clinician in order to circumvent cumbersome competency proceedings? Statutory solutions are hardly uniform (Plotkin, 1977).

Lastly, the problem of "who should preside" has posed the curious dilemma of whose professional toes are to be trodden upon, those of the jurists or those of the clinicians. Competence has long been a legal term of art; judges may accept expert testimony in the determination of a testator's competence but the ultimate decision in that context lies with the court. Yet courts, in the hope that psychiatry might pin down the term, invoke "deference to professional judgment" when they wish to escape the competence thicket surrounding the mental patient. Psychiatrists, equally uncomfortable with bearing the burden of this conceptual will-o'-the-wisp, ask the courts to decide. Yet, neither group fully trusts the other and a mutually satisfactory sharing of the task remains to be achieved (Stone, 1979).

The niceties of competence and of the delicate balance between the common law right to refuse and the counterpoised state interests traditionally have fallen away in the presence of "an emergency" (Stone, 1981). Unlike the rose, an emergency is apparently not necessarily an emergency, as was made painfully clear in the recent Rogers litigation (*Rogers v. Okin*, 1979, 1980). Opinions as to the nature of an emergency ranged from a likelihood of immediate physical harm to the possibility of deterioration (Ford, 1980; Stone, 1981).

It was against this patchwork legal background of common law *cum* state statutory provisions that patient-plaintiffs turned to the federal courts. The elevation of the common law right to refuse to federal constitutional status would, it was hoped, bring numerous advantages in its wake. At common law, recovery in tort depends upon proof of damages sustained as a result of the violation of one's claimed right (Stone, 1981). Federal law eases the plaintiff's burden in establishing grounds for recovery in a suit brought for violation of a recognized, constitutional right (Wright, 1983). Suits at common law are generally confined to state courts while the establishment of a federal cause of action grounded in constitutional provisions allows access to federal courts under "federal question" jurisdiction. Federal courts afford procedural advantages to civil rights plaintiffs including more liberal discovery. Furthermore, federal courts are usually viewed as adopting a more indulgent stance toward civil rights. Changes in federal class action law had also, in recent years, made access to federal courts in the absence of a federal cause of action more difficult. The availability of suit directly under the federal constitution, it was hoped, would remedy that difficulty as well.

Above all, a federal court holding establishing a constitutionally-based right to refuse psychiatric treatment, especially one eventually backed by a Supreme Court pronouncement, would guarantee state uniformity and enforcement under the Supremacy Clause. States would have to act to conform their hitherto multifold interpretations of the common law right to a single, federally-guided standard (Hart & Wechsler, 1973).

Plaintiffs' constitutional theories for relief took three routes: They drew upon the First, Eighth, and Fourteenth Amendments to the Constitution as the foundations for a constitutional right to refuse.

The First Amendment "free speech" theory maintained that the nonconsensual administration of psychotropic medications amounted to "mind-altering" and as such interfered with patients' rights to mold their own thoughts. Free thought, it was insisted, is a necessary predicate to free speech. Therefore, logic would have it that a right to refuse was encompassed by the First Amendment and applicable to the states through the Fourteenth Amendment (*Rogers v. Okin*, 1979).

The Eighth Amendment guarantee against "cruel and unusual punishments" seemed another potentially fertile constitutional source upon which to draw (*Mackey v. Procunier*, 1973). But there are patent difficulties in translating from the criminal context, in which Eighth Amendment jurisprudence has developed, to the civil context of commitment to a state medical-psychiatric facility.

In light of Supreme Court history over the past 15 years, the Fourteenth Amendment held out the greatest promise of constitutional hope for right to refuse plaintiffs in federal court. The Fourteenth Amendment mandates that "due process" be employed when a state deprives any citizen of "life, liberty, or property." For many years, the Supreme Court had restricted its Fourteenth Amendment holdings to interpretations of due process while avoiding any expansion of the life, liberty, or property interests which due process was to protect. Beginning in the mid-60s, however, a series of "substantive due process" opinions were handed down which opened the door toward including within the life, liberty, or property rubric a somewhat amorphous "right to privacy" (*Griswold v. Connecticut*, 1965; *Roe v. Wade*, 1973). "Zones of privacy" could be read into "penumbras formed by emanations" from the guarantees of the Bill of Rights (*Griswold v. Connecticut*, 1965).

Zones of privacy came to embrace fundamental rights to bodily integrity, rights which could be intruded upon only in the event of compelling state interests (Tribe, 1978). It would seem intuitive, then, that a right to refuse treatment ought be accorded the status of a fundamental right within this particular constitutional doctrine, and that any attempt by a state to invade that right ought be subjected to the strictest scrutiny (*Rogers v. Okin*, 1980).

In 1982, the Supreme Court declined to furnish the denouement to this saga of constitutional litigation. In *Mills v. Rogers* (1982), the Court took note of a quite recent, far-reaching opinion of the Massachusetts Supreme Judicial Court (*In re Roe*, 1981) which had held that in the case of a psychiatric outpatient under guardianship, only a judge, not the patient's guardian, could consent to the administration of antipsychotic medication, absent an emergency. The Supreme Court, recognizing that states are at liberty to go beyond the minimum protection of individual rights required by the Federal Constitution (Brennan, 1977), asked the Court of Appeals for the First Circuit to reconsider its decision in light of *In re Roe*. The Court stated that:

> Until certain questions have been answered, we think it would be inappropriate for us to attempt to weigh or even to identify relevant liberty interests that might be derived directly from the Constitution, independently of state law. It is this Court's settled policy to avoid unnecessary decisions of Constitutional issues. (p. 415)

Similarly, the Supreme Court remanded another "right to refuse" case to the Third Circuit without opinion (*Rennie v. Klein*, 1982). In *Rennie v. Klein* (1981) the Third Circuit Court of Appeals had focused its attention upon procedural safeguards for the right to refuse. The Supreme Court recommended that the Third Circuit rethink its holding, and take into account the Supreme Court's opinion in *Youngberg v. Romeo* (1982). This latter case was the first instance in which the Court had commented upon the substantive due-process rights of involuntarily committed retarded persons; the *Youngberg v. Romeo* opinion emphasized the deference due the judgment of "qualified professionals."

Thus, the common law contours of the right to refuse remain viable today. The Supreme Court has left a vacuum to be filled with a state-by-state determination of patient rights and their procedural fortifications; the catch-phrase is deference to professional judgment, and the long-awaited uniformity has not been forthcoming (Brant, 1983; Mills, Yesavage, & Gutheil, 1983).

THE CLINICAL PHENOMENON
OF THE REFUSING PATIENT

Who refuses treatment? Studies suggest that a minority of hospitalized psychiatric patients reject psychotropic medications and that of that minority only a fraction become "symptomatic refusers" by persistent refusal over significant periods of time during their hospitalization (Appelbaum & Gutheil, 1979). Persistent refusal, it is agreed, is much more likely to occur in underfunded public institutions than in well-staffed private hospitals (Ford, 1980; Michels, 1981).

Of great interest to clinicians have been the reasons which patients proffer in their exercise of the right to refuse (Amarasingham, 1980, Appelbaum, 1983; Appelbaum & Gutheil, 1979, 1980b, 1982). The reasons most commonly asserted may be sorted into 10 categories:

1. *Popular misconceptions*: Patients often draw upon the notion that psychotropic medication is "mind-altering" or "mind-controlling" in rebuffing the suggestion that such drugs will be helpful. The *Cuckoo's Nest* vision of the imposition of treatment as the equivalent of oppression pervades the lay conception of the mental hospital. The acceptance of medication, then, becomes a submission to abuse by the system and an abdication of one's own personality. Cries of "You're taking me over!" or "You want to control me!" are not always the earmarks of paranoia but may derive rather from our cultural climate.

   The medicated patient as "zombie" is a concept auxiliary to the idea of mind-control. The refusing patient's fear of being overpowered may be reinforced when he or she sees other patients who suffer from the side effects of major tranquilizers, which do often impose upon them a robotlike appearance. Certainly, if refusing patients have had occasion to view heavily medicated patients in the community, their fears of becoming permanently dehumanized may be firmly grounded.

2. *Eccentric beliefs*: The fads of the past 2 decades also often furnish the foundations for a patient's refusal. In particular, patient-adherents of the "natural foods school" object to psychotropics as unnatural, foreign substances. Those patients who have attempted self-cures prior to hospitalization may insist upon peculiar diets, megavitamins, or even herbal teas in lieu of Thorazine or Stelazine.

3. *Convictions*: Convictions run the gamut from those tenacious beliefs with which the clinician can most easily sympathize to those which are frankly psychotic. Religious convictions are among the most "sympathetic," especially when the individual's history establishes a consistent pattern of refusal of all forms of medical intervention. Religious objections to medication, moreover, receive significant legal support under the First Amendment.

   One notable conviction is the credo of "self-help" (i.e., that one must overcome adversity without the "crutch" of medication). It is evident that this tenet of "pulling oneself up by the bootstraps" is frequently overdetermined, finding its roots in popular conceptions of mental illness as abnegation of responsibility and perhaps in the patient's idiosyncratic belief that he or she is somehow unworthy of being helped.

4. *Drug side effects*: Patients do experience unpleasant fallout from the administration of psychotropics. The discomfort of akathisia and the derealization accompanying most psychoactive medications can be as disturbing to a patient as are the more dramatic manifestations of side effects: the acute dystonic reaction, sudden and severe hypotension, or tardive dyskinesia. Refusals based on allegations of side effects involve the clinician in what may constitute the most sensitive of therapist-patient dialogues. The evaluation of side effects depends in large part upon the patient's subjective reports, and while

wishing to respect those reports, the clinician must also ask whether the patient's complaints truly stem from physiological phenomena or are a product of the illness itself.

5. *Theories of the illness*: Patients suffering from psychotic illnesses devote a substantial amount of their attention to formulating "theories" of the origin of their disturbance in the hope that by arriving at the correct theory, the cure will become apparent (Arieti, 1974). Such theories sometimes masquerade as delusions but, although distorted and irrational at first blush, proceed from a coherent wish to feel better. If the theory assumes the form that the illness was itself acquired from some external source, from a medication, for example, the patient may feel compelled to refuse any further medications for fear that they will *exacerbate* the problem. Similarly, if the theory holds that the illness was caused by a physician or a nurse ("I haven't been the same since my operation"), any medical intervention will be shunned.

6. *Delusions*: The warping of reality which induces a patient to refuse medication is extremely far-reaching, probably more so than is usually verbalized. In retrospect, recovering patients may explain the rationale for their earlier refusal to accept medications: "I thought you were trying to poison me, but the voices told me not to say anything"; "I thought you were giving the meds to the wrong person." The paranoid patient will brusquely repel drugs while concealing an elaborate delusional system which is ever warning him or her about the malice of his or her treaters. The grandiose patient who recognizes no illness will recognize no need for treatment.

7. *Transference*: The vicissitudes of the patient-therapist relationship account on occasion for the patient's refusal not only to take medications but also to participate in other aspects of the treatment plan. Transference implies that the patient is distorting a current reality to conform to a past perception and while this phenomenon certainly

may lie behind a refusal, many times there is no real distortion but rather a miscommunication. The patient whose therapist misses an appointment may display his or her hurt and anger by refusing a dose of medication; the patient who feels ignored by ward staff may, in a similar manner, express his or her protest. Again, the reasons for refusal may not be clear at the time and are often reconstructed only in a later dialogue with the refusing patient.

8. *Legal rights*: The language of rights is also employed by the refusing patient. Those who were conversant with current events or who participated in patient advocacy organizations before hospitalization offer their constitutional rights to privacy or freedom as their rationale for refusing. Some mimic their fellow-patients and mouth the "buzzwords" of due process, life, and liberty to escape undesired treatment.

9. *"Pseudorefusals"*: Reasons for refusal may be incoherent or irrelevant (e.g., "I don't like the way you look"). Clinicians whose training demands that they constantly ask "Why?" may be frustrated in encountering the refusing patient who simply gives no reasons or who cannot think of any. Whether to term refusals in the absence of reasons true refusals is problematic. The mute, catatonic patient, in effect, refuses treatment by not assenting; the severely depressed person may refuse out of a lack of incentive to acquiesce; the negativistic patient can refuse medications just as he or she refuses food, cigarettes, and verbal contact. These patients may all ultimately possess reasons for refusal but those reasons remain unarticulated and inaccessible.

10. *Familial influence*: Whether or not reasons for refusing medications are vocalized, the refusal itself may arise from subtle, familial pressures exerted upon the patient. Families may convince their hospitalized relatives to refuse for reasons deriving from any of the foregoing categories or because of intrafamilial dynamics which require that the patient remain a patient. Patients who in

most instances will return to the family upon release from the institution must reasonably heed familial demands; the family, not the hospital staff, is and will continue to be their lifeline, and they may thus find themselves subscribing to viewpoints which are not truly their own.

The modes in which a patient chooses to refuse medication are variable and belie any easy translation from clinical reality into legal conceptualization (Gutheil & Mills, 1982; Hoffman, 1976). There are those patients who verbalize their refusal and those who do not. There are those who agree to take medications and actually "tongue" them (Appelbaum & Gutheil, 1980b). There are those who voice refusal at the same moment they roll up a sleeve to receive a shot. And there are, of course, those who neither by words nor action indicate their instant wishes.

That persistent refusal is the exception rather than the rule is a fact worthy of emphasis (Appelbaum & Gutheil, 1980b). Patients who adamantly refuse medication during the initial phase of hospitalization are more often than not agreeable to it as they become familiar with their surroundings and with ward routine. Refusal, once acclimatization has occurred, is likely to be episodic and short-lived.

The establishment of a reasoned dialogue between patient and staff is obviously recommended as the tool most likely to succeed in resolving dispute over the advisability of taking medication (Appelbaum, 1983; Appelbaum & Gutheil, 1982). Only through enlightened discourse can the patient be assured that the medication will not harm him or her; that it may enhance his or her sense of control rather than vitiate it; that side effects are manageable; that his or her anger at his or her therapist should not stand in the way of receiving a treatment which can alleviate his or her confusion. Through dialogue, the clinician can gain valuable allies among the family which has previously perceived the psychiatric system as blaming and accusatory. Through dialogue, the clinician may avoid an ultimate showdown in a court of law.

PERCEPTIONS OF RIGHT TO
REFUSE IN THE CLINICAL COMMUNITY

The arrival of refusing patients at the courthouse doors has received mixed reviews within the clinical community. Quite inconsistent with portraits of psychiatry as a brutalizing and sadistic discipline (Appelbaum & Gutheil, 1979; Plotkin, 1977) is the current, painful, intraprofessional debate over how best to accommodate both patient rights and needs. The centrality of a right to refuse treatment to the exercise of autonomy and to cherished values of individualism and equality has hardly gone unnoticed by treaters (Roth, 1981).

But the good will of clinicians has been sorely tested as their expertise has been called into question, their altruism doubted, and their practices denounced (Cocozza & Melick, 1977; Plotkin, 1977). Professional self-esteem is made fragile and it is against this background that the responses of the clinical community to the right to refuse debate must be seen.

One perspective on the right to refuse litigation—a perspective which is amenable to the bolstering of professional self-esteem—maintains that the controversy has become most germane at a time when psychiatric science has become most powerful; the right to refuse treatment debate has gained momentum as more effective treatment has at last evolved (Byrne, 1981; Roth, 1981). Because clinicians now know so much more, patients have a lot more to refuse than they ever did in the past.

If this is indeed so, what explanation can there be for the fact that courts, except, perhaps, the Supreme Court, continue to view treatment as inherently suspect, deserving of a circumspect approach rather than a presumption of validity? How is it, in other words, that the legal system has not willingly embraced the advances in clinical science and has instead retained an attitude of skepticism and doubt?

Answers to these questions have not appeared, but criticism of judicial attitudes has abounded. It is said that legal minds simply fail to comprehend the complexity of clinical phenomena (Gutheil, 1980b; Gutheil & Mills, 1982). There exists a form of cognitive dissonance between legal and clinical theorizing; the former is inductive, the latter deductive. Interdisciplinary miscommunication results in judicial holdings which fail both to grant clinicians the elbowroom necessary for adequate patient care and to safeguard patient rights without allowing patients to sabotage their treatment programs.

Legal norms, moreover, are rigid and fixed (Appelbaum & Gutheil, 1980b; Gutheil & Mills, 1982; Hoffman, 1976). The clinical phenomena, on the other hand, which these legal norms purport to embrace, demand a fluid conceptualization, one capable of encompassing the subtleties of patient-staff interactions and of recognizing that clinical reality shifts over time. There are no discrete quanta of autonomy. Rights are forever, while a patient's refusal of treatment is rarely so.

It is said that while clinical science has come into its renaissance, legal practitioners cling to medieval prejudices against mental health professionals (Appelbaum & Gutheil, 1979, 1980a; Mills & Gutheil, 1981). Legal training reaffirms the popularly-held misconceptions of the "snake pit," misconceptions which at one time may have borne some grain of truth but are now sorely outdated.

It is said that the judiciary has now forced clinicians into a position either of practicing law or of serving as an ancillary police force (Ford, 1980; Stone, 1979). Clinicians may no longer attend to their clientele at their liberty *qua* clinicians but must be constantly on guard lest they violate rights. Individuals committed to a state facility who may refuse medication, can, in the absence of treatment, become prisoners, not patients.

It is said that far-reaching legal prescriptions have been handed down based upon a dearth of empirical clinical data (Gutheil & Mills, 1982; Roth & Appelbaum, 1982); that judges err when they tie the hands of clinicians without adequate provision for follow-up studies. What becomes of those patients who exercise their newly fortified right to refuse is not known, and in the absence of such knowledge, legal decisions which restrict the business of treatment for years to come are to be avoided.

Angrier words have flowed from both sides of the right to refuse fence. The lawyers who call for an end to the "therapeutic orgy"—the unsupervised clinical practices which are alleged to make a mockery of human dignity (Plotkin, 1977)—are in turn accused of misguided advocacy of the "psuedoliberation" of the mental patient (Tanay, 1980). Such rhetoric furthers polarization in the medico-legal sphere and heightens the sensitivities of those earnestly seeking to secure an acceptable compromise.

But polarization there is and, although it may find itself being played out in the arena of the right to refuse debate, it may be fueled by unstated concerns fundamental to both lawyers and clinicians. These concerns are: What is treatment and how do we provide it? It remains to be seen how clinicians, themselves, may have unwittingly participated in the deflection of attention from those questions to fine points of informed consent and refusal.

TOWARD A NEW CLINICAL
AGENDA IN THE RIGHT TO REFUSE DEBATE

Two major themes seem to dominate any consideration of the right to refuse. First is the assumption that treatment is medication (or electroshock therapy or psychosurgery). Second is the belief that the language of rights has been *inappropriately* thrust upon clinicians as the proper vocabulary with which to address dynamic, clinical experiences. Somehow, despite the best of intentions, the right to refuse debate has been *allowed* to proceed with a focus on somatic therapies and has been *allowed* to transform interactional phenomena into concrete, fixed terminology.

Treatment is not reducible to the restricted realm of somatic therapies. While the acute schizophrenic patient may show marked improvement with rapid, high-dose administration of antipsychotics, treatment does not end with the normalization of mental status. Treatment may require assisting the patient in reorganizing his or her disrupted life, restoring lost community supports, and examining the precipitants of his or her illness, to name just a few of the nonsomatic aspects of treatment. Yet treatment, at least for the purposes of litigation, is equated with nonverbal clinical tools.

Rights imply conflict while the essence of treatment is alliance. Rights pit patient against doctor when any successful therapy demands that patient work *with* doctor. One's rights are always held forth as *against* the interests of another entity—state, family, or professional. Yet rights remain the battle cry of the refusing patient.

Equating treatment with medication and adopting the inapposite jargon of rights is not, however, without significant basis. These themes persist and dominate the debate over treatment refusal because they serve a hidden, but clearly present *clinical* agenda. This hidden agenda is the avoidance of professional pain (Minow & Kraft, 1982).

The clinician who is faced with the refusing patient commended to his or her care is simultaneously confronted with an ethical quandary which eludes any facile solution. It is extraordinarily difficult to "subject" another person to one's will, however evident it may be that the one refusing is deluded, incompetent, or merely suffering from impaired judgment. No matter how certain they are that the patient who receives a drug today will feel better tomorrow, clinicians still emerge from the fray with a sense of their own sadism and grandiosity. This is not to say that they are in fact cruel. Quite likely they are not. Yet they will nevertheless perceive themselves as such and, in the process, feel demeaned.

The pain of insisting that one knows better than the patient is exacerbated by the fact that forthright clinicians suffer pangs of doubt as to the safety of the treatment which they press upon their patients. Antipsychotics do ameliorate psychotic symptomatology; but they bring along in their wake the dangers of tardive dyskinesia, dystonias, and, more unusually, fatal blood dyscrasias, the possibilities of which must all be weighed against the potential benefits for the patient. It is a tough clinical call, for example, whether to recommend antipsychotics for the flagrantly psychotic patient who is also showing early signs of tardive dyskinesia.

The language of rights gets clinicians "off the hook" in these delicate contexts. The internal struggle, whether to force a treatment which has decided drawbacks upon the nonconsenting patient, is suddenly displaced onto grander planes: the individual v. the state, freedom v. repression. Clinical issues are magically transformed into legal issues (Appelbaum & Gutheil, 1982). And the busy state hospital psychiatrist is relieved of the necessity for painful decision making once the patient has uttered the simple formula: right to refuse treatment. The language of rights has not, then, been inappropriately foisted upon protesting clinicians. It has its usefulness in creating conflict where there ought to be process and in substituting legal neatness and finality for the open endedness and frustration of clinical interaction.

The avoidance of professional pain has also stoked the fires of clinical complicity in allowing the definition of treatment to devolve to the administration of psychoactive medications. Medication has come to symbolize the effectiveness of mental health practitioners (Baldessarini & Lipinski, 1981). When medication works, its effects are often rapid, overt, and dramatic. The advent of antipsychotics on the institutional scene has made possible the release of thousands of patients from mental hospitals across the country. Antipsychotics are the glory of the trade. When medication is challenged by patients and in turn by the courts, professional self-esteem is placed in jeopardy. If patients are encouraged to reject such eminently effective treatment, it is feared that the entire *raison d'etre* of the helping professions will be called into question.

Whatever doubts clinicians may covertly entertain regarding the advisability and efficacy of antipsychotics and other somatic therapies, they are a minor matter when compared with the currently overwhelming disbelief in the usefulness of psychotherapy for the severely mentally ill. The results of psychotherapy have never been quantified to anyone's satisfaction; if there are positive results, they are most often agonizingly slow. Even then, the therapist is hard put, despite the clarity expected of hindsight, to know exactly which psychotherapeutic interventions were successful and which were not.

If the courts were to establish a firm right to refuse somatic therapies, what tools would survive for the clinician who remains devoted to the care of the severely ill? All that would be left are the "talking therapies," which stubbornly defy empiricism. It is a fear of being relegated to clinical impotence which raises the stakes in the right to refuse debate.

Thus, the right to refuse treatment has come to mean the right to refuse medication because clinicians have placed all their bets on medications. They have done this all the while knowing that medications are not enough; that they are most helpful when administered on a short-term basis (Appelbaum, 1983), but that they are insufficient in solving such extended problems of the severely disturbed as the "revolving-door" syndrome, the lack of community placements, the need for rehabilitation, and the reintroduction into normalcy. To conspire with the legal system's tunnel vision of treatment as drugs is to court professional disaster. For just as clinicians know the limitations of such treatment so do their patients and, in the last resort, so do the courts. The right to refuse controversy undoubtedly has become more heated because clinicians know more; but they do not yet know enough. And to pretend to know enough is fraudulent.

Mary is a chronic schizophrenic patient in her mid-20s, who was recently committed to a state facility for violent behavior. Three days into her admission, having consistently refused oral medication, Mary approached a mental-health worker and demanded angrily that he give her a cigarette. The mental-health worker, otherwise unoccupied, handed her a cigarette and instructed her to return to her room and calm herself. Shortly thereafter, Mary again sought out the worker, this time screaming that she wanted her radio, which was held for safekeeping at the nurses' station. Mary appeared frantic. The worker, fetching the radio, once again told her to return to her room and quiet down. Five minutes later, Mary ran wildly from her room, grabbed a chair, and began beating it against the locked door of the nurses' station. Workers from other units were quickly summoned to assist in escorting Mary to locked seclusion. She refused oral Chlorpromazine: "I don't want your drugs! I wanna' talk to somebody!" She received an intramuscular injection of 100 mgs. of Chlorpromazine and remained in seclusion for the balance of the shift. A note in her chart documented the emergency as justification for the injection.

It is a mistake to assume that there can be no hope for the severely mentally ill until the right medication—the one with permanent, restorative powers and the one free of troubling side effects—is discovered. Nevertheless, it is this very assumption which lies at the heart of the right to refuse controversy. The essence of the unspoken dialogue between clinicians and jurists seems to be the following:

CLINICIAN: (1) The only real hope we have for severe mental illness lies in the development of an appropriate medication (somatic therapy).

(2) The medications presently in our therapeutic arsenal don't do the trick. They solve only a piece of the problem. They don't cure; they merely temporize.

(3) We don't believe, however, given the state of the art, that anything else is effective.

JUDGE: (1) If the only promise you can hold out to the patient is one of temporary relief, what compelling inducement is there for the law to override that patient's fundamental right to personal integrity?

(2) You have promised much more than you are evidently able to deliver.

(3) Until you develop something more hopeful, patients ought to have the right to refuse.

These are the premises upon which the superstructure of the medico-legal confrontations of the past decade has been erected. Were they recognized as such, clinicians and lawyers might be able more realistically to offer the severely disturbed and their families what they truly seek, namely some glimmer of hope. The core clinical fear is that should patients be empowered to reject somatic therapies, they will thereby be barred from the only real bit of hope clinical science can offer at this stage in its evolution.

No matter how sensible the advocacy of "talk" as a means toward resolution of the right to refuse disputes which arise daily on any busy, state inpatient unit, so long as clinicians continue to believe that medication and nothing but medication is effective, talk will remain a rarity, a second-best alternative entered into halfheartedly with no real hope of success. Mary made it quite clear that what she desired was talk. Perhaps she was unable to articulate that wish in her initial irate sallies onto the ward, but, oddly enough, no one stopped to wonder at the outset whether it might be conversation she was pursuing—not cigarettes or her radio. No one paused to ask why the cigarettes and radio failed to placate her. No one thought to ask what was bothering her. The message which had permeated the treatment team was that Mary was refusing her medications and that without them nothing could be done for her.

There is always hope. It does not follow inexorably that because clinicians do not know how to cure schizophrenia, schizophrenia must be incurable or "hopeless." Likewise, the fact that psychotherapy defies measurement does not necessarily imply that talk is worthless.

Almost 10 years ago, in *O'Connor v. Donaldson* (1975), the Supreme Court deftly side-stepped the establishment of a right to treatment. The Court stated that "a State cannot constitutionally confine *without more* a nondangerous individual who is capable of surviving safely in freedom by himself or with the help of willing and responsible family members or friends" [emphasis added] (p. 576). Since the landmark opinion, the push toward a right to psychiatric treatment has been derailed (Brant, 1983; Stone, 1979; Weiner, 1982). In its stead, the courts have dealt with the right to refuse psychiatric treatment. The right to refuse may be the right to treatment turned inside out. In the absence of the something more to which the Supreme Court alluded as a possible justification for involuntary civil commitment of the nondangerous patient, courts have increasingly permitted the committed patient to refuse the something less.

The desire to improve the quality of care for committed patients and the search for pledges of adequate resources lie behind the right to refuse psychiatric treatment (Appelbaum & Gutheil, 1981; Michels, 1981; Stone, 1979). But quality of care can improve only when clinicians, after first confessing to their own hopelessness, set about defining with greater confidence and precision the clinical ingredients essential to a prescription of hopefulness.

For perhaps, in the end, what Rubie Rogers and her fellow patients at Boston State Hospital (*Rogers v. Okin*, 1979) sought was the right to refuse *nontreatment*: the right to say "no" to the hollow assurances that medications would cure. In responding to the manifest content of patient complaints, the accusations of cruelty inflicted upon patients through restraints both chemical and physical, clinicians and lawyers alike may have overlooked the latent content of the right to refuse litigation, namely the patients' simple plea: "Offer us some realistic measure of hope." The Supreme Court has indicated its willingness to defer to professional judgment. Clinicians must respond to that grant of authority by providing the something more which the Court found wanting in 1975. Finding and providing something more is the task of the 1980s.

Philip B. Kraft, M.D., J.D., is a Clinical Instructor in the Department of Psychiatry at Harvard Medical School. Formerly a Fellow in Emergency Psychiatry at Cambridge Hospital and Medical Director of the Fresh Pond Day Treatment Program in Cambridge, Massachusetts, Dr. Kraft recently graduated from Harvard Law School.

RESOURCES

Amarasingham, L. R. (1980). Social and cultural perspectives on medication refusal. *American Journal of Psychiatry, 137,* 353-358.

Appelbaum, P. S. (1983). The patient's right to refuse medication. *Schizophrenic Outpatient, 1,* 10-12.

Appelbaum, P. S., & Gutheil, T. G. (1979). "Rotting with their rights on": Constitutional theory and clinical reality in drug refusal by psychiatric patients. *Bulletin of the American Academy of Psychiatry and the Law, 7,* 306-315.

Appelbaum, P. S., & Gutheil, T. G. (1980a). The Boston State Hospital case: "Involuntary mind control," the Constitution, and the "right to rot." *American Journal of Psychiatry, 137,* 720-723.

Appelbaum, P. S., & Gutheil, T. G. (1980b). Drug refusal: A study of psychiatric inpatients. *American Journal of Psychiatry, 137,* 340-345.

Appelbaum, P. S., & Gutheil, T. G. (1981). The right to refuse treatment: The real issue is quality of care. *Bulletin of the American Academy of Psychiatry and the Law, 9,* 199-202.

Appelbaum, P. S., & Gutheil, T. G. (1982). Clinical aspects of treatment refusal. *Comprehensive Psychiatry, 23,* 560-566.

Arieti, S. (1974). *Interpretations of Schizophrenia* (2nd ed.). New York: Basic Books.

Baldessarini, R. J., & Lipinski, J. F. (1981). Rights of antipsychotic drugs overemphasized. *New England Journal of Medicine, 305,* 588.

Brant, J. (1983). The hostility of the Burger Court to mental health law reform litigation. *Bulletin of the American Academy of Psychiatry and the Law, 11,* 77-90.

Brennan, W. J. (1977). State constitutions and the protection of individual rights. *Harvard Law Review, 90,* 489-504.

Byrne, G. (1981). Conference report: Refusing treatment in mental health institutions: Values in conflict. *Hospital & Community Psychiatry, 32,* 255-258.

Cocozza, J. J., & Melick, M. E. (1977). The right to refuse treatment: A broad view. *Bulletin of the American Academy of Psychiatry and the Law, 5*, 1-7.

Ford, M. (1980). The psychiatrist's double bind: The right to refuse medication. *American Journal of Psychiatry, 137*, 332-339.

Freedman, B. (1981). Competence, marginal and otherwise: Concepts and ethics. *International Journal of Law and Psychiatry, 4*, 53-72.

Griswold v. Connecticut, 381 U.S. 479 (1965).

Gutheil, T. G. (1980a). Restraint versus treatment: Seclusion as discussed in the Boston State Hospital case. *American Journal of Psychiatry, 137*, 718-719.

Gutheil, T. G. (1980b). In search of true freedom: Drug refusal, involuntary medication, and "rotting with your rights on." *American Journal of Psychiatry, 137*, 327-328.

Gutheil, T. G., & Mills, M. J. (1982). Legal conceptualizations, legal fictions, and the manipulation of reality: Conflict between models of decision making in psychiatry and law. *Bulletin of the American Academy of Psychiatry and the Law, 10*, 17-27.

Hart, H. M., & Wechsler, H. (1973). Further note on the power of congress. In P. M. Bator, P. J. Mishkin, D. L. Shapiro, & H. Wechsler (Eds.), *The Federal Courts and the Federal System* (2nd ed., pp. 330-360). Mineola, NY: Foundation Press.

Hoffman, P. B. (1976). The right to refuse psychiatric treatment: A clinical perspective. *Bulletin of the American Academy of Psychiatry and the Law, 4*, 269-274.

Mackey v. Procunier, 477 F.2d 877 (9th Cir. 1973).

Michels, R. (1981). The right to refuse treatment: Ethical issues. *Hospital & Community Psychiatry, 32*, 251-255.

Mills v. Rogers, 457 U.S. 291 (1982).

Mills, M. J., & Gutheil, T. G. (1981). Guardianship and the right to refuse treatment: A critique of the Roe case. *Bulletin of the American Academy of Psychiatry and the Law, 9*, 239-246.

Mills, M. J., Yesavage, J. A., & Gutheil, T. G. (1983). Continuing case law development in the right to refuse treatment. *American Journal of Psychiatry, 140,* 715-719.

Minow, M., & Kraft, P. (1982, December 4). *Deinstitutionalization: Professional Prescriptions and Ideologies.* Paper presented at the Conference on Chronic Mental Patients in the Community, Harvard University Division on Health Policy, Stanford University Department of Psychiatry, Stanford, CA.

O'Connor v. Donaldson, 422 U.S. 563 (1975).

Plotkin, R. (1977). Limiting the therapeutic orgy: Mental patients' right to treatment. *Northwestern Law Review, 72,* 461-525.

Reiser, S. J. (1980). Refusing treatment for mental illness: Historical and ethical dimensions. *American Journal of Psychiatry, 137,* 329-331.

Rennie v. Klein, 476 F.Supp. 1294 (D.N.J. 1979), *aff'd in part,* 653 F.2d 836 (3d Cir. 1981).

Rennie v. Klein, 102 S.Ct. 3506 (1982).

Roe v. Wade, 410 U.S. 113 (1973).

In re Roe, 383 Mass. 415, 421 N.E.2d 40 (1981).

Rogers v. Okin, 478 F.Supp. 1342 (D. Mass. 1979).

Rogers v. Okin, 634 F.2d 659 (1st Cir. 1980).

Roth, L. (1981). The right to refuse treatment. *Hospital & Community Psychiatry, 32,* 233.

Roth L, & Appelbaum, P. S. (1982). What we do and do not know about treatment refusals in mental health institutions. In A. E. Doudera & J. P. Swazey (Eds.), *Refusing Treatment in Mental Health Institutions—Values in Conflict* (pp. 179-196). Ann Arbor: AUPHA Press.

Stone, A. A. (1979). Legal and ethical developments. In L. Bellak (Ed.), *Disorders of the Schizophrenic Syndrome* (pp. 560-584). New York: Basic Books.

Stone, A. A. (1981). The right to refuse treatment: Why psychiatrists should and can make it work. *Archives of General Psychiatry, 38,* 358-362.

Tanay, E. (1980). The right to refuse treatment and the abolition of involuntary hospitalization of the mentally ill. *Bulletin of the American Academy of Psychiatry and the Law, 8,* 1-14.

Tribe, L. H. (1978). *American Constitutional Law.* Mineola, NY: Foundation Press.

Weiner, B. A. (1982). Supreme Court decisions on mental
    health: A review. *Hospital & Community Psychiatry*,
    33, 461-464.
Wright, C. A. (1983). *The Law of Federal Courts* (4th ed.).
    St. Paul, MN: West.
Youngberg v. Romeo, 457 U.S. 307 (1982).

INTRODUCTION TO SECTION III: PSYCHOLOGY, PSYCHIATRY, AND FAMILY LAW

The relationship of psychology and psychiatry to family law is well established and firmly rooted in the conviction that mental health professionals can assist the courts in resolving family-related disputes. Indeed, there seems to be no other area of the law in which psychology and psychiatry are regarded as so vital to the process of legal decision making.

The traditional and primary role of mental health professionals in family law matters has long been that of providing consultation and expert testimony to the courts, particularly in litigation over child custody and placement. In recent years, however, many mental health professionals have grown disenchanted with the adversary system of dispute resolution and the limited role that system affords them. As a result, psychologists, psychiatrists, and other mental health professionals have sought not only to reconceptualize their roles within the adversary legal framework but also to develop alternative, nonadversary methods of resolving family-related disputes.

The chapters in this section—each of which reflects aspects of this recent trend—address the mental health professional's role in the resolution of conflicts between parents over divorce and child custody and disputes between parents and state over allegations of child abuse and neglect.

In the first of these three chapters, Joan Kelly, Carl Zlatchin, and Joel Shawn describe divorce mediation, an emerging alternative method of resolving disputes surrounding the dissolution of marriage. These authors, all of whom are professional mediators, recount the history of divorce mediation including the reasons for its emergence as an alternative to the adversary system, review the small but growing body of research done to date in the area of divorce mediation, and describe in some detail the various theoretical models and practices which comprise this form of family dispute resolution. Written from the perspective of two clinical psychologists (Drs. Kelly and Zlatchin) and a lawyer (Attorney Shawn), the chapter also describes the roles of both mental health professionals and legal professionals in divorce mediation.

In the second chapter, Andrew Musetto, a psychologist and marriage counselor, examines the role of mental health professionals in conducting child custody evaluations and in mediating custody disputes between parents. While advocating a mediation approach to such disputes, Dr. Musetto recognizes that mediation is not always successful. Thus, in addition to describing the custody mediation process, he also explores the many factors mental health professionals must consider when they assume the role of evaluator and consultant to the adversary system.

In the final chapter in this section, Melvin Guyer, an attorney and psychologist, and Peter Ash, a clinical and forensic psychiatrist, discuss the multiple roles played by mental health experts in the legal system's handling of child abuse and neglect cases. While their discussion is clearly tied to the existing legal framework—which is presented in some detail—Drs. Guyer and Ash also explore the contributions psychologists, psychiatrists, and other mental health professionals can make in abuse and neglect cases outside of formal judicial proceedings.

DIVORCE MEDIATION: PROCESS, PROSPECTS, AND PROFESSIONAL ISSUES

Joan B. Kelly, Carl Zlatchin, and Joel Shawn

The number of divorces obtained each year in the United States nearly tripled from 1962 to 1981, and in the past decade, more than a million divorces were recorded each year. As the divorce rate accelerated, it was accompanied by a growing dissatisfaction with the traditional adjudicatory process for resolving family law matters. In 1982, for the first time in 20 years, the number of divorces declined by 3%, but there is no indication that this represents a consistent trend (National Center for Health Statistics, 1983).

The concern with the impact of the adversary process in settling disputes has permeated all levels of society and its institutions. The increased burden on the court system, coupled with an alarming increase in our society's tendency to litigate grievances which were previously settled in family, neighborhood, or religious forums, has caused grave concern among judges and lawmakers. Citing the enormous expense, time, stress, and frustration resulting from the dramatic rise in state and federal lawsuits and appeals of all types, Chief Justice Burger (1982) sounded an urgent call for more reliance on mediation and arbitration as alternatives to courtroom litigation.

Divorce cases are estimated to account for one-half of all civil suits now filed (Bahr, 1981a). Reacting not only to crowded court calendars, lawyers and judges have noted as well the high financial and psychological costs to clients of pursuing a divorce settlement through the courts. Many have urged changes in lawyers' training and roles and in methods of reaching agreement (Feldman, 1977; Folberg, 1983; Folberg & Taylor, 1984; King, 1979; Mnookin & Kornhauser, 1979; Pickrell & Bendheim, 1979; Vroom, Fassett, & Rowan, 1982; Winks, 1980-1981). And researchers and mental health professionals studying and assisting families in the midst of divorce have repeatedly observed increased hostility and prolonged turmoil engendered and sustained by the adversarial divorce for most couples and their children (Gardner, 1977; Hess & Camera, 1979; Hetherington, 1979; Kelly, 1982; Wallerstein & Kelly, 1980; Weiss, 1975). Equally important, as the public has recognized the enormous costs of divorce litigation in monetary and human terms, people have turned to alternatives outside the legal system for resolving their disputes. The "Do your own divorce" literature, the first popular manifestation of this growing discontent, was followed by increased requests to attorneys and mental health professionals to change their roles and assist both parties conjointly in reaching a mutually acceptable settlement.

This chapter focuses on the field of divorce mediation which has emerged in response to the search for a more rational and beneficial alternative to the adversarial process. Included will be a brief recounting of the emergence of this new field, its beginning research efforts, various models and practices, the mediation process, and the role of the lawyer and mental health professional in the mediation process. As with any new field on the threshold of assuming a more coherent and permanent identity, ethical issues, standards of practice, and training considerations are important to consider, and a limited discussion of these aspects of divorce mediation is also contained in this chapter.

THE EMERGENCE OF DIVORCE MEDIATION

Mediation is a voluntary dispute resolution process in which a third impartial person, engaged by the two disputing parties, assists the disputants in resolving their dispute and reaching agreement. Various forms of mediation have been practiced for centuries. In some countries, most notably China and Japan, and within some religious groups, particularly the Jewish and Quaker, mediation has long been an established and preferred mode for resolving those disputes that arose among families and neighbors. In the United States, the Federal Mediation and Conciliation Service was established in 1947 to provide dispute resolution services to labor and industry. Within the past decade, in response to the overwhelming numbers of cases before the courts, the scope of the Federal Mediation Service was broadened to provide conflict resolution in community disputes such as landlord-tenant, neighborhood, environmental, and consumer complaints.

But despite the growing acceptance of mediation in labor-management and community disputes, mediation was not utilized for the settlement of divorce disputes. Until recently, divorce was possible only if a party were proven to be "at fault" or "guilty," and the adversarial process was indispensable in determining fault. Mediation had little opportunity to flourish in a cultural setting in which one party was presumed to be guilty and the other "innocent" prior to settlement, and in which the distribution of property and children was awarded accordingly. The possibility of mediation as applied to divorces became a reality with the gradual acceptance of no-fault divorce statutes on a state-by-state basis in the 1970s. Thus, the development of divorce mediation, first as a technique and increasingly as a field, began in the mid-1970s. Despite its growing acceptance, mediation is a field still in its infancy (see Brown, 1982 for a detailed description of the earliest years of the family and divorce mediation field).

Divorce mediation is a field and practice which has emerged through the integration of theory, technique, and content from diverse related fields. Law, labor relations, accounting, and the behavioral sciences (those which have focused on negotiation strategies, conflict resolution, the psychology of the divorce experience, and counseling or psychotherapeutic techniques appropriate for individuals and couples dealing with the stress of divorce) have all contributed in substantial ways. The resultant combination of expertise and knowledge into this alternative form of dispute resolution has the potential to be collectively more efficient, productive, and beneficial for its clients than any of its separate contributing parts.

RESEARCH IN MEDIATION

Because divorce mediation is a relatively new phenomenon, research regarding kinds of services, types of clients, the mediation process, and outcomes is in its early stages. Existing research has been focused primarily in the area of court-connected mediation services for custody and visitation disputes.

DESCRIPTION OF SERVICES

In a questionnaire survey of private (N=256) and public (N=53) mediation services, Pearson, Ring, and Milne (1983) found that more than one-half of all private mediation cases were self-referred and an additional 19% were referred by attorneys. In the public sector, however, 82% of the clients were referred or mandated by the court to mediation. The private mediation services were found to be more comprehensive in scope, with two-thirds of private programs mediating all aspects of their clients' divorce (e.g., property distribution, spousal and child support, custody, visitation). In contrast, more than two-thirds of the court programs mediated only custody or visitation disputes. These differences in scope may account, in part, for the finding that the average number of sessions needed to reach agreement in private mediation (6.2) was nearly double that of the court services. More than half of the the private mediations required 9 or more hours to reach agreement. Private mediators also reported terminating mediation more quickly if agreement did not seem possible. In terms of successfully completed mediations, the private mediators reported agreement in 65% of the cases, whereas public mediators reached agreement 56% of the time. All of the preceding differences described by Pearson et al., were statistically significant. Public and private sector mediation services seemed to be attracting more affluent clients, yet thus far, social status indicators did not appear to affect outcome.

COSTS

Bahr (1981b) and Parker (1981) noted that couples who used mediation paid less for their divorces than those using the traditional adversary proceeding. Pearson and Thoennes (1982) also found that clients in the Denver Custody Mediation Project (seen without charge) paid less in legal fees than either a control adversarial group or a second group that initially rejected the invitation to mediate custody-related disputes. A closer look at the mediation group revealed that the greatest savings were achieved by those who sought mediation early in the divorce dispute. Those mediation clients who sought later modification of permanent custody orders actually had higher fees than the two control groups. However, savings to the taxpayer in custody disputes were substantial when comparing the entire group served by mediation with their adversarial counterparts.

EFFECTIVENESS

In a review of several mediation studies whose experimental design included control groups, Sprenkle and Storm (1983) noted that the mediation groups reached a higher rate of pretrial stipulations and agreements than did control groups using the traditional adversary method. Further, in those studies conducting follow-up research, the mediated groups were involved in considerably less litigation after the final divorce decree. There is also some evidence that with custody and visitation disputes, mediation is more likely to succeed if the couple enters mediation early rather than late in the divorce process (Sprenkle & Storm, 1983).

SATISFACTION

One of the consistent early findings has been the greater satisfaction of mediation clients with the process and resulting agreement than control groups of litigating clients (Bahr, 1981b; Parker, 1981; Pearson & Thoennes, 1982, 1984; Sprenkle & Storm, 1983). Because mediation produces a substantially higher degree of satisfaction and feeling of fairness regarding the agreements reached in child and property matters, it is anticipated that mediated agreements will have a higher rate of compliance post-divorce than lawyer negotiated settlements or court judgments. Further follow-up research utilizing adversarial control groups will be needed to determine whether this expectation is warranted.

POST-DIVORCE RELATIONSHIPS AND ARRANGEMENTS

Improved communication between spouses is reported significantly more often in mediated couples (Pearson & Thoennes, 1982). Further, three separate studies have found a significantly higher rate of co-parenting, joint custody, and visitation among clients choosing mediation as contrasted to adversarial couples (Bahr, 1981a; Kelly, 1984; Parker, 1981; Pearson & Thoennes, 1982). A higher rate of shared parenting was evident even for clients who were unsuccessful in mediating their custody disputes as compared to those groups of clients who refused or did not receive mediation services (Pearson & Thoennes, 1982).

Thus, initial research regarding costs, effectiveness, and post-divorce relationships appears to support some of the early claims that mediation is more beneficial to its clients and related family members than the adversary process.

MEDIATION MODELS

In the short period that divorce mediation has become a viable alternative to the adversary proceeding, different models and methods of practicing mediation have emerged (Folberg & Taylor, 1984; Milne, 1983; Saposnek, 1983a, 1983b; Waldron, Roth, Fair, Mann, & McDermott, 1984). The theoretical underpinnings of the "practitioner" models have not yet been established. Therefore, variations exist in the mediators' training, previous personal and professional experience, and the settings in which the mediation takes place. Although mediation models differ in the content of the disputes they address, the procedures and techniques used to reach agreement, and the role of the mediator, they all share the common goal of reaching a settlement of the differences between the disputing parties which is fair and acceptable to both.

There are various ways of characterizing the differences in mediation models, but the following broad dimensions seem useful to consider: (a) mediation services in the public and private sectors; (b) the identity of the mediators and their role; and (c) the degree of structure imposed on the mediation process.

PUBLIC AND PRIVATE SECTOR MEDIATION

Within the public sector, in the past decade, mediation services have been provided in court-connected programs which have sought less destructive and longer lasting alternatives for resolving visitation and custody disputes. Conciliation and family courts took an early lead (Brown, 1982; Elkin, 1962, 1977) in providing counseling which had the goal, if divorce was inevitable, of diminishing the parents' hostility so they could continue to exercise their parental responsibilities post-divorce. Conceptualized in this manner, such short-term conciliation counseling was the forerunner of divorce mediation as applied to custody and visitation disputes. Numerous court-connected mediation programs have been established throughout the United States and Canada. In California, Connecticut, and Massachusetts, recent legislation has made mediation mandatory for parents engaged in contested custody and visitation disputes. Most public mediation programs are staffed by social workers or marriage and family therapists who have expertise in family evaluation and custody and visitation matters. With rare exceptions, the content of the dispute mediated does not extend beyond custody and visitation issues.

Private mediation services, in contrast, serve clients whose participation is entirely voluntary and mediate a broader range of disputes (Pearson et al., 1983). Depending on the discipline and orientation of the mediator, the mediation may encompass all aspects of a divorce dispute, including spousal and child support, property distribution, and post-divorce parent-child arrangements, or may focus more narrowly on any of these issues. As might be expected, lawyers functioning as mediators are more likely, without additional training, to focus primarily on those issues of property division and support which traditionally have been the domain of family law. Therapists without additional training in family and tax law are more likely to restrict their mediation practices to custody, visitation, and, sometimes, support issues.

MEDIATOR IDENTITY AND ROLE

Mediation models in the private sector vary according to whether mediators practice individually or in teams and how they view their professional identities in that regard. Mediators working in teams divide essentially into two groups representing different philosophies about their role in the mediation. In the first instance, the lawyer and mental health professional work collaboratively with the divorcing client, but their function is clearly delineated along disciplinary lines. The lawyer handles the legal and factual issues, and the therapist deals with the emotional and process issues relevant to the dispute. While there are variations in this mediation model (Black & Joffee, 1978; Gold, 1982; Wiseman & Fiske, 1980), the notable feature is the retention by the mediator of his or her professional identity and function, and the resultant division of responsibility within the mediation team.

In the second variant of the co-mediation model, mediators view themselves as interdisciplinary mediators and do not separate their role and function in working with the divorcing couple. These mediators, often (but not necessarily) a lawyer and mental health professional working together, have prepared themselves for their cross-disciplinary roles by taking additional training in relevant areas outside of their professions of origin and by working together in an integrated manner. In this model, each mediator deals with factual, child-related, and emotional issues as appropriate, conducts negotiations, manages conflict, and shares responsibility for drafting the Memorandum of Understanding. This particular mediation model provides an excellent training opportunity for mediators with legal or mental health backgrounds who wish to prepare for and develop an identity as an interdisciplinary mediator.

Proponents of both variants of co-mediation teams share a belief in the flexibility and symmetry provided by this model (Gold, 1982). The support the co-mediators offer each other during the process and the opportunity to balance perceptions and potential mediator biases is viewed as an important advantage of co-mediation. Some mediators (Gold, 1982) state that the male-female co-mediation presence is indispensable to the success of divorce mediation because each client can be supported or challenged by a mediator of the same or opposite sex on any given issue without disturbing the balance and neutrality of the overall process. Thus far, there is no evidence that co-mediation teams, at least in custody disputes, are more effective than single mediators (Pearson et al., 1983). Preliminary findings from the research project of the Northern California Mediation Center (NCMC) indicate that while some clients view the male-female team balance as important, others who successfully completed mediation with an all-male mediation team did not feel the absence of a woman was detrimental. NCMC clients described the psychological balance *within* the mediation team and the mediators' respective qualities and contributions as more important, *per se*, than the sex of the mediator. Further Northern California Mediation Center research efforts will investigate psychological, educational, social, and role-identity factors that may be related to the sex of mediators and mediation success or failure.

A similar division holds for single mediators as well. There are those who solidly retain their original professional identities and restrict their mediation activities to issues most compatible with their training. And there are mediators who seek to develop the broader and more integrated identity of the interdisciplinary mediator (Coogler, 1978; Haynes, 1981, 1982).

THE DEGREE OF STRUCTURE IN MEDIATION

The mediation models described thus far in the mediation literature or in training programs vary according to the amount of structure associated with the process. Structure can be imposed either through external rules and guidelines or by the directiveness of the mediator's style.

At one end of the spectrum is Coogler's (1978) model of Structured Mediation which relies heavily on rules and structures the manner in which clients move through the process. Coogler, for example, has a predetermined ordering of disputed issues to be handled in the mediation. His model also requires that emphasis and effort be placed on restructuring the marital relationship into a post-divorce relationship that is capable of cooperation and joint problem solving.

Other practitioners, including the authors, have developed mediation models which are considerably less structured and generally more flexible in terms of number and type of meetings (separate or joint), the ordering of issues, the handling of emotional issues, and the use of attorney review (Erickson, 1984; Folberg & Taylor, 1984; Haynes, 1981). Haynes, for example, sees the mediator's primary goal as helping the couple reach an agreement which they both feel is acceptable, has an expectation of good faith negotiations and full disclosure, but does not require a signed agreement to mediate which specifies these and other issues. In the Haynes context, mediator control of the process, but not the content or clients' decisions, is emphasized so that the couple can successfully negotiate the disputed issues. Others (see Folberg & Taylor, 1984) also do not have rules or procedures, but views the mediator's role as one of active and pragmatic involvement in helping the couple develop options and positions which lead to negotiations. Other mediators let the couple decide on the pace and issues to be discussed, and view the mediator as a more neutral and nondirective facilitator.

Clearly, mediator styles will vary from the more direct and active to the more *laissez faire*, depending on philosophical and personality differences. To the extent these styles do not reach the extremes of authoritarian control over clients' decisions or passive acceptance of an unfair agreement, there is a legitimate need in a newly developing field for different styles and mediation models to adequately meet clients' differing needs and disputes.

Most mediators espouse a standard of fairness and mutual acceptability to the clients, rather than an absolute standard against which the mediated outcome is measured. And mediators in the private sector, serving clients who come voluntarily to the mediation process, generally share the belief that the divorcing couple, rather than the mediator, has the responsibility to resolve their differences and arrive at an agreement which reflects their particular wishes and needs. In the event the couple fails to reach agreement, most mediators do not arbitrate the outcome but instead terminate the mediation process (see Coogler, 1978, for a model incorporating arbitration in the event of impasse).

THE PROCESS OF MEDIATION

In examining the process of divorce mediation, it is important to recognize that there may be at least two major components simultaneously at work. The first is the process by which agreement on terms of the divorce settlement is reached and recorded, the overall structure and the concrete tasks of the mediation. The second, and equally important, is the psychological process. This process can assist clients in accepting the finality of the divorce, gaining a growing degree of individual autonomy, developing an increased ability to handle their own financial and other matters, and developing an understanding of the redefined post-divorce relationship with their ex-spouses and children. Many mediators (e.g., Coogler, 1978; Gold, 1982; Haynes, 1981, 1982) believe that the ability to be aware of and work with both processes is critical to the success of mediation.

The mediation process may be conceptualized as occurring in three primary phases. While for the most part these phases occur sequentially, there may be an overlap and interweaving from one phase to another.

THE BEGINNING PHASE

The first contact with clients most often occurs on the telephone. The mediator describes the process and attempts to determine whether mediation is appropriate for the dispute. If so, the mediator speaks with the other party to the dispute to explore the same issues and to initiate a balance in the interaction with the couple during this stage.

An initial consultation is scheduled if the parties decide they are interested in exploring mediation. In this first face-to-face meeting with the divorcing couple, the mediation process is described in detail; distinctions between legal representation, psychotherapy, and mediation are made; and expectations that the mediator and the clients may have of each other are explored.

The clients are advised that the results of the mediation will be summarized in a written agreement, encompassing all aspects of their dispute, which will then be reviewed by their respective attorneys. Further, the steps necessary to achieve a final divorce are explained so the place of the written agreement in the larger context of the legal process of divorce is made clear.

The use to be made of various experts, including attorneys, during the process is generally discussed. Some mediators prohibit contact with individual attorneys during the process (Coogler, 1978), while others encourage contact, as necessary, with individual attorneys throughout the process (Folberg & Taylor, 1984; Haynes, 1981; Samuels & Shawn, 1983). Whatever the nature of the contact clients have with their attorney during mediation, most mediators will *not* agree to proceed unless ongoing litigation is suspended.

If the couple decides to proceed, they enter into a mediation agreement, which may be either written or oral. Generally, such an agreement emphasizes that participation in mediation is voluntary, requires full disclosure of all data relevant to the negotiations and requested by the mediator, and specifies that the parties treat the process as confidential and waive the right to subpoena the mediator. This agreement often includes a description of fees for services and the manner in which they are to be paid.

Once contracting is concluded, many mediators take a brief, focused history to get an understanding of each client's perception of the reasons for the failure of the marriage and the decision to divorce (Kelly, 1983). Some mediators collect additional information about children, current visitation patterns, and the legal status of the divorce (Gold, 1982).

Implicitly and explicitly, the mediator communicates to the clients that he or she will work to create a safe setting for productive discussions where each will be heard, and assures the clients that their conflict will be managed so that they can achieve their goal of reaching agreement.

Prior to ending the initial consultation, clients may be assigned tasks to complete in preparation for the first mediation session. Most mediators request detailed income statements, preparation of a detailed budget based on current expenses, and a comprehensive description of all assets and liabilities. Most often, the initial consultation ends without any need to engage in negotiations except, perhaps, around the sharing of mediation fees. Sometimes, however, it may be necessary to help the couple reach a rapid and temporary agreement about an area of significant dispute (e.g., access to children, or the desperate financial need of one party and the necessity of transferring money from one spouse to the other).

Throughout this consultation most mediators assess the patterns of communication and interaction (both verbal and nonverbal) between the parties; the level of anger, hostility, guilt, and fear; and evidence of psychological difficulties, such as significant depression. Finally, an assessment of the overall emotional readiness of the individuals to proceed with mediation is usually made (Gold, 1982). Among the important issues in this assessment are: (a) the readiness and/or potential of the disputants to see themselves as separate individuals able to begin to disengage from each other and from the marriage; (b) the extent of the nonmutuality of the divorce decision and the implications for current psychological functioning; and (c) the ability of the participants to engage fully, emotionally, and intellectually in the mediation. In almost every divorce a state of psychological crisis exists for one if not both spouses, and ambivalent and powerful feelings are experienced. The mediator should recognize that if the spouses can express their divorce-engendered feelings in relatively appropriate ways, the mediation may be facilitated. The feelings experienced often include anger and a sense of deprivation; however, clients who are able to grieve for and eventually accept the loss of the spouse and relationship can more readily proceed with their own lives. During the course of the divorce mediation, the mediator will often observe real changes in clients' ability to cope with and accept the divorce.

During this initial phase, the mediator has intervened by structuring the session, clarifying expectations, beginning the development of trust and empathy, and describing (at least implicitly) the behaviors likely to produce a satisfactory mediation.

THE MIDDLE PHASE OF MEDIATION

In this phase the mediator assists the clients in collecting, analyzing, and understanding the data, and in so doing helps them begin to identify the issues and their positions. Many mediators begin by examining budgets, which gives the spouses the opportunity to come to grips with the details of their current financial needs and expenses in relation to the income they have available. Spouses invariably come to understand that an often sizable discrepancy exists between income and projected or actual expenses and that the expense associated with maintaining two households is surprisingly high. The mediator's task is to help the clients understand that developing and scrutinizing budgets is the only rational way to arrive at support figures. For those with children, it is helpful to list separately the costs associated with basic care, education, and recreational activities of the children. This lays the groundwork for cooperative efforts by both spouses to address how costs associated with their children are to be met. Major questions often confronted at this point include: where the spouses can afford to live, given the costs associated with supporting two households; whether a major geographical move may be necessitated due to insufficient income; and whether the part-time or nonworking spouse will need to enter the work force full time and what the costs associated with such a change will be.

Attitudes toward money, which are often only thinly veiled reflections of attitudes toward one's spouse and self, often emerge powerfully in this process. Careful attention to these attitudes can provide clues to how the issues of fairness, generosity, and respect for the other will be dealt with, and about the ability of each to separate ideas from feelings and remain task focused.

Most mediators agree that it is important to communicate in both direct and indirect ways to the couple. The mediator is not responsible for the data that describe the couple's condition. "Shortfalls" are the couple's problem to deal with and these data form the basis for discussions about support payments for a spouse and/or children. The beginning articulation of the needs and wishes of the individual spouses often emerge at this point, and mediators encourage and attempt to shape the expression of these needs. Frequently, there are shared needs and desires concerning the children. Where these overlapping self-interests can be identified, it is helpful to note and reinforce their expression. In this way, the couple quickly learns that the greater the number and wider the circle of overlapping self-interests, the easier their task is to develop an agreement that has major elements of mutual fairness and satisfaction.

Next, there often follows the development of a comprehensive inventory of the assets and liabilities associated with the marriage. The mediator performs an educational and exploratory function here. Consideration is given to whether an outside expert, such as a real estate appraiser, accountant, pension evaluator, and so forth, might be needed. Joint selection and consultation with a *single* expert has at least two benefits: The expense is usually one-half of what it would be in the adversary process; and the spouses benefit from their ability to reach a cooperative decision despite often high levels of conflict.

Given the amount and considerable complexity of the data and issues under consideration, clients may often feel overwhelmed. The mediator should be aware that the divorce process often significantly impairs both intellectual and emotional functions (Kelly, 1982; Wallerstein & Kelly, 1980). Careful and detailed explanations are frequently provided by the mediator for each area or issue examined, recognizing the specific needs of the client at the particular time.

Throughout the early part of this phase, the mediator has intervened by eliciting data and explaining its importance, by providing an understanding of aspects of the divorce process and the accompanying psychological issues, by encouraging the expression of individual and family needs, by identifying areas of overlapping interests, and by managing conflict to enable the couple to remain task focused. Numerous techniques are used to keep communication open and to remove negatively charged emotional content from the ideas, thereby permitting the reframing of the initial proposals into relatively neutral language (Haynes, 1981; Kelly, 1983; Ury & Fisher, 1981). In this less emotionally charged climate, the details of the tentative proposals can be examined and consequences explored, thereby increasing the likelihood of agreement.

The mediator pays close attention to relative imbalances in power between the clients at this juncture. Clients must be able to speak for themselves, articulate their desires and positions, and do this in a climate free from intimidation. If this cannot occur, the mediator must work to adjust the power balance so the "weaker" spouse becomes "empowered" and is able to enter the negotiations with a relatively equal position. Empowering can be accomplished by directly providing knowledge to a client so he or she gains an equal footing with a spouse; by assisting in the organization of material so the weaker spouse may make his or her case most effectively; by referring to outside experts, if necessary; and by assuring that the more threatened or fearful spouse expresses his or her desires and opinions (Kelly, 1983). The power imbalances may shift dramatically during the course of a mediation, with each spouse at various times appearing to be the weaker.

With respect to child-related issues, the mediator assists in the exploration of the children's needs and those of the parents through parental discussions or, in some mediation settings, in direct consultation with the children. If likely to be helpful, explanations may be offered regarding the effects of divorce on parents and children and the various ways in which parenting responsibilities can be shared post-divorce (Kelly, 1984). As parents understand the child's psychological need to maintain a relationship with and love both parents, they can then explore possible structures or patterns for post-divorce parenting that may apply to their family circumstances and their children's needs. Clients with children gradually come to realize that they are relinquishing a spousal role but maintaining the role of parent (Ahrons, 1980; Gold, 1982; Wallerstein & Kelly, 1980). This recognition is often the start of important efforts to restructure the family unit that many families struggle with for a period of years post-divorce. In mediation, this difficult process is often enhanced and considerably shortened.

THE END PHASE OF MEDIATION

This phase includes the negotiations that enable the clients to reach agreement, and the preparation of the clients for the attorney review, which leads to the finalization of the divorce. As do the two previous phases of the mediation process, this phase also has highly focused tasks and psychological components, both of which must be addressed for closure to be reached successfully.

The primary task of the mediator in this phase is to help organize the material and conduct negotiations without wresting control from the clients. Some mediators will formally order the sequence in which issues will be negotiated (Coogler, 1978). Others believe that starting with what appears to be a relatively simple, straightforward difference that may lend itself to rapid and satisfactory resolution is the best way to proceed (Brown, 1982). In this manner, couples gain the experience of a successful negotiation, and the resultant satisfaction, especially when actively reinforced, often has carry-over effects to the more difficult issues.

Whatever the order in which the issues are negotiated, the mediator is typically quite active throughout the negotiations. The mediator encourages clients to develop their positions and make clear their self-interests. As proposals are developed, their objectives and implications are explored. The parties are often asked to argue for the other side, that is, to indicate the advantages inherent in their proposals for their spouse. When clients are stymied, the mediator assists by providing other options for further exploration. Finally, the mediator continuously assists the clients in testing the reality of their proposals—will they work now and in the future?

The mediator strives to go beyond compromise and "splitting the difference" (Haynes, 1983). The goal is to reach a degree of consensus where both spouses feel engaged in a "win-win" rather than a "win-lose" encounter (Ury & Fisher, 1981).

Once agreement has been reached on all of the issues in dispute, the mediator drafts the Memorandum of Understanding or settlement agreement, preferably in language that is easily understandable. This document usually describes the important considerations which underlie the agreements. Clients then have an opportunity to review the draft and "fine tune" both the content and language so their agreements are carefully and fully detailed.

Clients have a significant and sometimes difficult role in the attorney review process. They must shift from the mediative and cooperative posture of the mediation to a posture of advocate for the final agreement when they meet with their respective attorneys. For some clients, the prospect of having to meet with an attorney can be intimidating, either because they fear the unraveling of the agreement or doubt their ability to be persuasive. In addition, powerful and at times ambivalent feelings may lead some clients to actively or unwittingly undermine the agreement at this point. They may be experiencing some unexpressed dissatisfaction with an aspect of the agreement, suffering considerable depression or fear about the ending of the marriage, or panicked about what the future holds for an "independent" individual. Any of these feelings lead clients to resist completion of the attorney review process. Sensitivity to such resistance by the mediator is important, and some intervention may be required to assist in the completion of the attorney review process. However, if clients have participated fully in the mediation and understand not only the final result but the manner and process by which final agreements were reached, the attorney review is likely to be a manageable and satisfactory experience (Samuels & Shawn, 1983).

There is a psychological termination in the mediation process as well. Bringing about closure with a respect for the significance of this process in the clients' lives is important. Termination has been described in great detail in the literature on psychotherapy, but little attention thus far has been given to this aspect of mediation (Gold, 1982). Other than the separation itself, no event that the clients have experienced to this point brings home as vividly as the final settlement agreement that the marriage is ending. A mediator, being party to this realization, may be placed in a position of considerable importance in the clients' lives, despite having had relatively little face-to-face contact. Adequate time for the clients to say good-bye to each other and the mediator seems to be an important final step.

THE LAWYER'S ROLE IN
THE MEDIATION PROCESS

LAWYER AS MEDIATOR

Legal training in the adversarial approach to divorce is generally antithetical to successful mediation of disputes. In the usual divorce proceeding, the lawyer will avoid responding to personal feelings or value judgments regarding the controversy at stake and find refuge in advocating a client's position regardless of its merit or underlying motivation. The lawyer generally views any issue presented as one that is either good or bad for his or her client as opposed to what might be good or bad for the larger family unit. The outcome most often disposes of the immediate problem in dispute and is less concerned with the possible long-term consequences or survival of the judgment or agreement.

In the adversarial process, a lawyer will sometimes create issues that have little substance in order to achieve an advantageous bargaining position for the client. As a result, the process often becomes extremely expensive. For example, in litigating support, the objective pursued by the husband's attorney would be to minimize the amount and duration of support for the wife by attempting to prove that her support needs are less than she claims, and by stating the lowest possible income for the husband. The costs associated with resolution are often doubled when each side uses its stable of experts to convince the court or opposing counsel of the merit of its claim. Over all, the lawyer's role is to protect his or her client and because of that, personal contact between the parties is generally discouraged.

In practicing as a mediator, a lawyer must put aside this adversary training and orientation and begin to view himself or herself as a facilitator of cooperation between two people in conflict who have the objective of bringing about a "win-win" situation (Ury & Fisher, 1981). Therefore, the lawyer-mediator must first deal with the question of representation in the initial interview with clients. Lawyer-mediators clarify that they do not represent either client and will not provide in mediation the legal protection usually provided in the adversarial context. Although it may be necessary or helpful during the mediation for the lawyer to role play each client's lawyer in presenting the range of possibilities, this presentation should be balanced. In the mediator role, the lawyer refrains from overly emphasizing a proposal he or she believes is beneficial for one or the other spouse, avoids attacking a proposal because of a dislike for one party, and does not lend support to a proposal which fails to acknowledge the needs of the other party.

Since mediation proceeds on the assumption that the negotiations are in good faith and that full disclosure has been agreed to, the lawyer's training and temptation to cross-examine or engage in unproductive challenges to the offered evidence needs to be resisted and rechanneled into more creative problem solving. The task of the lawyer in mediation is to encourage rather than discourage the private ordering of the parties' affairs (Mnookin & Kornhauser, 1979). Thus, the lawyer-mediator must be content with agreements reached which do not comply with present legal precedents, but nevertheless fall within broad standards of fairness.

MEDIATION REPRESENTATION

There is ongoing debate as to whether the lawyer-mediator can avoid the mantle of representation while participating in the mediation process. Some contend that a lawyer is always representing someone when imparting legal knowledge and that representation cannot be avoided because the clients are relying on that knowledge to assist them in formulating proposals.

Canon 5 of the present American Bar Association, Canons of Professional Responsibility, prohibits representing clients with conflicting or potentially conflicting interests (American Bar Association, 1980). Dual representation contemplates one lawyer representing both parties to a conflict and such representation has been criticized in State Bar Association opinions across the country. In California, dual representation has been indirectly approved in *Klemm v. Superior Court* (1977), where the Court held that representing both parties in an uncontested divorce was not unethical. The Court upheld the judgment resulting from that dual representation on the grounds that the attorney had fully disclosed all facts, circumstances, and risks; had advised the parties that they were entitled to independent legal counsel; and had obtained their informed consent to a sole attorney proceeding in the matter.

The dual representation question is not new in the area of the law. Lawyers, for example, have long planned wills with husbands and wives present and have formed corporations with all of the prospective shareholders present. These activities have been found acceptable because there was presumably no conflict at hand, but rather a common objective. It seems equally plausible that the lawyer-mediator can function under this "common objective" theory in conflict resolution so long as the common, mutually agreed upon objective is to avoid the adversary process and reach a mutually beneficial result. By mandating mediation in contested custody disputes, several states have in essence validated the common objective theory by defining the common objective as the best interest of the child.

CONFIDENTIALITY AND PRIVILEGE

Lawyers and mental health professionals have in most states been cloaked with an evidentiary privilege. This privilege is separate and distinct from any concept of confidential relationship. The privilege, a creature of the law, allows the lawyer and the mental health professional to avoid disclosing any information obtained from a client/patient, unless the client/patient waives the privilege. Currently, however, *neither the lawyer nor the mental health professional providing private mediation services has a statutory privilege preventing disclosure.* Therefore, the mediator can be called to testify by anyone. Thus, the mediator can rely only upon an agreement for confidentiality entered into between the parties, and in most states even this agreement does not prevent either party from calling the mediator at a subsequent trial.

California, however, has provided an instructive ruling in *Simrin v. Simrin* (1965), a case in which the parties had engaged the presumably confidential services of a rabbi to counsel with them in regard to their marital dispute. The wife in a subsequent trial attempted to call the rabbi to testify. In ruling against the wife's position the Court of Appeals recognized that, "For the unwary spouse who speaks freely, repudiation [of the agreement] would prove a trap; for the wily, a vehicle for making self-serving declarations" (p. 95). The Court further encouraged such counseling as a meaningful way of avoiding family litigation and stated that to permit one party to void the contract of confidentiality would discourage such efforts.

The law also protects from court disclosure settlement discussions between parties to a dispute on the premise that settlement discussions are to be encouraged. Mediators may find refuge from disclosure in court by asserting that mediation is in effect a settlement negotiation.

THE LAWYER/THERAPIST TEAM MODEL

Lawyers who mediate in teams with mental health professionals are faced with claims that the lawyer is involved in the aiding and abetting of the unauthorized practice of the law. This is true to the extent that in the mediation the lawyer and the therapist engage in giving legal advice to the clients (assuming that there is a representational aspect to the mediation process). The same claim may arise when the mediator prepares the Memorandum of Understanding.

There are, however, other professional disciplines interfacing with the law where "advice" is given and no such claims are raised. The accountant is permitted to provide advice about the legal consequence of certain tax planning, the realtor is permitted to prepare deposit receipts and other contracts affecting real property, and bank officers prepare various financial documents affecting the legal rights of people. Mediators who draft a document reflecting the agreement reached between the parties, that is subject to later lawyer review, may successfully claim as well that they are merely scriveners of the parties' wishes and not drafters of legally binding documents.

The co-mediation model has additional problems when the lawyers/therapists charge a single fee for their services. In this instance, the lawyer may be faced with the charge of illegal fee splitting. Although there is an unpublished Oregon State Bar Opinion criticizing such a lawyer/therapist model, there are adequate means to avoid such illegal fee splitting claims by structuring the service and fee collection in a way that avoids fee splitting. To date, however, there is no clearly safe harbor for the lawyer/therapist model.

THE ROLE OF THE LAWYER
OUTSIDE THE PROCESS

Under present day standards, clients are more likely to come first to lawyers rather than mediators to deal with their divorce. Therefore, one of the functions of the lawyer outside the mediation process might be to consider the appropriateness of referring the client to mediation (Samuels & Shawn, 1983).

In making this determination, the lawyer should consider the capabilities of the client as well as the dispute to be resolved. The lawyer might explore with the client why mediation may be an appropriate choice and explain the benefits of mediation: That it gives them the opportunity to apply their own standard of fairness to the solution of the problem, that they can avoid engaging in accusatory and unpleasant statements about the other party, that it is often a speedier process, and that the process and result are controlled by them and not the lawyers. Further, the lawyer may explain the additional benefit of lower cost.

The lawyer will also consider whether the client is capable of assuming the responsibility of self-determination. Certainly there are clients who are too timid, unsophisticated, or emotionally unable to participate fully in mediation, and lawyers would generally retain these clients. Similarly, there are clients who do not wish to take responsibility for the result and would much rather hide behind the excuse, "That was what my lawyer told me to do," or "That's what the judge decided." Some clients need the adversarial process to obtain validation for themselves or to inflict pain or financial hardship on the other party who is trying to leave.

The referring lawyer continues to have a role during mediation. Many clients return to their lawyers between mediation sessions in order to obtain additional information regarding the law, alternatives for solving various matters considered in mediation, and referrals to experts needed to validate agreements made in mediation. Consultation with the referring lawyer can be supportive of the work in mediation. The lawyer can help the client develop proposals and compare such proposals with the results likely to be achieved by going to court. The lawyer must be sensitive to the fact that clients may be making choices which reflect their own sense of fairness and should be willing to validate those choices so long as they fall within reasonable limits.

At the conclusion of the mediation, most mediators prepare a Memorandum of Understanding which reflects not only the final result reached by the clients on each issue, but also the negotiations and "trade offs." The Memorandum is usually accompanied by all of the documents that the clients relied upon in the mediation process, including tax analyses, appraisal reports, and other formal or informal evaluations when appropriate.

Another role of the attorney in the mediation process is that of reviewing the Memorandum of Understanding and preparing a final, legally binding document which will be a part of the Final Judgment of Divorce. The reviewing lawyer should be sensitive to the fact that the clients have reached an agreement that meets not only their sense of needs, but their moral and ethical values and their sense of responsibility to each other and their children. The lawyer must, nevertheless, probe the underpinnings of the agreement to be certain that nothing has been overlooked, that all factors influencing the result have been considered—in short, that the result is comprehensive.

To the extent that the reviewing lawyer finds that the Memorandum of Understanding is in some way incomplete or requires additional work, it is appropriate for the lawyer to refer the clients back for mediation in order to conclude their work.

Some lawyers find great difficulty in addressing a mediation agreement because they have not conducted what they consider to be full and complete discovery as they might in litigation. It is curious that participating in review of a Memorandum of Understanding and the final preparation of an agreement stresses many lawyers, since business lawyers have been providing a similar function for many years. For example, securities and tax lawyers give counsel and prepare investment letters or other opinions in security offerings. They have traditionally written opinions based upon facts outlined by the client and have accepted those facts as true and have not allowed that to impede their work. Similarly, lawyers involved in the review process of the mediation agreement can provide the client with a letter indicating that the review process they have conducted and the final legal document they have prepared is based upon facts outlined by the client, and that the client has not required that the lawyer look behind those facts in order to arrive at the final agreement as prepared.

ROLE OF MENTAL HEALTH
PROFESSIONALS IN THE MEDIATION PROCESS

Mental health professionals who become mediators must be aware of issues and dilemmas which arise in relation to their own training and experience. More specifically, it is important for them to understand the distinctions between mediation and psychotherapy or counseling, and to be aware that in providing competent mediation services, they may be vulnerable to attorneys' claims that they are engaging in the unauthorized practice of law.

DISTINGUISHING MEDIATION FROM PSYCHOTHERAPY

The mediation process is viewed by many mediators as distinct from counseling or psychotherapy (Kelly, 1983). Whereas clients seeking therapy or counseling do so for relief of internal distress, behavioral or relationship change, the explicit goal of clients in mediation is to negotiate a settlement of the issues mutually identified as in dispute. If a negotiated settlement and written agreement is not obtainable within a brief period of time, the mediator's responsibility is to terminate the mediation. By concretely focusing upon divorce-related matters, the mediator *creates a setting* for personal and relationship change, and thus a successfully completed mediation can be highly therapeutic for one or both clients. This beneficial result can be seen in reduced tension, depression, and hostility; renewed self-confidence; and improved communications. But clients can successfully reach agreement in mediation *without* any psychological change, be totally satisfied with the result, and have no desire to work on altering either their own behavior or that of their spouse. In this case, the mediator with a therapeutic background needs to resist the temptation to insist that therapeutic work take place.

In mediation, the mediator is not concerned *per se* with the client's symptomatic or neurotic behavior, and does not seek to change long-standing personality problems. Unlike the counselor-therapist, the mediator's primary responsibility is *not* the client's mental health. The mediator's conflict management skills and focus on the tasks necessary for reaching agreement serve to *contain*, to a considerable degree, the exploration and expression of emotional reactions, whereas in psychotherapy the therapist's goal is to *expand* and build upon such exploration (Kelly, 1983).

As noted earlier, feelings in relation to the failed marriage are often intense in divorce mediations, but they are not the *major* focus of the mediation. To the extent their expression facilitates progress toward reaching agreement, mediators see that acknowledging, labeling, and allowing emotional reactions to emerge is an important part of the process. The task of the mediator with therapeutic training is to make careful judgment about how much emotional discharge is actually necessary for each couple's mediation. Just as the lawyer may lapse into authoritarian advice giving without sufficient training and experience in mediation, so too the therapist may face the possibility of moving into a therapeutic mode when the emotional content is inviting. Mediators with therapy experience need to be especially sensitive to the possibility that exploration of the marital relationship and emotional issues can dominate and obscure the purposes of the mediation. They may need to remind themselves throughout that clients contract for issue-focused dispute resolution services when they come to mediation. If there is an expressed or observed need for psychotherapy, the mediator's obligation to both clients is to make a referral to another psychotherapist outside the mediation process.

THE MENTAL HEALTH PROFESSIONAL AS MEDIATOR

To the extent that mental health professionals mediate disputes which are generally within the realm of their usual professional sphere, they are least vulnerable to scrutiny from professionals in other fields. Counselors or therapists who mediate custody or visitation disputes are generally familiar with the psychology of the divorce experience, have training and experience in those developmental issues relevant to post-divorce custody and visitation decision making, and generally obtain specific training in conflict management and negotiation or bargaining skills which enables them to mediate rather than provide therapy. The major issue, it would seem, for mental health professionals is to experience and understand the distinction between mediation and counseling so that they can be explicit and clear in their contracting and role with clients.

It is when mental health professionals broaden their scope and offer comprehensive mediation which includes the complex issues of asset identification and valuation, property distribution, support, and the associated tax consequences, as well as parent-child issues that there are potential hazards. In offering to mediate *legally* based, factual issues, the nonlawyer mediator promises expertise and experience in these areas, and to the extent such expertise does not exist, the mediator is extremely vulnerable to malpractice claims.

Mediated divorce settlements usually have a profound impact on each participant's future financial well-being and thus deserve and require the most competent attention possible. Therefore, cross-disciplinary mediators must add to their original training and experience course work in family law, taxation, and property distribution, and gain whatever business and financial acumen is necessary to understand real estate transactions, partnership and corporate issues, and pension structures (Haynes, 1982). This process of actively integrating the most relevant aspects of law and psychology may take 1 to 2 years of training and experience in order to enable the nonlawyer mediator to offer high quality services.

Further, as discussed earlier, cross-disciplinary mediators who are not lawyers face the potential charge that in mediating financial and property issues (which are generally the domain of lawyers) they are giving legal advice and thereby engaging in the unauthorized practice of law (Silberman, 1982). Mediators from the disciplines of law and mental health recognize three areas in which the unauthorized practice of law may occur: (a) in the drafting of a legally binding agreement which is intended to be the final legal result; (b) in misrepresenting to the public that the mediator is providing legal services; and (c) in giving legal advice. It is this third area which creates the greatest concern for lawyers and nonlawyer mediators alike. Most mediators make the distinction between *sharing* information to help clients make decisions (e.g., giving clients information about taxes, support needs, visitation and custody, and options for dividing property) and *advising* people what to do. Nonlawyer mediators often pointedly refer their clients back to their attorneys whenever legal advice is needed or sought. Further, they refrain from placing values on assets, suggesting what result clients might obtain in court, and making decisions for their clients or telling them what is best for them.

An increasing number of professionals, recognizing the complexities as well as the benefits of cross-disciplinary mediations, are now entering the mediation field with dual degrees and licensure in law and a mental health profession.

ETHICAL CONSIDERATIONS FOR MEDIATORS

Although each of the professional disciplines of individuals who would mediate has its own ethical standards, the issues raised in the mediation process begin to demand evaluation of those standards to see if they are applicable to mediation. The issue of ethical standards for mediators is being addressed by a committee of the Academy of Family Mediators, the American Bar Association Family Law Section, the Association of Family and Conciliation Courts, and other national organizations with an interest in the developing field of mediation (Bishop, 1984; Milne, 1984). What is presented here is a brief survey of much of the work in progress combined with some additional thoughts of the authors.

TERMINATION OF MEDIATION

The mediator must be constantly aware of the parties' approach to mediation and their attitudes within the process in order to determine whether the process has the potential for concluding in an agreement. When the mediator determines that the process is no longer functioning for one or both clients, it is incumbent upon the mediator to explore with the parties the validity of that conclusion. If the conclusion is validated, then the mediation must be terminated.

While there is not yet agreement regarding the circumstances under which mediation should be terminated, the following are some instances where termination of mediation should be given serious consideration:

1. If it becomes apparent that one or both of the parties are not committed to the process but have adopted a "wait and see" attitude;
2. If the efforts of the mediator to empower the weaker party in the mediation process have been unsuccessful and significant imbalance remains in the negotiation phase;
3. If the overwhelming guilt felt by one of the parties results in willingness to reach an agreement which is unfair to himself or herself;
4. If educational, mental, or psychological limitations prevent the client from assimilating the information being developed in the process;
5. If it is determined that a party is not acting in good faith, particularly as evidenced by nonnegotiable demands or proposals that totally ignore the needs of the other party;
6. If the parties have reached a partial or overall agreement which offends basic standards of fairness; and
7. If a client persists in a refusal to disclose relevant information.

SEPARATE SESSIONS

In an extension of the labor mediation model, some divorce mediators utilize separate sessions with each client. There is concern that separate sessions may be inappropriate because they interfere with the trust a mediator attempts to develop with both parties, particularly if the mediator takes the position that anything said in the private session will remain confidential. If, on the other hand, the content of the private session is brought back into the conjoint mediation session, much of that concern may be alleviated. Some mediators believe that they cannot avoid the inherent concern of the excluded party that some alliance was developed between the mediator and the other party during the private session.

MEDIATOR DISCLOSURE TO OTHERS

It may be helpful for the mediator to discuss the

content of the process with third parties in order to assist the clients in either clarifying or obtaining information. Discussion with the clients' lawyers, either during the process or thereafter when they are reviewing the Memorandum of Understanding, is the most common need. If such discussions take place, there needs to be a written waiver of confidentiality, in general or with respect to a particular issue, so that the mediator may freely discuss the subject area with the attorney. In such circumstances, the disclosure should be made in writing with copies to the parties so that there is no misunderstanding as to its scope.

OTHER RELATIONSHIPS WITH THE PARTIES

The development of a relationship of trust and confidence between the parties and the mediator is critical, and thus the mediator should not have previously served either party in a legal or counseling capacity. Many believe that after mediation is successfully completed, or ends prior to completion, the lawyer-mediator should not further represent either or both of the clients, should not proceed to conclude an uncontested dissolution, and should not prepare the final settlement agreement or any other document implementing the content of the mediation (Bishop, 1984). The therapist and mental health professional would be similarly constrained by ethical considerations from providing any further services to one of the mediation clients.

There is considerable variation in the functioning of both the private and public mediator when a custody or visitation dispute must be resolved. In the event a child needs to be evaluated in the midst of such dispute, some mediators switch roles and conduct the evaluation, then return to the couple as a mediator and convey the results of the evaluation. It is the view of the authors that such a change in role compromises the mediator's effectiveness and impartiality. Thus, it may be preferable that such child evaluation be performed by a party other than a mediator in order to preserve the ability to mediate whatever result is communicated to the parties.

GENERAL CONSIDERATIONS

As discussed earlier, it is incumbent upon the mediator during the contracting process to clearly disclose to the clients what they can and cannot expect from mediation, and to delineate their respective responsibilities in the process so that the clients can make the determination that they are willing and capable of proceeding.

The mediator cannot remain passive during the information-gathering phase of the process, but has the responsibility, when clients are not considering vital aspects of the mediation, to raise legal, business, and financial issues not raised by the clients.

Although the mediator should be neutral and impartial, it is not uncommon for mediators to have biases in a particular area. Therefore, such predispositions should be disclosed to the parties within the mediation process, so that it is clear that a recommendation or proposal being made by the mediator emanates from such bias. For example, the parties may wish to have an unstructured visitation schedule leaving reasonable visitation to be worked out in the future. If the mediator believes that such unstructured agreements do not work well and that a schedule is more appropriate, that recommendation should be made with the disclosure that it is the mediator's preference, but that the clients are free to continue, if they wish, with their arrangement for reasonable visitation.

CERTIFICATION

There is an ongoing debate regarding certification, accreditation, and standards of practice for mediators (Bishop, 1984). No clear direction has been established at this time with regard to such certification or licensing. It has been argued by some that certain minimal knowledge, both of the psychological and legal issues, is required in order to effectively mediate and that those minimum requirements should be the basis of certification (see Milne, 1984). Therefore, a field of mediator training has evolved which attempts to provide mediators with that knowledge.

It will be several years before the issues of ethical standards and certification for mediators are settled. Most mediators currently express the need to err on the side of being scrupulously ethical and extremely knowledgeable in order to avoid the possibility of mediation becoming fraught with malpractice claims.

Joan B. Kelly, Ph.D., a clinical psychologist, is Director of the Northern California Mediation Center and was formerly Co-Director of the California Children of Divorce Project. Dr. Kelly has written extensively in the area of divorce and is co-author of *Surviving the Breakup: How Children and Parents Cope with Divorce.*

Carl Zlatchin, Ph.D., a clinical psychologist, is Associate Director of the Northern California Mediation Center and an Assistant Clinical Professor of Psychiatry at the University of California at San Francisco Medical Center. Dr. Zlatchin is the former Director of Community Crisis Services at Mt. Zion Hospital and Medical Center and is currently in private practice as a psychologist.

Joel Shawn, J.D., an attorney, is Associate Director of the Northern California Mediation Center and maintains a private law practice in San Francisco. Mr. Shawn, a graduate of the Hastings College of Law of the University of California, chairs the Custody and Visitation Committee of the California State Bar's Family Law Section and is an arbitrator with the American Arbitration Association.

RESOURCES

Ahrons, C. (1980). Redefining the divorced family: A conceptual framework for postdivorce family system reorganization. *Social Work, 25*, 437-441.

American Bar Association. (1980). *Model Code of Professional Responsibility.* Chicago: National Center for Professional Responsibility.

Bahr, S. (1981a). An evaluation of court mediation: A comparison in divorce cases with children. *Journal of Family Issues, 2*, 39-60.

Bahr, S. (1981b). Mediation is the answer: Why couples are so positive about this route to divorce. *Family Advocate, 3*, 32-35.

Bishop, T. (1984). Mediation standards: An ethical safety net. *Mediation Quarterly, 4*, 5-18.

Black, M., & Joffee, W. (1978). A lawyer/therapist team approach to divorce. *Conciliation Courts Review, 16*(1), 1-15.

Brown, D. (1982). Divorce and family mediation: History, review, future considerations. *Conciliation Courts Review, 20*(2), 1-44.

Burger, W. (1982, January). Address by the Chief Justice. Presented at the mid-year meeting of the American Bar Association, Chicago, IL.

Coogler, O. J. (1978). *Structured Mediation in Divorce Settlement: A Handbook for Marital Mediators.* Lexington, MA: Heath.

Davis, H. (1977). Let's get divorced out of the courts. *Florida Bar Journal, 51*, 501-504.

Elkin, M. (1962). Short-contact counseling in a conciliation court. *Social Casework, 18*, 184-190.

Elkin, M. (1977). Post-divorce counseling in a conciliation court. *Journal of Divorce, 1*, 55-65.

Erickson, S. (1984). A practicing mediator answers the questions most asked about divorce mediation. *Mediation Quarterly, 3*, 99-108.

Feldman, S. (1977). A statutory proposal to remove divorce from the courtroom. *Maine Law Review, 29*, 25-46.

Folberg, J. (1983). A mediation overview: History and dimensions of practice. *Mediation Quarterly, 1*, 3-14.

Folberg, J., & Taylor, A. (1984). *A Comprehensive Guide to Conflict Resolution.* San Francisco: Jossey-Bass.

Gardner, R. (1977). *The Parents Book about Divorce.* New York: Doubleday.

Gold, L. (1982). The psychological context of the interdisciplinary co-mediator team model in marital dissolution. *Conciliation Courts Review, 20,* 45-53.

Groner, E. (1982). Social workers as mediators in child custody disputes. *Family Law Reporter, 8,* 4059-4063.

Haynes, J. (1981). *Divorce Mediation.* New York: Springer Publishing.

Haynes, J. (1982). A conceptual model of the process of family mediation: Implications for training. *American Journal of Family Therapy, 10,* 5-16.

Haynes, J. (1983). The process of negotiations. *Mediation Quarterly, 1,* 75-92.

Hess, R., & Camera, K. (1979). Post-divorce family relationships as mediating factors in the consequences of divorce for children. *Journal of Social Issues, 35,* 79-96.

Hetherington, E. M. (1979). Divorce: A child's perspective. *American Psychologist, 34,* 851-858.

Kelly, J. (1982). Divorce: The adult experience. In B. Wolman & G. Stricker (Eds.), *Handbook of Developmental Psychology* (pp. 734-739). Englewood Cliffs, NJ: Prentice Hall.

Kelly, J. (1983). Mediation and psychotherapy: Distinguishing the differences. *Mediation Quarterly, 1,* 33-44.

Kelly, J. (1984, April). *Mediating Parent-Child Issues in Divorce: Research and Clinical Observations.* Paper presented at the meeting of the American Orthopsychiatric Association, Toronto, Canada.

King, D. (1979). Child custody—A legal problem? *California State Bar Journal, 54,* 157-158.

Klemm v. Superior Court, 142 Cal. Rep. 509, 75 Cal. App. 3d 893 (1977).

Milne, A. (1983). Divorce mediation: The state of the art. *Mediation Quarterly, 1,* 15-32.

Milne, A. (1984). The development of parameters of practice for divorce mediation. *Mediation Quarterly, 4,* 49-60.

Mnookin, R., & Kornhauser, L. (1979). Bargaining in the shadow of the law. *Yale Law Journal, 88*, 950-995.

National Center for Health Statistics. Provisional 1982 data. (1983, March 16). *San Francisco Chronicle*, p. 16.

Parker, A. (1981). Type of divorce process linked with custody preferences. *Marriage & Divorce Today, 6*, 2.

Pearson, J. (1982). Child custody: Why not let the parents decide? *Judges Journal, 4*, 4-12.

Pearson, J., Ring, M., & Milne, A. (1983). A portrait of divorce mediation services in the public and private sector. *Conciliation Courts Review, 21*(1), 1-24.

Pearson, J., & Thoennes, N. (1982). The benefits outweigh the costs. *Family Advocate, 4*, 26-32.

Pearson, J., & Thoennes, N. (1984). A preliminary portrait of client reactions to three court mediation programs. *Mediation Quarterly, 3*, 21-40.

Pickrell, R., & Bendheim, A. (1979). Family dispute resolution—A new service for lawyers and their clients. *Arizona Bar Journal, 15*, 33-35.

Samuels, M., & Shawn, J. (1983). The role of the lawyer outside of the mediation process. *Mediation Quarterly, 1*, 13-20.

Saposnek, D. (1983a). *Mediating Child Custody Disputes.* San Francisco: Jossey-Bass.

Saposnek, D. (1983b). Strategies in child custody mediation: A family systems approach. *Mediation Quarterly, 2*, 29-54.

Silberman, L. (1982). Professional responsibility problems of divorce mediation. *Family Law Quarterly, 16*, 107-145.

Simrin v. Simrin, 233 Cal. App. 2d 90 (1965).

Sprenkle, D., & Storm, D. (1983). Divorce therapy outcome research: A substantive and methodological review. *Journal of Marital & Family Therapy, 9*, 239-258.

Ury, W., & Fisher, R. (1981). *Getting to Yes.* New York: Basic Books.

Vroom, P., Fassett, D., & Rowan, A. (1982). Winning through mediation: Divorce without losers. *The Futurist, 16*, 23-34.

Waldron, J., Roth, C., Fair, P., Mann, E., & McDermott, J. (1984). A therapeutic mediation model for child custody dispute resolution. *Mediation Quarterly, 3,* 5-20.

Wallerstein, J., & Kelly, J. (1980). *Surviving the Breakup: How Children and Parents Cope with Divorce.* New York: Basic Books.

Weiss, R. (1975). *Marital Separation.* New York: Basic Books.

Winks, P. (1980-1981). Divorce mediation: A nonadversary procedure for the no-fault divorce. *Journal of Family Law, 19,* 615-653.

Wiseman, J., & Fiske, J. (1980). Lawyer-therapist team as mediator in a marital crisis. *Social Work, 25,* 442-445.

EVALUATION AND MEDIATION IN CHILD CUSTODY DISPUTES

Andrew P. Musetto

Child custody, in one sense, refers to the control of and right to make decisions about a child (Committee on the Family of the Group for the Advancement of Psychiatry, 1980). In most cases it means that one parent, the custodial parent, is in charge and the other, the noncustodial parent, has visitation. Child custody, in another sense, refers not only to parental rights but also to parental responsibilities. Custody then means the accountability of parents for meeting children's needs, being available to children emotionally as well as physically, and raising them to maturity. Thus, the concept of custody is defined not only by rights and privileges, but also by responsibilities and obligations. This was, however, not always the case. Until modern times children were regarded as the property of their parents and laws demanded of them few reciprocal responsibilities to their children.

Decision making regarding child custody evolves with the times and is influenced by the cultural trends and social values of the day. The social sciences could be counted among the current influences. Laws, which follow practice, usually change at a slower rate.

Those involved in child custody decisions, such as mental health professionals who advise families and courts, are called upon to apply their expertise in helping to shape judicious, humane decisions. If they are to succeed in that task, they must examine their assumptions, share their experience, and be open to learning from each other. With that thought in mind, my purpose in this chapter is to suggest ways that mental health professionals can contribute positively to the practice of resolving child custody disputes. The chapter begins with an examination of some of the more common issues encountered in child custody disputes and then explores a theoretical framework helpful in understanding and assessing these issues. The chapter then goes on to posit guidelines for child custody decision makers and to suggest a viable role for mental health professionals in the custody decision making process.

CHILD CUSTODY TODAY

Deciding child custody is inherently difficult. Though divorce does not necessarily damage children, it does put them at high risk. Children of divorce are frequently faced with conflicts of loyalty, especially when—as is often the case—they are implicated in their parents' ongoing hostility toward each other. Furthermore, such children are often confronted with a disruption or loss of their relationship with one of their parents (Scheiner, Musetto, & Cordier, 1982). One recent longitudinal study found that the psychological significance of both parents survives divorce and that depression in children of divorce is associated with "disrupted or diminished parenting by one or both parents" (Wallerstein & Kelly, 1980, p. 309). Not only does custody impose difficulties upon children, but it also brings hardships to parents as well. Financial pressures, the loss of a significant relationship, grief, anger, pressures to re-enter the social world, the demands of single or weekend parenting, feelings of failure or guilt, an increased sense of isolation, the interference of family, and the opinion of peers, all place demands on divorced parents. And some of these demands conflict. The aftermath of divorce leaves many parents with little rationality or energy to deal constructively with child custody issues. As parents and children have and assert conflicting needs and rights, child custody stands as an ongoing dilemma (Musetto, 1982b).

Decision makers have their own difficulties. Judges face a backlog of cases with little time or information; decisions often rest upon cultural and personal prejudices. Vague guidelines prompt uncertain choices. Faced with hidden emotional agendas of their clients, attorneys are baffled by individuals who seem intent upon beating each other rather than settling issues. Constricted by role expectations of being advocates and winning a case, and by an adversary system that fosters competition and dishonesty, attorneys have little recourse (and sometimes little motivation) but to press their client's interests at the expense of the other party and to the detriment of the children. The entire procedure often resembles emotional warfare in which each party fights for personal gain while waving the banner of parental concern.

Decision making is not only intrinsically difficult, but it has also become extremely complex. Previous rules of thumb, for example, that a mother is the preferred custodial parent (Maternal Presumption) especially in cases of very young children (Tender Years Doctrine), are being challenged and have become unreliable (Derdeyn, 1976). Today more fathers compete for custody. And while previously they had to demonstrate a mother's incompetence, they now assert, at least in theory, an equal claim to custody. The uncertainty of current social values as to what constitutes viable caretaking, healthy relationships, appropriate parent-child interaction, reasonable expectations regarding the family, and acceptable alternative life styles, makes any easy solution to the complex issue of custody virtually unattainable.

Today many different questions confront decision makers. Is a mother naturally the better choice? Should grandparents have a legal claim to visitation or custody? What about joint custody? Should siblings be separated? What specifically are a child's best interests, especially in a mobile society where a geographical distance often separates family members? How important are a child's interests? What about alternative life styles; the mental health of either parent; their personal morality and conduct? What constitutes parental fitness and capacity? Should someone other than a biological parent be considered for custody? What is the effect of stepparents and stepsiblings? The list is as long as the answers are hard to ascertain.

The complexity of child custody decision making, finally, is matched by its urgency. Divorce is prevalent and rising, with many more children involved. Numbers alone demand careful, humane choices, not prejudicial, uncritical, self-seeking decisions.

RELATIONAL APPROACH

The field of mental health, which is becoming more intimately involved with contested custody, has been undergoing a shift in emphasis and theoretical perspective. No longer are individual dynamics alone on center stage. Now, relational or contextual theories (sometimes called systems theories), which include but go beyond intrapsychic variables, have captured the attention of researchers and clinicians. The relational approach (Beavers, 1977; Boszormenyi-Nagy & Spark, 1973; Bowen, 1978; Minuchin, 1974; Minuchin & Fishman, 1981) attempts to explain human behavior in terms of the interdependence common to all people, especially as found in families.

Self-identify does not arise out of a vacuum. Individuals, rather, acquire an identity through satisfying, meaningful, and well-defined interaction with significant others, especially their families. As mediators of cultural values, families shape and regulate individual behavior and give form and substance to the important life choices that make up individual identity. Bound by ties of loyalty, implicit and explicit rules, and patterned ways of behaving, the family, while including individual variation and uniqueness, is not simply an aggregate of individuals but exists as a distinct entity. And in the context of family relationships, individuals either grow to maturity or are pressed into twisted lives and distorted identities.

The relational approach concerns itself with two broad areas: the structure and quality of family relationships. Structure or "the invisible set of functional demands that organizes the ways in which family members interact" (Minuchin, 1974, p. 51) refers to (a) the principles which govern family members' participation in various tasks and decisions (e.g., the notion that parents not children must decide custody); (b) how close or how distant family members are allowed to be; (c) how power is divided and expressed; (d) how much and what kind of affection is permitted; and (e) how much autonomy and individuality is allowed.

The quality of relationships, what Boszormenyi-Nagy and Spark (1973) call "relational ethics," refers to whether family members are treated fairly or exploited by each other, whether one member is favored at the expense of another. How members treat each other leads to a ledger of merit—whether a person feels emotionally entitled or indebted, owed or owing. In the extreme, the former go through life with a proverbial chip on the shoulder, while the latter become martyrs, doing for others while neglecting themselves.

Relational ethics, a balance between what individuals have received and what they have given in return, and trust, the cornerstone of human development, go hand in hand. Exploited individuals do not invest much trust in human relationships and expect relationships to result in frustration. Besides trust, the relational approach also emphasizes how children have a natural, unbreakable tie with their parents—a bond of loyalty that survives a legal divorce, geographical distance, or attempts by one parent to subvert it.

Just as the relational dimension of human living has advanced the field of mental health, it also offers much hope of aiding families and decision makers out of the morass of contested custody. Decision makers, first and foremost, need to recognize and honor the emotional universe to which children belong and through which they forge their identities. Recognition must be given not only to one psychological parent but to a large network of significant others, all of whom are potential sources for identification, support, and trust-building. If either parent or any part of the network is denigrated, the child suffers, for that parent or that network is an essential part of a child's self-concept and identity.

Sometimes it is the family even more than decision makers which fails to appreciate the child's relational and emotional network. It is a task of each parent to endorse a child's positive loyalty to the entire network, to work actively to keep the network available to the child, and to demonstrate a willingness to deal with the network and the other parent as mutual collaborators trying to minimize harm to the child and protect the child's interests.

Children, then, need continuity; not the continuity of just one parent at the expense of the other, but the continuity of both parents and the entire emotional network. It is better for children to have a distorted relationship with a parent than no relationship at all; so committed are children to maintaining continuity with both parents that if thwarted in the present they will tend to recreate the same type of relationship in the future, with their spouses or their own children (Cotroneo, Krasner, & Boszormenyi-Nagy, 1981). The unfinished business of the past is acted out in present and future relationships. In a word, parents are irreplaceable and families invaluable.

Custody decision makers must take into account the interdependence intrinsic to families; despite divorce, children and their parents are forever related through blood and bound by loyalties. Custody decisions which ignore this interdependence are likely to be viewed by the child as unfair and exploitative and to leave the child cynical about life and distrustful of relationships.

CHILD CUSTODY CONFLICTS

Between 1975 and 1982, as a staff member of a community mental health center, I did custody mediation and evaluations for the local courts. Since 1982 I have been doing this work in private practice. My experience has taught me that custody conflicts are not solely the by-products of the divorcing process; they are continuations of unresolved marital and family problems. Parents who fought to control each other while married fight to control each other through custody. Custody conflicts are also exacerbated by adversary legal proceedings, which pit one parent against the other and by the stress of a family breakup, which makes great demands on all family members. Contested custody arises when parents put personal gain ahead of their children, or when parents, overwhelmed by divorce and family disruption, are so preoccupied with their own problems as to neglect their children.

Divorce is a transition in the life of a family. Throughout its history a family faces many transitions or choice points. While all are stressful, some transitions are natural and expected (e.g., the birth of children, marriage, the eventual death of a family member, a member leaving home, and the normal developmental epochs that mark individual functioning). Others, such as divorce, are unexpected and people have no adequate way to prepare for them; no rite of passage is provided by society. Divorce is similar to but not the same as death, which is final and does not encourage in family members fantasies of reconciliation. Divorce is a transition of such magnitude as to qualify as a crisis. It represents itself as part challenge and part catastrophe, and it demands considerable adjustment.

Contested custody indicates that parents have failed to finish the transition of divorce; their adjustment is incomplete. The lack of a resolution of custody issues means a lack of emotional resolution of marital issues, for parenting is one of the key issues that must be negotiated by any divorcing couple with children. Contested custody also signifies that the quality of family relationships, the accountability of family members to each other, has turned into an exploitative, trust-reducing emotional warfare, which blocks the adjustment of each member. Parents, in short, are often fighting more *against* each other than *for* their children.

The practical problems of divorce also militate against adjustment. Moving may mean new friends, neighborhoods, and schools. Reduction of income curtails leisure activities and perhaps cuts into necessities. Working parents are more tired and less available parents. Single parents are more taxed parents, with less leisure time and less relief from the daily cares of child rearing. Parents' new love relationships confront children with new adults and possibly new children in their lives, often endangering their already strained loyalty to the absent parent or siblings.

Emotional tasks, no less than practical concerns, impinge on parents and children alike. As an emotional process, divorce signals the death of a marriage, the need for mourning, the acceptance of at least partial responsibility for its breakup, and a period of aloneness and uncertainty as a new life style is being developed. For children, divorce means a changed, usually reduced if not totally abrogated relationship with one parent and possibly siblings. Anger, sadness, grief, feelings of abandonment, guilt, and lowered self-esteem follow as by-products and must be dealt with.

PARENTS SEEKING CUSTODY

Besides genuine parental concern, parents press for custody for a variety of reasons, many self-serving, leaving their children victims of neglect or inappropriate involvement in parental battles (Musetto, 1982a). Parental desire for revenge turns children into weapons: What better way to hurt parents than by depriving them of their children? Blame and self-vindication make children the judges and jury of marital fault. When one or both parents secretly wishes to hold onto the marital relationship, children become the spies or go-betweens who pass information back and forth between parents. Anxiety about uncertain futures or about re-entering the social world inclines parents to use their children as rescuers, who by their symptoms direct attention away from a parent's problem or attempt to re-engage an estranged spouse. Dependency on children places them in parental roles, while parents in effect become the children in the family. Inadequate self-esteem converts children into trophies, supposed signs of parental competence. Wanting to control the other party leads parents to use custody and their children as pawns, and greed relegates to children the role of bargaining chips in the divorce settlement, as if they were property to bargain with or about. Lastly, guilt feelings pressure some parents to sue for custody to reassure and exonerate themselves.

PRINCIPLES FOR
MAKING CUSTODY DECISIONS

Based on the above observations, the following conclusions are presented (see also Musetto, 1981).

1. Children belong to and develop their identities primarily through a relational and emotional network, which includes parents and siblings, grandparents, and extended family members. Continuity with this entire network is in a child's best interests.

2. Treating either parent (or any part of the network) as unimportant or peripheral or denigrating either parent violates a child's natural loyalties and is harmful.

3. Because of children's natural loyalty to their parents and extended families, contested custody exploits children when it places them in the middle of parental conflict or pushes them to take sides between their parents or extended family members.

4. The family is part of the problem and therefore must be part of the resolution. Families have a right and responsibility to come together to resolve a custody dispute. Contested custody should be mediated and decided by the parents as the first priority, and only if this fails should a court decide custody.

5. Two primary dangers threaten children on account of contested custody: a loyalty conflict in which children are involved in the ongoing hostilities of their parents, and the loss or major disruption of a child's relationship with one or both parents. Both should be guarded against.

6. In deciding custody the justice and merits of each member's position, especially the children's, must be honored. Injuring children's sense of justice reduces their trust in themselves and others and their commitment to society. Such injury

eventually threatens society with individuals who lack sufficient regard for the rights of others.

7. Contested custody represents a continuation of unresolved marital and family problems, exacerbated by adversary legal proceedings and the demands placed on family members by divorce and its aftermath.

8. Parents contest custody for a mixture of motives: self-interest, parental concern, and the overwhelming stresses of divorce which turn their attention away from parental accountability.

9. The best interest of the children (and the family), although difficult to concretize, is the ultimate criterion for deciding custody. Parental preference or self-interest, often disguised by a pretense of parental concern, should not be the deciding factor.

10. Co-parenting or joint custody (shared responsibilities but not necessarily shared living arrangements) preserves continuity, protects loyalty ties, and minimizes inappropriate involvement of children in parental hostility. Such arrangements stand as the ideal for deciding custody, but parents must be able to cooperate enough to carry them out. Adversary legal proceedings or emotional warfare between parents injures children.

11. Decision makers should focus on continuity (with the child's emotional universe), co-parenting, negotiation, and keeping both parents involved, more than unfitness or which parent is more capable. Parental accountability, not parental condemnation, is the goal. Even when it is clear that one parent has more parental capacity, custody should be mediated to preserve continuity and to encourage the accountability and involvement of both parents. Fitness becomes important when parents have tried but failed to negotiate and a court must decide custody.

12. The best custodial parent promotes a child's positive loyalty to the other parent and relational network and is willing to work with the other parent for the child's benefit.

THE ROLE OF A MENTAL
HEALTH PROFESSIONAL IN
CUSTODY MEDIATION AND EVALUATION

There are three basic approaches used by mental health professionals regarding custody contests: the advocate, the impartial, and the mediator.

ADVOCATE

An advocate, except in exceptional cases where the clinician's involvement is clearly to protect the immediate well-being of a child, is a "hired gun." An advocate, hired by one parent or attorney, works on the premise that you can be paid by one party and still be impartial. Or an advocate believes that an evaluation can be made by seeing only one parent (or seeing the other parent only briefly), or by seeing both parents separately. At best, an advocate is misinformed: He or she overestimates his or her ability to maintain objectivity and/or underestimates the family's ability to distort the issues. At worst, an advocate is driven by greed, despite protestations of impartiality and a veneer of concern.

IMPARTIAL

Elsewhere (Musetto, 1982b), I have contrasted an impartial (evaluator of competence) with a mediator (facilitator of change). Gardner (1982) presents the impartial role at its best. The impartial, except in rare cases of unambiguous neglect when he or she will be an advocate, works for the "best interests of the family." The impartial tries to be exactly that, an *impartial* evaluator who collects as much information as possible and necessary regarding parental capacity in order to make a recommendation for custody.

While Gardner will urge the family itself to settle custody, the impartial's chief goal is to determine the more capable parent. The role is diagnostic and the emphasis on competence and fitness. As described by Gardner, the impartial tries to interview all pertinent family members and others (e.g., housekeepers) who may have relevant information. The impartial advises the parents that the process is one of evaluation not therapy; that confidential information may be revealed to the other parent if necessary to determine parental capacity; that information will be requested from any relevant source; that, in order to insure impartiality, the evaluator's fee will be collected before the evaluation and placed in escrow; and that once the final recommendation is discussed with parents, the impartial will have no further contact with them until he or she has testified in court. A signed agreement detailing the ground rules of the evaluation is required from both parents.

MEDIATOR

The mediator is, most importantly, a skilled therapist who intervenes in the family system in order to facilitate sufficient change so that the family can resolve custody. Involved but impartial, the mediator follows the ideal presented by Cotroneo et al. (1981)—"a multilateral advocate," who articulates and advocates the relative merits of each family member's position and does not favor one member at the expense of another. Not just an impartial expert who collects information, evaluates it, and recommends, a mediator *intervenes* to help the family negotiate. Though not a judge, a mediator explores the justice of each member's point of view, especially that of the children. Though not a faultfinder, the mediator helps parents admit mistakes and calls them to accountability to their children.

The basis for this mediator role comes from several sources, including Boszormenyi-Nagy and Spark (1973), Cotroneo et al. (1981), Bowen (1978), Erickson and Rossi (1979), Minuchin (1974), and Beavers (1977). By listening to and trying to understand each family member and by inviting other members to understand each other, by establishing rapport, by expressing an expectation of success, by joining and pacing the family, by being fair to all, by preventing interruptions when one member speaks, by keeping the sessions from deteriorating into shouting matches, the mediator sets an ambience of dialogue. Next, the mediator attempts to remove the barriers to resolution of the custody conflict—dysfunctional family transactions such as blaming, accusing, discounting, mindreading, speaking for one another, giving mixed or incongruous messages, triangulating the children or courts or attorney or mediator, and parental maneuvers to control each other. The mediator blocks the parents' usual response to each other and challenges rigid patterns that have solidified through the divorce and adversary process. As the mediator looks for the positive in the negative—parental love in the miasma of their fighting, a small point of agreement hidden by their mutual contempt—he or she practices reframing. As the mediator rules out certain issues such as marital fault or who did what for the children, he or she uses redefining and urges cooperation. As the mediator affirms parental resources in spite of intractable marital problems, he or she confirms the inherent potential of each party to work out a compromise. The mediator continually implies that a resolution is possible despite the ongoing conflict, if only the parents will set aside their conscious, learned, cognitive limitations and tap into their own creativity. As the mediator removes the children from parental transactions of hostility, he or she circumscribes parental boundaries and calls parents to accountability. The mediator stands for cooperation, negotiation, and mutual respect and against the pervasive human tendency to blame another and exonerate oneself when things go wrong, to deny what is painful or awkward, to hide one's bitterness and self-centeredness under a mask of loving concern.

COMPARISON OF IMPARTIAL AND MEDIATOR MODELS

The impartial and mediator models, the evaluator and facilitator roles, have different purposes, based on different assumptions, and operate in different ways. Though each has advantages and drawbacks, it should be clear that I favor the mediator model.

The impartial collects as much "objective" information as possible in order to evaluate and recommend. The mediator gathers the family together in order to help them negotiate a resolution. The impartial tries to be just that—impartial in all dealings with the family and courts;

without strict impartiality (no favoritism, prejudgment, or special treatment) the evaluator becomes a "hired gun" and the evaluation meaningless. The mediator is partial to all family members, enunciating the relative merits, needs, and legitimate rights of each party. Individually oriented, the impartial assumes that parental capacity can be deduced from "objective" information provided by the family and other relevant parties. Family oriented, the mediator believes that the family has the responsibility and resources to settle its problem and that information in custody contests is notoriously biased and unreliable.

While the impartial stresses competence—determining which parent is more fit or finding at least one psychological parent—the mediator works towards family change, co-parenting, maintaining continuity with the children's entire relational network. Parental competence becomes second to family change and resolution; it becomes primary only if the parents fail to mediate a resolution and a court must decide.

The impartial approach has several drawbacks. First, reliable information is scarce during emotional wars and is probably inversely proportionate to the degree of emotional conflict. Also, individuals lie. Second, there may not be a better choice. As Gardner (1982) himself indicates, at times the impartial must "split hairs." Third, an emphasis on evaluation and recommendation over facilitation runs the risk of making decisions for others. Decisions made for someone else are often made, despite best intentions, more in the interest of the decision maker than in the interests of those being decided for. Fourth, the impartial may unwittingly become an accomplice in the emotional warfare, for the impartial's express purpose is to find the "better" parent, a position that encourages defensiveness and ends up with a winning and losing parent. And if one parent loses, he or she may withdraw from parental accountability and increase a child's loss.

The chief advantage of the impartial approach is that it arrives at a definite conclusion, thus ending the uncertainty of unresolved legal custody. At least the family will know who will have custody. Moreover, certain cases cannot be mediated. Parents may refuse mediation or try it and fail. Then an impartial evaluation becomes necessary. Certainly the impartial role far outstrips that of the advocate or hired gun, which offers no value to the family whatsoever.

The mediator's main problem is in doing a form of therapy when it was not explicitly requested. Most mediation is court ordered, and families come reluctantly, with the expectation of doing battle not therapy. Another disadvantage occurs if mediation fails and the family must go through the added strain and expense of impartial custody evaluation. A final disadvantage concerns inadequately skilled individuals doing mediation. Mediation is not common-sense bargaining which requires taking courses and then practicing. It is a psychotherapeutic enterprise, requiring the highest clinical acumen available in the field of mental health. It requires extensive skill in individual, marital, and family therapy. And it is among the most difficult work engaged in by mental health professionals.

Nevertheless, the mediator approach has several advantages. It stresses contested custody as a family problem, making a resolution more likely. Oriented towards problem solving and negotiation, the mediator seeks out any leverage available to encourage the *family* to solve the problem. And parents cooperating with parents is the very best resolution and is in the best interests of all family members.

If mediation works it shortens litigation, making resolution of custody less expensive and less emotionally debilitating for family members. Since the emphasis is expressly on maintaining the continuity and involvement of both parents, mediation decreases defensiveness and aids negotiation. I have seen many parents, given a chance to communicate outside the adversary framework and relieved of the pressure of being evaluated, begin to admit their fears and real intentions regarding custody and commence sincere negotiations.

CONDUCTING THE SESSIONS

Since the initiative for mediation usually comes from the court and since the family is often mired in anger, the task facing the mediator is formidable. The sessions must be conducted with great clinical skill and a thorough understanding of custody conflicts. I will outline the way I go about mediating, although I think it is more important to follow sound principles creatively rather than be enslaved in specific details.

Appointments are set through the court in a variety of ways. In one approach, the judge orders mediation and provides a list of local mediators from which the family selects one. The court's mediator coordinator, from the Probation Department, makes the arrangements. In another court, the judge suggests a mediator and the family makes an appointment. In a public agency, court personnel makes referrals to the staff who are assigned on a rotating basis.

In my approach, both parents attend the first session together, thus underscoring that contested custody is a *family* problem, requiring a joint decision and that parents must engage one another in negotiation. In some cases, extreme animosity necessitates seeing the parents separately for part or all of the first session. But they must come together before too long.

Clarifying expectations and appropriate roles for clinician and family members is imperative. From the outset I spell out the ground rules. The family is responsible to negotiate and my role is to help them do this. I mediate regarding custody and visitation and nothing else (e.g., finances). Primary is the children's well-being, but all members are to be treated fairly. The rights and merits of each member will be affirmed. I may invite other significant individuals, including grandparents and extended family members, to participate if I think their presence could help mediation.

Confidentiality is limited: I reserve (but do not always exercise) the right to communicate something I hear in an individual session if I think it is necessary. Charges of abuse or neglect cannot be kept confidential if the parent refuses to bring them up in a joint session.

I will see the family for approximately four to eight sessions and longer if progress is being made. If mediation fails, I inform the court and wait for their direction as to whether or not to submit a report including recommendations (this may require additional evaluation sessions). I request from both parents signed releases for my report (if necessary) and to obtain information from other professionals or agencies if indicated. The fee, payable at each session, is discussed, including who will pay it (if it will be split or if one will pay more). When fees are not split equally, it becomes more difficult to insure impartiality, yet the mediator must continually assert and demonstrate fairness regardless of who pays. This is a delicate and problematic area. The mediator must never come to be considered a "hired gun."

I cite the advantages of mediation over the more costly, more stressful, and more time consuming adversary contest. I explain that sessions will be individual (for parents and children), family, and conjoint (parents with each other).

I stress that mediation is a joint venture, requiring choices, exploration, negotiation, and clear communication of wants and opinions of all parties. I will not decide for the family; family accountability cannot be abdicated without harming children. Participatory decision making also promotes greater parental cooperation. And most parents want to control their lives by making their own choices.

After enunciating the ground rules, I ask about the current "facts": Who now lives with whom, for how long, and who is suing for what? I ask each parent to clearly specify what he or she wants to result from mediation and why. Mind reading, speaking for someone else, blaming, and denying fault work against a settlement and suggest parental irresponsibility. I tell the family that I expect each member to speak for him or herself and to honor what others say. Instead of vague generalities, I ask for specific examples.

During individual sessions, I take an intergenerational family history with special attention to whether each parent feels owed or owing and might be using the children or spouse as a way of paying off an emotional debt or collecting on one (Boszormenyi-Nagy & Spark, 1973). Emotionally deprived parents, for example, may be using their children to meet hidden, unmet needs. I also look to see how much emotional support is available to each spouse. I may try to explicate each parent's life script (Steiner, 1974) and determine whether he or she is used to being, for example, a rescuer, victim, or persecutor, a role likely to be continued in the custody fight. Reliance on themes of abandonment, being helpless as a way of controlling others, martyr-like overdevotion as a way of finding meaning and self-esteem, and other life scripts are explored, especially as they influence the custody drama. I try to determine if either parent's custody script is bogus. He or she may file a petition for custody but actually sabotage it (not coming for appointments, not paying, not cooperating). The parent's sabotage may also bespeak defensiveness, justified or not, a common reaction to mediation or evaluation.

In joint sessions, I observe the verbal and nonverbal signs that indicate family structure and patterns, including boundaries, communication styles, receptivity to each other's opinions, methods of problem solving, power issues, expectations of success or failure, autonomy (including taking responsibility for one's own behavior and feelings and expressing oneself clearly) (Beavers, 1977), and hidden agendas that underlie the custody contest, such as control, dependency, blame, revenge, or ambivalence regarding the divorce. As stated earlier, I join each member by listening attentively and respecting his or her point of view.

Redefining the problem from who is the better (or worse) parent to how to achieve co-parenting marks the sessions as therapeutic and less threatening. As in therapy, I may use authoritative advice, pose paradoxes, be humorous or confronting, refuse to side with one parent against the other, or clearly state my opinion regarding parent-child issues. I advise them of their ability and power to decide custody themselves and ask them if they want to use it or abdicate it to the court. If one parent admits a mistake or is willing to change his or her mind, or if either parent shows any support for the other, I congratulate that person. I may cite research findings, or read from various experts to put across a point, or tell the family that I am pessimistic about a resolution given their animosity and that I worry about the children.

I may ask the parents, if they appear to be better able to communicate with one another, to meet together without me to continue negotiation. After all, they will need to do this when the mediation is finished. I point out to them how their children suffer on account of their strife; firsthand observations of frightened, distressed children sitting in the waiting room or crying during one of the sessions, bring home the point. Affidavits of neglect, charges of misconduct, the chorus of blaming, and the manifestos of condemnation by family and friends are irrelevant; what is relevant is co-parenting, negotiation, and cooperation.

Most important is how parents respond to the mediation process—do they compromise, admit mistakes, listen to me and the other family members, or do they hold on to their self-righteous accusations of each other or their desire to keep the other parent on the periphery; do they avoid the issue of parenting while reopening old marital sores? I believe that this information is among the most valid upon which to base a custody recommendation. What parents do in mediation often belies what they say. Self-interest often comes to court dressed in a garment of parental love.

MAKING A RECOMMENDATION

Though the ideal is negotiation and cooperation, the reality often remains antagonism and discord. Mediation, while promising, often fails. Then the mediator must be prepared to offer a recommendation. Actually having witnessed the family struggling throughout mediation provides the mediator with the best base available from which to offer an opinion.

If mediation fails, determining who should have custody becomes the primary although difficult task. The recommendation should follow from the theory expounded throughout this chapter. Cotroneo et al. (1981) state, and I agree, that the "best custodial parent is one who most fully tolerates and cooperates in helping children maintain contacts with all significant persons in their relational context" (p. 476). The spirit of responsible parenthood is the spirit of cooperation.

The best custodial parent, elsewhere called a "psychological parent" (Goldstein, Freud, & Solnit, 1973; Musetto, 1982b), demonstrates throughout mediation a willingness to negotiate, an endorsement of a child's contact with the other parent and extended family, an open admission of some fault in the marital breakup and custody conflict, an awareness of how the very battle over custody jeopardizes a child, and repeatedly states personal preference as such without masquerading self-interest in the disguise of children's best interests.

The best custodial parent has already demonstrated parental capacity. By building an ongoing, continuous, affectionate relationship with a child, he or she has engendered trust. A child will go to this individual when troubled, and the child will want to live with him or her. Such a parent will spend and enjoy time with a child, doing things the child finds important and stimulating. He or she knows the child's individual preferences, unique abilities, sensitivities, likes and dislikes. Such a parent listens to all of a child's feelings, not censoring the child's pain, anger, or awkward feelings, and is alert to a child's nonverbal cues, thus demonstrating empathy.

The best custodial parent prizes parenthood but not to the exclusion of personal goals, outside interests, social and intimate relationships. The best custodial parent provides guidelines and allows for individual differences. He or she walks a narrow ridge between leadership and tyranny, freedom and permissiveness.

The best custodial parent does not propagandize a child against the other parent, yet provides truthful and accurate information. He or she does not hide the other parent's faults, nor does he or she attest to the absent parent's love despite mounting evidence to the contrary, neglect, lack of contact, or a failure to provide financial or emotional support. At the same time, the best custodial parent recognizes the positive as well as the negative aspects of the other parent and affirms the value of staying in contact with that parent even if the relationship falls short of the ideal. Respecting a child's developmental age and not exploiting a child by parentification (Boszormenyi-Nagy & Spark, 1973)—placing a child in the role of a parent—characterizes the best custodial parent. Nor does the best custodial parent place the child in other inappropriate roles: as a spy or mediator between parents; as a weapon of revenge; as a trophy of self-esteem; as a peer who provides the bulk of a parent's social life; as a protector who keeps the parent from facing the uncertainty of new involvements; as a judge of parental fault; or as a commodity or bargaining chip to be used to obtain a better divorce settlement.

The best custodial parent, furthermore, helps a child adjust to the separation and divorce—but at the child's pace. He or she is likely to have told the child about the impending separation without idealizing or maligning the other parent. He or she will answer a child's questions about what is happening truthfully and candidly, not detailing intimate marital problems, but outlining a general reason for the breakup. If a certain question seems inappropriate, he or she will be honest about not answering. The best custodial parent allows the child a full range of emotions likely to emerge during a divorce and afterwards: anger, fear, anxiety, sadness, loss, grief, guilt, fantasies of reconciliation, shame, uncertainty, and rage.

No single trait assures good parenting. Mental or emotional problems in themselves do not preclude adequate parenting (Committee on the Family of the Group for the Advancement of Psychiatry, 1980). An anxious but loving mother may be a better custodial parent than a successful, self-centered father. The question is rather how the emotional problems disturb the parent-child interaction and how much adequate parenting is available, in spite of the problems.

Alternative life styles, including homosexual parents, will be argued about in the years to come. Whatever consensus decision makers reach, I believe that the ultimate criterion for deciding child custody remains the best interest of the child (and family) and how much effective parenting is available in the conventional or unconventional life style.

Though I devote little space to joint custody, it is not because of its unimportance. Joint custody (that is, joint responsibility and decision making), if possible, embodies the ideal co-parenting arrangement. But it is often impractical or contraindicated. If two responsible parents cooperate with each other, joint custody, not necessarily shared living arrangements, insures the most continuity with the child's entire relational universe. On the other hand, if two parents cannot negotiate regarding child rearing, joint custody will provide a further arena for launching marital offensives, thus robbing the children of either parent rather than providing them with both.

MEDIATORS AND ATTORNEYS

Finally, since divorce almost invariably requires the services of attorneys, the relationship between mediators and attorneys is worth examining, at least briefly. Attorneys and mediators should strive for a cooperative relationship. Each is, or should be, working for the best interests of the children and family. Working at cross-purposes decreases the value of each, confuses the family, and militates against a resolution.

Problems may arise on the part of the mediator or the attorney. Mediators must maintain their impartial position, as advocates of the merits of each member's position, pressing the interests of children above all and working toward a resolution. They must avoid being drawn into adversary ploys, however subtly disguised, by attorneys who are promoting their client's interests above all else. They must not encourage an attorney's ill will by doing more than custody mediation, such as trying to settle finances or give legal advice.

Attorneys, on the other hand, need to respect the legitimate role of mediators. The clamor of some that mediators are practicing law is, to my mind, self-serving. But it is encouraged by unskilled or unscrupulous mediators who go beyond their mandate. Cooperation is just as important between mediators and attorneys as it is between parents.

Andrew P. Musetto, Ph.D., a psychologist and marriage counselor, is a member of the Psychological Services Associates, a private group practice in Haddonfield and Cherry Hill, NJ. Dr. Musetto's professional interests and publications are in the areas of custody and visitation, agoraphobia, and marital and family therapy.

RESOURCES

Beavers, W. R. (1977). *Psychotherapy and Growth: A Family Systems Perspective.* New York: Brunner Mazel.

Boszormenyi-Nagy, I., & Spark, G. M. (1973). *Invisible Loyalties: Reciprocity in Intergenerational Family Therapy.* New York: Harper & Row.

Bowen, M. (1978). *Family Theory in Clinical Practice.* New York: Jason Aronson.

Committee on the Family of the Group for the Advancement of Psychiatry. (1980). *New Trends in Child Custody Determinations.* New York: Harcourt Brace Janovich.

Cotroneo, M., Krasner, B. R., & Boszormenyi-Nagy, I. (1981). The contextual approach to child custody decisions. In G. P. Sholevar (Ed.), *The Handbook of Marriage and Marital Therapy* (pp. 475-480). New York: Spectrum Publications.

Derdeyn, A. P. (1976). Child custody contests in historical perspective. *The American Journal of Psychiatry, 133,* 1369-1376.

Erickson, M. H., & Rossi, E. L. (1979). *Hypnotherapy: An Exploratory Casebook.* New York: Irvington Publishers.

Gardner, R. A. (1982). *Family Evaluation in Child Custody Litigation.* Cresskill, NJ: Creative Therapeutics.

Goldstein, J., Freud, A., & Solnit, A. J. (1973). *Beyond the Best Interests of the Child.* New York: Free Press.

Minuchin, S. (1974). *Families and Family Therapy.* Cambridge, MA: Harvard University Press.

Minuchin, S., & Fishman, H. C. (1981). *Family Therapy Techniques.* Cambridge, MA: Harvard University Press.

Musetto, A. P. (1978a). Child custody and visitation: The role of the clinician in relation to the family. *Family Therapy, 5,* 143-150.

Musetto, A. P. (1978b). Evaluating families with custody or visitation problems. *Journal of Marriage and Family Counseling, 4,* 59-63.

Musetto, A. P. (1981). Standards for deciding contested child custody. *Journal of Clinical Child Psychology, 6,* 51-55.

Musetto, A. P. (1982a). *Dilemmas In Child Custody: Family Conflicts and Their Resolutions.* Chicago: Nelson Hall.

Musetto, A. P. (1982b). The role of the mental health professional in contested custody: Evaluator of competence or facilitator of change. *Journal of Divorce, 6,* 69-89.

Scheiner, L. C., Musetto, A. P., & Cordier, D. M. (1982). Custody and visitation counseling: A report of an innovative program. *Family Relations, 31,* 99-107.

Steiner, C. M. (1974). *Scripts People Live: Transactional Analysis of Life Scripts.* New York: Grove Press.

Wallerstein, J. S., & Kelly, J. B. (1980). *Surviving the Breakup: How Children and Parents Cope with Divorce.* New York: Basic Books.

LAW AND CLINICAL PRACTICE IN CHILD ABUSE AND NEGLECT CASES

Melvin J. Guyer and Peter Ash

The problems of child abuse and neglect, which are today so much in the public consciousness, are of complex origin. They raise issues about the nature of the parent-child relationship, pit prerogatives of the "family" against those of the state, and challenge our judgment as to what is "right" or "best" for children. Even as this chapter is being written, the newspapers are reporting a juvenile court's emergency order taking into protective custody 66 children who, with their parents, have resided in a religious community in a rural Michigan county. Police, social workers, and Department of Social Service employees have abruptly removed those children, at least temporarily, from the care and custody of their parents following the death of one of the children after a whipping for "disobedience." Judicial and public concern was triggered because the religious tenets of the "cult" called for vigorous physical discipline of both adults and children for a variety of transgressions against Biblical teachings. Perhaps too, memories of the Jonestown deaths lent urgency to the intervention.

In this particular episode we see at work the ability of the state to exercise its authority over children when there is concern about their safety or their parents' fitness. Weighed against that authority is the issue of the ambit of prerogatives parents may be allowed in raising their children according to family standards of conduct and family morals, beliefs, and codes of conduct.

Complicating these questions in this and other situations are constitutional guarantees of religious freedom which allow parental behavior which may adversely affect children.

What also contributes to the dilemma in so many situations is our lack of adequate knowledge of the consequences for the child of a state initiated intervention and placement outside the home. Often, a sequence of foster placements is the alternative to an "unfit" parental environment. The need and duty of the courts to move quickly and decisively to protect children who are at clear risk of physical injury is settled and case law and statutes provide for such intervention. The determination of which cases require intervention, and what those interventions should be, often requires psychological expertise. This expertise is often provided by caseworkers in social service agencies. But in the more difficult cases, other experts, such as psychologists and psychiatrists, are asked to consult.

HISTORY OF CHILD
ABUSE/NEGLECT LEGISLATION

The laws of the United States have their historical, intellectual, and ethical origins in the English common law, the centuries-long body of court decisions which enunciate principles and rules for resolving conflicts and ordering society. In that body of law little is found that anticipates the current status of child abuse/neglect legislation in the United States. Under English common law virtually all rights of control over children in a family were delegated by the Crown to the father. While this delegation of control was not absolute, there was virtually no scrutiny by any outside authority of the conduct of parents toward their children. Children had no independent legal status or rights within the family, at least none which they could assert against a parent, and their status in the home was similar to that of chattel, that is, "personal property" (*Black's Law Dictionary*, 1979, p. 215). There was a property-like relationship, in a legal sense, between parent and child. Having great respect for property in general, the English courts and Parliament did little to interfere with the ways parents cared for their children.

The history of legislative response to the problem of child abuse in the United States began in 1874 with the often cited case of the child, Mary Ellen. An abused child in New York City, the account of her situation is cited as the first reported case of child abuse (Katz, Ambrosino, McGrath, & Sawitsky, 1977). Public awareness of the problem of child abuse resulting from Mary Ellen's case was heightened when those seeking to assist her discovered no law on the books that protected a child from parental abuse. Ironically, the only avenue for legal intervention on Mary Ellen's behalf was an appeal to the Society for the Prevention of Cruelty to Animals on the premise that Mary Ellen was entitled to the same legal protection afforded members of the animal kingdom. This irony led to the founding of the Society for the Prevention of Cruelty to Children and the subsequent enactment in New York State of the nation's first child protection law.

Later developments in legislation intended to protect children from parental abuse/neglect came quite slowly, were weak, and were not zealously enforced. Most early legislation was intended only to permit courts to assume jurisdiction over children who had been physically abused by their parents. Severe instances of abuse might result in bringing criminal charges against a parent, but in the past, as today, use of the criminal justice system is especially cumbersome and often undesirable for handling cases of family violence.

The early statutes represented a new and unfamiliar intrusion by the state into the usual privacy accorded the family. Moreover, the scope of the problems of child abuse were little understood. No systematic reporting of abuse was being done by state or local agencies of government. Even the definition of child abuse was quite vague. Community standards of appropriate methods of child discipline permitted far more corporal punishment than is accepted today. Thus, historically, the combination of definitional problems as to what constitutes "abuse," the reluctance of the state to intrude itself into areas traditionally left to parents, the absence of any systematic reporting agencies, and the lack of a statutory or case law basis for dealing with suspected abuse kept the problem of child abuse/neglect far from the public consciousness and conscience.

Early efforts to allow state intervention in cases of child abuse were made through enactment of statutes which sought to excuse certain professional persons (e.g., physicians, social workers, and nurses) who regularly came in contact with children from confidentiality constraints which ordinarily would preclude the reporting of child abuse/neglect. Health professionals, by licensure provisions, rules of evidence, and the rights of privacy of their patients are ordinarily prevented from making unauthorized disclosures of patient records. Since parents ordinarily control the medical records of their children, physicians and other health professionals who had knowledge of possible child abuse were constrained from disclosing such evidence without the consent of the parent. Unwarranted disclosures could be grounds for a lawsuit against the professional. In addition, a number of other and more diffuse factors served to discourage the reporting of suspected child abuse. Included among these factors was the desire of many professionals to avoid being called as a witness in protracted adversarial proceedings, especially one with an uncertain outcome and directed against a patient or a patient's parent. Historically, however, at least prior to 1962, the most salient reason for nonreporting was that most people found the issue of abuse quite troubling and often failed to notice evidence that was plainly before them.

A watershed event in the history of child abuse/neglect legislation occurred in 1962 with the publication by Kempe and his colleagues of their now famous paper "The Battered Child Syndrome" (Kempe, C. H., Silverman, Steele, Droegemuller, & Silver, 1962). In that paper, the Kempe group identified a cluster of physical signs and behavioral patterns associated with children who had a history of physical abuse inflicted upon them by a parent. Combining hard medical evidence obtained from physical examinations (e.g., x-ray films showing old bone fractures) with "accident explanations" offered by a parent which were inconsistent with the nature of the child's injury, Kempe and his colleagues inferred the existence of a characteristic pattern of child abuse which had previously been unreported. The Kempe paper accomplished several things: It alerted the medical profession to the prevalence of physical abuse of children by their parents, it provided physicians and other health care workers with diagnostic indicators of possible physical abuse, and, most importantly, its impact upon public opinion and the legislative conscience contributed to the enactment of various child abuse/neglect reporting laws.

These laws, unlike previous legislation which focused upon the punishment of child abusers, were intended to *identify* instances of abuse and then provide services to an abused child and his or her family. Kempe's (Kempe, C. H., et al., 1962) designation of child abuse as a "syndrome" whose identification turned on *medical evidence* brought the problem of child abuse into the ambit of "medical" problems with the associated orientation of approaching it in terms of diagnosis and treatment. Thus, the new child abuse reporting laws, enacted following Kempe's article have focused upon the identification (or diagnosis) of child abuse and abusing parent(s) and the initiation of remedial interventions (or treatment), rather than punishment.

The medical approach to child abuse problems emphasized reliance upon physicians and other health care providers to detect child abuse and possibly intervene in families where it was suspected. Kempe's (Kempe, C. H., et al., 1962) article clarified specific medical diagnostic procedures to be employed by medical personnel for the detection of the battered child syndrome. The article also suggested some techniques for interviewing and confronting suspected abusers. As to psychological interventions, Kempe and his coauthors took a rather guarded view of the outcomes in treating the psychological problems of the abusing parent. Instead, they emphasized affording direct protection to the child:

Up to the present time, therapeutic experience with the parents of battered children is minimal. Counseling carried on in social agencies has been far from successful or rewarding. We know of no reports of successful psychotherapy in such cases. In general, psychiatrists feel that treatment of the so-called psychopath or sociopath is rarely successful. Further psychological investigation of the character structure of attacking parents is sorely needed. Hopefully, better understanding of the mechanisms involved in the control and release of aggressive impulses will aid in the earlier diagnosis, prevention of attack, and treatment of patients, as well as give us better ability to predict the likelihood of further attack in the future. At present, there is no safe remedy in the situation except the separation of battered children from their insufficiently protective parents. (p. 23)

Much of the work in child abuse since 1962 has aimed at fulfilling this hope for knowledge so that children can be maintained in their homes without being subject to continuing abuse.

The evolution of child protection laws followed fairly rapidly after the U. S. Children's Bureau developed a Model Reporting Act for Suspected Abuse and Neglect in 1963. These efforts in the 1960s were significant in that they were undertaken at the federal level rather than on a state-by-state basis. A federal strategy was more efficient and far-reaching in its impact. Of even greater significance, to an extent not yet fully appreciated, is that child abuse legislation brought the federal government into the arena of regulation and/or intervention of family matters, an area of legislation usually reserved for the states. The introduction of federal agencies into matters affecting children and their families has resulted in a continuing shift of regulatory power from the states to the federal government and its various agencies.

During the 1970s the provision of federal funding incentives to states which adopted a version of the Model Reporting Act, as well as the granting of federal funds to defray the costs to states of establishing child protection services, caused almost all jurisdictions in the United States to enact one or another version of what are called "mandatory reporting acts" for suspected child abuse/neglect. These mandatory acts have several important common characteristics although there are state-to-state variations.

First, the mandatory acts require members of certain named professions (such as physicians, teachers, social workers) to report both abuse and *suspected* abuse/neglect either to the police or to some legal or social agency. The acts waive or abrogate any confidentiality or privilege which might otherwise prevent a report of suspected abuse/neglect from being made. The acts also prescribe sanctions to be imposed against those who are required to report suspected abuse but fail to do so. Some state laws rely only upon a civil sanction to encourage compliance (i.e., a lawsuit for money damages to compensate a child for any harm which results from the failure to report). Other states use a criminal sanction and make failure to report a misdemeanor punishable by a jail sentence and/or fine.

Another common characteristic of reporting laws is that they afford some measure of anonymity to the reporting person and provide the reporting person/agency with a measure of immunity from criminal prosecution or civil lawsuits which might arise from reporting.

Yet another common aspect of reporting laws and modern abuse/neglect statutes is their allowance of a certain measure of parental freedom to pursue their religious beliefs even when such beliefs are the basis for their treating their children in ways not ordinarily acceptable. Thus, Jehovah's Witnesses and Christian Scientists may be allowed to deny their children certain types of medical treatment, such as blood transfusions, vaccinations, radiation and chemotherapy, and surgery, at least where the child's life is not at stake. Without religious convictions to justify the denial of medical treatment for their children, such parents might be subject to abuse/neglect proceedings. In this regard, child reporting acts and related statutes recognize that some sort of balance must be struck between parents' rights to raise their children in accordance with family beliefs and the state's interest in protecting children from harm.

In looking back over the proliferation of child protection laws during the last two decades, several clear lines of development are evident. Obviously, both the reach and scope of child protection laws have been greatly expanded. One dimension of expansion has been the move from permissive reporting laws—those which *allow* reporting—to mandatory reporting laws— those which *require* reporting. Another dimension of expansion has been in terms of the diversity of professional groups whose members are obligated to report suspected abuse/neglect. Early mandatory acts required only physicians to report. In more recent acts, however, the reach of the mandatory obligation has been expanded to include those persons whose professional activities involve working with children and/or families, such as social workers, teachers, licensed child care workers, nurses, dentists, and psychologists. It should be noted too that the reporting acts do not *restrict* reporting only to those mandated to report. Instead, they are permissive as to reporting by others, allowing any person to report and affording the same assurances of anonymity and immunity from retaliatory lawsuits given those mandated to report. Even children may report suspected abuse, as, for example, when they know that a friend or schoolmate has been subjected to abuse.

During the last several years, the effects of the mandatory reporting laws have been dramatic (Besharov, 1983). Part of the increase in reporting rates has been the result of greater public awareness and professional responsibility. Another component of the increase, however, is related to the manipulation of the incentives associated with reporting. By requiring a report on *suspicion*, the reporting laws encourage "false positive" errors (i.e., reporting abuse/neglect when it is not present). One study reports that of the approximately one million reports now made per year, about 60% appear, upon investigation, to be "unfounded" (Besharov, 1983).

Despite their apparent efficacy, however, mandatory reporting acts have not been free of criticism. Civil libertarians, for instance, have assailed the anonymity accorded the reporting person. Normally, under our system of law, the accused has the Constitutional right to be confronted with the witnesses against him. Also, under the Fourth Amendment, various guarantees of privacy and protections against unreasonable searches are granted. Critics argue that these rights are sometimes strained under the actions and investigations triggered by reports made pursuant to the various mandatory reporting acts. A number of the constitutional issues arising from the anonymity guarantees and investigatory processes of the mandatory acts have already been addressed by the courts and controversy over them is certain to continue as the courts wrestle to strike the proper balance between the individual's (and the family's) constitutional rights and the state's authority to act under its police power to protect children from societally defined risks.

COURSE OF A CHILD ABUSE CASE

THE REPORT

Despite the passage of mandatory reporting laws, there remain many obstacles to reporting child abuse. Even with the safeguards provided by the various reporting laws, many health professionals are still reluctant to report suspect child abuse or neglect. This reluctance stems from several sources.

First is the traditional confidentiality and privilege usually accorded to the physician-patient relationship, which typically bar the physician from either giving testimony about medical care or releasing to others any material in a patient's medical record without first obtaining the patient's consent— or, if the patient is a minor, without the prior consent of a parent. For many health professionals, it simply goes against the grain of tradition to report without consent.

A second barrier to reporting abuse stems from professionals' reluctance to become involved in the legal system's adversarial process. By reporting suspected abuse/neglect, the health provider is cast in the role of an "accuser" of the family of the abused child. Quite likely, too, the reporting professional will be called upon to testify in judicial proceedings. The prospect of being called as a witness, subject to examination and cross-examination, is distressful to many. In most cases, a psychologist is not the person who reports child abuse. There are occasions, however, when in the course of evaluation or treatment a psychologist is made aware of or comes to suspect that abuse may be taking place. Many psychologists share the general professional's reluctance to become involved in the adversary legal process.

The reporting acts have broadened the definition of the harm or risk which must be reported. The earlier permissive reporting and mandatory reporting acts were directed against clear physical abuse which produced physical injuries and instances of neglect which demonstrated a parent's clear failure to provide food, clothing, and shelter. Successive legislation has broadened and generalized the definitions of "abuse and neglect" so that considerably more parental conduct (or omissions) may be construed as abuse or neglect. With broadening definitions has come an invitation for more subjective standards as to what should be reported. Some reporting statutes now include terms such as "emotional abuse," "psychic injury," and "emotional neglect." Because of the lack of clarity in definitions of this "new" category of abuse or neglect, mental health professionals have been placed in a particular quandary.

For instance, a psychologist conducting an evaluation or providing treatment of a child might conclude that the child's psychiatric symptoms are a consequence of parental behavior (emotional injury) or parental inadequacy (emotional neglect). It is evident that mental health professionals only rarely report parents who are suspected of being responsible for their children's psychiatric problems. Instead, a more complicated, and more troublesome relationship develops between the psychologist, the child, and the family. The mental health professional will make treatment recommendations to the parents and will refrain from making an abuse/neglect report if, and so long as, the treatment recommendation is followed.

Not uncommonly, the treatment recommendation is that the child and the parents enter into a treatment relationship with the professional with the understanding, tacit or expressed, that if the treatment is unilaterally terminated by the parent it will lead the professional to initiate an abuse/neglect report against the parent. It should be noted as well that it is not only emotional abuse which often gets managed this way by some mental health professionals. In the course of their practice they may be made aware of ongoing *physical* abuse of children and justify not reporting it on the grounds that they are providing treatment. Such behavior is simply not in conformity with the requirements of the mandatory reporting acts.

In many cases, a report by a therapist will not trigger a protective service investigation because agencies are generally willing to let professionals, who are already treating the family, continue to manage a case as long as the agency is apprised of progress made. The fact that a report of emotional abuse or neglect will not result in any significant agency investigation, however, does not free the mental health professional from the obligation of reporting.

INVESTIGATION

What begins with a report of suspected abuse leads to an investigation by a protective services (PS) worker. This investigation may be informal, for example, encompassing inquiries to family members, the child, and neighbors. At this point, the PS worker is accorded a considerable amount of discretion in deciding how to proceed. The worker may close the case after a determination that there is no appreciable risk to the child. Alternatively, the PS worker may counsel the family and offer various social services to assist an inadequate parent. All of this is done without any court involvement and is considered to be the voluntary offering, and presumably voluntary acceptance by a family, of state-funded social services.

If the investigation results in concern of risk to the child, a process of coercive persuasion may begin in which the PS worker encourages the family to cooperate in obtaining various evaluations, including medical, psychiatric, and psychological examinations. A strong implication in this phase of negotiation with the family is that failure to cooperate with the PS worker's recommendations will lead the worker to seek court orders for compliance or to petition the court to assert jurisdiction over the child and family.

The mental health professional who becomes involved in assessment or treatment at this prepetition "informal" point is well advised to clearly define for the family members and the PS agency exactly what the expectations of the respective parties might be. For example, the PS worker may anticipate receiving the medical records and recommendations which result from the evaluation. Family members may believe that they are obligated to release such records to the PS worker, and the mental health professional may assume that the "client" is the PS agency which is likely paying for the services. From a legal perspective, mental health professionals should understand, and make it clear to all concerned, that until there is a court order or stipulation for the release of medical records, such records can be released only with the written consent of the parents, who control both their own medical records and those of the minor children in their custody. Parents should be told that even if they voluntarily release their medical records they are free to withdraw that consent up until the time that the information has been released to a third party. If the evaluator believes that it is important to bind the patient to their consent to release the medical record, the patient may be asked to agree to a consent order to be issued by the court so that a change of mind is precluded. If the patient is represented by counsel it could be suggested that a stipulation for release of records be entered into prior to the start of the evaluation.

An additional warning, which the evaluator should provide in obtaining the informed consent of persons evaluated on a "voluntary" basis, is that subsequent circumstances might result in their medical records being subpoenaed by a court order and that absolute confidentiality cannot be assured. Moreover, it is advisable to inform such persons (those seeking a voluntary evaluation upon referral by a PS agency) that at some time in the future what they say might be used in a judicial hearing in a manner adverse to their interests and that the evaluation should proceed only with this point well understood and documented. The mental health professional should keep the patient's situation clearly in mind when discussing and informing the patient of his or her rights to confidentiality. If patients are present for evaluation on a voluntary basis they may believe that their refusal to participate will result in the PS agency seeking a court order requiring their participation. Whether this belief is correct or not, the evaluator should make clear that the patient has rights of confidentiality and that medical records concerning the patient will be released to third parties only with the expressed consent of the patient or upon a court order (to which the patient's attorney may object).

This explicit waiver of confidentiality must be handled tactfully by the evaluator. If he or she frightens the patient too much, the evaluator will be unable to form the working alliance necessary to be helpful to abusing parents. Abusive parents generally have considerable difficulty in forming alliances. The evaluator must help them see that working with the evaluator is an important component of assessing their capacity for change, a capacity which needs to be demonstrated prior to return of the child. This assumes the usual case in which the purpose of the evaluation is *not* to establish the fact of abuse. Such a fact is usually established by independent physical evidence, information provided by other adults, or information provided by the child. Thus, the evaluator can attempt to ally with the parent's wish to improve and indicate the ways he or she can be helpful to the parent, despite the absence of a confidential relationship.

If during the investigation it is decided that the family is in need of and receptive to social services, the mental health professional who provided the evaluation may make treatment recommendations to both the family and the PS worker. If the family complies with the treatment recommendations (which may include parent guidance, psychotherapy, or substance abuse counseling) the PS investigation will be placed "on hold" for a period of time to determine whether the family utilizes the services and benefits from them. The service provider may be a PS employee or a private mental health worker. In either case, although there is some similarity to a private treatment relationship, it should be understood that the child protection agency will be provided information as to how well treatment is progressing and whether treatment is continuing according to plan.

If, after a period of time, treatment appears to be going well, the case will be closed by the PS worker and the investigation of abuse/neglect allegations will be ended. However, the PS worker may continue to make occasional informal contacts with the family to determine if further assistance is needed. Additionally, a closing or summary progress report may be requested of the mental health professional by the PS worker. The family in this case almost certainly will consent and, with written release of information, such a report may be forwarded.

In more serious cases, the investigation following a report may lead the PS worker to formally petition the court to assert jurisdiction over the child at risk. The decision to petition may result from the nature of the initial report and PS investigation, from the family's refusal to accept services, or from a determination that such services are not sufficient to protect a child from future harm. In this latter circumstance, the family may have voluntarily participated in a psychological evaluation, the report of which has served to heighten the PS worker's concern for the child's safety.

The petition to the court to take jurisdiction marks the beginning of formal judicial process. The petition contains assertions and allegations of fact intended to prove to the court that a statutory basis exists for the court to take jurisdiction (control and custody) of the child. In most states, due process requirements call for the appointment of a guardian *ad litem* for the child, the appointment of counsel for the parents (if they are indigent), and a formal series of hearings with proper notice, rights of discovery, and the calling of witnesses—all to take place before a judge or referee of the court of jurisdiction. The PS agency, in advancing its petition, is typically represented by its own attorney, by an attorney from the prosecutor's office, or by a case worker with some experience in court procedures.

ADJUDICATION

In the petition the court is asked to determine that the factual matters alleged in the petition are sufficient, that proper procedures have been followed, and that the court has jurisdiction under the law. If the court agrees to these matters it will schedule evidentiary hearings (adjudicatory phase) to determine whether the petition should be granted. In preparation for the evidentiary hearing, the court may issue broad orders allowing discovery and examination of various records including medical and psychological records of parents and the children. The court may order the parent(s) and child(ren) to undergo psychological testing and evaluation. Here, it is clear that any material prepared by a mental health evaluator is *not* privileged but instead will be turned over to the court and the various attorneys involved in the proceedings. When the mental health professional is called upon to provide an evaluation under these circumstances, it is essential that the persons being evaluated be fully advised of the absence of any privilege or confidentiality, that the purpose of the evaluation is to provide information to a court, that the information they provide may be detrimental to their parental interests, and that they do not have to respond to the evaluator's questions if they do not wish to do so. The evaluator should clearly document that a psychological "*Miranda* warning" has been provided.

Furthermore, the mental health professional who evaluates persons under a court order, in preparation for an evidentiary hearing, must anticipate being called upon not only to submit a report but also to provide expert testimony at a formal hearing. The expert witness will be called upon to testify as to his or her findings, conclusions, and recommendations. The expert should also expect to be subject to cross-examination as to such findings, conclusions, and recommendations. For this reason, it is very important that careful records be made and documentation kept throughout the course of the court ordered evaluation. Because proceedings in child protection matters can continue for several years, it is important that records be maintained in some type of permanent storage.

If the case goes to trial and the PS petition is granted, the legal result is that the court asserts temporary jurisdiction over the child and can make placement decisions, issue orders affecting the parents, and gather further information to determine what is in the child's best interests, both in the immediate future and long run. The court may again direct that evaluations be undertaken to determine the child's medical and psychological needs and seek treatment recommendations to be implemented under the supervision of the department of social services (DSS).

Because of the strong public policy that families should be kept together and that efforts at rehabilitation must be undertaken whenever possible, the DSS will seek evaluations to determine what, if anything, can be done to assist the family in reducing the risk to the child. This is done in preparation for a "dispositional" hearing which follows the evidentiary hearing in which the court granted the PS petition.

In preparation for the dispositional hearing, the DSS must obtain information to help the court determine whether the child should continue in the parental home or be placed elsewhere under court supervision. A number of alternative placements, including foster care, placement with relatives, and hospital or group home care, are ordinarily available. The mental health professional may be called upon at this point (or called upon again) to assist the court and the DSS in planning services for the child and the parents. The DSS is committed by law to attempt rehabilitation and efforts to that end will almost certainly be made, even if there is good reason for pessimism about the ultimate ability of the parents to meet even minimal standards of parental adequacy.

It should be mentioned here that a common misunderstanding exists as to just what must be proved if the state is to prevail in its action seeking termination of parental rights. The misunderstanding arises because many people (including some attorneys) incorrectly assume that the "best interests of the child" test is applicable to termination proceedings. Although this test is used in matters of disputed custody arising out of divorce proceedings and certain other child placement decision making, it is *not* the standard for termination nor the matter at issue in a termination hearing. Instead, the burden upon the state in such proceedings is to prove, by at least clear and convincing evidence, that there is parental *unfitness* or one of the other statutorily defined criteria of parental inadequacy (i.e., chronic mental illness, criminal incarceration for certain felonies, abandonment, etc.). A mere showing by the state that it would be in the child's "best interests" to terminate parental rights does not fall within the statutory bases which permit termination. The fact that the more stringent test of "parental unfitness" rather than "best interests" is required to terminate parental rights reflects in large part the public policy that the integrity and privacy of the family should be protected and should be intruded upon by the state only when there is a clear showing of harm or serious risk to a child.

Evaluations conducted between the evidentiary stage and the placement phase differ from earlier evaluations in that the children are now under the custody of the court and parental consent is not usually required for routine examinations requested by the court and the DSS. The situation as to the adults is not significantly different. They may or may not be cooperative in seeking treatment recommendations and they may or may not be under court order to participate in evaluations. Obviously, the period of time between adjudication and placement is one in which a certain amount of negotiation takes place between the DSS and the parents and their attorney. If the parents wish to retain physical custody of their child, they will be especially amenable to treatment measures suggested by DSS if such measures include continued placement of the child in the parental home. For the DSS, it is usually preferable that placement be in the home if it does not present an unwarranted risk to the child. This preference arises both from the expense and managerial problems of arranging alternative placement and the previously mentioned policy orientation toward ultimately returning the child to the custody of the parents.

The psychological evaluator who is called upon to offer or assess proposed treatment plans may find his or her recommendations for out of home placement greeted with a certain lack of enthusiasm by DSS, the parents, and the court. The evaluator should be careful to make an assessment and recommendation independent of any negotiations which may be going on between the parents and the DSS and avoid becoming caught up in an unwarranted enthusiasm for the early return of a child to a home, especially one where there has been a history of chronic abuse or neglect. If the expert's recommendations are relied upon at the dispositional hearing and afterwards things turn out badly for the child, it will be the mental health expert's recommendations which will be remembered, not the pressures upon him or her to be overly optimistic regarding the parents' ability to overcome long-standing limitations.

At the placement hearing the court generally will rely heavily upon DSS recommendations. These in turn will rely heavily upon recommendations and evaluations made by outside mental health experts. The placement decisions will also incorporate treatment plans for both child and parent. The placement hearing may be a proceeding in which the outside expert is called upon again to testify as to placement and treatment recommendations. The psychological evaluator may be called upon to justify his or her conclusions and may be subject to cross-examination. Again the caveat of careful record keeping, adequate preparation, and attention to the requirements of privileged communications and informed consent should be kept in mind. Here, too, as in other stages of the process, the mental health professional called upon to provide evaluation, testimony, or treatment should clarify *who* is the client: court, DSS, patient, or child. As part of this clarification the matter of fees for services should be expressly addressed. A contract or letter of understanding between the mental health worker and the party seeking services should be negotiated at the outset.

For families with little or no prior history of PS involvement, the dispositional hearing will emphasize rehabilitation efforts and orders to provide services to the family as well as placement of the child with continuing court supervision. At the same time, the court may set a "review hearing" to be held some months in the future. At that later hearing, the degree of progress toward treatment goals will be assessed and the extent of parental compliance with DSS recommendations and court orders will be examined. If the child has been placed outside the parental home, the child's adjustment in the placement environment will be evaluated. The mental health professional is typically involved in one way or another during the period between the dispositional hearing and the review hearing.

The professional may be providing ongoing treatment to the child, the parent(s), or to the family. Or the process of evaluation of the parents and child may still be continuing under court order for the child and voluntarily or court ordered for the parents. If the parents' treatment involvement is voluntary, it should be clear that any claim to confidentiality is illusory. If the court wishes to know the status and progress of treatment it can and will simply compel testimony, even over objections of parent and therapist. The juvenile courts typically weigh the parents' claim of privilege against the child's best interests, which are arguably furthered by an abrogation of privilege, and the best interests prevail. It is naive and mistaken to assure a "voluntary patient-parent" who is involved in the child protection system, that the relationship is and will remain confidential. The professional should be aware that at some future date he or she may be called upon to testify concerning the parent and may be an adverse witness at either a review or termination of parental rights proceedings.

One possible way to avoid this difficult situation is to obtain, prior to the start of the treatment relationship, a court order or stipulation between the parties that discovery of medical records will not be sought. Even this, however, is not a guarantee of confidentiality. Material may emerge during treatment which will require the therapist to make a PS report (for example, if the child is abused by the parent in the home or if placed elsewhere, during visits). Also, if the current case is closed, and a future child protection action is begun, the medical records may be sought and the previous court order or stipulation will be without effect.

The mental health professional who works with a parent during this interim period is in a difficult position. The therapist must encourage openness and the trust and cooperation of the patient-parent. Both know or should know, however, that what the patient divulges may be detrimental and that the trust, though well intended, may be regretted. The therapist is in the position of working with a patient whose "involvement" in treatment may represent nothing more than court-ordered or otherwise coerced "cooperation." Few therapists are willing to risk the contempt powers of the court in the service of protecting privileged communications.

At a review hearing, written reports and testimony from mental health experts will be examined. Progress reports from DSS will also be presented. The decision the court weighs at these hearings is whether to alter the placement, continue the placement and end the court's jurisdiction, or instead move to take permanent jurisdiction of the child (a termination of parental rights). Alternatively, the court may issue new treatment orders and schedule a review hearing some months later. This cycle of placement, service provision, and periodic review may be repeated a number of times, with several years passing before the court faces the decision of whether to end jurisdiction or terminate parental rights. If a child is in foster or institutional placement, the pressure to make a termination decision is heightened, although in actual practice many years may go by punctuated only by the child's birthdays and review hearings. For cases of long duration there may be a gradual disengagement of the parent and child. Occasional visits between parent and child may be scheduled and telephone calls and letters may be exchanged. For children who are institutionalized for long periods of time, the parents may abandon efforts to obtain custody and drop out of treatment or "parent guidance," especially if they live some distance from their child and are billed for missed visits even when they have a legitimate excuse.

TERMINATION OF PARENTAL RIGHTS

When the DSS concludes that efforts to rehabilitate a family have failed and that parental behavior is such as to constitute a continuing risk to the child, the court will be petitioned to take permanent jurisdiction over the child, that is, to terminate parental rights. This type of hearing is the most somber undertaking of the juvenile court and the proceedings are governed by strict procedural rules and as many trappings of due process as the court can muster. Termination proceedings have received considerable appellate review and there is considerable case law which guides their conduct. This is so because public policy affords fundamental importance to the integrity and privacy of the family. The courts and legislatures view the permanent severing of the parent-child relationship as the ultimate state intrusion into a relationship the state generally wishes to foster.

When the court is petitioned to terminate parental rights, the use of expert psychological or psychiatric witnesses is virtually imperative. In most states, there is specific statutory language which sets out the state's basis for termination of parental rights. Abandonment, chronic mental illness which interferes with parenting, parental unfitness, and certain criminal behavior leading to lengthy jail terms are among the bases for terminating parental rights. The most common reason for seeking a termination, however, is "parental unfitness" without reasonable prospect of parental rehabilitation and only after the clear failure of good faith efforts made by the state to assist the parents and facilitate a continuation of the family unit. Further, under the U. S. Supreme Court's recent holding in *Santosky v. Kramer* (1982), the burden of proof of "unfitness" is upon the state and the standard of proof is set at the stringent "clear and convincing" level or higher. Given the procedural safeguards, high evidentiary standards, and the need for proof of the state's good faith efforts to reunite the family, heavy reliance upon psychological data, reports, and conclusions is an essential aspect of the state's case. In the event termination proceedings are inevitable, all those mental health professionals who have been involved in the case, at any stage, may be called upon to testify.

In a termination hearing, the mental health expert can expect to be called upon to give testimony as to his or her credentials in order to qualify as an "expert" (the process of *voir dire*). Once "qualified" as an "expert" the witness may testify as to *conclusions* or *opinions* in his or her area of expertise, unlike ordinary witnesses, whose testimony is restricted to matters of *fact*. The attorney for whom the expert's testimony is expected to be adverse will attempt to prevent the mental health witness from being qualified as an expert.

During the preliminary examination of the witness, the opposing counsel may question the training, experience, or credentials of the witness. Questions may also be raised at this stage as to whether the material the expert is to testify about was obtained from the respondent (parent named in the termination petition) in a manner which bars its admission into evidence. For example, if a psychological evaluation was court ordered but the evaluator failed to inform the parent of the nonprivileged nature of the evaluation, evidence obtained in that evaluation may be deemed inadmissible. This is essentially an exclusionary rule not unlike the requirements set out in the famous *Miranda* decision (*Miranda v. Arizona*, 1966).

During this *voir dire* proceeding the witness may also be questioned as to possible prejudices he or she might hold toward the respondent and possible conflicts of interest which might bias his or her testimony. If the witness is qualified as an expert (a decision made by the presiding judge), he or she will be called upon later to offer direct testimony, including opinions and conclusions relevant to the issue of termination. The expert should also anticipate being subject to cross-examination. For this reason, it is advisable to clearly formulate one's opinions upon a well-defined data base of clinical observations.

The process of inference from data to opinion should be sound rather than merely speculative and recognition should be allowed that reasonable experts might well differ in the conclusions which they reach. To claim an absolute degree of confidence in one's opinions and conclusions or to assert that psychology and psychiatry are exact sciences is an invitation to devastating cross-examination at the hands of a skilled attorney. Because there is such wide disagreement among psychological experts regarding diagnoses and the causes of behavior, and because of the mediocre ability in the behavioral sciences to make accurate predictions concerning future behavior of individuals, an appropriate degree of modesty is becoming to an expert witness. In general, experts who provide psychological testimony do best when they rely heavily upon behavior which they have personally observed and/or objective tests which they have administered or reviewed.

Highly conjectured inferences are also a trap which should be avoided. In most proceedings involving the termination of parental rights, the state can make its case only by establishing that a child has suffered harm or is at clear risk. It must also be shown that the parents' behavior is the cause of the harm (or risk). Moreover, it must be shown that remedial efforts to aid the family have been made and have produced no ameliorative result. Most importantly, it must be shown that there is no prospect in the foreseeable future (or in a reasonable period of time) for a positive change in the parents' ability to adequately care for the child.

This last element of the parental rights termination case obviously calls for both an opinion and a prediction. Because the state must prove its case by at least clear and convincing evidence, this particular opinion/prediction is often the most difficult to sustain. It requires the expert to conclude that there is no available treatment program that would allow the parents to improve their parenting capacity and that their inadequacies are so severe as to constitute parental unfitness. The expert who testifies to this conclusion must carefully review all the available history of the family and seek to supplement the social history of parental failure with a psychological diagnosis consistent with the pessimistic conclusion that there is little likelihood of parental remediation.

The ultimate decision as to whether there is sufficient evidence to support a finding of parental unfitness is the responsibility of the trier-of-fact—either judge or jury. The expert is ordinarily not asked, and should not be asked, whether there should be "a termination of parental rights." This is a legal not a psychological question and hence lies outside the proper scope of the expert testimony. After the evidence is in, it is the role of the court to decide whether termination of parental rights is a disposition which is supported by the evidence. This, too, is a legal conclusion and determination of whether the proper evidentiary standard to support this finding has been met is a question for the court and not the expert.

Although experts will typically testify in court, there are circumstances in which their reports, prepared outside of court, may be entered into evidence. This can come about in several ways. There may be specific evidentiary rules in juvenile court which permit the admissibility of reports into evidence even though they would ordinarily be excluded by the hearsay rule. Alternatively, expert reports may be entered into evidence through a prior stipulation by petitioner and respondent that no objection to admissibility will be raised when the report is offered into evidence. Other reports may be regarded simply as medical records and entered into evidence if the custodian or preparer of the record is available in court to establish a proper foundation for its admissibility.

BEYOND TERMINATION

Even where termination of parental rights has been ordered, the mental health professional may continue to have a significant diagnostic and treatment role to play. Once the parent-child bonds have been severed legally, there remains the question of the most appropriate placement for the child. Should the child remain in permanent foster care, be moved to or from an institutional or group home setting, or placed for adoption? In addition to offering the court and social service personnel assistance in answering the question of placement, the mental health professional also will often be called upon to continue or initiate treatment of the child. Such treatment will be aimed at helping the child cope with the stress which so often follows legal proceedings which put a permanent end to even the most tenuous or damaging parent-child relationships. Here, as throughout the legal process in child abuse and neglect cases, the work of mental health professionals often proves critical.

Melvin J. Guyer, J.D., Ph.D., a psychologist and attorney, is Director of the Family and Law Program and Associate Professor in the Department of Psychiatry at the University of Michigan in Ann Arbor.

Peter Ash, M.D., a clinical and forensic psychiatrist, is an Assistant Professor in the Department of Psychiatry at the University of Michigan. Dr. Ash's research is in the areas of child abuse, contested custody, and divorce mediation.

RESOURCES

Adams-Tucker, C. (1982). Proximate effects of sexual abuse in childhood. *American Journal of Psychiatry, 139*, 1252-1256.

Besharov, D. (1983). Child protection: Past progress, present problems and future direction. *Family Law Quarterly, 17*, 151-172.

Black, H. C. (1979). *Black's Law Dictionary* (rev. 5th ed.). St. Paul, MN: West.

Defrancis, V., & Lucht, C. L. (1974). *Child Abuse Legislation in the 1970s.* Denver, CO: American Humane Association, Children's Division.

Friedrich, W. N., & Wheeler, K. K. (1982). The abusing parent revisited—a decade of psychological research. *Journal of Nervous and Mental Disease, 170*, 577-587.

Green, A. H. (1983). Child abuse: Dimensions of psychological trauma in abused children. *Journal of the American Academy of Child Psychiatry, 22*, 231-237.

Grumet, B. R. (1970). The plaintive plaintiffs: Victims of the battered child syndrome. *Family Law Quarterly, 4*, 296-317.

Guyer, M. J. (1982). Child abuse/neglect statutes: Legal and clinical implications. *American Journal of Orthopsychiatry, 52*, 73-81.

Helfer, R. E., & Kempe, C. H. (Eds.). (1976). *Child Abuse and Neglect: The Family and the Community.* Cambridge: Ballinger.

Kaplan, S. J., Pelcoritz, D., & Salzinger, S. (1983). Psychopathology of parents of abused and neglected children and adolescents. *Journal of the American Academy of Child Psychiatry, 22*, 238-244.

Katz, S. N. (1971). *When Parents Fail: The Law's Response to Family Breakdown.* Boston: Beacon Press.

Katz, S. N., Ambrosino, L., McGrath, M., & Sawitsky, K. (1977). Legal research on child abuse and neglect: Past and future. *Family Law Quarterly, 11*, 151-184.

Kempe, C. H., Silverman, F. N., Steele, B. F., Droegemuller, W., & Silver, H. K. (1962). The battered child syndrome. *Journal of the American Medical Association, 181*, 17-24.

Kempe, R. S., & Kempe, C. H. (1978). *Child Abuse.* Cambridge: Harvard University Press.

Miranda v. Arizona, 384 U.S. 436 (1966).

Mnookin, R. H. (1973). Foster care—in whose best interest? *Harvard Educational Review, 43,* 599-638.

Newberger, E. H., Newberger, C. M., & Hampton, R. L. (1983). Child abuse: The current theory and future research needs. *Journal of the American Academy of Child Psychiatry, 22,* 262-268.

Rootman, H. (1973). Children under the law. *Harvard Educational Review, 43,* 487-514.

Santosky v. Kramer, 102 S.Ct. 1388 (1982).

Stan, R. H. (Ed.). (1982). *Child Abuse Prediction: Policy Implications.* Cambridge: Ballinger.

Weiss, E. H., & Berg, R. F. (1982). Child victims of sexual assault: Impact of court procedures. *Journal of the American Academy of Child Psychiatry, 21,* 513-518.

INTRODUCTION TO SECTION IV: PSYCHOLOGY AND PSYCHIATRY IN TORT LAW AND WORKERS' COMPENSATION

Anglo-American law has long provided legal mechanisms by which individuals harmed by others may seek and receive compensation for their injuries. The most prominent of such mechanisms is tort law, that branch of jurisprudence which governs private lawsuits brought by victims against those allegedly responsible for their injuries. While such lawsuits provide remedies—primarily in the form of money damages—for most legally recognized private wrongs, claims for compensation for certain kinds of injuries are dealt with through specialized administrative mechanisms which have grown up outside of traditional tort law. Workers' Compensation, the statutory system which provides economic redress of job-related injuries, is the best known example in contemporary law. In most cases, injured workers may not sue their employers but must seek legal remedies through quasi-judicial mechanisms which operate under Workers' Compensation laws in every American jurisdiction.

The chapters in this section explore some of the many and various roles played by psychologists, psychiatrists, and other mental health professionals in tort lawsuits and the adjudication of Workers' Compensation claims. In the first of these three chapters, Harold Smith, a clinical and forensic psychologist, examines some of the more common psychological aspects of personal injury and the role played by mental health experts in personal injury litigation. In particular, Dr. Smith's contribution deals with post-traumatic stress disorders, psychological sequelae of closed-head trauma and cervical ("whiplash") injuries, and malingering.

Dr. Smith's contribution is followed by Martin Kurke's chapter on the use of multispecialty forensic psychology teams in products liability litigation, lawsuits against manufacturers and distributors whose products are alleged to have resulted in injuries to others. Dr. Kurke, a psychologist with a law degree, begins by offering an overview of the law of products liability. He then demonstrates how a team of forensic experts—including human factors engineering psychologists, clinical psychologists, and vocational counseling psychologists—can work together to make the most effective use of psychological expertise in products liability lawsuits.

This section concludes with Herbert Weissman's chapter regarding the role of psychological factors in Workers' Compensation claims and the psychological and psychiatric evaluation of Workers' Compensation claimants. After detailing the legal history of the Workers' Compensation system, Dr. Weissman, a clinical and forensic psychologist, describes the psycholegal aspects of Workers' Compensation evaluations. Dr. Weissman concludes with a detailed description of what the Workers' Compensation clinical report should include and how it should be organized.

PSYCHODIAGNOSTIC ASSESSMENT IN PERSONAL INJURY LITIGATION

Harold H. Smith, Jr.

The term "tort" refers to a "private or civil wrong, other than breach of contract, for which the court will provide a remedy in the form of an action for damages" (Black, 1979, p. 1335). Tort law includes remedies for wrongs such as assault and battery, trespass, nuisance, false imprisonment, invasion of privacy, defamation, misrepresentation, and professional malpractice, among others. Probably the most common tort actions, however, involve claims of some form of personal injury, negligently or intentionally inflicted upon the plaintiff by the defendant (i.e., tortfeasor).

Personal injury litigation runs the gamut from relatively small claims arising out of everyday motor vehicle accidents to multimillion dollar lawsuits resulting from disasters in which many people are killed or injured. In one recent suit, for example, the plaintiff, who was disabled as the result of a shipboard explosion, received a damage award of 25.8 million dollars.

In modern tort law, the term *personal injury* encompasses not only physical harm but mental distress and psychological symptomatology as well. Many physical injuries have psychological components (e.g., chronic pain) or sequelae (e.g., emotional disturbance following head injury), the presence of which may increase a plaintiff's entitlement to money damages. But even absent physical injury, a plaintiff may, in some jurisdictions under certain circumstances, recover damages for psychological harm caused by a tortfeasor.

Over the course of time, the courts have developed several rules which determine a plaintiff's right to recover for psychological injuries. A minority of jurisdictions follow the "impact" rule which disallows recovery for psychological harm unless the plaintiff also sustained some physical impact as a result of the defendant's actions. In such jurisdictions, for example, a plaintiff who was frightened or otherwise psychologically traumatized by mere exposure to the defendant's conduct would be denied recovery for any resulting psychological harm.

The majority of jurisdictions, however, follow the so-called "zone of danger" rule, which allows recovery for psychological harm, absent physical impact or injury, if at the time of the defendant's tortious action the plaintiff was within the zone of risk or threat of physical harm. Some jurisdictions, however, have rejected the spatial limitations posed by the zone of danger rule and have applied, instead, a test of "foreseeability." In applying this test, the court's determination that a plaintiff's psychological distress was foreseeable and thus compensable will depend on whether: (a) the plaintiff was located near the scene of the accident or tortious act; (b) the plaintiff's distress resulted from direct observation of the accident or tortious act; and (c) the victim and plaintiff were closely related (*Culbert v. Sampson's Supermarkets, Inc.*, 1982; *Dillon v. Legg*, 1968).

Whatever the source of the plaintiff's psychological harm, his or her right to damages will depend, in most cases, upon proof that such harm resulted from the defendant's conduct. Thus, not surprisingly, psychologists and psychiatrists with expertise in assessing psychological injury and its causation, have come to play a significant role in personal injury litigation. Ordinarily, in litigation over alleged psychological harm, the mental health expert will be called upon to conduct a careful and thorough evaluation of the plaintiff and to testify regarding the nature, degree, and causation of any psychological impairment found to exist. The ability of psychologists and psychiatrists to render such testimony is now well accepted by the courts. It has been held, for example, that "psychodiagnostics has moved beyond problems of classification to the more mature objective of completely describing the [etiological] factors causative of disorder" (*Sandow v. Weyerhaeuser*, 1969, p. 429) and that "medical science has unquestionably become sophisticated enough to provide reliable and accurate evidence on the causes of mental trauma" (*Culbert v. Sampson's Supermarkets, Inc.*, 1982, p. 463).

The purpose of this chapter is to examine some of the more common psychological aspects of personal injury and the role that psychologists and psychiatrists play in personal injury litigation. Specifically, this chapter will deal with post-traumatic stress disorders, the psychological sequelae of closed head trauma and cervical ("whiplash") injuries, and malingering. Because of space limitations, other important aspects of trauma commonly the subject of personal injury litigation (e.g., psychological impairment related to disfigurement, amputation, burns, loss of teeth, chronic pain, sensory loss, and sexual dysfunction) will not be considered.

POST-TRAUMATIC STRESS DISORDER

Post-traumatic stress disorder (often referred to in the past as "post-traumatic neurosis") involves "the development of characteristic symptoms following a psychologically traumatic event that is generally outside the range of usual human experience" (American Psychiatric Association, 1980, p. 236). Such traumatic events include not only stressors such as rape, military combat, and natural disasters, but also automobile accidents, plane crashes, and other personal catastrophes, many of which result in tort actions. "Frequently there is a concomitant physical component to the trauma which may even involve direct damage to the central nervous system" (American Psychiatric Association, 1980, p. 236), but post-traumatic stress disorder may occur without physical injury and there is often an inverse relationship between the clinical features observed and the severity of the provoking injury (Miller, 1961a, 1961b).

The symptoms of post-traumatic stress disorder (Modlin, 1967; Thompson, 1965) include: (a) *anxiety* of a free-floating or near phobic quality, including panic attacks whenever conditions similar to or reminiscent of the traumatic incident occur or are recreated; (b) *muscular tension,* as reflected in insomnia, fatigue, restlessness, impatience, and tension headaches; (c) *irritability,* which may include inability to tolerate noise, startle response to sudden auditory stimuli, and difficulty in controlling anger; (d) *impaired concentration and memory,* which is not demonstrated psychometrically but instead reflects inattention; (e) *repetitive nightmares* or intrusive recollections of the traumatic event; (f) *sexual inhibition;* and (g) *social withdrawal.* Depression may also occur, superimposed upon the anxiety state. All of these symptoms may not be present in a given case. Moreover, many patients will not report some of these symptoms spontaneously. Thus, careful clinical evaluation is generally required.

Once having diagnosed post-traumatic stress disorder in a personal injury tort victim, the mental health professional will generally be called upon to provide some statement as to the level of impairment and the patient's prognosis (i.e., the permanency of the injury). The *Diagnostic and Statistical Manual of Mental Disorders* (3rd ed.) (American Psychiatric Association, 1980) describes impairment resulting from post-traumatic stress disorder in the following terms:

> Impairment may either be mild or affect nearly every aspect of life. Phobic avoidance of situations or activities resembling or symbolizing the original trauma may result in occupational or recreational impairment. "Psychic numbing" may interfere with interpersonal relationships ....Emotional lability, depression, and guilt may result in self-defeating behavior or suicidal actions. Substance Abuse Disorders may develop. (p. 237)

In every case the clinician should carefully specify the impairments determined to have resulted from the patient's exposure to the traumatic event.

As to permanency of the injury, Thompson (1965) has reported that post-traumatic stress disorder symptoms may last as long as 15 years, but that in 52% of cases some improvements will occur without treatment. "When the symptoms begin within six months of the trauma and have not lasted more than six months...the prognosis for remission is good" (American Psychiatric Association, 1980, p. 237). In many cases, improvement will occur with psychotherapy. Specific intervention techniques, such as hypnotic age regression for catharsis, have been successful in alleviating some patients' symptoms (Watkins, 1971).

PSYCHOLOGICAL SEQUELAE
OF CLOSED HEAD INJURIES

The head is the most frequently injured part of the body in vehicular accidents (Heiskanen & Sipponen, 1970). Severe and irreversible brain damage may occur without skull fracture or blemish on the scalp, and not all damage in head injury cases occurs at the moment of impact (Adams, Mitchell, Graham, & Doyle, 1977). Even minor injuries may result in widespread neuronal and axonal damage, and the post-concussional syndrome may have an organic basis without clear neurological or psychometric signs (Merskey & Woodforde, 1972).

The clinical characteristics of individuals presenting with post-concussional syndrome will vary according to the severity of the injury. Commonly, patients complain of impairments in concentration and attention, poor memory, headache, dizziness, vision disturbances, fatigue, tinnitus, and a variety of nervous or psychic symptoms, including anxiety, depression, emotional instability, irritability, and anger. Many of these symptoms are not reported spontaneously by the patient and must be elicited through careful questioning of the patient and significant others.

Closed head injury (CHI) may include not only post-concussional state, a mild form of head injury, but also more severe forms of injury including contusion and compression injuries. There exists a voluminous literature regarding the clinical features of CHI, much of which has recently been reviewed by Levin, Benton, and Grossman (1982). The patient, or significant others, may report a variety of symptoms, including anterograde and retrograde amnesia, immediate and long-term memory deficits, various cognitive impairments, language difficulties, altered perceptual and motor functions, and personality changes. Reports from many countries have documented the universality of symptoms that result from CHI and their acceptance by the medical and psychological professions.

The means by which these symptoms are identified and quantified are also valid and reliable. The neurological bases for various symptoms may be established by computerized axial tomography (CAT scan) or photon emission tomography. Cognitive and neurobehavioral consequences of CHI may be evaluated through a variety of psychological tests. The Halstead-Reitan Neuropsychological Battery (Reitan, 1955) has been shown to compare favorably to the diagnostic value of the CAT scan in head trauma cases (Tsushima & Wedding, 1979) and to provide superior clinical data when compared with more traditional psychological assessment procedures (Goldstein, S. H., Deysach, & Kleinknecht, 1973). This objective test battery, which evaluates intellectual, cognitive, sensory-perceptual, and motor functions, has been shown to be capable of differentiating neurologic and "pseudo-neurologic" patients (Matthews, Shaw, & Klöve, 1966), assessing the likelihood of patient employment (Heaton, Chelune, & Lehman, 1978; Newman, Heaton, & Lehman, 1978), and providing information about a patient's everyday functioning (Heaton & Pendleton, 1981).

Receptive and expressive language is often affected as a result of CHI, and deficits in verbal fluency, anomic disturbance, and dysarthria are reported (Hagen, 1981; Sarno, 1980). It is characteristic of CHI patients, however, to cope with such language deficits by reducing verbal output, falsely acknowledging an understanding of communication, or substituting different words for those they intended to say. Demonstrating to a judge or jury the existence of these deficits, particularly when they occur in intelligent and highly educated patients, is a challenging task.

Personality changes directly attributable to CHI have been established and will vary according to the severity of the injury (Dikman & Reitan, 1977; Finlayson & Bloch,

1980). Such changes may include the development of symptoms of post-traumatic stress disorder, anxiety, depression, and psychotic adjustment. K. Goldstein (1952) has drawn attention to impairments in abstract capacity, memory and attention, and capacity for pleasure, joy, friendship, love, and humor. All of these changes alter the quality of the patient's life, often reduce or eliminate employability, and place a significant burden on family members (Lezak, 1978; Thomsen, 1974).

Gronwall and Wrightson (1975) have demonstrated that concussion produces a decrease in the rate of information processing and that the effects are cumulative. Numerous reports have documented the presence of unequivocal cognitive and emotional deficits related to CHI (Dencker, 1958; Fahy, Irving, & Millac, 1967; Heiskanen & Sipponen, 1970; Levin, Grossman, Rose, & Teasdale, 1979). Not only are work, leisure activities, and social relationships affected, but CHI patients also manifest increased fatigability, lowered tolerance to alcohol, decrease in interests, and occasional impotence (Ruesch, Harris, & Bowman, 1945). Paranoid trends, often leading to social isolation, have also been observed in CHI patients (Ruesch & Bowman, 1945).

The mechanism of closed head injury is clearly understood. Pudenz and Sheldon (1946) administered various forms of trauma to monkeys, the convex portion of whose skulls had been replaced with a lucite calvarium. Through this "window" it was observed that a blow to the head caused the brain to move within the cranial cavity. The pathophysiological consequences of CHI, including hemorrhages, contusion, and diffuse degeneration of white matter have been documented at autopsy (Bloomquist & Courville, 1947; Strich, 1956).

Damage to the central nervous system in humans appears to be permanent, even in cases of mild head injury (Ewing, McCarthy, Gronwall, & Wrightson, 1980). Although Becker, Grossman, McLaurin, and Caveness (1979) have noted that it may take from 6 months to 2 years for the post-concussive syndrome to resolve, it is perhaps better stated that the greatest amount of recovery will occur within the first 2 years after the trauma.

When called upon to testify in a personal injury action involving closed head injury, the mental health professional may be asked to specify the nature of the injury and its psychological consequences, to describe the level of impairment resulting from the injury, and to provide a prognosis for recovery from such impairment. Furthermore, the clinician may be asked to differentiate those symptoms which are the result of the injury and those which may have other causes unrelated to the injury in question.

In specifying the nature of the injury and its psychological consequences, the clinician should rely most heavily upon objective test results (such as those derived from the Halstead-Reitan Battery) and the clinical interpretation of such results, but should not neglect to mention clinical findings apparent in the more subjective psychological or psychiatric interview. In any event, the clinician should be well-versed in the literature (some of which has been reviewed briefly above) documenting the relationship between various psychological symptoms and closed head injuries.

Differentiating symptoms attributable to the injury and those of other etiology requires careful differential diagnosis. Other possible causal factors which must be ruled out include alcohol and drug abuse; senility; developmental disabilities; pre-existing psychiatric disorders; endocrine, metabolic, and nutritional disturbances; infections; and ingestion of toxic substances. In every case, the clinician should carefully assess and report the patient's history (including pre-traumatic functioning in all currently affected areas) as well as his or her current functioning. In addition to specific tests and the clinical examination and interview of the patient, the clinician should look to significant others (e.g., friends and family members) as well as documentary evidence (e.g., school, military, and vocational records) for pertinent diagnostic information.

Prognosis in closed head injuries is difficult to specify and clinicians should be wary of offering firm statements of the likelihood of full recovery. Often, rather than specifying a firm prognosis for a given case, the clinician will be more helpful if he or she provides the court with a general understanding of prognostic considerations in closed head injury cases. Thus, for example, the clinician might note that certain factors, such as older age, prolonged unconsciousness, amnesia, severe dysphasia, and evidence of brainstem lesions, portend a poorer prognosis while others, such as higher intelligence and greater adaptability suggest a more positive prognosis.

CERVICAL INJURIES

Rear-end vehicular collisions, as well as other forms of sudden impact, often result in acceleration injuries which are described by the patient as causing neck pain, interscapular discomfort, chest pain, headaches, dizziness, loss of balance, blurring of vision, dysphagia, tinnitus and hearing difficulties, numbness of the extremities, and emotional problems. Spasms, tenderness, and limited mobility of the neck muscles are also often reported (MacNab, 1974; Toglia, 1976).

These patients frequently complain of chronic pain for which physical therapy, medication, and rest provide little relief. The "whiplash" injury can be incapacitating, yet Gorman (1979) notes that extensive documentation shows that objective signs of injury are found in only about 2% to 20% of cases. Most neurologists and orthopedists are likely to diagnose the condition as myofascitis, myofibrositis, or fibrositis. Many of these patients, particularly if they are involved in litigation, receive little aid from medical treatment. Some patients develop neurotic adjustment patterns as a result of the chronic pain.

The mechanism of whiplash injury is well understood. In 1882, Erichsen wrote, "I have often remarked that in railway accidents those passengers suffer most seriously from concussions of the nervous system who sit with their backs turned towards the end of one train which is struck" (cited in Trimble, 1981, p. 15). Rear-end collisions account for about 20% of all motor vehicle accidents, and Gorman (1979) has noted that a 10 mile per hour collision produces a force of 9 G at the neck, an impact which can produce severe injury.

Diagnosis of cervical ("whiplash") injury may not occur for as long as 3 months post injury. Treatment may include physiotherapy, heat, bedrest, biofeedback training, and hypnosis. Although symptomatic recovery occurs in about 57% of whiplash patients, degenerative changes (including intervertebral disc narrowing, spur formation, and the development of arthritis) may occur in about 39%, and some 27% will continue to have symptoms without degenerative changes (Hohl, 1974, 1975). Injury to the lower back may be a complication in about 30% of patients (Gay & Abbott, 1953). Short-term studies of the permanency of effects of cervical injury have shown them to persist as long as 5 years; long-term studies have not been reported.

The "cry of whiplash" following an accident is well recognized and criticized by laymen and professionals alike. Given the frequent lack of objective signs of injury (Gorman, 1979), whiplash claims are frequently disputed and often the subject of heated litigation. The role of the mental health expert in such litigation has a number of aspects. First, the expert may be called upon to testify regarding the possibility of malingering (an issue discussed in some detail below). Second, he or she may provide evidence regarding the psychological sequelae of the patient's claimed injury (e.g., neurotic adjustment in response to the chronic pain). Third, the expert may be asked to testify to clinical findings, such as psychological test results and electromyographic biofeedback recordings (which measure the amount of muscle tension present in the head, neck, and shoulders), which help to document or refute the patient's claim of injury. Finally, the expert may testify regarding the prognosis for successful psychological intervention (e.g., psychotherapy, relaxation techniques, biofeedback treatment, hypnosis, vocational rehabilitation, etc.).

MALINGERING AND THE
EFFECTS OF LITIGATION

Inevitably the issue of malingering will be raised at some point in personal injury litigation. Malingering is the conscious, planned simulation of illness or disease for some type of gain. It is a condition not often diagnosed or labeled, in part because of the subjectivity involved but also because of "reaction formation to the hostility engendered in doctors by certain patients with non-organic disorders who are almost invariably called hysterical no matter how transparently conscious the deceptive behavior may be" (Chodoff & Lyons, 1958, p. 736).

Nevertheless, malingering is a legitimate diagnosis and one which should be made where appropriate. In every case, however, the clinician must be careful to differentiate malingering and other possible diagnoses, such as conversion disorder. Conversion disorder, like malingering, may present loss or alteration of physical functioning. But the conversion "hysteric," unlike the malingerer, has no voluntary control over manifest symptomatology. Conversion reactions, rather, seem to reflect an unconscious psychological conflict or need. Malingering should also be differentiated from the factitious disorder in which the patient presents voluntarily controlled symptoms for which "there is no apparent goal other than to assume the patient role" (American Psychiatric Association, 1980, p. 285).

Malingering is difficult to detect in many cases. But the diagnosis should be given serious consideration if any combination of the following signs is present:

(1) medicolegal context of presentation, e.g., the person's being referred by his attorney;
(2) marked discrepancy between the person's claimed distress or disability and the objective findings;
(3) lack of cooperation with the diagnostic evaluation and prescribed treatment regimen;
(4) the presence of Antisocial Personality Disorder (American Psychiatric Association, 1980, p. 331).

Psychological testing may also be helpful in diagnosing malingering. Bash (1978) has demonstrated that malingerers may be differentiated on the basis of their performance on the Wechsler Adult Intelligence Scale (WAIS), the Bender-Gestalt, Rorschach inkblots, and a Listening Task. Furthermore, Gough (1947) found that psychiatrists, psychologists, social workers, and personnel consultants—all knowledgeable in the field of psychopathology—were unable to simulate neurotic and psychotic profiles on the Minnesota Multiphasic Personality Inventory (MMPI). The validity scales of the MMPI have long been used to detect dissimulation, prevarication, and the exaggeration (or minimization) of psychological impairments.

The mental health professional who suspects malingering by a personal injury litigant is well advised to conduct a thorough evaluation, including a battery of appropriate psychological tests, and to be fully prepared to address this issue in trial or deposition testimony.

Closely related to the issue of malingering is the effect of litigation. Clinicians should always be aware that a patient's symptoms and complaints may be unconsciously influenced by the status of ongoing personal injury litigation. Miller and Stern (1965), for example, report that subjective complaints in severe head injury cases are nearly always resolved after the patient receives a financial settlement. On the other hand, others (e.g., Merskey & Woodforde, 1972) note that CHI symptoms persist even when compensation is no longer an issue. Furthermore, Allodi (1974) reports that post-traumatic neurosis does not appear to be affected by settlement of the patient's legal claim. Likewise, Balla and Moraitis (1970) suggest that the "green poultice" (i.e., a compensation award) has no significant effect on the functioning of patients suffering from neck or back injuries. Finally, Peck, Fordyce, and Black (1978) have found that neither litigation nor legal representation seem to bring about any alteration in a patient's pain-related behavior.

Despite these conclusions, the belief persists among many mental health professionals and certainly many attorneys that concern over compensation often exacerbates symptoms and that the *prospect* of financial gain frequently deters recovery. Thus, the clinician who is involved in a personal injury case in which there is pending litigation should always at least consider the possible effects of such litigation on the patient's symptoms, complaints, and prognosis.

Harold H. Smith, Jr., Ph.D., a clinical and forensic psychologist, is a Diplomate of both the American Board of Professional Psychology (Clinical Psychology) and the American Board of Forensic Psychology. Dr. Smith is in private practice in Largo, FL and is a member of the adjunct faculty at the University of South Florida. He also directs the Domestic Violence Pre-Trial Intervention Program in conjunction with the Pinellas County State Attorney's Office. Dr. Smith's professional practice includes not only forensic evaluations, but also psychotherapy, neuropsychology, and treatment of chronic pain.

RESOURCES

Adams, J. H., Mitchell, D. E., Graham, D. I., & Doyle, D. (1977). Diffuse brain damage of immediate impact type. *Brain, 100,* 489-502.

Allodi, F. A. (1974). Accident neurosis: Whatever happened to male hysteria? *Canadian Psychiatric Association Journal, 19,* 291-296.

American Psychiatric Association. (1980). *Diagnostic and Statistical Manual of Mental Disorders* (3rd ed.). Washington, DC: Author.

Balla, J. E., & Moraitis, S. (1970). Knights in armour. A follow-up study of injuries after legal settlement. *Medical Journal of Australia, 2,* 355-361.

Bash, I. Y. (1978). Malingering: A study designed to differentiate between schizophrenic offenders and malingerers (Doctoral dissertation, New York University, 1978). *Dissertation Abstracts International, 39,* 2973B.

Becker, D. P., Grossman, R. G., McLaurin, R. L., & Caveness, W. F. (1979). Head injuries. *Archives of Neurology, 36,* 750-758.

Black, H. C. (1979). *Black's Law Dictionary* (rev. 5th ed.). St. Paul: West.

Bloomquist, E. R., & Courville, C. B. (1947). The nature and incidence of traumatic lesions of the brain.

Bulletin of the Los Angeles Neurological Society, 12, 174-183.

Chodoff, P., & Lyons, H. (1958). Hysteria, the hysterical personality and "hysterical" conversion. *American Journal of Psychiatry, 144,* 734-740.

Culbert v. Sampson's Supermarkets, Inc., 444 A.2d 433 (Me. 1982).

Dencker, S. J. (1958). A follow up study of 128 closed head injuries in twins using co-twins as controls. *Acta Psychiatriaca et Neurologica Scandinavica, 33,* 9-121.

Dikman, S., & Reitan, R. M. (1977). Emotional sequelae of head injury. *Annals of Neurology, 2,* 492-494.

Dillon v. Legg, 68 Cal.2d 728, 69 Cal. Rptr. 72, 441 P.2d 912 (1968).

Erichsen, J. E. (1882). *On Concussion of the Spine: Nervous Shock and other Obscure Injuries of the Nervous System in their Clinical and Medico-Legal Aspects.* London: Longmans, Green & Co. Cited by M. R. Trimble, *Post-Traumatic Neurosis.* New York: Wiley, 1981.

Ewing, R., McCarthy, D., Gronwall, D., & Wrightson, P. (1980). Persisting effects of minor head injury observable during hypoxic stress. *Journal of Clinical Neuropsychology, 2,* 147-155.

Fahy, T. J., Irving, M. H., & Millac, P. (1967). Severe head injuries. A six year follow up. *Lancet, 2,* 475-479.

Finlayson, M. A. J., & Bloch, R. F. (1980, June). *Cognitive and Emotional Changes in Head Injury: A Follow-Up Study.* Paper presented at the annual meeting of the International Psychological Society, Italy.

Gay, J. R., & Abbott, K. H. (1953). Common whiplash injuries of the neck. *Journal of the American Medical Association, 152,* 1698-1704.

Goldstein, K. (1952). The effect of brain damage on the personality. *Psychiatry, 15,* 245-259.

Goldstein, S. G., Deysach, R. E., & Kleinknecht, R. A. (1973). Effect of experience and amount of information on identification of cerebral impairment. *Journal of Consulting and Clinical Psychology, 41,* 30-34.

Gorman, W. F. (1979). "Whiplash": Fictive or factual? *Bulletin of the American Academy of Psychiatry and the Law, 7,* 245-248.

Gough, H. G. (1947). Simulated patterns on the Minnesota Multiphasic Personality Inventory. *Journal of Abnormal and Social Psychology, 42*, 215-225.

Gronwall, D., & Wrightson, P. (1975). Cumulative effect of concussion. *Lancet, 5*, 995-997.

Hagen, C. (1981). Language disorders secondary to closed head injury: diagnosis and treatment. In *Topics; Language Disorders.* Rockville, MD: Aspen Systems Corporation.

Heaton, R. K., Chelune, G. J., & Lehman, R. A. W. (1978). Using neuropsychological and personality tests to assess the likelihood of patient employment. *Journal of Nervous and Mental Disease, 166*, 408-416.

Heaton, R. K., & Pendleton, M. G. (1981). Use of neuropsychological tests to predict adult patients' everyday functioning. *Journal of Consulting and Clinical Psychology, 49*, 807-821.

Heiskanen, O., & Sipponen, P. (1970). Prognosis of severe brain injury. *Acta Neurologica Scandinivica, 46*, 343-348.

Henderson, S., & Bostock, T. (1977). Coping behavior after shipwreck. *British Journal of Psychiatry, 131*, 15-20.

Hohl, M. (1974). Soft-tissue injuries of the neck in automobile accidents. *Journal of Bone and Joint Surgery, 56*, 1675-1681.

Hohl, M. (1975). Soft-tissue injuries to the neck. *Clinical Orthopedics and Related Research, 109*, 42-49.

Levin, H. S., Benton, A. L., & Grossman, R. G. (1982). *Neurobehavioral Consequences of Closed Head Injury.* New York: Oxford University Press.

Levin, H. S., Grossman, R. G., Rose, J. E., & Teasdale, G. (1979). Long-term neuropsychological outcome of closed head injury. *Journal of Neurosurgery, 50*, 412-422.

Lezak, M. D. (1978). Living with the characterological altered brain injured patient. *Journal of Clinical Psychiatry, 39*, 592-598.

MacNab, I. (1974). The Whiplash Syndrome. *Clinical Neurosurgery, 20*, 232-240.

Matthews, C. G., Shaw, D. J., & Klöve, H. (1966). Psychological test performances in neurologic and "psuedo-neurologic" subjects. *Cortex, 2*, 244-253.

Merskey, H., & Woodforde, J. M. (1972). Psychiatric sequelae of minor head injury. *Brain, 95*, 521-528.

Miller, H. (1961a). Accident neurosis. *British Medical Journal, 1*, 919-925.

Miller,H. (1961b). Accident neurosis. *British Medical Journal, 1*, 992-998.

Miller, H., & Stern, G. (1965). The long-term prognosis of severe head injury. *Lancet, 1*, 225-229.

Modlin, H. (1967). The post accident anxiety syndrome: Psychosocial aspects. *American Journal of Psychiatry, 123*, 1008-1012.

Newman, O. S., Heaton, R. K., & Lehman, R. A. (1978). Neuropsychological and MMPI correlates of patients' future employment characteristics. *Perceptual and Motor Skills, 46*, 635-642.

Peck, C. J., Fordyce, W. E., & Black, R. G. (1978). The effect of the pendency of claims for compensation upon behavior indicative of pain. *Washington Law Review, 53*, 251-278.

Pudenz, R. H., & Sheldon, C. H. (1946). The lucite calvarium - a method for direct observation of the brain. *Journal of Neurosurgery, 3*, 487-505.

Reitan, R. M. (1955). Investigation of the validity of Halstead's measures of biological intelligence. *Archives of Neurology and Psychiatry, 73*, 28-35.

Ruesch, J., & Bowman, K. M. (1945). Prolonged post traumatic syndromes following head injury. *American Journal of Psychiatry, 102*, 145-162.

Ruesch, J., Harris, R. E., & Bowman, K. M. (1945). Pre- and post-traumatic personality in head injury. *Association for Research in Nervous and Mental Disorders, 24*, 507-543.

Sandow v. Weyerhaeuser, 449 P.2d 426 (Wash. 1969).

Sarno, M. T. (1980). The nature of verbal impairment after closed head injury. *Journal of Nervous and Mental Disorder, 168*, 685-692.

Strich, S. J. (1956). Diffuse degeneration of the cerebral white matter in severe dementia following head injury. *Journal of Neurology, Neurosurgery, and Psychiatry, 19*, 163-185.

Thompson, G. N. (1965). Post traumatic psychoneurosis - a statistical survey. *American Journal of Psychiatry, 121*, 1043-1048.

Thomsen, I. V. (1974). The patient with severe head injury and his family. *Scandinavian Journal of Rehabilitative Medicine, 6,* 180-183.

Toglia, J. V. (1976). Acute flexion—extension injury of the neck. *Neurology, 26,* 808-814.

Tsushima, W. T., & Wedding, D. (1979). A comparison of the Halstead-Reitan Neuropsychological Battery and computerized tomography in the identification of brain disorder. *Journal of Nervous and Mental Disease, 167,* 704-707.

Watkins, J. G. (1971). The affect bridge: A hypnoanalytic technique. *International Journal of Clinical and Experimental Hypnosis, 19,* 21-27.

THE MULTISPECIALTY FORENSIC TEAM APPROACH IN PRODUCTS LIABILITY LITIGATION

Martin I. Kurke

A variety of psychologists with competence in different areas of specialization may be involved in litigation in which products liability is at issue. This chapter examines the roles played by clinical, vocational counseling, and human factors psychologists in such litigation. The chapter begins with a brief overview of the legal theories of products liability and the legal elements attorneys must prove in products liability lawsuits. This introduction is followed by a discussion of the specific contributions to be made in such lawsuits by psychologists with different sorts of expertise. The chapter concludes with a demonstration of how a multispecialty team of forensic psychologists, using a systems approach, can have a synergistic impact upon products liability litigation not available to the aggregate of experts acting independently of each other.

THE LAW OF PRODUCTS LIABILITY

Producers and distributors of any product have a legal duty to assure that their product does not impose upon the public unnecessary hazard or risk of serious injury or death. Failure to meet that duty gives rise to a class of lawsuits known as products liability litigation. A products liability lawsuit may be brought on three separate legal theories: strict liability, breach of implied warranty, and negligence. A detailed discussion of the distinctions among these three theories is beyond the scope of this brief overview. For present purposes, however, it may be helpful to distinguish among products liability lawsuits on the basis of whether or not there is a claim of negligence involved.

Where negligence is not a factor in products liability litigation, the focus of the legal inquiry is on the quality of the product. If the product was sold in a defective condition unreasonably dangerous to the user or consumer or to his or her property, the defendant (producer and/or distributor) is liable for the harm done—regardless of the care taken by the defendant in the preparation and sale of the product. If the plaintiff's claim is that the product is defective because of a design feature, the probability and gravity of harm must be considered in balancing the risk inherent in the design against the product's utility. In sum, the focus in such cases is on the reasonableness of the product in the environment of its use.

If the theory of the lawsuit is one of negligence, the focus of litigation is the conduct of the parties. The defendant has a duty to protect a reasonable person against possible harm arising from use of the product (Weinstein, Twerski, Piehler, & Danaher, 1978). The plaintiff's claim may be challenged on the grounds of contributory negligence if it can be established that he or she did not act as a "reasonable person" in using the defendant's product, that is, as a person exercising "those qualities of attention, knowledge, intelligence and judgment which society requires of its members for the protection of their own interests and the interests of others" (Gifis, 1975, pp. 170-171).

Where the products liability lawsuit is predicated upon a theory of negligence, the plaintiff's attorney must prove that:

1. The defendant's product was instrumental in causing harm;
2. There was a defect in the product that made it possible for the product to be instrumental in causing that harm;
3. The defendant had a duty to see that the plaintiff was not harmed by the product; and

4. The defendant was negligent in that duty to the plaintiff.

In every negligence action, the court must consider the probability of occurrence of the harm, the gravity of the harm, and the burden of precaution to protect against that harm.

INDIVIDUAL ROLES OF FORENSIC PSYCHOLOGISTS IN PRODUCTS LIABILITY LITIGATION

Broadly speaking, psychologists are capable of providing two kinds of expertise and information in products liability litigation. One group of psychologists focuses upon the product while another group focuses upon the victim or other persons involved in the incident that precipitated the legal action.

The first group of psychologists, usually human factors engineering psychologists and other applied experimental psychologists, examines the product and the environment in which it is used in order to determine whether the product, its use, or its maintenance procedures contributed to the incident. Psychologists from this group testify as experts regarding the product's safety with reference to its human-machine-environment interfaces.

The second group of psychologists, usually clinical or counseling psychologists, examines the people involved in the incident. Generally these psychologists testify as to the mental health consequences of injuries caused by the incident and the loss of vocational or educational skills resulting from such injuries.

Where both types of psychologists serve as experts for the same party in a products liability lawsuit, they generally do so independently. Rarely is one even aware of the content of the other's testimony. While this is currently the general practice in products liability lawsuits, the failure to integrate the activities and testimony of the various psychological experts results in a failure to capitalize fully upon their combined expertise. In what follows, it will be urged that the use of an integrated, systems-oriented team approach, in which the psychological experts work together, is more appropriate to the evidentiary demands of the products liability lawsuit.

THE MULTISPECIALTY FORENSIC TEAM

A team of psychologists whose skills encompass the ability to focus on the person(s) involved in the incident, the human factors aspects of the product design, and the interaction of both can be a powerful tool for the attorney in products liability litigation. Figure 1 (p. 355) illustrates how such a team (consisting of a clinical psychologist, a vocational counseling psychologist, and a human factors engineering psychologist) can pool the specialized expertise of its members to provide twice as many elements of testimony as would be available if these members provided independent and uncoordinated advice to the attorney.

As a practical illustration of how such a team makes its contribution, consider the following hypothetical case. A worker parked a forklift on a ramp, setting the handbrake. However, due to a design feature on that model forklift, it was possible for the driver unknowingly to release the brake tension while setting the brake. After the worker dismounted, the brakes slipped and the vehicle rolled down the ramp, but the two left wheels went off the edge, leaving the forklift hung up on its axles. The driver asked two other workers to help push the vehicle back onto the ramp, but as they lifted the forklift it overturned, seriously injuring the driver and one of the helping workers. Subsequently a lawsuit was filed alleging that the brake design was faulty, that the design fault had caused the vehicle to slip, and that the plaintiffs were injured as a result.

Rothenberg (1982) has noted a number of ways in which a consulting forensic psychologist may contribute to the planning, development, and implementation of trial strategies. Assume that in the above hypothetical, the plaintiffs' attorney chooses a variant of Rothenberg's approach. A forensic psychologist who is retained as a consultant reviews the allegations, pleadings, and other documentation available to the attorney at the outset of

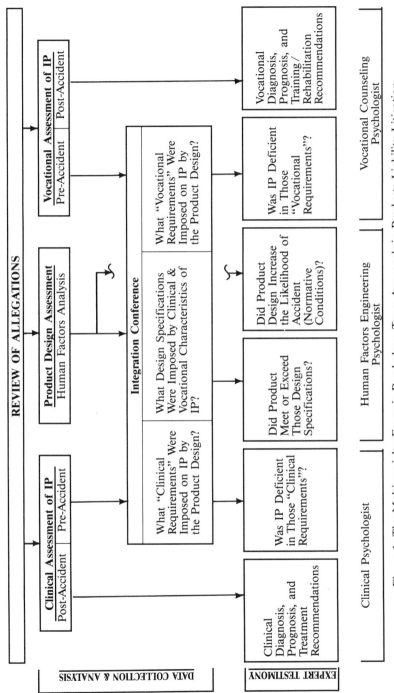

Figure 1. The Multispecialty Forensic Psychology Team Approach in Products Liability Litigation

litigation. The consultant then prepares a proposal for a team consisting of a clinical psychologist, a vocational counseling psychologist, and a human factors engineering psychologist, and a strategy to be followed by the attorney and the team.

Upon acceptance of the proposal, the clinical and counseling psychologists focus on assessment of the involved parties (IP), in this case the plaintiffs. Such assessment might include measures of intellectual, cognitive, and mental health status of the IP both before and after the incident. Such assessment might also include an evaluation of the psychosocial, organizational, or other pressures that might have contributed to the incident. Also to be included are demographic variables such as age, sex, ethnicity, marital status, and any language or cultural considerations which might be relevant to the case at bar. If relevant, vision, hearing, or other physical abnormalities of the IP should also be assessed.

Meanwhile the human factors psychologist focuses on the product. The actual product involved in the incident (or one just like it) is examined, as are photographs and/or engineering drawings. User and maintenance manuals, training documentation, and training devices (if any) are likewise reviewed. Information is collected or inferred concerning the intended uses of the product as well as the expected conditions of use. Similar information is obtained or inferences are made concerning the users for which the product was designed—including demographics, anthropometrics, mental and physical capacities. The psychologist then applies the human factors/safety assessment model described by Christensen (1980). This assessment reviews the product's design, recommended training, warning labels, and other caveats in terms of adequacy in:

1. Designing the danger out of the product;
2. Removing people from any danger which cannot be designed out;
3. Guarding people from danger if they cannot be removed from it;
4. Training people to avoid the danger if it cannot be guarded against; and

5. Warning of potentially dangerous situations stemming from the use of the product.

In short, the human factors psychologist will be prepared to testify as to his or her evaluation of the "accident proneness" of the product under optimal operating conditions. An expert opinion will be given as to whether the design of the product was a direct cause of the incident in light of the caveats and warnings provided, the training and procedures followed, and the conditions extant at the time of the incident.

By the time the human factors psychologist is ready to testify about the product, the clinical psychologist is prepared to give expert testimony about the IP's pre- and post-incident mental health status and intellectual and cognitive capacities. Expert opinion will be available as to whether the combination of pre-incident characteristics and stress levels at the time of the incident contributed to the incident. Prognosis and treatment recommendations (type, time, and cost considerations) will also be available for use in assessing damages.

The vocational counseling psychologist will be prepared to testify as to the IP's pre- and post-incident skill levels, vocational capabilities, and potential earning power. Expert opinion will be available as to whether the combination of the IP's intellectual, cognitive, and physical capabilities; training; education; and experience level; or the organizational and social milieu of the work setting was a proximate cause of the incident. Also available for consideration when assessing damages will be a statement of need for vocational counseling, rehabilitation, and/or training to bring the IP to subsistence income or pre-incident income level.

Having completed three independent assessments, the team members will exchange reports and meet to determine whether the IP's idiosyncratic characteristics might have imposed additional design requirements or modified operational procedures to assure product safety in the instant case. As a result of their joint efforts, the three psychologists may be able to offer additional expert opinion on the following questions:

THE CLINICAL PSYCHOLOGIST

Are the mental health, intellectual, cognitive, and stress level characteristics exhibited by IP at the time of the incident to be expected of users of this product?

Did those same characteristics in IP, in combination with the accident proneness of the product (as testified to by the human factors psychologist), contribute to the incident?

THE VOCATIONAL COUNSELING PSYCHOLOGIST

Are the educational, training, vocational skill, and experience level characteristics exhibited by IP at the time of the incident typical of those expected to be found among the population of users of this product?

Did those same characteristics in IP, in combination with the accident proneness of the product, contribute to the incident?

THE HUMAN FACTORS PSYCHOLOGIST

Could the product have been designed to accommodate safely people with the idiosyncratic characteristics of IP? How could this have been done?

Given the degree of commonality of those characteristics in the user population, should such design changes have been considered for this product?

Now suppose that in the hypothetical case the plaintiff's attorney expected the defendant's attorney to attempt to exculpate the defendant on a theory of contributory negligence (i.e., by relying on the fact that an operator's training manual gave explicit and detailed instructions on how to park the forklift on a hill, and that the driver did not follow those instructions). The forensic psychology team met and, in addition to other activities, the human factors psychologist was asked to examine the readability of the operator's manual, while the counseling psychologist was asked to assess the driver's capacity to read and follow instructions in that manual. After completing these tasks, the team meets again to integrate the results of their separate investigations, and to prepare their testimonies accordingly.

In addition to the normal testimony expected of a vocational counseling psychologist, this expert is now capable of offering the following opinion:

1. I have tested and otherwise examined Mr. Driver and have determined that he now reads at the fourth grade level, and that at the time of the incident his reading level was the same.
2. I have reviewed the relevant literature and concluded that 50% of the operators of ZYX forklifts have not completed an eighth grade education, and that 30% of ZYX operators read at or below the fourth grade level.
3. Mr. Driver, as a member of the class of ZYX operators, would be unlikely to study user manuals written at the 12th grade reading level. Indeed, if he did attempt to study such a manual, the text would be incomprehensible to him.
4. In my opinion, the failure to provide a training manual more comprehensible to Mr. Driver contributed to the likelihood that he would not operate the brake on the forklift in accordance with the manual's instructions.

In addition to the normal testimony expected of a human factors psychologist, this expert is now in a position to add the following opinions:

1. I have examined the human factors aspects of the ZYX forklift. It is my opinion that the human factors engineering design of the brake handle was deficient to the extent that it contributed significantly to the incident in which Mr. Driver was injured. In my opinion, a better engineered design would have reduced significantly the likelihood of this incident.
2. Although a safer design is feasible, the ZYX company may have relied upon the driver to follow the operational procedures described in considerable detail in the user manual.

3. I conducted a readability analysis of the manual and have determined that it was written at the 12th grade reading level.
4. It can be demonstrated that the operational procedures that should have been followed to avoid brake slippage could have been written at the fourth grade reading level.
5. Given (a) the assumption that the designer relied upon a description of correct and safe operational procedures and other safety warnings in the text of the manual to prevent incidents such as this one, (b) the comparative difficulty of preparing user manuals at the fourth and 12th grade reading levels, and (c) the manufacturer's awareness that 30% of the class of individuals operating its forklifts do not read above that fourth grade level, it is my opinion that a reasonable designer would consider any user manual written at the 12th grade reading level to be inadequate.

The plaintiff's attorney then ties together the opinions of the two experts to point up the defendant's culpability and to preclude the defense of contributory negligence.

CONCLUSION

Returning now to the four objectives of the attorney litigating a products liability case, it can be seen how the expert testimony of psychologists can help the attorney achieve these objectives:

1. *Was the defendant's product instrumental in causing harm?*

The facts about the incident in question are testified to by other witnesses (e.g., those actually present at the time of the incident), but the psychologist may testify regarding the IP's condition before and after the incident and to the extent of the harm done by the incident. This sort of expert testimony helps the court to assess money damages.

2. *Did a defect in the product (or its design) make harm likely?*

A psychologist may testify to the existence of a human factors defect in design, training, or operational procedures which makes the defendant's product accident prone for a significant portion of the user population.

A psychologist may also testify as to whether the plaintiff may reasonably be expected to fall within the user population, and whether the plaintiff's individual characteristics, when combined with the accident proneness of the product, caused the incident in question.

3. *Did the defendant have a duty to see that the plaintiff was not harmed by the product?*

This is a legal question in which psychologists ordinarily do not become involved.

4. *Given such a duty, was the defendant negligent?*

A psychologist may testify that the product could have been made safer from a human factors engineering standpoint and that a safer design should have been considered by the defendant, in light of the nature of the product and characteristics of its users. Utilization of a multispecialty forensic psychology team makes it possible to relate the product design to the idiosyncracies of the involved parties in such a way as to greatly increase the credibility of expert opinions concerning whether the defendant was negligent in design decision making.

Martin I. Kurke, Ph.D., LL.B., is a founding director of the American Board of Forensic Psychology. For many years, Dr. Kurke served as Chief Psychologist of the Drug Enforcement Administration of the United States Department of Justice and as an Adjunct Professor of Psychology at George Mason University. He is currently a member of the professional staff, the Select Committee on Narcotics Abuse and Control, United States House of Representatives. Dr. Kurke's chapter was adapted from his article, "Multi-Specialty Forensic Psychology Teams in Products Liability Litigation," which appeared in the first issue of the new journal, the *American Journal of Forensic Psychology.*

RESOURCES

Christensen, J. M. (1980, May 28-30). Human factors in hazard/risk evaluation. In *Human Factors and Industrial Design in Consumer Products.* Symposium conducted at Tufts University, Medford, MA.

Gifis, S. H. (1975). *Law Dictionary.* Woodbury, NY: Barron's.

Rothenberg, D. (1982). The psychologist as a trial strategist. *Bulletin of the American Academy of Forensic Psychology, 3,* 1.

Weinstein, A. S., Twerski, A. D., Piehler, H. R., & Danaher, W. A. (1978). *Products Liability and the Reasonably Safe Product.* New York: Wiley.

PSYCHOLOGICAL AND PSYCHIATRIC EVALUATION OF WORKERS' COMPENSATION CLAIMANTS

Herbert N. Weissman

Workers' Compensation is the primary mechanism for compensating victims of work-related illnesses or injuries. Every state and jurisdiction in the United States has adopted a Workers' Compensation program of one sort or another. While the details of these programs vary from state to state, such programs have a number of common features. Most significantly, these programs are essentially "no fault" systems. Injured employees are not required to prove negligence or fault on the part of the employer, but must establish that their injuries arose out of and in the course of their employment.

This chapter will briefly explore the historical and legal development of Workers' Compensation programs and the legal standards under which these programs currently operate. The chapter will then examine in some detail the role of psychological factors in Workers' Compensation claims and the psychological and psychiatric evaluation of Workers' Compensation claimants.

HISTORY AND LEGAL DEVELOPMENT

The Workers' Compensation system first developed in late 19th century Europe. Originally a German conception, Workers' Compensation developed as an integral part of the overall social security system. Under this system, economic responsibility for industrial injuries was shared by employer and employee.

This European model was never adopted in the United States, which had no organized independent system of Workers' Compensation until industrial and labor reforms of the early 20th century provided the impetus for such a system. Until that time, the injured American worker had to rely upon traditional procedures of tort law, which provided the right to money damages upon proof of negligence or fault on the part of the employer (Larson, 1979).

At common law, however, employers had available three defenses which virtually insulated them from liability for an employee's injury. First, the doctrine of "contributory negligence" denied recovery if the employee was in any way partially at fault. Under this doctrine, the injured employee had the burden of proving that the employer's negligence was the *sole* cause of the injury. Second, under the "assumption of risk" doctrine, recovery was disallowed if the employee knew or should have known that the job was dangerous. Employees were assumed to have accepted the risks attendant upon their jobs. Thus, unless the injury was completely unforeseeable to the employee, no recovery was allowed. Finally, the "fellow servant" rule denied recovery if the employee's injury was in any way the result of carelessness on the part of another employee.

These three defenses, combined with the cumbersome and often protracted procedures of tort litigation, resulted in a system in which few workers were compensated for employment-related injuries. Thus, the burden of caring for injured workers fell largely upon their families or upon private charities. By the second decade of this century, however, dissatisfaction with this system (and with its economic and social consequences) led to a variety of legislative changes aimed at lifting many of the common law barriers to employee recovery for on-the-job injuries.

The major thrust of these changes, which ultimately provided the basis for the modern Workers' Compensation system, was to assure at least limited benefits to the injured worker while shielding the employer from civil suit for additional damages (Larson, 1979). In essence, injured employees were forced to give up the right to sue their employers in exchange for guaranteed benefits regardless of fault. The economic justification for this "exchange" principle was provided by the "trade risk" theory, which defines the risk of injury as a production cost to be passed on to consumers, and by the "least social cost" theory, which asserts that the cost of industrial injuries should be distributed between consumers and producers so that it does not excessively burden any one sector or individual (National Commission on State Workmen's Compensation Laws, 1973).

THE MODERN WORKERS' COMPENSATION SYSTEM

The modern Workers' Compensation system, which derives from legislative enactments in every American state and jurisdiction, affords protection to between 70% and 95% of the labor force, with the cost borne solely by employers. Under this system, employees are automatically entitled to benefits once it is established that they have suffered a "personal injury by accident arising out of and in the course of employment." Benefits generally include about two-thirds of lost wages plus reasonable costs of medical care and rehabilitation services (National Commission on State Workmen's Compensation Laws, 1973). Injured workers need not prove negligence or fault on the part of the employer and are entitled to benefits even if their own negligence contributed to their injuries (Ewing, 1981).

Workers' Compensation plans are similar throughout the jurisdictions of the United States. Differences exist, however, as to the type of insurance carrier that issues and regulates the plan (e.g., state agency, self-insurance trust, or private carrier), the extent of coverage, amounts paid for temporary and permanent disability, and limits on medical and other health-related, restorative, and rehabilitative services. Uncontested claims are paid either directly, on the basis of legally prescribed claims schedules, or on the basis of agreement between the carrier and the injured worker. Disputed cases are resolved variously throughout the jurisdictions by arbitration, courts, commissions, or administrative boards (Herlick, 1979).

LEGAL STANDARDS

While earlier Workers' Compensation programs were highly circumscribed in their range of coverage and their definition of accidental job-related physical injuries, developing case law has broadened definitions of both injury and accident, thereby expanding the coverage of most modern programs. "Injury" has come to include "any harmful change in the body" as well as most psychological disorders (Larson, 1979). "Accident" has been modified to include not only injuries resulting from a single time-limited traumatic event, but also those which develop over extended periods of exposure to work-place hazards (O'Brien, 1979). This trend toward definitional expansion of the concepts of accident and injury has been joined in the courts by another trend, that of more liberally interpreting the statutory requirement that a compensable injury must be one "arising out of and in the course of employment." A major result of this latter trend has been the increased recognition of psychological disorders as compensable injuries (Ewing, 1981).

The statutory basis supporting coverage for claims based upon psychological grounds derives from language in the law specifying that injuries may be either specific or cumulative. A *specific* injury is one which results from a single incident or exposure which causes impairment, disability, or the need for medical treatment. *Cumulative* injuries are those which occur as a result of repetitive mentally or physically traumatic activities extending over a period of time. Psychological trauma, like physical trauma, may be either specific or cumulative and is compensable if caused by employment. Job-related aggravation of a pre-existing condition, whether physical or psychological, may also entitle an employee to compensation (O'Brien, 1979).

In cases involving mental or emotional elements, the causal nexus between employment and impairment or disability is often infused with subjectivity and complexity. Concepts of proof and causation become particularly acute concerns. The burden of proof rests with the claimant (i.e., the injured employee), who must show by a preponderance of the evidence (essentially, at least 51%) that the illness, disorder, or impairment is indeed job related. Reasonable scientific *probability* (i.e., more likely than not) is the legal standard to which examiners must adhere in reports and testimony relating the alleged accident to impairments found on examination of the claimant. Mere *possibility* of a work connection is insufficient to sustain an employee's claim.

Employment may be related to a claimant's impairment or disability in a variety of ways. It may be the sole source of the injury or simply an aggravating or exacerbating element. It may be something which produces impairment on a short-term or long-term basis. And it may be something which aggravates or exacerbates a latent condition or causes a completely asymptomatic condition to become symptomatic for the first time. Whatever the relationship, the legal "key" to Workers' Compensation is proof of causation.

Of the two standards commonly applied to causation—one termed "proximate cause" and the other "actual cause"—it is the latter which has meaning and bearing in Workers' Compensation cases (Larson, 1979). The doctrine of proximate cause developed in the context of personal injury litigation where fault and negligence are the criteria for determining liability. In Workers' Compensation cases, however, fault and negligence are irrelevant and actual cause is the legal yardstick for determining whether a connection (or "nexus") exists between employment and the impairment or disability for which the employer is being asked to compensate. A "but for" test is the standard commonly applied. If the impairment or disability would not exist but for the claimant's employment, the causal nexus is established. Yet the job-related injury need not be the *sole* cause of impairment in Workers' Compensation cases; it need only be an *actual* and *significant* cause (Larson, 1979).

Modern Workers' Compensation programs also generally require not only a finding of disability, but also a differentiation between permanent and temporary disability as well as between partial and total disability. Disability is legally defined as any condition which diminishes one's capacity to perform one's usual occupation or to compete for employment in the open labor market. Permanent disability is assumed when the claimant's condition has become stationary and will not be improved by further reasonable medical and/or psychological treatment (O'Brien, 1979). Permanent disability may be partial or total. If total, the injured worker receives "temporary disability" compensation for the rest of his or her life. Permanent partial disability implies continued ability to be employed, but where a competitive handicap in the open labor market has resulted, the employee is entitled to compensation based upon the degree of disability.

If and when a disability is considered permanent, the examiner may "apportion" it as between the claimed job-related injury and any pre-existing conditions. Apportionment is necessary because, as a rule, an employer will not be liable for those aspects (or that "portion") of the employee's permanent disability attributable to factors other than employment-related injury. The employer is liable for the direct effects of such injury, but not for pre-existing impairments or those which would have existed as a result of the normal progression of some underlying disease or disorder in the absence of the injury (O'Brien, 1979). In order to support an apportionment to the normal progression of a pre-existing condition, medical and psychological evidence must clearly document the relationship between the claimant's impairment and what would have been the normal development of his or her pre-existing condition in the absence of the work-related injury.

ASPECTS OF CLINICAL EVALUATION

Psychodiagnostic evaluation in Workers' Compensation cases is always initiated in response to specific referral questions which guide the course of the examiner's evaluation. While such questions may vary as a function of the nature of the claim and the referral source (e.g., claimant, employers, insurance carrier, or Workers' Compensation board), they generally call for the kinds of conclusions outlined above. Regardless of the source or form of the referral questions, however, the examiner is generally asked to provide the kind of information and conclusions needed to assess the claimant's entitlement to statutory benefits.

As has been noted, Workers' Compensation programs vary from state to state. Thus, examiners must be familiar with the statutory requirements in the state in which they practice. As a general rule, however, the examiner must determine the degree to which the claimant's current clinical status represents a new disorder that is work related or the degree to which it represents a pre-existing disorder with or without a significant aggravation or acceleration due to work-related stresses. Clearly, examiners must also assess the degree of the claimant's disability or impairment, whatever its cause.

Formal clinical evaluation in Workers' Compensation cases requires an understanding of psychosocial and somatic stress factors operating both within and upon the claimant as well as an understanding of the claimant's particular personal characteristics, such as the nature and quality of his or her psychological resources for coping with stress. Moreover, the evaluation requires analysis of the interactional effects of both stimulus (*incident*) and mediating (*personal*) factors upon the claimant's reactions, relative to impairments which may diminish his or her ability to compete in the open labor market (*disability*). Table 1 (p. 370) sets out the major components of each of the elements, the interaction of which must be addressed in any comprehensive evaluation.

The precipitating or aggravating incident (i.e., the alleged job-related stimulus or stimuli) may be distinguished as to its *origin* (e.g., the activity that produced the impairment), *type* (e.g., the specific nature of the activity), *intensity* (i.e., a judgment as to its expectable effects on people in general and the claimant in particular), and *duration* (i.e., the temporal period over which it occurred). Cognitive appraisal refers to the claimant's personalized interpretation of the symbolic and actual meaning of the incident and is understood through examination of the claimant's past history, current functioning, exposure to other environmental stresses, and trait- and state-level personality factors.

TABLE 1: COGNITIVE APPRAISAL

INCIDENT	PERSON	IMPAIRMENT	DISABILITY
— Origin — Type — Intensity — Duration	Determinants of cognitive appraisal: — Needs — Values — Expectations — Motivations Determinants of stress sensitivity/tolerance: — Available defense and coping mechanisms and resistance resources, including pain tolerance — Ego strength — Self-concept, personal and vocational — Personality traits/disorders — Psychosocial conflicts — Health status generally	Disorders of — Affect — Mood — Cognition — Consciousness — Psychophysiology — Neuropsychology — Behavior — Adjustment — Other *DSM-III* — Clinical disorders	Rated according to levels, ranging from partial to total, based on description of work limitations, restrictions or preclusions that are directly related to functional impairments which serve to diminish worker's ability to compete in the open labor market.

370

The "person" component in Table 1 pertains to personality factors which determine the importance of the accident to the claimant as well as his or her sensitivity to and tolerance of stress in general. The claimant's cognitive appraisal of the incident and its meaning for him or her obviously will depend upon considerations such as currently active need systems, personal values, motivation, and expectations as to probable outcomes. Personality characteristics which determine stress sensitivity and tolerance (e.g., ego strength, adjustive resources, general health status, self-concept, etc.) are also important determinants which must be considered by the examiner.

The significance of such "person" characteristics becomes readily apparent when one considers the wide variation in human response to stress, even under controlled circumstances where the level of the stressor is held constant between or among individuals. For example, strict deadlines and other performance pressures in a competitive work environment may constitute an exhilarating challenge for persons whose needs, values, and expectations are compatible with such environments and whose personality attributes, skills, and adjustive resources are robust and well integrated. Yet the same work environment may result in unrelieved tensions and stress-related disorders among persons otherwise predisposed. Likewise, what may generally be regarded as a mild physical injury may result in relatively mild reactions and rapid recovery among some individuals. Yet others may respond to the same injury with elevated and protracted complaints of pain and distress as well as delayed recovery—the result, at least in part, of predisposing psychological and/or somatic vulnerabilities coupled with the individual's personal appraisal of the injury in the context of his or her current life circumstances.

The "impairment" and "levels of disability" components in Table 1 refer to examination-based data that will ultimately form the basis for opinions as to the presence of clinical symptomatology, if any, and its relationship to the claimant's ability to function on a job. Disability in the Workers' Compensation context has been defined as "impairment of earning capacity, impairment of the normal use of a member, or competitive handicap in the open labor market" (*State Compensation Insurance Fund v. I.A.C.*, 1963, p. 47). A significant part of the examiner's task is to describe and specify whatever relationships may exist between functional impairments caused by the job-related injury and any compromise in the claimant's ability to function in an occupational setting. Standard rating scales, which graduate levels of disability into categories such as "slight," "moderate," "severe," or "pronounced" are available in most jurisdictions but fail to specify the correspondence between particular impairments and their respective effects on job functioning. The task can more effectively be accomplished by gathering detailed clinical and vocational information, including information on the specific nature of the claimed injury and its consequences in subjective complaints and objective symptoms as well as information about the specific duties and operational requirements of the job itself. In approaching this task, the examiner may find it helpful to arrive at a diagnosis of the sort specified in the *Diagnostic and Statistical Manual of Mental Disorders* (3rd ed.) (American Psychiatric Association, 1980), commonly referred to as *DSM-III*. The primary benefit afforded by *DSM-III* lies in its use of behavioral descriptors and multiaxial diagnostic format, both of which assist the examiner in linking types and levels of functional impairment to opinions regarding levels of disability.

ASSESSMENT METHODS

Psychodiagnostic evaluation of psychological functioning and its interaction with physical impairment is ordinarily accomplished by means of a systematic and comprehensive clinical interview. When relevant, a wide variety of well-researched, standardized psychodiagnostic assessment instruments is also available. Before examining the application of the clinical interview and standardized assessment instruments to Workers' Compensation evaluations, it is important to note that laws vary from state to state as to who may conduct such evaluations. Psychological testing is clearly the province of the qualified clinical psychologist, but in some states even that aspect of the Workers' Compensation evaluation must be conducted, if at all, under medical referral and/or supervision. In a number of states (such as California), however, qualified psychologists are statutorily recognized as independent providers in Workers' Compensation cases and thus, like psychiatrists, may autonomously provide all evaluative and treatment services. Since legal standards vary across jurisdictions, it behooves the examiner (particularly the nonphysician) to become acquainted with the laws, regulations, and administrative procedures operative in his or her own jurisdiction.

THE CLINICAL INTERVIEW

The detailed clinical interview, a standard component in any comprehensive psychodiagnostic assessment, seeks to acquire both historical and contemporaneous information and focuses not only upon the facts and events surrounding the incident but, more importantly, upon the claimant's cognitive and affective appraisal of what has transpired. Additionally, interviewing addresses level and quality of psychosocial functioning, ego integration, coping skills, and adaptive resources, both before and since the claimed injury.

The clinical interview also addresses ways in which the claimant has reacted to, symbolized, and attempted to manage stressful events and medical or psychological impairments, both in the past and at present. In addressing these issues, the examiner looks for evidence of emotional, cognitive, and behavioral effectiveness as well as the presence of early vulnerabilities, sensitivities, conflicts, and rigidities which may have rendered the claimant more highly susceptible to the impact of stressful events and their consequence in protracted stress-related disorders. The examiner also seeks information regarding the psychological purposes that functional and somatic symptoms have served and are currently serving for the claimant. In so doing, the examiner will note and explore with the claimant any disparity between subjective complaints and objective medical or psychological findings (Weissman, 1984).

Additionally, the clinical interview should include the fundamentals of a mental status examination—that is, an inquiry into the claimant's current level of consciousness, mood, cognition, motor behavior, social behavior, and the presence or absence of cerebral and psychophysiologic disturbances.   The claimant's current and past involvement with prescribed medication as well as with alcohol, and nonprescription and illicit drugs should also be identified.

Finally, since referral questions in Workers' Compensation cases ask, among other things, whether the claimed impairment is causally related to psychological and/or physical stress factors associated with the claimant's job, the clinical interview also seeks a full description of the claimant's job and the claimed injury or exposure. Such description, which should generally be supplemented by resort to job descriptions and any records of the incident, is also essential to assessment of the claimant's relative capacity to continue performing the operational requirements of the job.

TEST BATTERIES

In many cases, the examiner will find it necessary to supplement clinical interview findings with data that can only be derived from psychological testing procedures. Such procedures often yield data which serve to further the examiner's understanding of the claimant's impairment and its relationship, if any, to stresses in the work environment.   Psychological testing includes measures of personality, intelligence, memory, general cognition, neuropsychological functioning, aptitude, and vocational interest— all of which can be useful in providing baseline information, in evaluating the claimant's status pre- and post-treatment, in differential diagnosis, in planning and guiding therapeutic and rehabilitative interventions, and in rendering contingent predictions regarding future behavior. In all of these areas, psychological testing permits focused observation under standard conditions in ways that reduce subjective bias and allow different individuals to be compared quantitatively along relevant dimensions of psychological functioning (Korchin, 1976). This quantitative aspect of psychological test data is especially useful in cases of protracted impairment, where repeat assessment allows for a comparison of functioning over time, thus helping to establish whether the impairment is temporary or permanent.

Personality Measures. Among the multitude of psychological test instruments designed to measure personality functioning, four seem particularly well suited for use in the Workers' Compensation context. The first, the Minnesota Multiphasic Personality Inventory (MMPI) (Hathaway & McKinley, 1943) not only allows for personality assessment on a wide variety of dimensions but also offers validity scales which detect dissimulation, prevarication, and responses which tend either to minimize or exaggerate psychological impairments. Moreover, configural interpretation of MMPI results reflects the presence of psychological disorders, somatic focus, and psychophysiologic involvement.

A second well-referenced, self-administered, objective measure of personality functioning is the Millon Multiaxial Clinical Inventory (Millon, 1977), whose 20 scales organize into four categories relating to basic personality styles, pathological personality syndromes, and symptom disorders. More transient clinical disorders (Axis I, *DSM-III*) are specifically differentiated from the more pervasive and enduring personality disorders and character patterns (Axis II, *DSM-III*). Such differentiation is clearly important in Workers' Compensation evaluations, where apportionment requires an understanding of the nature and contribution of pre-existing conditions.

The other two personality measures useful in Workers' Compensation cases are the Rorschach Psychodiagnostic (Rorschach, 1921/1942) and the Thematic Apperception Test (Murray, 1943), both of which are projective tests. These tests provide clinical data, the interpretation of which assists in the detection of disorders of thought and perception and helps clarify the claimant's perception of, reaction to, and ability to cope with stressful events. Exner (1974) has developed a comprehensive system of Rorschach interpretation which provides empirically based standardized data and thus increases the

Rorschach's usefulness in the Workers' Compensation context.

Measures of Intelligence. The Wechsler scales of intelligence are of primary importance in any assessment battery. These widely used, well-standardized test procedures sample a broad range of intellectual functions in both children (Wechsler, 1974) and adults (Wechsler, 1981) and yield reliable and valid estimates of general intelligence. A claimant's performance on the Wechsler scales, however, yields a great deal more than just quantitative measures of intellectual functioning. The claimant's behavior during testing as well as the characteristics of his or her test responses correspond to behavior in nontest, everyday life situations (Korchin, 1976). Thus, administration of these scales may be used to help assess, among other things, the particular ways in which the claimant's affective response to stressful events may compromise or otherwise negatively intrude upon his or her cognitive functioning.

Measures of Neuropsychological Dysfunction. A variety of clinical instruments serve as useful screening devices in the detection of neuropsychological dysfunction. Among the most notable of the highly formalized and comprehensive procedures in this domain are the Halstead-Reitan (Reitan & Davison, 1974) and Luria-Nebraska (Golden, Hammeke, & Purisch, 1980) Neuropsychological Batteries. Use of these batteries, which include highly sensitive measures which detect the presence and localization of impairments in brain-behavior relationships, is indicated where a claimant's impairments are associated with, or are a consequence of, brain trauma and/or where a history of cerebral dysfunction is present. Assessment measures sensitive to impairments in brain-behavior relationships facilitate understanding of the potential impact of such deficits on a claimant's performance in a given job and in the labor market in general. Data derived from such measures also greatly assists in the formation of appropriate rehabilitation plans.

Measures of Vocational Interests and Aptitude.
Vocational interests and aptitude are frequently assessed
by such instruments as the Strong-Campbell Inventory
(Johansson, 1974) and the Career Assessment Inventory
(Johansson, 1982), in combination with other measures of
intellectual and aptitude factors. Such instruments, used
in conjunction with interviews directed at previous
occupational activity and performance and self-report
measures, such as the Forer Structured Sentence
Completion Test (Forer, 1957), provide information which
may be applied in retraining the injured worker for
gainful re-employment consistent with his or her
capacities, limitations, and preclusions.

Measures Related to Chronic Pain and Its Tolerance.
Specialized self-administered instruments for assessing the
relative contribution of functional and somatic factors in
chronic pain and pain tolerance include the Wahler
Physical Symptoms Inventory (Wahler, 1973), the MMPI
(Hathaway & McKinley, 1943), and the Millon Behavioral
Health Inventory (Millon, Green, & Meagher, 1982). The
Millon provides data regarding "Basic Coping Styles,"
"Psychogenic Attitudes," and "Psychosomatic Correlates."

The Wahler, Minnesota, and Millon inventories, all
sensitive to the involvement of functional factors in the
production, promotion, and protraction of somatic
dysfunctions and chronic pain complaints, assist the
examiner in distinguishing subjective complaints from
objective medical and psychological findings. These
inventories also provide data useful in predicting whether
a claimant is likely to benefit from surgical or other
medical interventions or is likely to seek repeated medical
contacts and interventions and to demonstrate a
protracted pattern of pain and fear, multiple setbacks,
and/or retarded recovery.

Measures of Coronary-Prone ("Type A") Behaviors.
The "Type A" or "coronary-prone" behavior pattern, an
action-emotion complex characterized by competitive,
ambitious, achievement-oriented, time-urgent, and hostile
behaviors (Friedman & Rosenman, 1959) is now formally
recognized as a risk factor in the development of
coronary artery disease (Rosenman et al., 1975). Such

recognition reflects the growing understanding of the role played by psychosocial stress factors in the development of various symptoms and disorders. The principal instrument currently used in detecting the presence of a "Type A" behavior pattern (i.e., that set of overt behaviors which occur in susceptible individuals under appropriate eliciting conditions) is the self-administered Jenkins Activity Survey (Jenkins, Zyzanski, & Rosenman, 1979).

Measures of Psychosocial Stressors. In addition to interviewing a claimant with regard to job-related and other psychosocial stressors which may have contributed to his or her impairment, the examiner may wish to utilize a more comprehensive, standardized, and quantitative approach in cataloging the life stress to which the claimant has been exposed. The self-administered Social Readjustment Rating Scale, developed by Holmes and Rahe (1967) offers an ideal means of carrying out such an assessment. A significant body of empirical research has substantiated the value of the Social Readjustment Rating Scale in assessing vulnerability to symptom formation as a consequence of stressful life events (Rahe & Holmes, 1966; Rahe & Lind, 1971; Thiel, Parker, & Bruce, 1973).

Identifying, categorizing, and weighing psychosocial stress factors to which a claimant has been exposed is obviously pertinent in Workers' Compensation cases. Such information elucidates the degree to which various stressful life events may have contributed to the development or exacerbation of the claimant's current disability or impairment. Such information is also often significant relative to prognostic and dispositional considerations.

ORGANIZATION OF
ASSESSMENT STRATEGY AND REPORT

The strategy of the psychological or psychiatric examiner in Workers' Compensation cases may be conceptualized as encompassing several levels of analysis. First the examiner must determine whether or not and to what extent the claimant is disabled. Determining the extent of disability entails not only rating it as to severity on a scale of impairment, but also ascertaining whether it is partial or total, temporary or permanent.

Having identified the presence and extent of disability, the examiner must then move to a second level of analysis, that of determining causation. At this level, the examiner must establish whether the disability is a result of the normal progression of pre-existing pathology (which would have occurred regardless of employment), a result of a new disorder or exacerbation of a latent or previously asymptomatic condition (which would *not* have occurred *but for* the claimed employment-related injury or exposure), or some combination of both.

An employer is liable for the direct and aggravating effects of a job-related injury but is not liable for pre-existing impairments nor for those which would have existed as a result of the normal progression of some underlying disorder in the absence of the work-related injury. The employer is, however, liable if the injury aggravates or exacerbates a latent condition or causes an otherwise asymptomatic condition to become symptomatic for the first time. While in theory such categories of causation are clear-cut and apparently mutually exclusive, in practice the examiner will often find that a claimant's disability is attributable partly to the claimed work-related injury or exposure and partly to nonoccupational causes. It is in these cases that the examiner's analysis must extend to a third level—that of apportionment. The examiner must "apportion" the claimant's disability or impairment between or among the various factors determined to have contributed to it.

Apportionment usually involves assigning a specific percentage to each "causal" factor. But Workers' Compensation boards and courts have recognized the difficulties involved in such a quantitative approach and, in some jurisdictions, have allowed examiners to be less precise in their apportionments. For example, as a California Court states in *Gay v. W.C.A.B.* (1979):

We are cognizant that it may at times be a formidable task for a physician to state precise figures on apportionment. The physician must often make conclusions when faced with matters difficult to measure and with conflicting factual contentions made by the parties. [citation omitted]. Accordingly, it is permissible for the physician to state his opinion on apportionment in terms of the <u>reasonably medical probable range</u> [citation omitted] provided, however, that the physician states in his report the basis and variable facts determining the range of apportionment. The appeals board may then, after determining the true facts based upon the conflicting evidence, determine the issue of apportionment based upon the range of evidence in the record. (p. 565)

Appropriate procedures for apportionment will, of course, depend upon governing law in the particular jurisdiction. Recently, however, Lasky (1980), a California Workers' Compensation Judge, reviewed current judicial trends in apportionment and offered a set of precepts helpful to examiners in Workers' Compensation cases.

Lasky notes, for example, that a claimant's disability or impairment "cannot be attributed to different sources of stress, unless a discrete and discernible portion of the disability can be imputed to each source" (p. 12). He also observes that an examiner's opinion regarding apportionment "must be based upon stated factual findings which indicate either familiarity with a pre-existing disability or the relationship between the present disability and the normal progress of a pre-existing condition" (p. 12) and "must state not only the existence of pre-existing problems but must also explain the determination of the percentage figure which expresses the apportionment" (p. 13). Finally, Lasky notes that "to support an apportionment based on natural progression of a pre-existing disability, there must be medical evidence expressly stating that the apportioned disability is the result of the pre-existing nonindustrial condition and that [the] disability would have occurred even in the absence of the industrial injury" (p. 13).

The examiner fulfills his or her role most effectively by describing and defining psychological impairments in reference to a claimant's ability to work, describing any permanent disability or work limitations, and providing reasons for opinions, including all facts upon which such opinions are based. As Lasky (1980) has suggested, the comprehensive Workers' Compensation report should include the following elements:

- History of the injury;
- Patient's complaints;
- Source of all facts set forth in the history of injury and complaints, including all relevant prior records;
- Findings on examination;
- Opinion as to the extent of disability and work limitations, if any;
- Opinion as to cause of disability;
- Treatment indicated;
- Opinion as to whether permanent disability has resulted from the injury and as to whether or not such disability is stationary;
- A complete diagnostic formulation stated in terms of the *DSM-III* classifications; and
- Reasons for all opinions.

The essential point is that in Workers' Compensation cases, as in all legal matters, the examiner's report and expert testimony must be geared to the specific legal issues and questions presented. As a rule, that means the report and testimony must not only label but explain the claimant's condition and not only specify conclusions but detail the facts and reasoning upon which such conclusions are based.

As the California Supreme Court observed in *People v. Bassett* (1968)—in language more recently relied upon to reverse a Workers' Compensation decision because of an inadequate examiner's report (*Castellon v. W.C.A.B.*, 1981):

To make a reasonable inference, concerning the relationship between a disease and a certain act, the trier of facts must be informed with some particularity. This must be done by testimony. Unexplained medical labels—schizophrenia, paranoia, psychosis, neurosis, psychopathy—are not enough. Description and explanation of the origin, development and manifestations of the alleged disease are the chief functions of the expert witness. The chief value of an expert's testimony in this field, as in all other fields, rests upon the material from which his opinion is fashioned and the reasoning by which he progresses from his material to his conclusion in the explanation of the disease and its dynamics, that is, how it occurred, developed and affected the mental and emotional processes of the defendant; it does not lie in his mere expression of conclusion. (p. 126)

Herbert N. Weissman, Ph.D., is a psychologist in private practice and an Associate Clinical Professor of Psychology in the Department of Psychiatry at the University of California-Davis School of Medicine. Dr. Weissman is a Diplomate in Clinical Psychology, Forensic Psychology, and Behavioral Medicine and is an independent medical examiner for the California Department of Industrial Relations Division of Industrial Accidents. As a forensic clinician, Dr. Weissman provides psychodiagnostic evaluations, consultation, and expert testimony in family law, criminal, administrative and personal injury litigation. He is currently President of the American Board of Forensic Psychology.

RESOURCES

American Psychiatric Association. (1980). *Diagnostic and Statistical Manual of Mental Disorders* (3rd ed.). Washington, DC: Author.

Castellon v. W.C.A.B., 46 Cal. Comp. Cases 991 (1981).

Ewing, C. P. (1981, October). *Psychological Disorders and Employment: The Causal Nexus Problem in Workers' Compensation.* Paper presented at the Biennial Convention of the American Psychology-Law Society, Cambridge, MA.

Exner, J. (1974). *The Rorschach: A Comprehensive System* (Vol. 1). New York: Wiley-Interscience.

Forer, B. R. (1957). *The Forer Structured Sentence Completion Test Manual.* Los Angeles: Western Psychological Services.

Friedman, M., & Rosenman, R. H. (1959). Association of specific overt behavior pattern with blood and cardiovascular findings—blood cholesterol level, blood clotting time, incidence of arcus senilis, and clinical coronary artery disease. *Journal of the American Medical Association, 169,* 1286-1296.

Gay v. W.C.A.B., 96 Cal. App. 3d 555; 158 Cal. Rptr. 137; 44 Cal. Comp. Cases 817 (2d Dist. 1979).

Golden, C. J., Hammeke, T. A., & Purisch, A. D. (1980). *Luria-Nebraska Neuropsychological Battery Manual.* Los Angeles: Western Psychological Services.

Hathaway, S. R., & McKinley, J. C. (1943). *Minnesota Multiphasic Personality Inventory Manual.* New York: Psychological Corporation.

Herlick, S. D. (1979). *The California Workers' Compensation Handbook.* Los Angeles: Herlick Publications.

Holmes, T. H., & Rahe, R. H. (1967). The readjustment rating scale. *Journal of Psychosomatic Research, 2,* 213-218.

Jenkins, C. D., Zyzanski, S. J., & Rosenman, R. H. (1979). *Jenkins Activity Survey Manual.* New York: Psychological Corporation.

Johansson, C. B. (1974). *The Strong-Campbell Interest Inventory: Manual for the Augmented Interpretive Report.* Minneapolis, MN: National Computer Systems, Inc.

Johansson, C. B. (1982). *Manual for Career Assessment Inventory* (2nd ed.). Minneapolis, MN: National Computer Systems.

Korchin, S. J. (1976). *Modern Clinical Psychology.* New York: Basic Books.

Larson, A. (1979). *The Law of Workmen's Compensation.* New York: M. Bender.

Lasky, H. (1980). Psychiatry and California workers' compensation laws: A threat and a challenge. *California Western Law Review, 17,* 1-27.

Lasky, H. (1982). The usable psychiatric report, workers' compensation style. *Bulletin of the California Society of Industrial Medicine and Surgery, 3,* 2-6.

Millon, T. (1977). *Millon Multiaxial Clinical Inventory Manual.* Minneapolis, MN: National Computer Systems, Inc.

Millon, T., Green, C. J., & Meagher, R. B., Jr. (1982). *Millon Behavioral Health Inventory Manual* (3rd ed.). Minneapolis, MN: National Computer Systems, Inc.

Murray, H. A. (1943). *Thematic Apperception Test Manual.* Cambridge, MA: Harvard University Press.

National Commission on State Workmen's Compensation Laws. (1973). *Compendium on Workers' Compensation.* Washington, DC: Author.

O'Brien, D. W. (1979). *California Employer-Employee Benefits Handbook.* Los Angeles: Winter Brook Pub. Co.

People v. Bassett, 69 Cal.2d 122 (1968).

Rahe, R. H., & Holmes, T. H. (1966). Life crisis and major health change. *Psychosomatic Medicine, 28,* 774.

Rahe, R. H., & Lind, E. (1971). Psychosocial factors and sudden cardiac death. *Journal of Psychosomatic Research, 15,* 19-24.

Reitan, R. M., & Davison, L. A. (1974). *Clinical Neuropsychology: Current Status and Applications.* Washington, DC: Winston.

Rorschach, H. (1942). *Psychodiagnostics: A Diagnostic Test Based on Perception* (P. Lemkau & B. Kronenburg Trans.). Berne: Huber. (1st German edition, 1921).

Rosenman, R. H., Brand, R. J., Jenkins, C. D., Friedman, M., Straus, R., & Wurm, M. (1975). Coronary heart disease in the western collaborative group study.

Final follow-up experience of 8-1/2 years. *Journal of the American Medical Association, 233*, 872-877.

State Compensation Insurance Fund v. I.A.C., 59 Cal.2d 45 (1963).

Thiel, H., Parker, D., & Bruce, T. A. (1973). Stress factors and the risk of myocardial infarction. *Journal of Psychosomatic Research, 17*, 43-57.

Wahler, H. J. (1973). *Wahler Physical Symptoms Inventory Manual.* Los Angeles: Western Psychological Services.

Wechsler, D. (1974). *Manual for the Wechsler Intelligence Scale for Children-Revised.* New York: Psychological Corporation.

Wechsler, D. (1981). *Manual for the Wechsler Adult Intelligence Scale-Revised.* New York: Psychological Corporation.

Weissman, H. N. (1984). Psychological assessment and psycho-legal formulations in psychiatric traumatology. *Psychiatric Annals, 14*, 517-529.

INTRODUCTION TO SECTION V: PSYCHOLOGY AND PSYCHIATRY IN THE COURTROOM

One of the major avenues through which psychologists and psychiatrists influence law and legal process is expert testimony. Psychologists, psychiatrists, and other mental health professionals are routinely called upon to serve as expert witnesses in a wide variety of legal proceedings. Most often their expert testimony relates to clinical findings resulting from examination or testing of a particular claimant or litigant. In a growing number of cases, however, mental health and behavioral science expert testimony is used to make judges and jurors aware of empirical research relevant to the issue being tried.

Regardless of its nature, expert testimony requires more than the basic clinical and/or research expertise possessed by most mental health and behavioral science professionals. The effective expert witness must also have a clear understanding of legal process and an ability to communicate technical data in terms readily intelligible to lay factfinders. Lacking such understanding and ability, many mental health professionals and behavioral scientists either fail as expert witnesses or avoid that role altogether.

In this section, psychologists Stanley Brodsky and Norman Poythress offer a chapter which might be described as a beginner's guide to being an expert witness. Drs. Brodsky and Poythress, experienced expert witnesses in a variety of legal matters, describe the basic knowledge, skills, and attitudes mental health and behavioral science experts need in order to be effective on the witness stand. Their chapter, of course, is no substitute for the experience and self-education needed to fully develop such knowledge, skills, and attitudes. It does, however, offer the would-be or beginning-level expert witness the kind of background information he or she will need to get started on the right foot in the courtroom.

EXPERTISE ON
THE WITNESS STAND:
A PRACTITIONER'S GUIDE

Stanley L. Brodsky and Norman G. Poythress

"The courtroom is a place best reserved for those who are brave, adventuresome, and nimble-witted" (Schwitzgebel, R. L., & Schwitzgebel, R. K., 1980, p. 241).

Expert testimony is not for everybody. Testifying in court is an experience with emotional peaks and valleys, and many mental health professionals have returned battered and beaten from a first, tentative foray into the legal arena, sworn never to return. The courtroom is not the place for thin-skinned individuals vulnerable to the sometimes caustic and scathing attacks on the witness' personal or professional worth. It is not the place for practitioners who are cynical about their professional activities or who carry substantial doubts about the fields of psychology or psychiatry in general; the Hans Eysencks of the mental health professions simply should not be testifying. It is also not the place for individuals with low tolerance for frustration and ambiguity, features which frequently permeate the field of litigation.

We are not saying that mental health practitioners are any more, or less, professional because they choose to participate in court as expert witnesses. We simply warn that this aspect of professional practice carries hazards which are not encountered in other activities, and particular attitudes, skills, and a certain constitution may be required in order for the experience to be emotionally rewarding. The purpose of this chapter is to help prepare those who would venture into the role of the mental health expert witness.

PROFESSIONAL SELF-CONCEPTS— GETTING COMFORTABLE IN EXPERT WITNESS ROLES

The most important preliminary issue to be resolved is for mental health practitioners to become comfortable regarding their anticipated roles as an expert witness in court. Being accorded the status of "expert" witness means two things: (a) that they have special training, knowledge, or experience that makes them privy to data not accessible to the ordinary lay person; and (b) that they will be allowed, encouraged, or directed to give opinions about how their special knowledge relates to legal decisions involving the client. People who have substantial doubts about the body of knowledge of the profession as scientifically respectable or valid (e.g., the unreliability of diagnosis, the lack of precision in predicting individual behavior) or who do not feel they have something potentially valuable to say, should avoid being expert witnesses. On the other hand, people who believe that imprecision is simply a part of life and feel comfortable talking in terms of probability and logical inference, have little to fear in the courtroom. Similarly, if professionals have reservations about opining on questions that are essentially social, moral, or legal in nature, then they may wish to avoid testifying on such issues, or develop mechanisms for limiting the scope of their testimony to keep them on safe and ethically proper grounds (Bonnie & Slobogin, 1980; Morse, 1978; Poythress, 1982).

If these two issues can be resolved, then much of the anticipatory anxiety associated with courtroom testimony can be allayed, and the witnesses can begin constructively and systematically to prepare for the battle of wits with the attorneys.

Having decided to become involved in forensic cases, with the potential for courtroom testimony appearances, mental health professionals should anticipate the problems inherent in this aspect of professional practice. The mental health professionals' best start for a successful courtroom experience is careful pretrial preparation. The preparation for courtroom testimony can be conveniently broken down into three segments: issues clarification, charting the course, and review of technical data.

ISSUES CLARIFICATION

The first task is to insure that the attorney's expectations and the experts' knowledge and plans to testify are congruent. As elementary as it may seem, attorneys do not always tell mental health professionals in clear terms the focus of the examination and testimony to be provided. Attorneys may confuse the different legal issues, or they may mistakenly assume that one examination will suffice for a variety of purposes. For example, an attorney may contract for a pretrial examination of a defendant's competency to stand trial, and later subpoena the mental health professional to testify on an entirely different issue (e.g., criminal responsibility or sentencing recommendation). This confusion may lead to problems which are ethically and legally insurmountable. Ethically, the professional may have been obliged, prior to undertaking the examination, to inform the defendant of any exceptions to confidentiality and the explicit purposes for the evaluation. Not having informed the defendant of other possible uses of the evaluation data, an expert may be legally prohibited from testifying in other stages of the legal proceedings (*Estelle v. Smith*, 1981).

This potential problem of confusion between the mental health professional and the attorney can be avoided by careful planning beginning with the initial contact with the attorney. Telephone consultation and a face-to-face meeting with the attorney a few days in advance of actual testimony will help to insure that there is mutual understanding of the goals and limits of the expert's testimony in the case.

CHARTING THE COURSE

Having decided where the evaluation is going, the next order of business is to determine how to get there.

Outlining the plan for direct examination with the attorney allows the goals to be accomplished.

The mental health professional's written report should have summarized the essence of the clinical examination with respect to techniques used and findings. The clinician's logic in proceeding from the clinical data to the legal opinions should also have been spelled out. The pretrial conference, then, should establish the means by which this information will be elicited in court. Brodsky (1977) emphasized the following guidelines in preparing for direct testimony:

—Examine the written list of questions that the attorney plans to ask on direct examination; suggest changes in the questions that are problematic.
—Insure that the questions are predominately open-ended, which allows the most latitude in responding.
—Avoid a "20 questions" format, to minimize the possibility of the testimony being perceived as "rehearsed."
—Avoid any questions which sound sour, phony, or which call for unprofessional opinions by the witness; assert the limits of the findings and professional expertise, and stay within them.

Preparation along these lines will help insure that the witness' direct testimony will be presented in a more fully developed and organized "narrative" format. The narrative style maximizes the opportunity for witnesses to integrate their various findings. It also capitalizes on the fact that listeners tend to associate greater personal competence with speakers who testify in narrative, rather than fragmented styles (Conley, O'Barr, & Lind, 1978; O'Barr, 1982).

When planning a direct examination, the issue of presenting contradictory data and counterarguments should be discussed. Clinical examinations are never perfectly reliable or valid, nor are clinicians' theoretical formulations or logical inferences above reproach. Research data are rarely uniformly supportive of a single inference. Discussing inconsistent data and counterarguments in advance serves two purposes. First, it gives full light to the different ethical demands on witnesses and the attorneys; clinicians may be obliged to present contradictory findings by virtue of their oath to "tell the whole truth" (Loftus & Monahan, 1980), while attorneys may feel obliged to present only that evidence which advances their clients' legal interests. Second, it allows attorneys to make tactical decisions about the inconsistent data and counterarguments—whether to ignore them on direct examination and hope that they go undiscovered by opposing counsel, or to bring them out on direct examinations in an attempt to increase credibility by showing "we have nothing to hide." If clinicians have good, sound reasons for rejecting contradictory data or counterarguments, the latter tactic may be indicated. The presentation of "negative" data, along with sound reasons for rejecting them, may serve as an "inoculation" against opposing positions (McGuire, 1964).

REVIEW OF TECHNICAL DATA

The pretrial plan is not complete until the necessary technical data have been reviewed. Mental health professionals must be prepared for a review of their professional credentials and knowledge of the tools of the trade. The review of technical data consists of preparing credentials, reviewing relevant published data, and noting legal guidelines.

In most jurisdictions, for most legal issues, trial judges exercise discretion in deciding which proposed experts will be allowed to give opinion and conclusion testimony. However, occasionally there will be statutory requirements that "expert" witnesses be of a particular discipline or background; thus, knowledge of the prevailing technical constraints on testimony should be the first order of business.

Assuming there are no technical constraints upon the proposed witness, preparing credentials consists of mentally organizing and updating a resume of professional activities. It may be helpful to provide the attorneys with a typed copy of the resumé, and a copy of sample questions for eliciting credentials on *voir dire*. Areas typically covered include:

— Formal education, including dates and places of degrees awarded, major area of study, title of thesis or dissertation if appropriate;
— Practical experience, including internship, residencies, professional positions held—including type of work (teaching, research, administration, or service provision), and kinds of clients served (adult, adolescent, child; inpatient or outpatient);
— Professional certification or licensure; Board Certification, where applicable;
— Membership in professional organizations (e.g., American Psychiatric Association, American Psychology-Law Society), and so forth;
— Professional publications—books, journal articles, and so forth;
— Prior court experience as an expert and in what kinds of litigation.

Credentials presentation should be prepared in such a way as to emphasize the clinicians' training and experience on issues before the bar in the present case. For example, clinicians might wish to emphasize their training in child development and family therapy when testifying in a child custody proceeding, with little mention of previous experiences assessing criminal defendants; in preparing to testify in an insanity case, just the opposite would hold. The importance of credentials preparation cannot be overemphasized; quite simply, experts who do not get their foot in the door are not going to be allowed to testify.

The review of relevant published data should attend to any formal assessment techniques which have been used in the forensic evaluation. Clinicians should be prepared to discuss these issues: (a) how the procedures were developed and standardized; (b) reference norms used in this case; (c) reliability and validity; (d) possible subjectivity in scoring and interpreting responses; and (e) the uses and limitations of the techniques. For psychological testing, witnesses might review the individual test manuals, recent reviews in Buros' *Eighth Mental Measurement Yearbook* (1978), and selected journal review articles. When clinical findings involve areas of substantial empirical research, the clinician should become familiar with the relevant literature, including specific findings, adequacy of design and analysis, and limits of generalizability.

Finally, mental health professionals should be familiar with pertinent legal statutes and case findings. Any time mental health professionals venture opinions on legal issues, they are engaging in translating the language of one profession into that of another. Specific guidelines often exist. For example, the law may utilize one definition of mental illness which, while flexible and elusive in some respects, is nevertheless discernably different from the definition used by mental health professionals in the clinic. Witnesses should know these definitions and be able to casually recite them, should testimony require. Similarly, judgments about how expert opinions should be formulated regarding particular behavior abnormalities may be specified in major appellate holdings. Thus, it is important that clinicians become familiar with the prevailing statutes and major legal holdings in the relevant legal areas.

IMPRESSION MANAGEMENT

In the context of the traditional adversary proceeding, the personality of the expert becomes more important than the subject about which he is testifying. The juror is more easily persuaded to a desired line of thinking by personable or friendly experts....This is true whether or not what he says is technically or medically truthful. Thus, a pleasant demeanor may mean more to a juror than the expert's knowledge. (Moenssens, 1978, p. 66)

For many mental health professionals, the most distasteful aspect of expert testimony is having to take part in a persuasive proceeding, and being forced to endure the opposing attorney's critical cross-examination. The persuasive aspect is distasteful because it smacks of selling something to the judge or jury. Cross-examination is unpleasant when clinicians fail to accept that the legal system's crucible for discovering the truth is not detached clinical investigation, but close scrutiny of the evidence in an adversary manner.

Regardless of clinicians' preferences, the persuasive aspect of testimony and adversarial cross-examination are integral parts of the typical court proceeding. If the journey through these unfamiliar regions is to be smooth, mental health professionals must master behaviors which facilitate being heard by the judge or jury, and withstand conventional attacks on testimony. These two issues fall under the headings of impression management and courtroom transactions. Impression management will be examined first.

From a technical point of view, mental health professionals become expert witnesses when a judge, after qualifying questions, declares them to be. From a phenomenological perspective, clinicians become "expert" when they behave in a manner which the jurors perceive as "expert." Impression management, in the courtroom setting, refers to a constellation of verbal and nonverbal behaviors which determine how witnesses are perceived by the jurors.

Impression formation begins as the witness is called to the stand. Rather than waiting timidly to be ushered to the stand, the witness can convey a sense of comfort and familiarity in the courtroom by striding confidently toward the stand. In preparation to being sworn in, the witness should stop, raise his or her hand, and face the person who will administer the oath. Having been sworn in, the witness can now take the stand in a calm manner, getting seated comfortably and casually making eye contact with the jury before accepting the first question from counsel.

While on the stand, several factors are important in conveying a sense of confidence and competence to members of the jury. Brodsky (1981) has labeled one important factor the Rumplestiltskin Principle. Mental health professionals should know the names of both sets of attorneys and use their names in responding from the stand. The names of the opposing attorneys are particularly important.

A general response to the question "Well, Dr. Freud, isn't that true?", is with the use of the attorney's title: "Yes, counselor, it is true." A stronger stance is for the witness to respond using the attorney's name, "Yes, Mr. Darrow, it is true."

A common error in style among witnesses unfamiliar with the courtroom is to engage in a question and answer session with an attorney, rarely addressing the jury while responding. It is important to make eye contact with the *jurors* during testimony. Eye contact affords witnesses nonverbal feedback from jurors as to how the testimony is being received—nods, glances, smiles, or smirks may help witnesses shape their testimony. It also allows witnesses to avoid looking at the attorney. This may be particularly important on cross-examination, as an attorney's stares, scowls, or looks of disbelief may be anxiety arousing.

If the witness is looking at the attorney, then chances are that the jurors will be also. This aspect of witness behavior requires special attention by inexperienced clinicians, for attorneys can be very subtle and adept at redirecting the witness' gaze away from the jurors. The attorney may start questioning at a podium next to the jury box, then pause in midquestion and casually glide one or two steps away, apparently lost in thought. As the questioning continues, the attorney moves across the room to the table, on the pretense of obtaining a book or note pad from which to refresh his or her memory. The witness who visually tracks the attorney will now be looking 90 degrees away from the jury. As the attorney comes forward toward the bench, perhaps to hold a piece of evidence or offer a report into evidence, the witness' gaze may be drawn nearly 180 degrees from the jurors, leaving them with a view of nothing but the back of the witness' head.

In delivering testimony, two factors are important. First, witnesses should speak in plain language, minimizing the use of jargon, labels, or professional idioms lay jurors are unlikely to comprehend. Undefined terms such as "flight of ideas," "registration amnesia," or even simpler terms like "the client's *affect*" will have little meaning to jurors, who may become alienated by the witness who insists upon using "big words." Second, mental health professionals should develop skills in testifying in what researchers have labeled a "powerful" style of speech (Conley et al., 1978; Erickson, Lind, Johnson, & O'Barr, 1978). The features of power*less* speech include the use of *intensifiers* (e.g., "most certainly"), *hedges* (e.g., "kind of," "I guess"), *hesitations* (e.g., "well," and "uh"), and so forth. Powerful speech, on the other hand, is unequivocal and straightforward. O'Barr (1982) has shown that audiences perceive powerful speakers as more believable, competent, intelligent, and trustworthy than powerless speakers. Thus, a witness' impact on jurors may be mediated by his or her style of speaking.

Responses should be relatively brief and, except to avoid possible misunderstanding, within the scope of the question asked. Even with a narrative style of responding, most answers can be delivered in four to five short sentences. The attorneys will have opportunities to go over the important material more than once or to tie it all together in their closing arguments. Expert witnesses should avoid being verbose.

Impression management extends also to the way witnesses leave the stand. Sulking off with shoulders slumped and head down conveys the impression of the warrior defeated in battle. Stumbling or excessive fumbling with records compromises credibility. Brodsky (1981) has provided an interesting anecdote in this regard:

> One friend of mine reports having tripped and fallen as he left the witness box, his papers flying all over the floor. Awkwardly and clumsily he scampered about picking up his papers, when the judge called out: "May I have the card please?" My friend was puzzled. The judge repeated the request, and finally my friend found a large card among his papers. The card had slipped off the witness box when he tripped, and in large letters warned: PLEASE BE CAREFUL STEPPING DOWN FROM THE WITNESS BOX. While the testimony went generally well, he believes this concluding episode undermined his opinions, and he grimaces about it to this day.

To avoid leaving any negative impressions after the testimony has been completed, Brodsky (1981) offers this model:

When I leave the stand after testifying, I always
stride as if I am supremely pleased, peaceful, and
confident about my testimony. Then I walk over
to the opposing attorneys' table and shake hands
with them. Because I am standing and they are
sitting, the very last impression in the viewer's
minds is of me as powerful and kind to these
attorneys who have challenged me.

A smile and a nod ("good day!") toward the jury box when
descending from the witness stand also helps to end the
performance on a congenial note.

It is beyond the scope of this chapter to cover
exhaustively the various factors related to impression
formation and persuasion in the courtroom, though some
of the more important ones have been summarized here.
(See also Bank & Poythress, 1982). It would certainly be
ethically improper to encourage the substitution of
showmanship skills for good clinical technique (see
Naftulin, Ware, & Donnelly, 1973). This section is
offered not as a substitute for, but as an adjunct to, good
informative clinical testimony, as part and parcel of the
whole experience of expert testimony.

COURTROOM TRANSACTIONS

The second component of successful testimony is
familiarity with fundamental cross-examination tactics
and appropriate responses. While careful pretrial
preparation of direct testimony is essential, witnesses
must also anticipate attempts by opposing counsel to
create turbulence sufficient to throw the testimony off
course. Opposing attorneys will do this by challenging
the witnesses, their credentials, methods, findings,
opinions, and, in rare cases, character.

The best defense against potentially damaging cross-
examination is to anticipate areas of potential weakness
and to deal with them openly on direct examination. In
this way the suspect areas can be dealt with by a
"friendly" counsel, whose patient manner of inquiry
should facilitate the expert's explanations without
creating an aura of doubt. Witnesses who wait to deal

with these issues on cross-examination, may find themselves confronted by a cunning lawyer who couches questions, loaded with innuendo, in such a manner as to permit only "Yes" or "No" answers.

In this section we will identify some of the more common areas of cross-examination and methods for dealing with them. The opposing lawyer's thrusts will generally emphasize one of three points: (a) what you are not; (b) what you did (or did not) do; or (c) what you do not know.

WHAT YOU ARE NOT

During cross-examination regarding credentials, the attorney will seek to emphasize what the witness is not, with the implication that they should be something other than what they are. This tactic takes many forms, depending on the credentials of the proposed witness and the circumstances of the case. The emphasis is frequently on lack of proper training, licensure, or certification. A common inquiry of this type is to the nonphysician who holds a doctoral degree; the attorney seeks to imply that the witness is not a "real" doctor and, therefore, should not be allowed to testify. A typical cross-examination might go like this:

— You are not a medical doctor, are you? You never completed, or even attended, medical school, did you?
— Are you allowed to prescribe medications to treat the mentally ill? You can't treat mental disorders like a real doctor, can you?

For physicians, lack of Board Certification is a common point of emphasis:

— Dr. Jones, are you certified by the American Board of Psychiatry and Neurology? Are you certified by the American Board of Forensic Psychiatry? NO? Then you really aren't a forensic psychiatrist, are you?

Parallel lines of inquiry can be seen in other areas the witnesses "are not":

To the recent graduate:

— You completed your doctorate only last year, is that correct? You really aren't very experienced, are you? How long will it be before you qualify to practice as a licensed psychologist?

To experts testifying in their first few cases:

— Doctor, how many times have you previously been qualified as an expert in custody proceedings? Only once?! Speak up, please!

To experts using cross-disciplinary data:

— Doctor, you are a psychiatrist, is that correct? I noticed in your report that your opinion is based on the consideration of psychological testing results—specifically the Rorschach. Are you also a psychologist? Are you trained in the Rorschach? Can you discuss for the court the reliability and validity of the test?

WHAT YOU DID (OR DID NOT) DO

Questions about what an expert did, or did not do, address the thoroughness of the evaluation. A broad range of issues, such as the depth of the clinical examination, utilization of corroborating data, and objectivity versus bias, may be probed. The attorneys will assert that whatever the expert did was *not* sufficient, that whatever he or she did not do *was* essential, and that, in any event, the conclusions were biased.

Adequacy of the clinical examinations may be probed by questions regarding the length of time spent with the client and tests that were or were not used. For example:

— How long did you interview Mr. Smith in assessing his competency to stand trial? Do you mean to tell this court that in a mere 1 1/2 hours you can assess a man's mental condition, his personality, and determine his competency?

— Doesn't a standard psychological evaluation include psychological testing? Did you administer the Stanford Binet? The TAT? The Rorschach? You did not? Why were you content to base an opinion on an incomplete examination?

Questions are often posed about the use of corroborating data:

— Isn't it common practice for psychologists to obtain records of prior psychiatric treatment in making a complete diagnostic assessment? Did you obtain and review all the records of Mr. Smith's prior treatment?

— You have given the opinion that Mr. Smith shot his neighbor because of persecutory delusions. Do you have it, on any source other than the self-serving word of Mr. Smith, that such delusions really existed at that time?

— You indicate that the mother in this case should have custody. Did you talk with the neighbors about this woman's tone of voice in scolding the child? Did you talk with the child's teachers about this woman's lack of interest in the child's progress at school? Wouldn't that be important?

The witness' objectivity may also be attacked:

— How much are you being paid by defense counsel for your testimony in this case? Eighty dollars an hour!!! Does that include the three hours you sat outside the courtroom this morning waiting to testify?

Of course, you wouldn't be able to collect this exorbitant fee if you had not reached the conclusion the defense wanted, now would you?

— You worked in therapy with Mr. Smith for several months prior to his filing for disability, didn't you? Is it possible that your therapeutic relationship and desire to further his personal goals may have biased your judgment about his disability?

—Doctor, you are a mother as well as a psychologist, is that correct? Might not your own maternal feelings influence your judgment about custody placement?

WHAT YOU DO NOT KNOW

Inquiries in this general area focus on what particular witnesses, or members of their field in general, do not know. Some inquiries focus on lack of accuracy or precision, while others emphasize differences in theoretical orientation. The fallibility of witnesses may also be asserted by showing their lack of familiarity with specific published research from their own field, or by confronting them with published findings which seem to contradict their statements or conclusions in the case at hand. For instance:

—Doctor, you have indicated that Mr. Smith is likely to commit further violent acts. Isn't it true that psychiatrists have no special expertise in predicting violent behavior? Hasn't the American Psychiatric Association issued a position statement that its members should not give unreliable testimony of this type?

—What really causes schizophrenia? What caused schizophrenia in Mr. Smith?

—Doctor, you've characterized Mr. Doe's unusual sexual behavior as a result of an unconscious fixation originating during his developmental years. Is it not possible that another psychologist might explain the very same behaviors on the basis of reinforcers in his current environment, not on unconscious factors? Isn't that just your pet theory about sexual behavior, Doctor? The bottom line, Doctor, is that you really don't know why he exhibits this unusual behavior, do you?

—You've testified that you do not believe Mr. Smith to be malingering. Are you familiar with Dr. Rosenhan's research which demonstrated, beyond any doubt, that perfectly normal individuals can fool psychiatrists into diagnosing them as schizophrenic simply by reporting one or two peculiar behaviors? I have the paper right here, Doctor!

WITNESS' COPING MECHANISMS

There are several coping mechanisms which allow the skilled witness to handle cross-examination questions with relative ease. A part of surviving on the witness stand, perhaps the most important part in terms of impression management, is the witness' attitude and sense of self. If a positive sense of self can be maintained, such that critical questions are handled confidently and nondefensively, half the battle is won.

Inexperienced witnesses may feel insecure because of what they are not. The fact is that there are thousands of things that each of us is not, and it is perfectly alright to not be everything. What little data has been gathered in cross-discipline evaluations of forensic expertise (Dix & Poythress, 1981; Petrella & Poythress, 1983) affirms that no particular discipline has demonstrated superiority in forensic matters.

Witnesses who get caught up in the content of testimony and feel that they have to be everything, must have done everything, or have to know everything, often slip into the posture of trying to defend indefensible (and occasionally trivial) points. They lose sight of the fact that in the process they concede their composure, which is the real concession the cross-examining attorney wants from them. General guideline No. 1, then, is maintain a calm, confident composure and a nondefensive tone. Make minor substantive concessions willingly.

General guideline No. 2 is to *listen carefully* and, where possible, answer only the question asked. Attorneys are notorious for loading questions, and loaded questions should be defused prior to attempting a substantive answer. Reconsider the earlier example:

— How long did you interview Mr. Smith in assessing his competency to stand trial? Do you mean to tell this court that in a mere 1 1/2 hours you can assess a man's mental condition, his personality, and determine his competency?

Note that in the first question, the clinician's task was to have assessed competency to stand trial. In the second question, the attorney loads the question with a considerably more complex and time-consuming clinical task, hoping the witness will claim to have accomplished much more than is realistic in the stated time frame. An appropriate response to the second question might be:

—The assessment was limited to his ability to function in role of a defendant as outlined in the competency criteria. A complete personality assessment, which was not attempted, would have required considerably more time and would not have been particularly relevant to answering the referral question about competency.

A third general guideline is for witnesses always to remember who the clinical expert is; it is the person on the witness stand, not the one conducting the cross-examination. Attorneys will construct various straw men with their questions, and naive witnesses may allow themselves to be knocked down by a straw man. Again, consider an earlier example:

—Doesn't a standard psychological evaluation include psychological testing?....

If the witness answers "Yes," but administered no tests, then he or she has been set up for being portrayed as having done an incomplete assessment. The key to handling such questions is *never* to let the attorneys define, through their questions, the standards for an evaluation. Thus, an appropriate response from an expert witness to this question might be:

—There is no *standard* psychological evaluation which applies in all cases; testing may or may not be needed, depending on the referral question and the clinician's discretion.

It is essential that witnesses maintain control in defining clinical expertise, practice, and procedure. Those who casually or carelessly allow the attorneys to gain this control will find themselves in for "a long afternoon."

These general guidelines will go a long way toward protecting witnesses during cross-examination. Elsewhere (Brodsky, 1977; Poythress, 1980) we have addressed more specific responses to cross-examination gambits, including the "learned treatise" techniques popularized by Ziskin (1975). A couple of the more specific response techniques are worth repeating here. These are the "push-pull" technique, and what Brodsky (1981) refers to as the "zang."

The push-pull technique is a method expert witnesses can use to convert a cross-examining attorney's point into one of their own. It is applicable when the attorney is pushing for a concession which, ultimately, the witness should make. The attorney hopes to have the witness make the concession grudgingly, as if it were a point he or she wished to conceal. The witness, however, can steal the attorney's thunder by enthusiastically agreeing with the point. The following example serves as a brief illustration:

Attorney: Doctor, isn't it true that the validity of the Rorschach and TAT has not been clearly demonstrated?

Doctor: That's a very important point, Mr. Darrow! No psychological tests are perfectly valid, which is the reason I supplemented the testing data with a clinical interview and family interviews.

Rather than trying to defend the validity of the tests, the witness agrees with the attorney, and even extends the point to other tests as well. Thus, the witness enhances his or her credibility through a transaction intended to discredit him or her.

The "zang" is a sudden and unexpected movement by expert witnesses which takes them out of the flow of the attorneys' line of cross-examination. Witnesses may take themselves out of uncomfortable situations in a number of ways, for example, giving an honest "No" to a question an attorney was certain would produce a "Yes," or by getting out of the "Yes-No" response mode altogether by answering "There is no 'Yes' or 'No' answer to that question." Witnesses might also assert that a "Yes" or "No" answer *must* be qualified in order not to be misleading. A "zang" may also consist of turning away from the cross-examining attorney to request guidance from the court about whether a particular question is appropriate (e.g., the attorney asks about a defendant's mental condition at the time of a crime during testimony at a pretrial competency hearing).

Finally, there is potential for the use of humor as a response to cross-examination. Witnesses will find times when the attorneys' questions are so repetitive, ridiculous, or inane that even the most patient, polite, candid, or serious responses will not bring an end to the badgering. In such cases, humor, tactfully injected, may have its place.

On one occasion one of us (NGP) was led through an increasingly ridiculous series of questions of the "Doctor, isn't it possible that..." type, in which increasingly improbable scenarios were offered for consideration. After conceding that "anything is possible" and politely responding that the hypotheticals were becoming increasingly improbable, the final response was:

—Well, Mr. Darrow, I guess if you sit a chimpanzee down in front of a typewriter with a large stack of paper, it is possible that he would kick out the Encyclopedia Brittanica for you—but I doubt it!

The attorney's outraged objection to the witness' flippancy was met by the court's admonishment to the attorney to cease being argumentative with the witness. While a humorous or flippant style is in no way appropriate as a general posture on the witness stand, it may be used with positive effect on rare occasions.

ADVOCACY PRESSURES
AND ETHICAL RESPONSIBILITIES

Mental health professionals who testify regularly find themselves subjected to pressures to join the attorney in the adversarial process. After all, the attorney who has engaged the expert is the person with whom the personal relationship has been established. A sense of loyalty exists. Furthermore, the expert will not have reached the point of testifying unless substantial consonance already exists between the expert's opinions and the attorney's trial objectives. It is not unusual, therefore, for some experts to find themselves committed to defending "their" attorney's position in a fierce and vigorous manner.

Some observers suggest that such a posture is appropriate for the role demands of the setting. Thus, Slovenko (1973) asserts:

> An expert who takes a neutral role does his party a disservice, for the opposing party's expert will undoubtedly assume his role as advocate and his advocacy would go without challenge. (p. 25)

We disagree. While it may be true that some opposing experts will be demonstrably partisan, such advocacy serves to compromise the integrity of expert testimony. Partisan testimony diminishes objectivity, the very foundation of the expert's role in the courtroom.

Blatant advocacy reduces the credibility of expert testimony, as it should. Subtle advocacy is a more widespread and difficult problem. Experts sometimes find themselves extending their findings beyond the data base because of their acquired adversarial identities. The pressures to infer excessively from their data come from the testimony dynamics of wishing to be seen as knowledgeable and certain in the face of challenging questions during cross-examination. A continuing alertness to this reaction is necessary. Occasionally, an alert expert who has gone too far might well say, for example, "I need to correct myself. When I said that Jamie would be seriously harmed in the custody of his father, what I should have said was that there was a greater probability he would be harmed in the custody of his father."

To whom does the loyalty of the expert belong? We have ruled out the position that some attorneys hold that the loyalty of experts belongs to the side that has called them. Sadoff (1975) has indicated that it is justice and the legal process to which loyalty and responsibility must be assigned. Sadoff writes:

> The psychiatrist is called by the defense counsel to help him prepare the best possible defense within the limits of his medical expertise....However once the expert takes the witness stand and begins testifying, his allegiance belongs to the court, in the interests of justice. (p. 35)

While the issues of truth and justice are surely central to expert testimony, expert witnesses must be cautious not to explicitly pursue such goals. That is, justice and the truth of a matter in controversy are determinations to be made by judge or jury. Experts who seek to draw such ultimate legal conclusions go beyond their legitimate role. Their task is not to see that justice is done because that process is not their responsibility. Courts often do defer to experts' opinions and do appear to seek just such guidance. However, these final findings and dispositions are the business of the court, not that of the expert witness.

The allegiance of experts is to their findings and to their professions. The responsibility is to insure that their findings and statements are founded on the best contemporary knowledge and that their testimony reflects the highest standards of their professions. The lawyers who have called the experts are not the reference point for duty. The court-defined tasks are not the reference point for duty, for sometimes the court defines problems in terms that are dissonant with professional frames of reference. The responsibilities of expert witnesses are to themselves, to their professional integrity as mental health professionals, and to the scholarly foundations of their testimony.

Stanley L. Brodsky, Ph.D., a clinical psychologist, is Professor of Psychology at the University of Alabama. Dr. Brodsky's primary scholarly interests are in the areas of psychology and law and psychotherapy with reluctant clients.

Norman G. Poythress, Jr., Ph.D., a clinical psychologist, is in independent practice. He has served as Acting Clinical Director and Director of Psychology at the Taylor Hardin Secure Medical Facility in Tuscaloosa, Alabama and worked for several years at Michigan's Center for Forensic Psychiatry. Dr. Poythress has long been interested and involved in training forensic clinicians.

RESOURCES

Bank, S., & Poythress, N. (1982). The elements of persuasion in expert testimony. *Journal of Psychiatry and Law, 10,* 173-204.

Bonnie, R., & Slobogin, C. (1980). The role of mental health professionals in the criminal process: The case for informed speculation. *Virginia Law Review, 66,* 427-522.

Brodsky, S. (1977). The mental health professional on the witness stand: A survival guide. In B. D. Sales (Ed.), *Psychology in the Legal Process* (pp. 269-276). New York: Spectrum.

Brodsky, S. L. (1981). *The Psychologist as Expert Witness.* Paper presented at the annual meeting of the American Society of Criminology, Washington, DC.

Buros, O. (Ed.). (1978). *Eighth Mental Measurement Yearbook.* Highland Park, NJ: Gryphon.

Conley, J., O'Barr, W., & Lind, E. (1978). The power of language: Presentational style in the courtroom. *Duke Law Journal, 6,* 1375-1399.

Dix, G., & Poythress, N. (1981). Propriety of medical dominance of forensic mental health practice: The empirical evidence. *Arizona Law Review, 23,* 961-989.

Erickson, B., Lind, E., Johnson, B., & O'Barr, W. (1978). Speech style and impression formation in a court setting: The effects of "powerful" and "powerless" speech. *Journal of Experimental Social Psychology, 14,* 266-279.

Estelle v. Smith, 451 U.S. 454 (1981).

Loftus, E., & Monahan, J. (1980). Trial by data: Psychological research as legal evidence. *American Psychologist, 35,* 270-283.

McGuire, W. (1964). Inducing resistance to persuasion. In L. Berkowitz (Ed.), *Advances in Experimental Social Psychology* (Vol. 1, pp. 191-229). New York: Academic.

Moenssens, A. (1978). The 'impartial' medical expert: A new look at an old issue. *Medical Trial Technique Quarterly, 25*, 63-76.

Morse, S. (1978). Law and mental health professionals: The limits of expertise. *Professional Psychology, 9*, 389-399.

Naftulin, D., Ware, J., & Donnelly, F. (1973). The Doctor Fox lecture: A paradigm of educational seduction. *Journal of Medical Education, 48*, 630-635.

O'Barr, W. (1982). *Linguistic Evidence: Language, Power, and Strategy in the Courtroom.* New York: Academic.

Petrella, R., & Poythress, N. (1983). The quality of forensic evaluations: An interdisciplinary study. *Journal of Consulting and Clinical Psychology, 51*, 76-85.

Poythress, N. (1980). Coping on the witness stand: Learned responses to "Learned Treatises." *Professional Psychology, 11*, 139-149.

Poythress, N. (1982). Concerning reform in expert testimony: An open letter from a practicing psychologist. *Law and Human Behavior, 6*, 39-43.

Quay, H. (1965). Psychopathic personality as pathological stimulation seeking. *American Journal of Psychiatry, 122*, 180-183.

Sadoff, R. (1975). *Forensic Psychiatry: A Practical Guide for Lawyers and Psychiatrists.* Springfield, IL: Thomas.

Schwitzgebel, R. L., & Schwitzgebel, R. K. (1980). *Law and Psychological Practice.* New York: Wiley.

Slovenko, R. (1973). *Psychiatry and Law.* Boston: Little, Brown.

Ziskin, J. (1975). *Coping with Psychiatric and Psychological Testimony* (2d ed.). Beverly Hills, CA: Law and Psychology Press.

INTRODUCTION TO SECTION VI: BEHAVIORAL SCIENCE AND OTHER ASPECTS OF THE LEGAL PROCESS

The preceding chapters have examined many of the more traditional roles played by mental health professionals and behavioral scientists in the legal system. The chapters in this section of the volume explore several less traditional but rapidly developing aspects of the relationship between law and the behavioral sciences. In particular, these chapters deal with eyewitness testimony, lie detection, and jury selection—all topics of growing significance to contemporary legal process.

EYEWITNESS TESTIMONY

In most forms of litigation, one of the major tasks, if not the major task, confronting the trier-of-fact is the reconstruction of past events. Indeed, many if not most civil lawsuits and criminal prosecutions come down to a simple question of fact: "Who did what to whom?" Generally, the answer to this question is sought from the testimony of those who actually observed the event in question—the so-called "eyewitnesses."

Yet, recent behavioral science research has demonstrated that eyewitness testimony is often mistaken. In their chapter on this important subject, psychologists David Hall and Elizabeth Loftus review recent advances in research on eyewitness identifications and testimony. In particular, Drs. Hall and Loftus focus upon the reliability of eyewitness testimony, strategies for preserving the integrity of eyewitness recollections, the impact of eyewitness testimony on jurors, and the use of expert behavioral science testimony to correct common misunderstandings regarding eyewitness identification.

LIE DETECTION

Another critical aspect of the task confronting triers-of-fact is that of determining who is telling the truth: "Who is to be believed?" Indeed, lie detection, a function commonly attributed to the polygraph examination, is of major importance not only in the legal process but also in government and many facets of the business world. Though generally inadmissible at trial, polygraph results are often used by attorneys, the police, and other legal authorities outside of court. Moreover, lie detection via the polygraph is becoming a popular, if not accepted, means of screening those who apply for or hold positions of trust in government and business.

In their chapter on psychological methods of lie detection, psychologists Benjamin Kleinmuntz and Julian Szucko describe the growing use of the polygraph in legal settings and other contexts. Drs. Kleinmuntz and Szucko then go on to examine the reliability and validity of polygraphy, ultimately concluding that, under current circumstances, the "lie detector's" main function may be more coercive than scientific.

JURY SELECTION

At trial in our system of justice, responsibility for determining "who did what to whom" and "who is to be believed" rests squarely with the trier-of-fact, judge, or jury. Our system of trial by jury is predicated upon the belief that a small group of lay persons (from 6 to 12 jurors) is capable of listening with an open mind to competing versions of the "facts," objectively weighing all of the evidence adduced at trial, and ultimately rendering a fair and unbiased verdict. In fact, however, lawyers, judges, and behavioral scientists have long recognized that jury decision making is far from this open-minded, objective, and unbiased ideal.

Like all human beings, jurors have attitudes, opinions, likes, dislikes, and prejudices which they cannot help but bring with them into the courtroom. And, of course, these aspects of their psychological make-up will influence the way they perform as triers-of-fact. Recognizing this truism, lawyers have long expended considerable energy in the art of jury selection (i.e., in attempting to make sure that those chosen as jurors in a particular trial are likely to be sympathetic—or at least not antagonistic—toward their clients). In the final chapter of this section, Diane Follingstad, a clinical and forensic psychologist, describes recent attempts to render the "art" of jury selection a "science," what Dr. Follingstad refers to as "systematic jury selection." For the most part, Dr. Follingstad's chapter provides a detailed review of the growing body of research aimed at assessing the influence of demographic and psychological variables upon jury decision making. Yet, her chapter also deals with many of the most significant practical and ethical problems encountered by both lawyers and behavioral scientists who seek to apply the results of this research in actual litigation.

RECENT ADVANCES
IN RESEARCH ON
EYEWITNESS TESTIMONY

David F. Hall and Elizabeth F. Loftus

An unusual instance of mistaken identification occurred to an Australian psychologist named Donald Thomson (Baddeley, 1982). Thomson took part in a televised discussion of the topic of eyewitness testimony. Within a short time of his appearance, he was arrested by the police and accused of rape. Much to his surprise, the rape victim identified him from a line-up. He pressed the police for details of the rape, and discovered it had occurred at precisely the same time as his television appearance. He explained that he had an excellent alibi, as he had been on television with the Australian Civil Rights Committee and an Assistant Commissioner of Police. They would be his witnesses. But the police were not convinced. One officer replied: "Yes, and I suppose you've also got Jesus Christ and the Queen of England, too." Further investigation into the case revealed that the woman had in fact been raped while watching the television program, and she had apparently merged her image of his face with her memory of this tragic episode.

Thomson is one of many psychologists now actively involved in research on eyewitness testimony. A number of investigators, over a period of decades, have established two crucial facts about eyewitness identifications: (a) false identifications occur in actual criminal investigations (e.g., Borchard, 1932; Hain, 1976; Sobel, 1972; Wall, 1965); and (b) eyewitness identifications often influence the outcomes of actual criminal trials (Devlin, 1976). In an early study, Borchard discovered 65 people who, because of false eyewitness identifications, were convicted of crimes that they apparently did not commit. In a more contemporary study, the Devlin Committee noted that, during 1973 in England and Wales, there were 347 criminal trials in which the only evidence was eyewitness testimony. Over 70% of these unsubstantiated prosecutions resulted in convictions. After many decades of outspoken concern from justice system professionals and from academic researchers, it appears that false eyewitness identification of suspects continues to be a major cause of false convictions.

The legal and social science research pertaining to eyewitness identification has been comprehensively reviewed by a number of authors (Clifford & Bull, 1978; Davies, Ellis, & Shepherd, 1981; Loftus, 1979; Starkman, 1979; Woocher, 1977; Yarmey, 1979). The existence of such a large number of recent and comprehensive reviews reflects, in part, a resurgence of interest in eyewitness research beginning in the early 1970s. Since those comprehensive reviews went to press, further progress has been made both in our theoretical understanding of eyewitness testimony, and in the extent of practical cooperation between psychologists and criminal justice professionals. Several researchers have attempted to provide a theoretical framework in which to encompass the growing body of eyewitness testimony research. Other recent research efforts have shed new light on a number of timely issues, for example: the risks entailed in the use of hypnotism in criminal investigations; the seemingly promising development of a technique for guiding, without biasing, the witnesses' recollection of an event; the remarkable and dangerous capacity of eyewitnesses to sway jurors' decisions; and the sometimes moderating impact on jurors of expert testimony delivered in courtrooms by academic researchers. The present chapter is not intended to be comprehensive in scope, but rather to give the flavor of recent progress in the aforementioned areas of eyewitness testimony research.

THE RELIABILITY OF
EYEWITNESS TESTIMONY

Within recent years, the body of research on eyewitness testimony has grown sufficiently large to require a broad conceptual framework. There have been several recent efforts to provide such a framework, and here we describe two such efforts: (a) Wells' (1978) distinction between system variables and estimator variables; and (b) Hall, Loftus, and Tousignant's (1983) categorization of variables affecting alterations in recollection of natural events.

SYSTEM VARIABLES AND ESTIMATOR VARIABLES

Wells (1978) notes that some of the variables that affect eyewitness testimony can be systematically controlled by justice system professionals in the course of actual forensic work. Such variables, referred to as system variables, include: the staging of line-ups, the use of mug shots for identification, the use of police sketch artists, open-ended unstructured interviews with witnesses, and other common procedures.

There is a distinctly different set of variables affecting eyewitness testimony that cannot be systematically controlled in the course of forensic work, for example: the racial or ethnic identities of suspects and of witnesses; the witness' state of anxiety while observing a crime; lighting, distance, and other perceptual factors; and the effects on memory of elapsed time. The latter variables, referred to as estimator variables, should no doubt be afforded careful consideration by triers of fact in criminal cases, but their precise impact in any given case can only be estimated, never known precisely.

Wells' (1978) distinction between system variables and estimator variables offers a tidy way of summarizing eyewitness research both for researchers themselves, and for lawyers, jurors, and other nonpsychologists. The distinction enables psychologists to more readily share their findings with professionals in the criminal justice system. In addition, Wells' distinction offers researchers a meaningful criterion for choosing new directions of investigation.

Much of Wells' (1978) own research is apparently intended to advance our understanding of procedures for which the criminal justice system can assume direct responsibility. For example, Wells, Leippe, and Ostrom (1979) note that the functional size of a line-up is a system variable that affects both the risk of false identifications and the likelihood of correct identifications of guilty suspects. The functional size of a line-up that contains a suspect is measured by asking a number of control subjects, who have never seen the suspect, to try to guess which member of the line-up is the suspect. The functional size is then defined as the ratio N/D, in which N is the total number of control subjects, and D is the number of control subjects who correctly detect the position of the suspect in the line-up. In less technical terms, the functional size of a line-up is the number of persons in the line-up who effectively share the risk of being identified by witnesses who are merely guessing. Clearly, increasing the functional size of a line-up lessens the individual risk for an innocent suspect of being mistakenly chosen.

Police want not only to avoid mistaken identification of innocent suspects, they want also to detect the presence in a line-up of the presumably-guilty suspect. Lindsay and Wells (1980) demonstrate empirically what could also have been predicted mathematically, that is, that any increase in the functional size of a line-up affords a corresponding increase in the detectional value of identifications made from the line-up. In the abstruse language of Bayesian statistics, "diagnosticity" (of any given eyewitness identification) is the probability that would have existed for an identification if the eyewitness really had seen the suspect commit the crime, divided by the probability that would have existed for the same identification if the eyewitness had not seen the suspect commit the crime, that is, pI(had seen)/pI(had not seen) (Wells & Lindsay, 1980). In any case, Lindsay and Wells showed that the Bayesian diagnosticity of identifications increased as subjects viewed line-ups having progressively larger functional sizes. The point of interest for police is that an identification from a line-up that has relatively large functional size can provide compelling evidence of a suspect's guilt.

As was the case with Wells' (1978) research, much of the research undertaken by Loftus (1979) appears to suggest practical improvements that could be adopted by criminal justice professionals. In particular, Loftus' research suggests ways of preventing the adulteration of witnesses' recollections by biased questions and misleading messages. We turn now to review of Loftus' recollection-alteration paradigm.

THE ALTERATION OF RECOLLECTION BY BIASING POST-EVENT MESSAGES

Hall et al. (1983) offer a conceptual framework in which to discuss the apparent alteration of eyewitnesses' recollections for complex natural events. The recollection-alteration model includes, first, a paradigm for demonstrating experimentally the alteration of recollection by exposure to misleading post-event information, and, second, two general principles that summarize the major variables that have been shown to affect the process of recollection change.

A Paradigm for the Alteration of Recollection. A growing number of experiments have demonstrated that memory for natural events can under some circumstances be affected by exposure to post-event information. The experimental paradigm used in such studies includes three steps:

1. Acquisition—experimental subjects are exposed to an initial complex event, such as a slide sequence depicting a crime or an automobile accident.
2. Retention and change—subjects are exposed to additional information subsequent to the initial event. The additional information might come from biasing suggestions or from potentially misleading questions, from viewing photographs, from exposure to a combination of illustrations and messages, or even from rehearsal of the initial event. Whatever the source, post-event misinformation is integrated indiscriminately with memory for the original event.

3. Retrieval—subsequent tests of memory for the initial event show that irreversible changes in recollection have occurred. Memory for the initial event often appears to have been altered or even wholly replaced by misleading post-event messages.

In a typical experiment (Loftus, Miller, & Burns, 1978), subjects were shown a slide sequence that depicted an automobile collision. For one group of subjects, the slides included a view of a yield sign, but for a second group of subjects, the otherwise-identical slides included a view of a stop sign. After viewing the original slides, subjects were given a questionnaire, which for some subjects contained a point of critical misinformation. For example, the item "Did another car pass the red Datsun while it was stopped at the yield sign?" presented misinformation when asked of subjects who had actually seen a stop sign. Finally, subjects were asked to recall whether they had viewed a stop sign or a yield sign. Depending on retention intervals, as many as 80% of the subjects showed that their memory for the sign had been affected by the misinformation. That is, they incorrectly recalled the sign suggested by the post-event questionnaire, rather than the sign that they had actually viewed.

As an experimental result, the alteration of recollection by post-event misinformation is robust and pervasive. We turn now to review two general principles that suggest a few discrete cognitive processes that may be common to many incidences of recollection change.

Two General Principles for Changes in Recollection

1. Change in recollection for a natural event is more likely to occur if memory for the event has been reactivated by post-event information.

Lewis (1979) distinguishes active memory and inactive memory. Inactive memory is memory that has been committed to long-term storage, but which has not been recently recollected. Active memory, by contrast, includes recently encoded memories and memories that have been recently recollected. Lewis cites research conducted with laboratory animals that hints that memory can be altered only if it is raised to an active status. The latter contention supports our own opinion that post-event experiences typically evoke from subjects malleable recollections of an event. Such malleable recollections can then be altered by the addition of new information, or by the excision or reworking of some of the original details. By contrast, recollection-alteration experiments typically include groups of control subjects who engage in irrelevant filler tasks during the interval between the exposure to the original event and final testing for memory. Irrelevant filler tasks generally leave original memory relatively unaffected presumably because they prevent original memory for the event from reaching an active, malleable status (during which contamination is possible).

The first principle of recollection change poses a dilemma for the investigator wishing to preserve a witness' memory. That is, a witness' memory can be altered during the process of retrieval and rehearsal, or the witness' memory can be allowed to fade with the passage of time if never retrieved and rehearsed. Although unretrieved memories are susceptible to fading with time, they do not, apparently, undergo spontaneous alteration of form or of essential content (Riley, 1962).

2. Change in recollection for a natural event is more likely to occur if discrepancies between the original event and post-event information are not initially detected.

Many experiments demonstrate that a diverse array of experimental variables can either cause or prevent alterations in recollection. This array of variables includes the attention-attracting prominence of particular details of an event; the time intervals between an event, exposure to post-event information, and final recollection of details; the format of the post-event information; the format of the final test of recollection; and warnings to the witness to expect to find misinformation in post-event messages. All of these variables apparently affect subjects' readiness to detect subtle errors in a post-event message.

In this vein, a number of experiments indicate that recollection of obscure details is more likely to be affected by post-event experiences than is recollection of salient details (Dristas & Hamilton, 1977; Marquis, Marshall, & Oskamp, 1972; Marshall, 1966). Marshall and his colleagues required subjects to view a film depiction of a crime. Certain details of the film had been found previously to be salient (likely to be recalled with accuracy) or relatively peripheral (difficult to recall). After viewing the film, subjects were presented with questions that contained misinformation. Results indicated that misleading information interfered with recall of peripheral details, but did not interfere with recall of salient details. Thus, subjects appear to be misled most frequently over details that initially attract only cursory attention.

A number of experiments that tested the effectiveness of warnings appear to offer support for the second principle of change in recollection. Greene, Flynne, and Loftus (1982) forewarned subjects that they might discover discrepancies between an event and a subsequent misleading message. Some of the warned subjects, in particular those who were warned just prior to being exposed to the misleading message, were more resistant to changes in recollection than were subjects who were not warned. Why was the warning effective? One possibility is that it caused subjects to search for inconsistencies between the post-event message and memory for the original event. Witnesses who had been warned were thus more likely to find such inconsistencies and to reject the misinformation.

Another variable that seems to affect the likelihood of a change in recollection is the syntax of the misleading post-event message (Loftus & Greene, 1980). Misleading information that has been placed in an auxiliary clause of a complex sentence has been shown to be highly effective in altering recollections. However, the same misleading information when placed in the main clause of a simple sentence is less likely to alter recollection. Apparently subjects readily assimilate information from an auxiliary clause, but fail to detect discrepancies between new information and old. By contrast, information contained in a simple declarative sentence is given more direct, critical attention. Thus, detecting discrepancies, and consequently rejecting false information, is more likely to occur when the subject reads simple declarative sentences. These findings suggest that it would be worthwhile for criminal investigators to carefully avoid complex, and potentially misleading, language in the course of interviews with witnesses.

In summary, experiments that support the second principle of change in recollection include studies of recollection of peripheral as opposed to central details, studies of the effects of warnings, and studies of the syntactic form of misleading messages. One practical implication of the second principle is that recollection alteration could to some extent be averted if witnesses were taught to recognize the biased content of certain presumptuous questions and messages.

STRATEGIES FOR PRESERVING THE INTEGRITY OF WITNESSES' MEMORIES

We have discussed research that addresses the alteration of witnesses' recollections. Such research has practical value insofar as it suggests techniques to preserve the integrity of witnesses' memories. For example, interview questions can be carefully written to avoid biasing language and suggestions, witnesses can be advised not to accept uncritically information provided by investigators or by other witnesses, and interviews with witnesses can be conducted promptly after an incident, rather than days or weeks later when the potential for distortion is increased.

Beyond instituting procedures to protect witnesses from misleading post-event messages, can other strategies be devised to enhance the accuracy of eyewitness testimony? Two lines of research have explored such strategies for memory enhancement. The first, which has proved rather unpromising, is research pertaining to the use of hypnotism; and the second, which has proved somewhat more promising, is research pertaining to methods of guided memory.

HYPNOTISM

A number of recent reviews have dealt with forensic applications of hypnotism (e.g., Hilgard & Loftus, 1979; Orne, 1979, 1981). On the whole, research indicates that the use of hypnotism to facilitate recollection entails considerable risk, and should be undertaken, if at all, only under rather limited circumstances. Claims of practitioners notwithstanding, hypnotism has rarely, if ever, been shown, under adequately controlled conditions, to improve the accuracy of subjects' recollections for details of complex natural events, such as crimes and accidents (Orne, Soskis, & Dinges, 1983; Timm, 1981, 1982). Furthermore, hypnotism appears to render many subjects increasingly susceptible to being misled by post-event questions (Putman, 1979; Zelig & Beidleman, 1981).

Equally damaging for proponents of hypnotism are experimental results which indicate that hypnotism creates a shift in subjects' response criteria, that is, a shift in subjects' level of caution or care in reporting information (Dywan & Bowers, 1982). Apparently disinhibited by hypnotism, subjects are likely to recall a greater number of details about an incident. However, such inflated recollection, while occasionally producing more correct details, can also include additional false details. Other experimental results indicate that hypnotism increases subjects' confidence in their recollections—without any corresponding increase in accuracy (Sheehan & Tilden, in press). In short, hypnotism often appears to evoke either more recollection, or more confidently delivered recollection, without adequate justification for either form of expansiveness.

GUIDED MEMORY

Somewhat more encouraging are recent efforts to enhance recall through methods of guided memory (Malpass & Devine, 1981). Malpass and Devine report an experiment in which subjects initially viewed a staged, but unexpected, vandalism. Five months later, subjects were at last given an opportunity to attempt to identify the suspect in a photographic line-up. One might expect that a 5-month delay would allow substantial fading of memory. Indeed, of subjects who were asked, rather unceremoniously, to simply attempt to identify the suspect, only 40% were able to do so. In comparison, other subjects were invited, prior to attempting identification, to recall each of the sequence of actions and objects that together constituted the original event. That is, their rehearsal was guided, and, in fact, entailed a vivid reconstruction of the event. After the guided rehearsal, subjects viewed the line-up. Sixty percent correctly identified the suspect—a significantly better performance than was obtained without guided rehearsal.

An experiment reported by Bekerian and Bowers (1983) also supports the notion that recollection can be enhanced through guided memory techniques. Bekerian and Bowers had sought, in part, to replicate earlier experimental results that had shown the alteration of recollection through exposure to misleading post-event messages. They found, however, that a careful ordering of final test questions can sometimes attenuate the usual deleterious effects of misleading post-event information. In particular, they showed that recollection is apparently unaffected by post-event messages if the order of test questions recreates the sequential unfolding of the original event. By contrast, a random ordering of test questions seemed to allow for many subjects the displacement of original memory by post-event misinformation. Apparently, systematic rehearsal of an event, especially a rehearsal that recreates the original sequence of events, facilitates retrieval of original memory for the event.

Taken together, these results suggest some promising strategies for investigative interviewers. However, it must be noted that guided memory, while apparently capable of facilitating recall, also contains the potential for abuse. In particular, guided recall depends upon someone, typically the experimenter, being able to accurately recreate the sequence of actions that constituted the original event. Thus, legal investigators would have to acquire quite reliable information about the essential stages of development of an event before guided memory techniques could be used reliably. Lacking reliable information about the actual unfolding of an event, efforts to employ the technique of guided memory might easily degenerate into a process of confabulation. In short, rehearsal of an incident has the potential both to enhance and to interfere with recollection.

In summary, research offers a certain amount of conditional support for the carefully undertaken rehearsal of an event as a means of enhancing recollection. In any case, witnesses often attempt spontaneously to rehearse events, and often discuss events with friends or acquaintances. The goal of police or other investigators is to obtain information from witnesses while avoiding procedures that contribute to the unnecessary deterioration of witnesses' memories. A promptly delivered set of questions, carefully worded to avoid bias, accompanied by warnings to disregard the interviewer's assumptions, but sequentially ordered to allow a retracing of the original course of the event, and fully recorded to allow critical examination at a later time, would appear to be a prescription for the ideal interview with a witness.

THE IMPACT OF THE
EYEWITNESS ON JURORS

Recent experimental results suggest that jurors are more likely to render a guilty verdict after hearing eyewitness testimony than after hearing only circumstantial evidence (e.g., Cavoukian, 1980; Loftus, 1974; Weinberg & Baron, 1982). Apparently, experimental subjects playing the role of jurors are highly accepting of eyewitness testimony. Such experimental results are consistent with the findings of the Devlin Committee's investigation in Great Britain which showed that many actual verdicts appear to have been influenced largely by the testimony of one or more eyewitnesses.

Thus, the credulity of jurors for eyewitness testimony has been reasonably well established. Can an eyewitness' impact on jurors be effectively neutralized by cross-examination? Obviously this question should be of practical concern to trial lawyers. Experimental studies of the latter question yield what appear, at first, to be inconsistent results. Some studies show that jurors tend to remain credulous of eyewitness testimony even after having heard pointed and seemingly damaging cross-examination (Cavoukian, 1980; Loftus, 1974; Saunders, Vidmar, & Hewitt, 1982, Experiment 3); whereas, other studies have shown that once discredited an eyewitness is no longer believed (e.g., Hatvany & Strack, 1980; McCloskey, Egeth, Webb, Washburn, & McKenna, 1982; Saunders et al., 1982, Experiment 1; Weinberg & Baron, 1982). The experiments that led to such varying results actually comprise a broad spectrum of differing designs and procedures. Thus, the conflicting results are not completely disconcerting, but still leave one wondering why cross-examination sometimes succeeds and sometimes fails. A reasonable goal for concerned researchers is to define precisely the circumstances under which cross-examination can be expected to be effective or ineffective.

It seems reasonable to expect that the eyewitness' reaction to a challenging cross-examination is one important factor. Indeed, the demeanor of the confederate portraying an eyewitness probably accounts for some of the variance observed between experiments. In several experiments, the eyewitness reacted to a discrediting challenge by stubbornly protesting the correctness of his or her testimony (e.g., Loftus, 1974). In other experiments, the eyewitness demurely acknowledged his or her error and even apologized for having appeared in court, or in full view of the jury failed a simple test of visual perception (e.g., Hatvany & Strack, 1980). It is hardly surprising that jurors lost faith in an eyewitness who collapsed with such melodramatic flair under cross-examination!

Unfortunately, the eyewitness' reaction to cross-examination does not fully account for all of the variance between experiments. For example, Weinberg and Baron (1982, Experiment 2) included a condition in which the eyewitness stubbornly maintained his or her identification of the defendant throughout a discrediting cross-examination. In spite of such staunch resolve on the part of the eyewitness, Weinberg and Baron's subjects were less likely to convict after the eyewitness had been challenged in cross-examination. Thus, a discrediting cross-examination sometimes succeeds in spite of the witness' refusal to admit fallibility.

Still other recent experiments indicate that jurors are much impressed by an eyewitness' proclamation of confidence, or proclamation of lack of confidence, when initially delivering testimony. For example, Wells, Lindsay, and Ferguson (1979) and Lindsay, Wells, and Rumpel (1981) obtained results indicating that jurors are swayed by an eyewitness' expressed confidence in making an identification, and are at the same time unable to discriminate accurate from inaccurate testimony. Wells' and his colleagues' experimental simulations included two stages. In the first stage, subject-eyewitnesses observed what appeared to be an actual theft, and later were asked to help the experimenter by trying to identify the culprit in a realistically simulated line-up. In the second stage of the study, subject-jurors viewed interviews of subject-eyewitnesses who had made either accurate, or inaccurate, identifications of suspects from the line-up. As a final dependent measure, jurors were asked to indicate whether or not they believed the eyewitness.

As had been found in earlier studies, subject-jurors were highly influenced by eyewitnesses, and, in fact, the eyewitness was believed about 80% of the time. Indeed, jurors believed inaccurate eyewitnesses nearly as often as accurate eyewitnesses. Jurors' apparent inability to detect inaccuracy is hardly surprising, since the degree of confidence expressed by witnesses was largely unrelated to their accuracy. Jurors tended to believe eyewitnesses who expressed confidence. However, such seemingly self-confident witnesses were often inaccurate. Thus, the capacity of jurors to evaluate the accuracy of an eyewitness was rather minimal.

Are there any circumstances under which jurors become more cautious, and perhaps even more discriminating? Fortunately, there is reason to believe that such circumstances exist, and can be systematically fostered. Occasionally, circumstances that increase jurors' caution occur through happenstance. For example, one recent study shows that current news events can affect the likelihood that jurors will bring guilty verdicts in cases involving eyewitness testimony (Loftus, 1982). Anecdotal reports indicate that journalistic accounts of false identifications or false convictions can temporarily enhance awareness of the problem of eyewitness unreliability in citizens called to serve on juries. However, such journalistic reports are sporadic occurrences, and their impact on potential jurors is probably brief and unpredictable.

A variable that could induce greater cautiousness on the part of jurors is the inclusion in the trial procedure of judicial instructions. In the United States, judges commonly explain to jurors the meaning of a presumption of innocence and the standards of proof regarded as sufficient for a verdict of guilty (e.g., "beyond a reasonable doubt"). The inclusion, or exclusion, of such judicial instructions has been shown to have interesting, even unexpected, effects on the way in which jurors weigh trial evidence. For example, Saunders et al. (1982) report that cross-examination of an eyewitness more effectively neutralizes jurors' credulity for the witness if judicial instructions are included in the trial procedure than if they are not. Judicial instructions do not, of course, pertain specifically to any particular witness or even to any particular criteria by which witnesses may be evaluated. The judicial instructions do, however, have an apparently salutary and generalized effect on the manner in which jurors scrutinize evidence, including evidence provided by witnesses.

In a similar vein, McCloskey et al. (1982) found fewer convictions when judicial instructions were provided to jurors. Thus, the presence of judicial instructions appears to dampen jurors' credulity somewhat, and to increase the care with which jurors evaluate evidence.

There is another variable that apparently has been shown to enhance jurors' critical assessment of eyewitness identifications. That other variable is the inclusion in criminal or civil trials of psychologists giving expert testimony about eyewitness reliability.

EXPERT TESTIMONY
REGARDING EYEWITNESS RELIABILITY

A number of recent surveys have revealed widespread misunderstanding of variables that affect eyewitness testimony. Such misunderstanding is apparently shared by potential jurors (Deffenbacher & Loftus, 1982; Loftus, 1979; Yarmey & Jones, 1983), as well as by many practicing attorneys (Brigham, 1981). Expert psychological testimony probably cannot wholly correct all of the common misconceptions, but studies have shown that expert testimony can at least induce subject-jurors to devote more time to a discussion of an eyewitness' questionable reliability (Loftus, 1980). In two experiments, subject-jurors were given information about a defendant, including the testimony of an eyewitness. Some subjects were given additional information about variables that, in the opinion of an expert, might be expected to have affected the eyewitness' testimony. Other subject-jurors were not given such additional information about eyewitness variables. Two dependent measures were obtained in the experiments: (a) the decision to convict or not to convict, and (b) the amount of time that jurors spent discussing the question of the eyewitness' reliability. Results indicated that the additional information about eyewitness variables caused subjects to render fewer guilty verdicts. However, it is perhaps even more significant that subject-jurors who encountered the added information about eyewitness variables spent more time discussing the eyewitness' reliability. Such results indicate that admitting expert psychological testimony in the courtroom is apparently one practical means of alerting jurors to the possibility that eyewitnesses might be partially or wholly inaccurate.

In a similar vein, Wells, Lindsay, and Tousignant (1980) reported that expert testimony reduces not only subject-jurors' credulity for eyewitness testimony, but also their over-reliance on the eyewitness' expressed confidence. However, Wells et al. noted that expert testimony did nothing to improve jurors' typical inability to discriminate between accurate and inaccurate eyewitnesses.

In summary, expert testimony appears to reduce jurors' general tendency to embrace uncritically virtually all witness' testimony. At the same time, expert testimony has not yet been shown to improve jurors' ability to discriminate an accurate from an inaccurate witness. In other words, current forms of expert testimony seem to reduce jurors' credulousness, but do not necessarily significantly improve their knowledge or discrimination. In view of the sometimes devastating and tragic consequences of unreliable eyewitness testimony, it behooves us to search for ways of not only increasing juror skepticism, but simultaneously increasing juror wisdom.

CONCLUSIONS

We began this chapter by noting that mistaken eyewitness testimony has long been recognized as a major cause of criminal convictions of the innocent. However, while the problem has long been recognized, it is still far from solved. Psychologists and other social scientists are attempting to contribute to a solution by presenting practical suggestions based on a growing body of recent theory and research.

Here we have reviewed research that leads directly to a number of practical proposals. Wells' distinction between system variables and estimator variables suggests that at least part of the variance in eyewitness performance can be attributed directly to the procedures of police and attorneys. Thus, law schools and police academies should include instruction in techniques for eliciting information from witnesses without attempting to coax the witness with potentially biasing hints or suggestions. Research by Loftus and others indicates that many variables contribute to the alteration of recollection, and such findings can also contribute to improved methods for interviewing witnesses.

Malpass' guided memory research offers the hopeful suggestion that police or other interviewers might be able to enhance the quality of witnesses' recollections by encouraging a witness to recall details of the crime according to the sequential order in which such details originally unfolded. However, the often used procedure of hypnotizing witnesses has come under serious fire by researchers. Hypnotism appears to make witnesses less cautious, but apparently does little to improve the quality of their recollection. While this research continues, much can be done to mitigate the typical over-reliance of jurors on eyewitness testimony. In particular, instructions from judges and expert testimony from eyewitness researchers have been shown to be effective in inducing jurors to regard eyewitness testimony with greater skepticism.

There is much that remains to be learned about eyewitness testimony. For example, the issue of individual differences between witnesses remains a vast and barely explored terrain. The attitudes of lawyers and police toward eyewitness testimony and eyewitness testimony research is, in itself, a topic worthy of increased research attention. Theoretical integration of eyewitness testimony research is still in initial stages. While theoretical advances are needed, it appears that eyewitness research will remain viable as long as researchers attend to the real needs of witnesses, jurors, professionals in the criminal justice system, and, of course, to the needs of those who are suspected of crimes.

David F. Hall, Ph.D., is an Associate Professor of Psychology at Thiel College. Dr. Hall's professional interests are in the areas of forensic psychology and alcohol and substance abuse.

Elizabeth F. Loftus, Ph.D., an experimental psychologist, is Professor of Psychology at the University of Washington. Dr. Loftus is the author of 10 books, including *Eyewitness Testimony* (Harvard University Press, 1979), which won a National Media Award from the American Psychological Foundation. Her professional interests and previous publications are in the areas of human perception and memory, eyewitness testimony, and psychology and law.

RESOURCES

Baddeley, A. (1982). *Your Memory: A User's Guide.* New York: Macmillan Publishing Co.

Bekerian, D. A., & Bowers, J. M. (1983). Eyewitness testimony: Were we misled? *Journal of Experimental Psychology: Learning, Memory, & Cognition, 9,* 139-145.

Borchard, E. M. (1932). *Convicting the Innocent: Errors of Criminal Justice.* New Haven: Yale University Press.

Brigham, J. C. (1981). The accuracy of eyewitness evidence: How do attorneys see it? *The Florida Bar Journal, 55,* 714-721.

Cavoukian, A. (1980). *The Influence of Eyewitness Identification Evidence.* Unpublished doctoral dissertation, University of Toronto.

Clifford, B. R., & Bull, R. (1978). *The Psychology of Person Identification.* London: Routledge & Kegan Paul.

Davies, G., Ellis, H., & Shepherd, J. (1981). *Perceiving and Remembering Faces.* London: Academic Press.

Deffenbacher, K. A., & Loftus, E. F. (1982). Do jurors share a common understanding concerning eyewitness behavior? *Law and Human Behavior, 6,* 15-30.

Devlin, Hon. Lord P. (Chair). (1976). *Evidence Identification in Criminal Cases* (Report to the secretary of state for the home departmental committee). London: Her Majesty's Stationery Office.

Dristas, W. J., & Hamilton, V. L. (1977). *Evidence about Evidence: Effects of Presuppositions, Item Salience, Stress, and Perceiver Set on Accident Recall.* Unpublished manuscript, University of Michigan.

Dywan, J., & Bowers, K. S. (1982, October). *Hypermnesic Patterns Over Time With and Without Hypnosis.* Paper presented at the annual meeting of the Society for Clinical and Experimental Hypnosis, Indianapolis, IN.

Greene, E., Flynne, M. S., & Loftus, E. F. (1982). Inducing resistance to misleading information. *Journal of Verbal Learning and Verbal Behavior, 21,* 207-219.

Hain, P. (1976). *Mistaken Identity.* London: Quartet Books.

Hall, D. F., Loftus, E. F., & Tousignant, J. P. (1983). Post-event information and changes in recollection for a natural event. In G. L. Wells & E. F. Loftus (Eds.), *Eyewitness Testimony: Psychological Perspectives* (pp. 124-141). New York: Cambridge University Press.

Hatvany, N., & Strack, F. (1980). The impact of the discredited witness. *Journal of Applied Social Psychology, 10,* 490-509.

Hilgard, E. R., & Loftus, E. F. (1979). Effective interrogation of the eyewitness. *International Journal of Clinical and Experimental Hypnosis, 27,* 342-357.

Lewis, D. J. (1979). Psychobiology of active and inactive memory. *Psychological Bulletin, 86,* 1054-1083.

Lindsay, R. C. L., & Wells, G. L. (1980). What price justice?: Exploring the relationship of lineup fairness to identification accuracy. *Law and Human Behavior, 4,* 303-314.

Lindsay, R. C. L., Wells, G. L., & Rumpel, C. M. (1981). Juror's detection of eyewitness-identification accuracy within and across situations. *Journal of Applied Psychology, 66,* 79-89.

Loftus, E. F. (1974, August). The incredible eyewitness. *Psychology Today,* pp. 116-119.

Loftus, E. F. (1979). *Eyewitness Testimony.* Cambridge, MA: Harvard University Press.

Loftus, E. F. (1980). Impact of expert psychological testimony on the unreliability of eyewitness identification. *Journal of Applied Psychology, 65,* 9-15.

Loftus, E. F. (1982). *Current News Events Can Change the Results of a Psychological Experiment: An Example from Juror-Simulation Research.* Unpublished manuscript, University of Washington.

Loftus, E. F., & Greene, E. (1980). Warning: Even memory for faces may be contagious. *Law and Human Behavior, 4,* 323-334.

Loftus, E. F., Miller, D. G., & Burns, H. J. (1978). Semantic integration of verbal information into visual memory. *Journal of Experimental Psychology: Human Learning and Memory, 4,* 19-31.

Malpass, R. S., & Devine, P. G. (1981). Guided memory in eyewitness identification. *Journal of Applied Psychology, 66,* 343-350.

Marquis, K. H., Marshall, J., & Oskamp, S. (1972). Testimony validity as a function of question form, atmosphere, and item difficulty. *Journal of Applied Social Psychology, 2,* 167-186.

Marshall, J. (1966). *Law and Psychology in Conflict.* New York: Bobbs-Merrill.

McCloskey, M., Egeth, H., Webb, E., Washburn, A., & McKenna, J. (1982). *Eyewitnesses, Jurors, and the Issue of Overbelief.* Unpublished manuscript, Johns Hopkins University.

Orne, M. T. (1979). The use and misuse of hypnotism in court. *International Journal of Clinical and Experimental Hypnosis, 27,* 311-341.

Orne, M. T. (1981). The significance of unwitting cues for experimental outcomes: Toward a pragmatic approach. *Annals of the New York Academy of Science, 364,* 152-159.

Orne, M. T., Soskis, M. D., & Dinges, D. F. (1983). Hypnotically-induced testimony and the criminal justice system. In G. L. Wells & E. F. Loftus (Eds.), *Eyewitness Testimony: Psychological Perspectives* (pp. 171-213). New York: Cambridge University Press.

Putman, W. H. (1979). Hypnosis and distortions in eyewitness memory. *International Journal of Clinical and Experimental Hypnosis, 27,* 437-448.

Riley, D. A. (1962). Memory for form. In L. Postman (Ed.), *Psychology in the Making* (pp. 402-465). New York: A. A. Knopf.

Saunders, D. M., Vidmar, N., & Hewitt, E. C. (1982). *Eyewitness Testimony and the Discrediting Effect.* Unpublished manuscript, University of Western Ontario.

Sheehan, P. W., & Tilden, J. (in press). Effects of suggestibility and hypnosis on accurate and distorted retrieval from memory. *Journal of Experimental Psychology: Learning, Memory, and Cognition.*

Sobel, N. R. (1972). *Eyewitness Identification: Legal and Practical Problems.* New York: Clark Boardman.

Starkman, D. (1979). The use of eyewitness identification in criminal trials. *Criminal Law Quarterly, 21,* 361-386.

Timm, H. W. (1981). The effects of forensic hypnosis techniques on eyewitness recall and recognition. *Journal of Police Science and Administration, 9,* 188-194.

Timm, H. W. (1982, August). *A Theoretical and Empirical Examination of the Effects of Forensic Hypnosis on Eyewitness Recall.* Paper presented at the 9th International Congress of Hypnosis and Psychosomatic Medicine, Glasgow, Scotland.

Wall, P. M. (1965). *Eyewitness Identification in Criminal Cases.* Springfield, IL: Charles C. Thomas.

Weinberg, H. I., & Baron, R. S. (1982). The discredible eyewitness. *Personality and Social Psychology Bulletin, 8,* 60-67.

Wells, G. L. (1978). Applied eyewitness-testimony research: System variables and estimator variables. *Journal of Personality and Social Psychology, 36,* 1546-1557.

Wells, G. L., Leippe, M. R., & Ostrom, T. M. (1979). Guidelines for empirically assessing the fairness of a lineup. *Law and Human Behavior, 3,* 285-294.

Wells, G. L., & Lindsay, R. C. L. (1980). On estimating the diagnosticity of eyewitness nonidentifications. *Psychological Bulletin, 88,* 776-784.

Wells, G. L., Lindsay, R. C. L., & Ferguson, T. (1979). Accuracy, confidence, and juror perceptions in eyewitness testimony. *Journal of Applied Psychology, 64,* 440-448.

Wells, G. L., Lindsay, R. C. L., & Tousignant, J. P. (1980). Effects of expert psychological advice on human performance in judging the validity of eyewitness testimony. *Law and Human Behavior, 4,* 275-285.

Woocher, F. D. (1977). Did your eyes deceive you? Expert psychological testimony on the unreliability of eyewitness testimony. *Stanford Law Review, 29,* 969-1030.

Yarmey, A. D. (1979). *The Psychology of Eyewitness Testimony.* New York: Free Press.

Yarmey, A. D., & Jones, H. P. T. (1983). Is the psychology of eyewitness identification a matter of common sense? In S. Lloyd-Bostock & B. R. Clifford (Eds.), *Evaluating Witness Evidence.* London: Wiley.

Zelig, M., & Beidleman, W. B. (1981). The investigative use of hypnosis: A word of caution. *International Journal of Clinical and Experimental Hypnosis, 29,* 401-402.

PSYCHOLOGICAL METHODS
OF TRUTH DETECTION

Julian J. Szucko and Benjamin Kleinmuntz

It is written in the Bible that when King Solomon had to decide to which of two women a disputed infant belonged, he asked for a sword and threatened to cut the living child in two, and give half to one and half to the other. This solution evoked an emotional reaction in the real mother who pleaded to let the other woman have the child. The woman who falsely claimed the infant, in contrast, coolly agreed that the child be cut in half so that neither of them could have it. On the basis of this ancient method of lie detection, King Solomon was able to establish the identity of the true mother.

Modern humankind, however, need not rely on so primitive and barbaric a method of lie detection. There is a technique that, like the one used by King Solomon, also relies on emotional reactions. Its users call it the polygraph examination and claim it to be scientific and highly accurate, sometimes suggesting that it is 90% to 100% accurate. But is it? While it is undeniable that the polygraph is more modern than King Solomon's sword, its accuracy and scientific merit have been the subjects of considerable debate. In fact, had the modern technique been used by King Solomon, it is quite possible that he would have been dead wrong. The theory of contemporary lie detection is that deceptiveness and lying evoke emotional reactivity. Therefore, according to modern practices, the second woman—the unemotional one who readily agreed to the destruction of the child—could

441

have been falsely judged as "truthful" and would have been given the child.

USES OF THE POLYGRAPH EXAMINATION

Since its introduction in the early part of this century, the polygraph procedure has gained wide acceptance within business as well as in government. This test is used for screening job candidates applying for sensitive positions in federal security agencies (FBI, CIA, NSA) and for many state and local police department jobs, as well as bank and armored truck work, all of which require honesty and integrity. Even in less sensitive positions, lie detection tests are often given in an effort to predict which applicants can best be trusted to handle large sums of money or other valuables. In some companies every employee must undergo an examination on a regular basis as a periodic "honesty check" to determine if any undiscovered pilfering has occurred. A recent survey indicated that 20% of the nation's major corporations use polygraph testing of employees and about 50% of fast-food companies like McDonald's 4,700 hamburger outlets and Burger Chef's 900 stores use pre-employment polygraphs for screening (Belt & Holden, 1978). These government agencies and retail outlets are mainly interested in identifying and hiring persons who can be trusted to fulfill their jobs faithfully and honestly.

Within the legal system there are many settings in which polygraph examinations also play an important role. These settings include those in which the test is given to suspects in criminal investigations of theft, rape, murder, or of lesser crimes (Cimmerman, 1981); to victims of crimes who may be so unfortunate as to reside in counties or states where the district attorney will not prosecute a complaint unless the victim agrees to a lie detector test; or to witnesses in a criminal trial who are requested by either the prosecuting or defending counsel to demonstrate the veracity of their testimony (Lykken, 1981c). Other legal contexts include those in which polygraph examinations are commonly given to plaintiffs or defendants embroiled in civil litigation in which conflicting testimony needs to be weighed. In most of these instances, the polygraph procedure, although generally not admissible as evidence in a court of law, nonetheless can contribute in important, and often disastrous, ways to the conduct and the outcome of a litigation.

With an estimated one million tests being conducted annually, it is quite likely that the average adult will be required to take the test at some point in his or her life. Recent estimates further indicate that reliance on this technique may be increasing at a rate as high as 10% to 15% each year. Such widespread use suggests that the social impact of this one psychological test may well be far greater than the impact of all other psychological tests combined.

A DESCRIPTION OF THE TECHNIQUE

Just what is this procedure that has achieved such a high level of acceptance, if not respectability? Basically, it is a specialized interview or interrogation technique that is conducted with the aid of an instrument which monitors and records physiological responsivity. The entire procedure consists of two phases—three if one includes the post-test interrogation. The first phase of the examination is usually the pretest interview which is conducted without the aid of the polygraph. This is a structured interview designed to obtain biographical data and to evaluate the subject's attitudes toward dishonesty, as well as to assess his or her attitudes toward the test itself. At this stage the individual might be asked to describe appropriate punishments for the suspected crime, reveal how the family feels about the fact of having him or her take a polygraph test, discuss his or her knowledge and theory of the crime, and suggest, as well as eliminate, other possible suspects. While the primary purpose here is to develop a data base from which to formulate questions for the polygraph phase, the responses and behaviors are also treated as interpretable data (Horvath, 1973).

The second phase of the examination is generally considered the polygraph test proper. It is only during this period that the subject's physiological reactions are monitored. The usual field examination, conducted by means of an elaborate and impressive looking piece of hardware; requires the continuous recording of three to four channels of physiological data. The variables measured typically include galvanic skin response (GSR), blood pressure, abdominal respiration, and thoracic respiration. The last two indices measure the amount of external stomach and chest movement by means of a system of attached tubes and bellows and give an indication of the rate and depth of breathing. Skin resistance, referred to above as the GSR, is also variously called the psychogalvanic response (PGR) or electrodermal response (EDR). It is obtained by placing two electrodes, usually on the fingers, but sometimes on other body sites, and passing through the electrodes an imperceptible current. This current varies with changes in skin resistance and registers as horizontal and vertical movements on the polygraph chart. Blood pressure and pulse are continuously monitored through a system that uses a sphygmomanometer cuff, usually attached to the biceps. An example of the tracings produced by the polygraph is presented in Figure 1 (p. 445) (for a further description of this instrumentation, see Reid & Inbau, 1977).

In the standard polygraph phase, the examiner asks a series of questions, each requiring a simple yes or no answer. These questions, which are represented by numerals in Figure 1 (the plus or minus represents a "yes" or "no" answer), are formulated during the pretest interview and are reviewed with the examinee just prior to the polygraph monitoring, a review that is intended to clarify unnecessary ambiguities. As the questions are presented, both verbal and physiological responses are recorded on the polygraph chart. This question sequence is usually repeated three or four times, often with a stimulation test inserted between the first and second presentation. The stimulation or "card test" procedure is usually used to impress on the respondent the infallibility of the instrument. That is, that the tracings produced by the hardware will immediately betray anyone intent on lying. During this test, the subject is presented with several numbered cards and is instructed to select one. After the selection, he or she is asked to respond with a

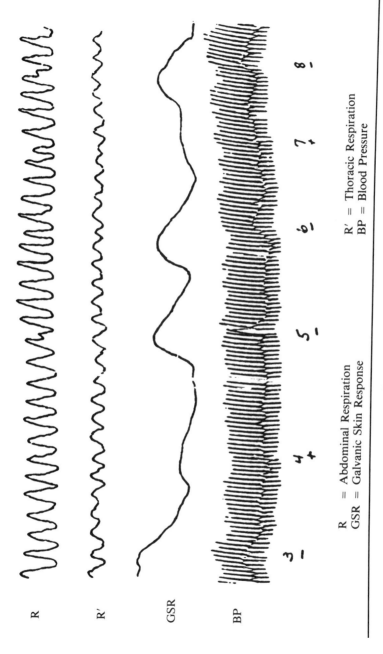

R = Abdominal Respiration   R' = Thoracic Respiration
GSR = Galvanic Skin Response   BP = Blood Pressure

Figure 1. Polygraph Tracings

445

"no" to all the alternatives as they are presented by the examiner. The polygrapher then tries to identify the chosen card, informing the subject that this will be done on the basis of the polygraph tracings. However, any number of deceptions may be used (e.g., memorizing the position of each card) to insure correct identification of the target card. At this point the subject may also be cautioned that it is difficult to "beat the machine."

The specific questions the subject is required to answer vary depending on the reasons for the examination, but most current examinations include three general types of questions. These are typically referred to as case-irrelevant, case-relevant, and control questions. Case-irrelevant questions deal with established biographic data (e.g., name, age, current address) and are designed to obtain a normal or base-line response level; case-relevant questions deal with the specific issues under investigation (e.g., "Did you shoot Jack Smith on Tuesday, September 12?"); and control questions attempt to force the subject to lie about some normatively shared transgression (e.g., "Did you ever steal anything in your life?"). The control questions permit the examiner to observe the subject's physiological reactions associated with emotional arousal.

In evaluating the polygraph charts, most interpreters look for signs of differential autonomic disturbance. If the disturbance associated with the relevant items seems to be greater or more persistent than that associated with the control questions, then the subject is judged to be deceptive. On the other hand, if the disturbance associated with the control questions appears to be greater than that of the relevant questions, then it is assumed that the subject is being truthful. Most interpreters use a global evaluation method without specific measurement or scoring in which they try to combine all the cues—polygraphic as well as pretest and other observable behaviors—in order to arrive at their decision. There are, however, many variations of this basic interpretive strategy, and more quantitative procedures have been suggested in which the autonomic differences between relevant and control questions must be assigned numerical scores (Backster, 1963; Raskin & Hare, 1978). These scores can then be used in evaluating the subject's responses.

If it is established that the subject has been deceptive during the test, or if he or she is suspected of deception, the examiner may proceed with the third and final stage, the post-test interrogation. It is here that the polygrapher will try to elicit a confession. It has also been suggested that for some examiners this may in fact be the most important part of the examination, and that the rest of the procedure serves only as an elaborate prop which is used to convince the subject that he or she has been discovered. The prop, of course, has all the trappings of scientific credibility because its instruments and print outs resemble those used by physicians and others presumed to be collecting important data. For most suspects, this is "science." The polygrapher is its spokesman and representative, even though he or she may have very modest scientific credentials (e.g., a 6-week to 6-month crash course).

RELIABILITY AND
VALIDITY OF POLYGRAPHY

So much for the details of the technique. It is now important to ask whether the polygraphic method of lie detection is accurate. That is, what, if any, is the relationship of the polygrapher's judgments about who is deceptive and who is telling the "ground truth"? In psychometrics this question addresses the issue of the procedure's reliability and validity.

Reliability deals with the consistency with which a test measures its dimensions. This consistency or stability can be assessed by measuring the extent of agreement in scores among individuals between test and retest, or by gauging the level of consensus attained among testers who score the same polygraph charts. Although several studies have reported rates of agreement in the 80% to 90% range (Hunter & Ash, 1973; Raskin, Barland, & Podlesny, 1978), it is difficult to determine whether this type of evidence indicates that the polygraph test is reliable.

The problem lies in the fact that total percentage of agreement is a poor measure of reliability. If a test has perfect reliability we would expect to obtain 100% agreement among interpreters. However, if a test has zero reliability, the expected percentage of agreement would not be 0%, but rather 50%. This is the lowest level of agreement, the chance level, against which to compare obtained agreement rates. This chance level percentage is arrived at due to the binary nature of the deceptive-nondeceptive decisions made by each interpreter.

Furthermore, under certain conditions, the chance level of agreement may be considerably higher than 50%. For example, if two examiners each randomly pass 90% of the subjects whose tests they interpret, then if they both evaluate the same tests, we would expect them to agree by chance on 82% of their decisions. We would expect examiner 1 to pass 81% of the subjects that were passed by examiner 2 (.9x.9), and to fail 1% of the subjects that were failed by examiner 2 (.1x.1). A more appropriate measure than total percentage of agreement can be obtained by using the correlation coefficient, or by using the average percentage of agreement. Unfortunately, most studies do not report such information and thus the reliability of the polygraph is difficult to gauge.

But even if a test achieves a high reliability it may still have little utility if its validity is low. Validity evaluates the extent to which a procedure measures what it *claims* to measure. In other words, the validity of a lie test deals with the correspondence between the test results and the subject's actual behavior, or the criterion of "ground truth." Thus, while a test may be reliable in the sense of obtaining similar scores when given on different occasions, or when given by different examiners, these scores will not be valid if they are not associated with the behavior that is of interest. Therefore, to assess the validity of the polygraph examination, a relationship must be established between the polygrapher's judgment and the truthfulness of each subject's statements.

FORMS OF VALIDITY

In order to evaluate the validity of the test there are four main types of information that must be examined. The first concerns the theory behind the technique and the plausibility of the psychological principles on which it is based. The second kind of evidence is empirical in that it is based on research dealing with the accuracy of the polygraph in laboratory studies using volunteer subjects lying on instruction about contrived "thefts." The third kind of evidence comes from field studies in which polygraph protocols of confessed thieves have been compared with those of innocent subjects. And the fourth type consists of case histories in which the test has not only been inaccurate, but where it has been dramatically and almost tragically wrong in the conclusions that were inferred from it.

The Psychophysiology of Lying. Regarding the first form of evidence, we must refer to the literature on psychophysiology since the lie detection test is concerned with psychophysiological responsivity. It purports to establish a relationship between lying and certain physiological changes. But the paradox here is that there is no reason to believe that lying produces distinctive physiological changes that characterize it and only it. In other words, there is no set of responses, physiological or otherwise, that humans emit only when lying versus those that they produce only when telling the truth. It has been shown that humans are quite variable in the pattern and form of their physiological reactions (Lacey & Lacey, 1958). Two individuals may show strikingly different physiological reactions when responding to a given stimulus, even when their outward behavior suggests that they are experiencing a similar emotional state. Similarly, the same physiological pattern obtained from two subjects does not necessarily indicate that they are experiencing the same emotion. No doubt when we tell a lie many of us experience an inner turmoil, but we experience a similar turmoil when we are falsely accused of a crime, when we are anxious about having to defend ourselves against accusations, when we are questioned about sensitive topics, and, for that matter, when we are elated or otherwise emotionally stirred. In short, as Lykken (1981b) recently suggested, "the polygraph pens do no special dance when we are lying" (p. 10).

What then is the basis of the polygraph examiner's decisions? Early polygraphers did indeed maintain that specific "lie patterns" could be identified and that these would be manifested by all individuals who were deliberately lying. Benussi (1914) argued that the respiration ratio of expiration to inspiration decreased after telling the truth but increased after lying. Marston (1938) placed the emphasis on blood pressure and claimed that an increase in systolic blood pressure could be used to identify a lie, while Summers (1939) believed that the response to critical items would habituate if the subject were telling the truth but not if he or she were lying. While it is unlikely that one would find any polygrapher who still maintains the specific lie pattern position, modern interpreters nevertheless assume that lying and truth telling can be discriminated on the basis of autonomic activity.

It is currently held that qualitative or quantitative differences in the subject's physiological reactions, rather than specific patterns, will betray the liar. Podlesny and Raskin (1977) explain that by using the control question approach one can set up a situation in which the guilty subject will respond most strongly to the relevant questions, while an innocent subject will respond most strongly to the control question. It is assumed that this can be accomplished by devising control questions that all subjects will answer deceptively, or at the very least, which will cause subjects to be concerned about their truthfulness. In formulating the control questions, the examiner will ask the subject about some transgression, one that is similar to, but much less serious than the issue under investigation. For example, in a theft investigation the examiner may ask about any previous thefts in which the subject has participated; whereas in an assault case, the polygrapher may ask whether the subject has ever hurt anyone intentionally. Since, for most subjects, the prior probability of such transgressions is generally quite high, a denial of such acts is assumed to be a lie. If this assumption is valid, the reaction on the control question can be used as a criterion against which to judge the relevant question reaction. If, however, the subject fails to deny these minor transgressions, then the examiner continues to ask about more serious acts, often behaving rather shocked that an apparently honest citizen would engage in such behaviors. The intent here is to keep the subject from telling the truth about all these minor acts and thus, in effect, forcing a lie.

Since it is assumed that the innocent subject has no reason to be concerned about the relevant items, he or she should show the greatest amount of physiological reactivity to the control questions. The guilty subject, on the other hand, because of the minor nature of the control questions, should be most concerned about, and should show the greatest reaction to the relevant items.

Based on an extensive analysis of the technique, Lykken (1974) has concluded that this theory, while plausible, is unlikely to be correct in all or even the majority of polygraph cases. First, since it is impossible to construct questions that will always be answered deceptively by all individuals, there is no guarantee that the response to the control question will be a lie. It may not be an example of the type of reaction that should be produced on the relevant questions if the subject lies in response to those. Second, it is not unreasonable to expect that even an innocent subject will be more concerned about the relevant questions. An innocent suspect being questioned about a theft may very well realize that to be judged deceptive on the control question, "Have you ever stolen anything in your life," might be the equivalent of being labeled dishonest. However, if the subject is judged deceptive on the relevant question, "Did you steal the missing $10,000.00 from the ABC Company," he or she will not only lose a reputation, but may be prosecuted and imprisoned as well. It is not unreasonable to assume that in such cases the reactions on the relevant questions will be greater than those on the controls. After all, the polygraph does not measure lying. It measures nonspecific emotional arousal. The greatest reaction will occur on questions which cause the subject the greatest amount of concern, and not necessarily on questions where the subject is lying. Thus, on the basis of the theory alone, one would not expect the test to produce results that are very high in accuracy.

Laboratory Evidence. The second kind of evidence is the empirical kind that involves laboratory studies and uses experimental subjects. Since the emotional impact of laboratory simulations, as well as the meaningfulness to the individual of the outcome, is unavoidably different than real life, such evidence must be interpreted with caution. A recent example is an experiment which was conducted by the present authors with 30 college students (Szucko & Kleinmuntz, 1981; see also, Szucko & Kleinmuntz, 1984). These students had volunteered for an advertised polygraph or "lie detector" experiment, and were randomly assigned to theft and no-theft conditions. The theft condition subjects were directed to an office on campus, where they were to enter without being seen, search through a desk containing a number of undesirable items plus a five-dollar bill, and steal anything they desired. After their departure from the office, the experimenter searched the desk to determine what was stolen. All 15 theft condition subjects stole the five-dollar bill. The 15 no-theft condition subjects were instructed to take a brief walk about campus before returning to the experimenter's office so that they would have no direct knowledge of the crime.

All subjects had previously been told that they would subsequently be administered a polygraph test and they were individually taken to a large polygraph firm where they were tested within an hour of fulfilling their instructions. Subjects in both conditions, furthermore, were told that "intelligent and well-adjusted persons can 'pass' the test without being judged guilty." The intent of this instruction was to involve the subjects in the experiment so that their motivational absorption in the outcome of their examination would resemble as closely as possible the level of involvement present in actual field examinations. The consequences of this instruction were that one-half of our subjects (i.e., the theft condition, or untruthful subjects) would be attempting to deceive the polygraph examiner, and the other half (i.e., the no-theft condition, or truthful subjects) would not. Upon completion of the experiment all subjects were thoroughly debriefed by the experimenter.

The polygraph tests were administered by four trainee-examiners at the polygraph firm. The examiners, who were not told that these were experimental subjects, asked the standard pretest, control, relevant, and irrelevant questions. The raw physiological data were then submitted to six experienced polygraph interpreters (judges), who were instructed to arrive at independent judgments of "truthful" or "untruthful" responses. These judgments were made on an 8-point rating scale anchored by "definitely truthful" at the low end of the continuum and "definitely untruthful" at the high end. The judges knew that half of the subjects had stolen something, but did not know what was stolen by whom, nor that the examinees were experimental subjects. The judges were informed about the proportion of guilty and innocent subjects in order to provide information that would allow them to adjust their intuitive selection ratios accordingly, although there is some evidence to suggest that such instructions do not influence the decision process in complex judgment tasks.

The data analysis consisted of determining whether the six polygraph interpreters, whose experience ranged from 3 months to 8 years, could use the information from the polygraph charts to arrive at accurate decisions.

Our results did not reflect favorably on the judges, two of whom could not even differentiate between the charts of guilty and innocent subjects at a better than chance level. What was even more surprising was the finding that greater amounts of experience, on the average, did not improve the interpreters' validities (i.e., accuracy or ability to differentiate between the two kinds of responses). And, much to our dismay, we also learned in this study that whatever level of accurate discriminability was achieved, it was done so at a considerable cost to the individuals who were telling the truth since many of them were misclassified as untruthful. As many as four of the six judges were biased in the direction of calling truthful subjects untruthful.

It is questionable whether the results of a game-like atmosphere of a laboratory study, with all its intellectual challenge and give-away qualities, are generalizable to the real-life situation of a criminal suspect who is being investigated regarding his or her guilt or innocence for some serious crime. Meaningful research on the accuracy of the lie test must be conducted in the field using tests that are administered to actual criminal suspects under real-life conditions. Such research must meet two minimum criteria: (a) the lie tests should be administered to criminal suspects under field conditions; and (b) the tests should be unselected and should be representative of the general run of tests administered.

Field Studies. Consequently, we conducted a field study, which is the third type of validity evidence that should be collected to support the technique's accuracy (Kleinmuntz & Szucko, 1982, 1984). The results of this study confirmed our earlier findings. We used as subjects persons accused of theft and later cleared of charges, as well as thieves who admitted stealing the money or items subsequent to their polygraph examination and interrogation. We postulated that polygraphers would not be able to differentiate between the two types of subjects from a reading of the polygraph tracings, and that their false-positive misclassification rates would be high. The results of this study are presented in Table 1 (p. 455). Regarding the first half of our hypothesis, we must note that the judges did rather well and obtained overall accuracy rates that were significantly better than a random sorting of the protocols. Among the six interpreters, accuracy ranged from a low of 63% to a high of 76%.

A careful examination of Table 1, however, also discloses that the false-positive rate—the proportion of innocent subjects classified as guilty—is alarmingly high, thus confirming our expectation that high valid positive rates (correct identification of guilty subjects) can be obtained only at the expense of a high false-positive rate. The range of false-positive diagnoses ranged from a low of 18% achieved by Judge 3 to a high of 50% obtained by Judge 5. The average false-positive rate was 37%.

That these high false-positive rates are not fortuitous findings has been confirmed by several other field studies. In one of these, Frank Horvath (1977), a Michigan State University criminologist and practicing polygrapher, found that polygraph interpreters called nearly half (50%) of innocent subjects as guilty. These charts were scored independently by 10 separate polygraphers who achieved an average accuracy rate of 63%, a rate that is only 13% better than chance. Gordon Barland, a physiological psychologist at the University of Utah and a practicing polygrapher conducted a similar study (with David Raskin, another psychologist

TABLE 1: VALID POSITIVE, VALID NEGATIVE, FALSE-POSITIVE, FALSE-NEGATIVE, AND OVERALL ACCURACY RATES OF POLYGRAPH JUDGMENTS FOR SIX JUDGES AND THE DISCRIMINANT FUNCTION ANALYSIS

	Valid Positive %	Valid Negative %	False-Positive %	False-Negative %	Overall Accuracy %
Judge					
1	78	60	40	22	69
2	64	62	38	36	63
3	70	82	18	30	76
4	82	66	34	18	74
5	80	50	50	20	65
6	82	56	44	18	69
Average	75	63	37	25	69

Note: The positive direction denotes a judgment of untruthful and the negative direction of truthful. Thus, a valid positive is a correctly identified theft subject and a valid negative is a correctly identified no-theft subject.

practitioner) and claimed to obtain accuracy rates of 86% and 88% (Barland & Raskin, 1977), findings that were seriously challenged by David Lykken (Lykken, 1960). The latter claims that since 78% of the suspects were actually guilty, one could have achieved 78% "hits" just by scoring every test "deceptive." Hence, not surprisingly, most of the "liars" were detected, but again at the considerable price (to the innocents) of a false-positive misclassification rate of 55%! In other words, of the known innocent suspects, 55% were scored "deceptive." Similar findings were recently reported in a U. S. Government sponsored review of the scientific validity of polygraph testing (U. S. Congress, 1983).

There is one series of studies, reporting accuracy rates in the 80% to 90% range, that is in conflict with the above findings (Hunter & Ash, 1973; Slowick & Buckley, 1975; Wicklander & Hunter, 1975). However, since all these studies were conducted by the same polygraph firm, it is unclear how many used the same cases or the same interpreters. Furthermore, it is unknown how the cases included in these studies were selected, nor is it always clear how "ground truth" or verification was established. In one of these at least, it is reported that certain cases were excluded because the indicators of truth or deception were too clear cut. We thus know that this study did not use a random sample. Hence, these studies do not present an accurate picture of the validity of the polygraph test.

Case History Evidence. Finally, regarding the last form of evidence, there are the case histories in which the test has been almost tragically wrong. An example is the celebrated case of Floyd Fay (Cimmerman, 1981). Fay was convicted of murder by virtue of the testimony of several polygraph examiners, and served a total of 2 1/2 years in prison before the real killers were tracked down. He considers himself lucky; he might have been sentenced to death, but the death penalty was ruled unconstitutional just a few weeks before his trial!

Yet other cases, much less dramatic than this one, suggest that many errors go unnoticed. For example, the junior author recently appeared as an expert witness for the defense in a case of a policeman who was accused of a burglary and subsequently gave a classic "deceptive" pattern on tests administered on two separate occasions by the same polygraph firm. Up to the time of the polygraph investigations, the prosecution had a weak case and was prepared to drop the charges if the defendant agreed to submit himself to a polygraph examination and "passed" the test. The officer's defense attorney firmly believed in the innocence of his client, and had faith in the test's ability to exonerate the police officer. He, therefore, counseled his client to accept the prosecution's offer. He also admonished the defendant of the consequences of "failing" the test—namely, the prosecution's case would be strengthened. Although the police officer was quite apprehensive about the consequences of "failing" the test, and somewhat concerned that a refusal to comply with the prosecution's request might be interpreted as evasiveness or even guilt, he was convinced of his innocence and, therefore, agreed to submit to a lie detection procedure. There was a great deal at stake for him. He was accused of a felony, was already suspended without pay, and was upset about the possibility of further disgrace, perhaps even imprisonment. All these factors made him a less than ideal candidate for polygraphy.

Predictably, the officer produced polygraph records on both testing occasions that were consistent with deception. In other words, his responses were more physiologically reactive to the following three relevant questions than to a set of control questions that dealt with some minor transgressions in his youth:

1. "Did you case Mr. and Mrs. X's house on the night of July 15th?"
2. "Did you steal the missing items from Mr. and Mrs. X's house on the night of July 15th?"
3. "Did you break into the rear door and enter the home of Mr. and Mrs. X on the night of July 15th?"

It should be mentioned that the home was indeed broken into on the designated night and that the break in was reported the following morning by the policeman under investigation. In fact, as it turned out, the police officer had been asked by Mr. and Mrs. X to "look after" the house during his off-duty hours, an arrangement which was against department regulations. The officer's strong polygraphic reaction may very well have been caused by his realization of the illegality of his moonlighting activities. Thus, although he was not casing the house, he was nonetheless in violation of a rule, but one whose violation was not a felony and did not carry a prison term. He was clearly upset. He became even more upset over the next question, and showed an even stronger emotional reaction because it became obvious to him that his case was becoming weaker with each question asked. Of course his emotional reaction to the third question was unmistakably greater than it had been to any of the control questions (e.g., "Did you ever steal anything of value?") because he was sensible enough to understand that his emotional responses to this question could jeopardize his future as a policeman, his reputation, and his pension, and might also confront him with the real possibility of going to prison—never a cheerful prospect for anyone, but especially not for a police officer who becomes a prime target for other inmates, some of whom he may have helped imprison. In short, the above three questions caused an inner and uncontrollable turmoil in the man which, quite predictably, showed up in the tracings of the polygraph pens. But he was also upset because he was innocent, a fact that is now confirmed.

Fortunately, two out of the three Commissioners were persuaded by the junior author's "expert" opinion that there is no such thing as a lie response that shows up when a person is telling a lie and does not register when that person is upset. They were also receptive to the cited evidence that polygraph interpreters, regardless of their many years of experience, sometimes perform at no better than 50-50 chance level and are often more likely to make false-positive errors (misclassifying an innocent person as guilty) than false-negative (misclassifying a guilty person as innocent) errors. Consequently, the case against the policeman was dropped and he was reactivated with pay and retroactive compensation. No doubt had the police officer's emotional reactions been monitored while he was listening to this happy outcome, he would have produced another set of "untruthful" responses.

IMPLICATIONS OF THE EVIDENCE

What conclusions can we draw from the evidence presented? Several, depending on who is drawing the conclusions. From the perspective of a corporation or business that hires a polygraph firm to help detect a suspected pilferer or embezzler, the high rate of "deceptive" decisions is in their best interest. Clearly, among the many misclassified innocent suspects there are at least some truly guilty ones. Likewise from the vantage point of a polygraph firm, the cost of misclassifying innocent subjects is low. Their task—and their vested interest—is not to err on the side of having too high a false-negative rate. A glimpse at Table 1 shows that they achieve this goal admirably. On the average, they call less than 25% of their guilty suspects "innocent."

However, from the viewpoint of the innocent person misclassified as guilty, our conclusions must be modified considerably. This modification must take into account the case of Floyd Fay, cited earlier, who spent 2 1/2 years in prison for a murder he did not commit. And it must consider the case of our police officer who was also misdiagnosed. The disgrace and humiliation that these proven innocents endured as a result of being considered guilty of murder, theft, or some other crime—even if ultimately freed of all charges— is not easily forgotten. And this does not even begin to touch on the personal tragedy of losing one's job, family, or, as in the unusual case of Fay, one's civil liberties or life.

AN ALTERNATIVE TO
TRADITIONAL POLYGRAPHY

An alternative and more promising method for detecting deception has been proposed, originally by Hugo Munsterberg (see Lykken, 1981a, p. 249), and more recently by David Lykken (1959, 1960, 1974, 1981a). This method, called the Guilty Knowledge Test (GKT), requires that the examiner be able to determine a number of facts that only a guilty subject can recognize. These facts are then presented to the respondent in the form of multiple choice items, embedded in a set of three, four, or five alternatives that would seem equally plausible to an innocent subject without guilty knowledge. For example, if the crime under investigation were a jewelry store robbery in which a diamond ring was taken, then the question presented to the suspect might be "Did you steal a _____?," with watch, necklace, ring, bracelet, and brooch included as the alternatives.

The basic assumption of GKT, according to Lykken and some others who have used it, is that the guilty subjects will show greater autonomic responsivity to what they recognize as the significant alternative than would subjects without such guilty knowledge. The amplitude of the autonomic responses to the significant alternative has little meaning by itself; hyperreactive subjects might respond strongly to that alternative without knowing that it was the "correct" one, while hyporeactive persons might yield a weak response even though they have guilty knowledge. But the same subjects' responses to the other plausible but incorrect alternatives of the guilty knowledge test provide a nearly ideal control against which to evaluate their responses to the significant alternative.

Is the GKT a reasonable alternative to current practices of lie detection? The empirical evidence seems to suggest that it may well be, although none of the studies to date have used actual criminal suspects as subjects. One early study by Lykken (1959) used student volunteers who enacted mock crimes of "theft," "murder," or both, and who were interrogated while having their electrodermal responses (EDR) recorded. The EDR is a wave-like change in the electrical resistance of the palms and soles associated with imperceptible sweating in those regions. Lykken presented the subjects with six multiple-choice questions for each of the two mock crimes. Some questions related directly to the criminal act, such as the location in which the stolen item was hidden, while others dealt with incidental matters, such as the presence of an artist's easel in the murder room. The test for each crime was scored by awarding 2 points if the EDR produced by the correct or "relevant" alternative to a question was the largest, 1 point if it was the second largest of the five associated with each question, and 0 points otherwise. Thus, with a six-item test, the highest guilt score would be 12 and the most innocent appearing score would be 0. A suspect was classified innocent if the total score for a test was 6 or less. The results were that of the 48 innocent subjects who were tested, all were identified as such; of the 50 guilty suspects tested, 44 received scores that permitted them to be correctly classified. Thus, the false-positive error rate was .00 while the false-negative error rate was .12; an average accuracy rate of 94%.

In a second study (Lykken, 1960), 20 subjects were offered a money prize if they could "beat" the test, either by inhibiting their responses to the correct alternatives (which is difficult) or by producing artificial responses to nonrelevant alternatives through self-stimulation (which is easier). These subjects were attached to the EDR apparatus and given time before the test to practice whatever technique they had decided to use, watching the pen trace out their EDRs as they experimented. All 20 subjects were correctly classified by the GKT, even though they had these opportunities to practice "beating" the machine.

These studies of the GKT have been successfully replicated in numerous laboratories (Ben-Shakhar, Lieblich, & Kugelmass, 1970; Davidson, 1968; Lieblich, Ben-Shakhar, & Kugelmass, 1976; Waid, Orne, & Orne, 1978), but not always with the high correct classification rate attained by Lykken. However, a virtue of the GKT method—one not shared by the more conventional procedures—is that the discrimination of guilty from innocent suspects can be increased simply by increasing the number of items. With 10 items, for example, each having five alternatives, one might expect to identify 97% of guilty suspects if persons scoring 5 or higher are classified as guilty. The odds against an innocent person scoring so high would be more than 100 to 1. According to Lykken (1981a, p. 298), this suggests that the experiments that failed to achieve good discrimination either had too few items or else used items in which the guilty subject could not recognize the "correct" alternative, or in which even the innocent subject could recognize this alternative. Lykken (1981a, p. 300) has developed an elaborate scheme for predicting precisely how accurate the GKT would be for tests of increasing length.

Two laboratory studies in fact reported results that fit reasonably well with Lykken's predictions. Geison and Rollinson (1981) required 20 guilty subjects to enact a mock crime and then tested them, along with 20 innocent suspects, using six well-constructed GKT items. The results were 100% and 95%, respectively, of innocent subjects who "passed" and guilty subjects who "failed." Podlesny and Raskin (1978) used five reasonably good items according to Lykken's criteria and correctly identified 100% and 90% of the innocent and guilty experimental suspect subjects.

In spite of these promising indications, professional polygraphers still have not taken up the Guilty Knowledge Test for use in criminal investigation. One reason for this is that the examiner may not have available to him or her the necessary items of information that only a guilty suspect would recognize and that could be translated into GKT items. But there are many instances of crimes which could provide the test constructor with information that would permit him or her to formulate good items. Given the reality of criminal investigation, particularly investigations of homicide cases, however, close cooperation between the investigating authorities and the polygrapher is essential. Such cooperation is necessary because it is important that the particulars of a crime be known only to the investigators, the polygrapher, and the truly guilty suspects. Moreover, polygraphers prefer conventional lie detection to the GKT because the latter may not be an appropriate technique for about 90% of the situations in which lie detectors are typically used. Business, as we indicated earlier, comes mainly from periodic "honesty checks" and from tests that are supposed to predict honesty and integrity in future (or present) employment situations. The GKT procedure is totally inappropriate for these purposes since it is only usable with reference to a specific past event. Unfortunately, traditional polygraphic investigation, which *is* considered appropriate for such use by its practitioners, is not valid for any of these purposes. At the present time the evidence seems to suggest that the lie detector's main function during criminal and other investigations may be similar to that of a gun-to-the-head threat: "You better confess or I'll blow your brains out." King Solomon's method was more subtle—but then again, he was a wise man.

Julian Szucko, Ph.D., a clinical psychologist, is a Research Coordinator with the Testing Division of the Student Counseling Service at the University of Illinois, Chicago Campus. Dr. Szucko's interests lie in the areas of psychometrics and clinical decision making, with special emphasis on the polygraph technique. He has conducted research into the validity and reliability of lie detection techniques.

Benjamin Kleinmuntz, Ph.D., is Professor of Psychology at the University of Illinois at Chicago. Dr. Kleinmuntz is a former member of the U. S. Army Military Intelligence Unit and was on the psychology faculty at Carnegie-Mellon University for 14 years before taking his current position. The author of numerous publications including the widely used text, *Personality and Psychological Assessment.* Dr. Kleinmuntz is currently researching the fallibility of human judgment in general and of lie detectors in particular.

RESOURCES

Backster, C. (1963). Total chart minutes concept. *Law and Order, 11*, 77-79.

Barland, G., & Raskin, D. C. (1977). *Validity and Reliability of Polygraph Examinations of Criminal Suspects* (Report No. 76-1, Contract No. 75-NI-99-0001). Washington, DC: Department of Justice.

Belt, J., & Holden, P. (1978). Polygraph usage among major U. S. corporation. *Personal Journal, 57*, 80.

Ben-Shakhar, G., Lieblich, I., & Kugelmass, S. (1970). Guilty knowledge technique: Application of signal detection measures. *Journal of Applied Psychology, 54*, 409-413.

Benussi, V. (1914). Die atmongs symptome der luge. *Archiv fur die Gesamte Psychologie, 31*, 244-273.

Cimmerman, A. (1981). The Fay case. *Criminal Defense, 12*, 7.

Davidson, P. O. (1968). Validity of the guilty knowledge technique: The effects of motivation. *Journal of Applied Psychology, 52*, 62-65.

Geison, M., & Rollinson, M. (1981). Guilty knowledge versus innocent associations: Effects of trait anxiety and stimulus contest on skin conductance. *Journal of Research in Personality, 14*, 1.

Horvath, F. (1973). Verbal and nonverbal clues to truth and deception during polygraph examinations. *Journal of Police Science and Administration, 1*, 138-152.

Horvath, F. (1977). The effects of selected variables on the interpretation of polygraph records. *Journal of Applied Psychology, 62*, 127-136.

Hunter, F. L., & Ash, P. (1973). The accuracy and consistency of polygraph examiners' diagnoses. *Journal of Police Science and Administration, 1*, 370-375.

Kleinmuntz, B., & Szucko, J. J. (1982). On the fallibility of lie detection. *Law and Society Review, 17*, 85-104.

Kleinmuntz, B., & Szucko, J. J. (1984). Lie detection in ancient and modern times: A call for contemporary scientific study. *American Psychologist, 39*, 766-776.

Lacey, J. I., & Lacey, B. C. (1958). Verification and extension of the principle of autonomic response-stereotype. *American Journal of Psychology, 71*, 50-73.

Lieblich, I., Ben-Shakhar, G., & Kugelmass, S. (1976). Validity of the guilty knowledge technique in a prisoners sample. *Journal of Applied Psychology, 61*, 89.

Lykken, D. T. (1959). The GSR in the detection of guilt. *Journal of Applied Psychology, 43*, 385-388.

Lykken, D. T. (1960). The validity of the guilty knowledge technique: The effects of faking. *Journal of Applied Psychology, 44*, 258-262.

Lykken, D. T. (1974). Psychology and the lie detector industry. *American Psychologist, 29*, 725-739.

Lykken, D. T. (1981a). *A Tremor in the Blood: Uses and Abuses of the Lie Detector.* New York: McGraw-Hill.

Lykken, D. T. (1981b, February). Letter: To tell the truth. *Discover*, p. 10.

Lykken, D. T. (1981c). The lie detector and the law. *Criminal Defense, 8*, 19-27.

Marston, W. M. (1938). *The Lie Detector Test*. New York: Smith.

Podlesny, J. A., & Raskin, D. C. (1977). Physiological measures and the detection of deception. *Psychological Bulletin, 84*, 782-799.

Podlesny, J. A., & Raskin, D. C. (1978). Effectiveness of techniques and physiological measures in the detection of deception. *Psychophysiology, 15*, 344.

Raskin, D. C., Barland, G. H., & Podlesny, J. A. (1978). *Validity and Reliability of Detection of Deception*. Washington, DC: National Institute of Law Enforcement and Criminal Justice.

Raskin, D. C., & Hare, R. D. (1978). Psychopathy and detection of deception in a prison population. *Psychophysiology, 15*, 126.

Reid, J. E., & Inbau, F. E. (1977). *Truth and Deception: The Polygraph ("Lie Detection") Technique*. Baltimore: Williams and Wilkins.

Slowick, S. M., & Buckley, J. P. (1975). Relative accuracy of polygraph examiner diagnoses from respiration, blood pressure, and GSR recordings. *Journal of Police Science and Administration, 3*, 303-309.

Summer, W. G. (1939). Science can get the confession. *Fordham Law Review, 8*, 334-354.

Szucko, J. J., & Kleinmuntz, B. (1981). Statistical versus clinical lie detection. *American Psychologist, 36*, 488-496.

Szucko, J. J., & Kleinmuntz, B. (1984). Statistical versus clinical detection reconsidered. *American Psychologist, 39*, 80.

U. S. Congress. (1983). *Scientific Validity of Polygraph Testing: A Research Review and Evaluation* (Tech. Mem. OTA-TM-H-15). Washington, DC: Office of Technology Assessment, U. S. Congress.

Waid, W. M., Orne, E. C., & Orne, M. T. (1978). Effects of attention as indexed by subsequent memory, on electrodermal detection of information. *Journal of Applied Psychology, 63*, 728.

Wicklander, D. E., & Hunter, F. L. (1975). The influence of auxiliary sources of information in polygraph diagnoses. *Journal of Police Science and Administration, 3*, 405-409.

SYSTEMATIC JURY SELECTION: THE QUEST FOR A SCIENTIFIC APPROACH

Diane R. Follingstad

Jury selection is like a Rorschach ink blot. It raises possibilities, stimulates ideas, generates concerns, and promotes a variety of approaches to a problem. But also like the ink blot, jury selection seems to raise far more questions than can be answered, and no one yet is sure how valid a method it is. Proponents, critics, constitutional authorities, methodologists, attorneys, and social scientists have all had their say regarding jury selection procedures. Experts in the area even dispute the *name* "jury selection," claiming that it misrepresents the process (Suggs & Sales, 1978).

Defining jury selection has been a difficult problem, as researchers mull over whether to consider informal decision making in the courtroom in the same manner as the recently established systematic procedures for selection of jurors. Many say the efforts of social scientists are merely a systematization of long-held notions by which attorneys predicted human behavior in the extremely specific setting of the courtroom. Others see any concentration on guessing juror behavior as useless or, at best, completely dependent on clinical judgment and intuitive hunches (Berk, Hennessy, & Swan, 1977). (One of the major trials utilizing systematic jury selection included a psychic on the defense team.) Still others feel that the potential benefits from effort expended in selection are too small; thus, they believe resources would be more productively placed into other aspects of a trial (Saks, Werner, & Ostrom, 1975).

Probably the best definition of jury selection is the determination of objective and valid indicators of attitudes in order to retain jurors from the venire (i.e., jury pool) favorable or neutral to one's position and to reject individuals with apparent biases against one's case. Since information about a juror may be extremely limited or possibly inaccurate, indicators of attitudes would aid the selection process by increasing the amount of data available for making decisions and by reducing the effects of deception or withholding information.

The contribution of social scientists in this legal sphere has been the development of *systematic* jury selection procedures. Knowledge of human behavior leads to the belief that patterns of actions and attitudes often can be predicted with some accuracy from information about category membership or other characteristics of individuals. This assumption has led to research assessing specific jury behavior demonstrated by "types" of people (e.g., demographically defined groups, possessors of certain attitudinal clusters, those with particular styles of cognitive activity, people who physically present themselves or act in nonnormative ways, and interactional styles exhibited by individuals in social settings).

The difficulty in choosing persons to sit on a jury lies in trying to predict a specific behavior (i.e., a verdict) when it is obvious that a trial is a highly complex and multifaceted affair. Should a jury selector believe an individual's predispositions toward someone with the defendant's characteristics will be universally applied toward all similar defendants, or should the selector believe a juror can find the evidence so persuasive that personal factors would have little bearing on the decision-making process? Will the jurors concentrate more on how much they prefer one attorney to the other and disregard evidence or their own beliefs about the case?

Anyone who has ever worked with an attorney in court to select jurors, with only the information given by the court administration regarding prospective jurors, has certainly experienced extreme frustration and uncertainty. It appears to make sense on the surface to add information systematically and collect the largest possible pool of data from which to make decisions. In the future, the most crucial considerations regarding jury selection may not be *whether* to gather significant amounts of data on juror characteristics, but how to disburse limited resources in a trial when jury selection has not been "proven" to be a critical variable. Another consideration may be the expertise of jury selectors. Huge amounts of data may be rendered useless if it is misinterpreted or the most accurate hypothesis for the results cannot be decided upon. For example, a juror's reactions during *voir dire* (i.e., the period of questioning conducted by attorneys and/or the judge prior to retaining or rejecting jurors) may be the result of a variety of personal and situational factors. Not knowing the source of or explanation for changes in a juror's body language may lead to inaccurate assumptions and, therefore, incorrect decisions regarding that juror.

Systematic and comprehensive jury selection as outlined in this chapter requires many professional skills as well as fiscal and human resources. The attorneys must be able to assess the issues and concepts involved in a case in light of the community in which the trial is to be held. Consultation with the legal team by social scientists must be a careful and continuing process. Questionnaire development, attitude assessment, and survey techniques all require specialists. Community interviews can be conducted by a wider range of individuals, but skilled professionals are needed to develop the questions to be asked and to train paraprofessionals in interviewing, collecting data, and handling problem situations. Data analysts with computer skills are needed to make sense of the mounds of collected facts and to provide interpretable results. Specialists in interviewing can develop attorneys' skills for questioning potential jurors during *voir dire*. Professionals with clinical experience are useful for interpreting physical cues (such as jurors' speech patterns and body language) and other courtroom behavior, while paraprofessionals can be trained as observers for informal assessments.

This chapter briefly examines a variety of ethical considerations raised by systematic jury selection as well as the major research conclusions on the effectiveness of jury selection procedures. The main thrust is a delineation of the variety of procedures which have been used or suggested. A number of sources are mentioned in the various sections which should be referred to for the most detailed outlines for carrying out specific techniques.

ETHICAL ISSUES IN
THE APPLICATION OF
JURY SELECTION TECHNIQUES

Jury selectors have been criticized on the grounds that they are trying to find jurors who are favorable to their point of view, thus distorting the "fair and impartial jury" tenet of our justice system. A few words regarding ethical issues are in order here.

The application of social science techniques seems justified as a sophisticated extension of attorneys' use of intuition, rules of thumb, and folklore that has been passed on through oral tradition and written suggestions (Christie, 1976; Daugherty, 1976; McConahay, Mullin, & Frederick, 1977; Saks, 1976). Not surprisingly, surveying attorneys regarding opinions and folk wisdom about jurors has failed to establish common and consistently held beliefs (Kallen, 1969). Selecting a favorable or at least a "fair" jury has certainly been viewed as an acceptable practice and is considered an essential part of the role of a trial attorney in protecting clients' rights. Ending up with a fair jury has rested on the assumption that both sides in a trial will eliminate biased jurors. Some writers have questioned the psychological impact on an individual who is "rejected" as a juror (McConahay et al., 1977), but most consider scrutiny of potential jurors by opposing attorneys an important safeguard in preserving a fair and impartial jury.

States vary in the extent to which they allow scrutiny of jurors, and certain of them limit the amount of choice attorneys have in selecting jurors. The jury pool, itself, may be selected in ways which influence which particular individuals are even available to be selected as jurors (e.g., the use of voter registration lists). The number of peremptory strikes (i.e., elimination of a juror simply on the basis of preference) is limited in all jurisdictions and varies according to the type of case. Challenges for cause (i.e., elimination of jurors by establishing that they hold biases which would not allow them to be impartial in a particular case) are often difficult to establish with limited *voir dire* questioning or judge-conducted *voir dire*.

Data mentioned by Bennett (1977) suggest that a preponderance of jurors come to a criminal trial with predispositions toward the prosecution, presumptions of guilt, expectations of the defense inconsistent with legal rights, and a tendency to believe police officers over other witnesses. Stephan (1975) has pointed to research which indicates that certain definable characteristics, both personal and demographic, have been linked with biases and predispositions which are expected to influence in-trial behavior. Research of this type certainly supports the case for the right to make choices among potential jurors.

The most critical ethical concerns raised regarding jury selection center around the following issues: (a) *who* will be allowed or able to have these additional techniques applied to their cases, (b) whether jury selection techniques may *increase* bias in juries, and (c) to what extent can selection procedures be applied and still protect the rights of jurors (Berman & Sales, 1977; McConahay et al., 1977; Saks, 1976). Several authors have raised concerns that the wealthy will have greater access to resources than the poor, or that the state may have greater ability to hire its own social scientists, thereby increasing its advantage in criminal proceedings. One side in a trial having additional expertise unavailable to the other side has been viewed as unbalancing the system. Because the most extensive and systematic jury selection has occurred with celebrated political cases, critics have suggested the state may be in jeopardy of not receiving a fair trial.

It might also be argued that jury selection procedures increase the risk of jury tampering, either deliberately by an unscrupulous individual or unintentionally through reactions of jurors to the investigation of their personal lives. Invasion of privacy becomes an ethical concern and civil suits conceivably might be brought for negative effects resulting from such investigations.

This may be a case where technology has advanced before ethical issues have been properly addressed.

However, because equally convincing arguments can be made by critics and advocates, the future of jury selection will most likely be determined by legal rulings, regardless of whether critical ethical questions are answered.

EFFECTIVENESS OF JURY SELECTION

Debates over the effectiveness of selection procedures are rendered inconclusive because of empirical limitations. To date, no rigorous evaluation of jury selection procedures, randomly conducted over a variety of trials, has been performed (Berk et al., 1977). The difficulty in controlling extraneous factors (e.g., attorney competence, type of defendant, type of trial) makes the outcome of trials a questionable dependent variable in research on jury selection.

Many social science advocates cite the tremendous effort and monetary resources required to adequately conduct systematic jury selection as one reason for the lack of research to support its efficacy. Also, the legal system frequently is not an appropriate place for manipulating variables, making naturalistic observations, and controlling extraneous factors.

Usually the most jury selectors will claim is that they possess some systematic techniques which may aid the attorney in making better decisions than those which rely upon conventional folklore (Berk et al., 1977). Diamond and Zeisel's (1974) study suggested that attorneys selecting juries appear to be responsive to some variables which may be potentially biasing even though such variables may be difficult to define or enumerate. Both randomly-selected jurors and attorney-rejected jurors were significantly more conviction prone than attorney-selected jurors when they all listened to the same case. Following some of the more recent systematic jury selection endeavors, selected and rejected jurors were interviewed. The jury survey producing a profile of the most favorable jurors was accurate 70% of the time. Moreover, combining the survey with out-of-court investigation of jurors and in-court observation further increased the accuracy rate (Kairys, Schulman, & Harring, 1975).

Even advocates are quick to point out limits to systematic jury selection (Christie, 1976). Aware of the probability of error, Christie stressed the need for use of multiple methods of assessing jurors. He also felt jury selection was not a magical formula which would work in all cases to acquit a defendant (e.g., where evidence was strongly against the defendant). In areas where feelings run high toward a particular case and a change of venue (moving the case to another jurisdiction) is not granted, the likelihood of picking unbiased jurors might be slim indeed.

Critics of the effectiveness of jury selection techniques argue that trials apparently demonstrating positive effects of selection mechanisms have not been typical trials and that, as yet, researchers have not been able to demonstrate that such techniques have been a significant factor in trial outcome (Berman & Sales, 1977). Zeisel and Diamond (1978), in looking at the state of the research on *voir dire* techniques, concluded that "on the whole, the *voir dire*, as conducted in these trials did not provide sufficient information for attorneys to identify prejudiced jurors" (p. 501). Decisions regarding retention of jurors based only upon *voir dire* examinations have been compared with *post hoc* interview data in several studies. Conclusions were that *voir dire* appeared ineffective in weeding out unfavorable jurors (Keeton, 1973), did not elicit relevant data from particular jurors which would have shown their unfavorableness (Broeder, 1965), did appear to reduce the effects of prejudicial information and to sensitize jurors to the facts and arguments which would be relevant to a case, and did seem to make jurors more aware of the importance of legal procedures (Padawer-Singer, Singer, A., & Singer, R., 1974). Two other studies (Saks, 1976; Saks et al., 1975) assessed the effectiveness of predicting juror attitudes on the basis of individual characteristics in conjunction with other trial variables. These studies concluded that the strength of trial evidence was more effective than juror characteristics in predicting bias toward conviction. In the Saks et al. (1975) research, the correlation of individual characteristics with the outcome of a trial accounted for only a small percentage of the variance.

While the data are insufficient to suggest that jury selection techniques are a clearly effective component in trial work (Berk, 1976), there is a definite danger in dismissing such techniques altogether without first assessing ways in which jury selection might be used more effectively. It appears that jury selection research has often made the same mistake as psychotherapy outcome studies in that such research has generally focused on gross assessments of overall predictors. A more refined examination of the association of techniques used and specific conditions (e.g., type of defendant, type of case) with prediction of outcome might be more useful. Ultimately, as Berman and Sales (1977) have suggested, research may indicate that no one component is all important. Rather, the increase in individuals involved in assessment of potential jurors and the increase in information regarding demographics, observable behavior, and attitudes of jurors might together decrease errors in judgment when selection occurs.

Jury research in general needs to address the following methodological concerns: (a) generalization problems arising from use of simulated juries which do not match typical jury pools or experience the typical influences on "real" jurors, (b) consideration of the effects of juror interaction upon the attributes of individual jurors, (c) generalization difficulties due to various types of trials, (d) control of variables such as the strength of evidence, (e) generalization problems resulting from a lack of comparability between simulated evidence and actual trial evidence, and (f) consideration of research results in light of the changing social attitudes, influences, and climate of the country. Methodological concerns for jury selection studies in particular include: (a) clear delineation of the jury selection techniques utilized; (b) comparisons between scientifically-selected juries, randomly-selected juries, and attorney-selected juries; and (c) clear scientific and theoretical understanding of the link between collected data and outcome, and between the characteristics of a juror and his or her actual behavior as a juror.

JURY SELECTION METHODOLOGY

Social scientists' contributions in the area of jury selection fall into several categories: (a) empirically assessing demographic characteristics similar to those suggested by legal folklore to determine the actual ability of such variables to predict jury behavior and to determine the relative predictive power of these factors with different populations, cases, geographical locations, and so forth; (b) introducing personality variables (e.g., attitudes, psychological make-up, cognitive styles) as mediating factors which may influence decision making by jurors and assessing their relative contributions to jury behavior; (c) developing increasingly sophisticated methods of assessing general community attitudes and collecting information about individual jurors (e.g., surveys, network models); (d) refining means for making inferences from nonverbal and verbal behavior of jurors in the courtroom; (e) developing more effective *voir dire* questioning, aimed at eliciting the most relevant and genuine self-report regarding attitudes and biases; and (f) bringing group dynamics research to bear in attempting to understand how individuals selected as jurors might behave once interaction with other selected jurors begins.

Proponents of systematic jury selection procedures believe that a combination of all of the above methodologies should be utilized to produce the most complete and adequate method of juror selection. Limits to applying and analyzing systematic procedures usually involve time, energy, monetary resources, physical resources (e.g., individuals to cover tasks, computer access), and limits imposed by the legal system (e.g., whether a judge will allow a questionnaire to be distributed to the entire jury pool).

Putting the various procedures of jury selection into play involves conducting analyses both in and out of the courtroom. The basic sequence of data collection is as follows: (a) Prior to the trial, data is collected suggesting ideal "profiles" for jurors expected to be neutral or biased in one direction. (b) Information is collected on the actual jury pool members from outside sources prior to trial. (c) In the courtroom, various techniques are used to assess individuals called from the venire as potential jury

members. The procedures used by social scientists to aid
in the collection of data, to weight the data to form
profiles, to collect self-reported information, and to
generate inferences from the data will all be discussed in
light of the three major sources of decision-making data
listed above.

"BEST JUROR" PROFILE DATA

It has long been believed that attorneys can predict
people's responses to a trial based on some characteristics,
either overt or covert. Clarence Darrow (1939) once gave
a prescription for selecting juries favorable to the
"underdog." He recommended rejecting prohibitionists,
Presbyterians, Baptists, Scandinavians, and the "well-to-
do," while accepting Jewish people, agnostics, the Irish,
and those who liked to laugh. Social scientists would like
to claim that they have certainly refined this selection
procedure. Methods for determining the type of
individual best suited to accept a particular point of view
include: analysis of general demographic indicators,
community analysis, surveys to assess attitudes toward
particular cases, and surveys to assess personality
variables with implications for juror decision making.
The "best juror," of course, will generally vary as a
function of the selector's "side" in the litigation (i.e.,
prosecution v. defense in criminal trials and plaintiff v.
defendant in civil matters).

Analysis of General Demographic Indicators. General
characteristics, such as sex, income level, or political
party affiliation, often are relied upon to the exclusion of
more subtle variables. As a result, attorneys are
frequently disappointed by jurors who do not behave as
expected when such global characteristics are relied upon
for jury selection. The fact that some consistent findings
reappear in the research literature does not imply that the
correlation between juror behavior and a particular
demographic characteristic will occur consistently, nor
does it mean that one or two characteristics can
necessarily predict subtleties in juror behavior.

The research findings discussed below must be
approached with caution. They may not apply to a

particular location or case and cannot be relied upon to predict behavior consistently. They may, however, be used as guidelines when no other information is available. Since much human behavior is influenced directly by situational components which account for a significant amount of the variance in individual responses, it appears unwise to place much confidence in predictions of juror responses based on only a few demographic characteristics.

Several commentators have reviewed available studies regarding demographic characteristics and the impact of these characteristics on jury decisions (Frederick, 1978; Fried, Kaplan, K., & Klein, 1975; Stephan, 1975; Suggs & Sales, 1978). These articles may be consulted for specific findings. Because of society changes, however, studies which utilize data collected decades ago should probably not be given strong consideration, particularly if their results conflict with those derived from more recent investigations.

Sex. Inconsistency of results makes sex a poor choice as a predictor of jury behavior. Differing types of criminal cases have often produced differential results by sex, but assessments of sex-linked verdicts in civil cases have been contradictory (Fried et al., 1975). While certain specific conditions have produced sex differences, the variable of sex appears to be too broad to serve as a basis for reasonable predictions of juror behavior.

Income Level. Adler (1973), Fried et al. (1975), Reed (1965), and Simon (1967) have all suggested that persons from higher income groups favor the prosecution more than do those from middle and lower income groups (Katz, 1968-1969). In civil cases, where large amounts of money are being sought in damages, Harrington and Dempsey (1969) have recommended that the plaintiff seek jurors in upper-income brackets. Reed (1965), however, found that jurors' income levels may have no differential effects in the awarding of damages.

Occupational Group. While information regarding this variable is hardly complete, some studies have suggested that bankers, engineers, and certified public accountants tend to favor the prosecution while butchers, other middle-range occupations, and social scientists are more likely to favor defendants (Adkins, 1968-1969; Katz, 1968-1969).

Political Party Affiliation. Hayes (1972) recommends selecting Democrats over Republicans as jurors if an attorney is handling the defense in a criminal case or representing a personal injury plaintiff seeking a high damage award.

Age. Age, in and of itself, is rarely found to be a predictor which consistently yields verdicts in one direction or the other (Reed, 1965).

Religious Preference. Religious preference is another demographic variable which by itself lends little information for predicting jury behavior. Much of the early psychological literature was optimistic that religious affiliation would prove to be a significant predictor of a wide range of attitudes, beliefs, and behaviors, but there were few consistent results reported. Psychologists have begun to assess the level of religious commitment and amount of actual religious activity. Because this approach to religiosity has yielded more pertinent and relevant findings, jury selection studies might successfully apply similar methods.

Ethnic Group. Several researchers have concluded that Teutonic ethnic groups (particularly Germans) and Anglo-Saxons are more conviction prone (Broeder, 1959; Campbell, 1972). On the other hand, the same authors have suggested that Latins, Jews, Slavs, and Italians favor the defense in criminal trials. Typically, blacks are found to favor defendants (Simon, 1967). Generalizations in this area should be cautiously applied.

Locale. People who live in rural areas are often harsher in criminal court judgments and less generous when civil court damage awards are decided (Grisham & Lawless, 1973; Rose & Prell, 1955). If a plaintiff is seeking a large award of money damages, he or she should hope for jurors from the eastern or western seacoasts, where juries have been found to be more generous than those in the midwest or the south (Broeder, 1959; Kalven & Zeisel, 1966).

Prior Jury Experience. Previous jury experience appears to predispose individuals toward finding the defendant guilty (Reed, 1965).

Perception of Juror Regarding Similarity between Self and Defendant. Jurors tend to assess their own demographic characteristics in relation to those of the defendant, and their perception of the degree of similarity frequently influences decision making. This phenomenon, called situational or personal relevance (Evenbeck, 1974), was investigated by Chaikin and Darley (1973), who found that a juror's perception of similarity between self and defendant produced a bias favoring the defendant, while a perception of similarity between self and victim resulted in a bias favoring the prosecution. These investigators, however, cautioned about possible exceptions, such as the case in which there is strong evidence for conviction and jurors are unlikely to believe the defendant's story despite any perceived similarity.

Demographic Rating Systems. The unreliability of most of the above-described generalizations has led social scientists to develop models for *individual* cases in court. The assumption has been that depending upon the particular region in which a case is coming to trial, some demographic characteristics *may be* predictive of attitudes toward the case. The model developed would determine which, if any, of such characteristics predict attitudes and what relative weights should be given to each predictive variable in the decision making process. Among the groups which have done the most to develop these and other techniques are the National Jury Project and Jay Schulman and his colleagues (Kairys et al., 1975; National Jury Project, 1979; Schulman, 1973; Schulman, Shaver, Colman, Emrich, & Christie, 1973). Their writings should be consulted for the most comprehensive discussion of each procedure.

To establish the relationship between demographic variables and attitudes toward a specific case, a survey must be conducted in the community from which the jury pool will be drawn. Choosing a sample from the population from which the venire is chosen (e.g., voter registration lists) will enhance the generalizability of the data. The National Jury Project (1979) has suggested that a minimum of 600 completed surveys is necessary to conduct a sophisticated analysis of the data.

While the survey is an expensive and time-consuming procedure, it is necessary in establishing the "best juror" profile where only limited data may be gleaned from the individual jurors. Information collected in the survey should include: (a) demographic characteristics (e.g., sex, race, age, occupation, place of residence); (b) personal information such as military experience, organizational affiliations, and primary reading materials; (c) attitudes toward the case in question, the participants on both sides of the trial, specific facts concerning the case, and any important legal issues that may be at stake in the trial; and (d) attitudes toward issues that may be indirectly related to the case, but nonetheless predictive of behavior in the case (e.g., attitudes toward sexuality in a case where criminal sexual assault occurred, attitudes toward police).

Great care must be taken in developing the questionnaire. Some general questions to consider when constructing attitude questions for the survey have been suggested by the National Jury Project (1979): (a) How do you think individuals will feel about the case? (b) What questions and concerns might prospective jurors have regarding this case? (c) What issues in the case might affect attitudes toward it? (d) What general attitudes might individuals hold that would bias their judgment on specific issues? (e) What demographic characteristics might be associated with prejudice regarding the case? Sometimes an actual description of the case or a hypothetical example will be stated to those being interviewed, followed by questions designed to elicit any recollection of the actual case and reactions to the facts and the issues involved.

Transformation of the mass of data into usable information requires computer analysis. An Automatic Interaction Detection (AID) program has been used by some jury selectors as a first step to identify subgroups of individuals holding similar attitudes. These subgroups are identified by common demographic characteristics. The data are then subjected to further analyses using multiple regression statistical techniques to generate equations elucidating those characteristics most likely to predict opinions toward the case. Multiple regression equations can also be used to assign numerical weights to demographics in order to compare potential jurors in light of several predictor variables.

The value of the ideal juror profile becomes apparent when one considers the difficulties often associated with in-trial questioning of potential jurors. Questions may be limited to specific factual content with attitudinal questions prohibited. Judges may do the questioning of jurors in the *voir dire* phase, the scope of questioning may be extremely limited, and genuine concern is often warranted regarding jurors' willingness to reveal true attitudes and beliefs. The profile, which relies on a small number of factual variables, permits more accurate assessment of jurors. Subsequent ranking of jurors as to desirability allows judicious use of peremptory strikes. Also, because juror assessment depends on questions of fact rather than attitude, jurors are less able to influence the assessment by masking feelings and opinions.

There are, however, significant methodological and statistical concerns which must be considered any time such techniques are employed (Berk et al., 1977). Berman and Sales (1977), for example, have pointed to three potential problems worth considering: (a) the uselessness of multiple regression techniques when a population is homogeneous, (b) the problems of generalizability when certain groups of individuals are automatically excused from jury participation, and (c) the weak link between potentially positive attitudes and actual behavior on a jury.

Community Analysis. An analysis of the community promotes understanding of the people living in the jurisdiction where a trial is to be held. Such analysis should typically occur far in advance of other procedures, as the information garnered regarding demographics and attitudes will be an excellent resource for the development of surveys. The analysis is also helpful in preparing *voir dire* questions and useful for case analysis and preparation.

The National Jury Project (1979) has suggested two major foci for case analysis in light of community attitudes: (a) development of a demographic profile of the community, and (b) interviews with representative people in the community. Specifically, the issues in a case must be understood in view of the particular community's feelings toward participants in, events surrounding, and legal aspects of the case. The goal is to tease out those issues important for making a case comprehensible and relevant to jurors. Thus, it becomes possible to experiment with strategies of evidence presentation (e.g., whether or not to use expert testimony) and ways of clarifying legal issues.

Developing a demographic profile requires thorough knowledge of the physical make-up of the jurisdiction, including counties, cities, towns, and neighborhoods. Jury lists should be consulted to determine which areas have the largest representation on the venire in order to focus data-gathering efforts on these areas first. Recommendations for information to collect (National Jury Project, 1979) include: size and composition of the population, amount of home ownership, income levels, racial and ethnic composition, mobility patterns, voting and registration patterns, and neighborhood histories. Major industries may be consulted for information as to principal occupational groups and unemployment rates. Libraries and election commissions may have attitudinal surveys or election results which can be used to identify geographical areas differing from the general patterns of public opinion.

After general patterns and exceptions in a community are identified, interviews of specific individuals are carried out. Randomly selected representatives of different groups in the area as well as the full range of community activists should be informally interviewed. Their background characteristics, perceptions of the community's attitudes toward legal issues in general, and specific perceptions regarding the case in question need to be elucidated.

Specialized Surveys

Evidence to Support Motions and Challenge Jury Composition. Surveys have been utilized by social scientists for very specialized purposes. When attorneys require evidence to support motions (e.g., change of venue) or to challenge the composition of a jury, social scientists frequently have the tools to produce the necessary information.

For example, the results of a survey of a randomly selected sample might be useful to establish the existence of a high level of awareness regarding a case and/or a high degree of presumption of guilt. The results of such a survey could be submitted to the court when a motion for change of venue is introduced. In one highly publicized case, a survey showing that Joan Little would not receive a fair and impartial trial in the community where she had been indicted appears to have been the major reason for the granting of her attorney's motion for a change of venue (Tivnan, 1975). The American Bar Association's *Standards Relating to the Administration of Criminal Justice* (1974) recommend that surveys assessing public opinion be admissible for just such a purpose.

Where a jury pool is not representative of the population from which the pool is drawn, survey data can be presented to demonstrate the discrepancies. In such cases, social scientists would provide the statistical data and significance level of the discrepancies upon which challenges to the composition of the jury could be based.

Attitudes and Personality Characteristics. Surveys are often designed to tap attitudes and personality characteristics which research has linked to the predispositions and likely behavior of jurors. Some of the techniques seem directly linked to behavior of an individual in court (e.g., the Legal Attitudes Questionnaire described below) while others assess mediating personality characteristics which imply probable attitudes and actions.

The courts are currently not very sympathetic to attorneys and social scientists who wish to assess jurors' actual attitudes through paper-and-pencil measures presented prior to *voir dire* questioning or through *voir dire* presentation of survey questions that do not seem directly linked to the case. Because of this inhibition of data gathering, social scientists often must make much more doubtful connections between small samples of *voir dire* behavior and juror demographics and the level of attitudes or personality characteristics they feel predict trial outcomes. For example, an estimate of authoritarianism based on a juror's nonverbal cues is more likely to be in error than one based on a score on a standardized measure of authoritarianism.

Surveys of personality variables and attitudes considered significant for the trial could be conducted with members of the community to determine the relationship between those variables and attitudes and various demographic characteristics. The ideal situation would be to know how personality variables relate to attitudes toward the case *and* to have prospective jurors complete those measures which show the most predictive power. Even if one were able to conduct personality measures with the actual jury panel, however, such measures would be useful only to the extent that they could be related to the issues of the specific case.

Boehm (1968) has developed a Legal Attitudes Questionnaire (LAQ) consisting of 30 items for use in criminal trials. This measure discriminates among individuals predisposed toward the prosecution, those predisposed to believe defendants, and those with no substantial predisposition. Predictions of juror bias based on LAQ scores have been validated in a study involving actual jurors. The LAQ is not only cost effective and quick to administer but it offers attorneys a valuable means of supplementing conventional *voir dire*. Moreover, because the LAQ taps a dimension relevant to both sides in a criminal trial, its use cannot be opposed on the basis of unfair advantage for one side. Refusal to allow for inquiry into similar bias has been held reversible error in some trials, but use of the LAQ, itself, in any given trial typically lies within the discretion of the court.

Tapp (Tapp & Kohlberg, 1971; Tapp & Levine, 1974) has proposed directly assessing jurors' "legal development" in relationship to jury decision making. She believes that jurors will base their attitudes and behaviors on their level of reasoning about laws, that is, either on (a) fear or deference, (b) conformity, or (c) ethics. Jurors at each of these levels should, according to Tapp, respond differently to events confronting them at trial. Those in the first group would view laws rigidly and perceive justice as a form of retaliation. Conformists would consider paramount the need to have law and order for maintaining society and would see majority rule and the standard application of laws as good practice. Individuals in the third group considering ethical principles would see the need for social systems to develop laws, but could independently assess situations in terms of ethical principles which a social system may not have considered.

Tapp's hypotheses have been indirectly inferred with some accuracy from the behavior of jurors in court (Tapp & Keniston, 1976), although a specific device for assessing legal development has been refined. For example, fearful and timid individuals might be regarded as functioning on the basis of fear and deference and thus not be considered fair jurors. Relaxed and outspoken persons, on the other hand, might be considered able to evaluate laws in light of ethics and thus be more desirable as jurors.

A variety of researchers have hypothesized that opinions for or against capital punishment might also imply other attitudes toward criminal populations (Bronson, 1970; Goldberg, 1970; Jurow, 1971; Wilson, W., 1964). Indeed, individuals favoring capital punishment have been found to be more conviction prone.

Much research and attention regarding personality variables affecting jury behavior has been focused on the authoritarian personality—a cluster of personality components which indicate "prefascistic" or antidemocratic trends. Originally defined in 1950 by Adorno and his colleagues (Adorno, Frenkel-Brunswik, Levinson, & Sanford, 1950), this personality type was described as "highly punitive, racist, politically conservative, rigid, and acquiescent to authority figures" (Frederick, 1978, p. 575). With that description, it is easy to understand why researchers interested in jury behavior in criminal trials would consider authoritarianism a fruitful focus of study. Both a mock jury study (Boehm, 1968) and a field study (Center, Shomer, & Rodrigues, 1970) found authoritarian individuals (as assessed by standardized measures) to be more conviction prone and more severe in their judgments against defendants. Furthermore, they were found to be willing to shift their opinions when an authority figure held an opinion opposite their own original opinion. Later studies have consistently supported these early results (Epstein, 1966; Jurow, 1971; Vidmar, 1974). Vidulich and Kaiman (1961) found high authoritarians more influenced by high status sources, while other researchers found authoritarians rigid in their thinking styles and quick to make decisions without reserving judgment or looking for additional information (Brown, 1953; Long & Ziller, 1965). These data have definite implications for decision making processes in court. Social scientists would predict that the presentation of arguments and evidence in criminal trials, where the prosecution proceeds first, would produce more guilty verdicts among authoritarian jurors.

Strong authoritarian attitudes, however, should not necessarily be expected to bias a juror toward conviction. Authoritarians, for example, upon confronting a defendant they considered similar to themselves, have been found to be less certain as to guilt than other jurors (Mitchell & Byrne, 1973). Further assessment of this personality type in the jury context requires investigation of the interaction between personal style and such situational variables as the nature of the litigation, type of evidence, and characteristics of the litigants.

Conformity and suggestibility have also been proposed as factors influencing jurors to acquiesce to presumed expertise or authority (McGuire, 1968). Unfortunately, conformity is typically inferred from actual behavior, is frequently a function of situational characteristics, and has often been proposed as a "symptom" of traits such as authoritarianism and low self-esteem rather than a consistent trait (Fried et al., 1975). Even if the concept could be operationalized and measured, further investigation would be needed to demonstrate the direction in which high conformers would be influenced and whether they would attach themselves to issues or persons on a random or idiosyncratic basis.

Internal versus external locus of control refers to peoples' beliefs regarding the degree to which they can exert control over events occurring in their lives. If jurors have strong beliefs in their own internal ability to affect outcomes (as opposed to believing that external factors such as luck or fate are primarily responsible for events), they seem more likely to consider defendants responsible for crimes (Phares & Wilson, K., 1972; Sosis, 1974) and tend to render harsher sentences (Sosis, 1974). Brodsky (1977) has also hypothesized that internals will not be favorable to civil defendants. Rotter (1966) has developed a measure for internal-external orientation and other researchers have refined the measure.

Cognitive styles (or modes of processing information through thought patterns) have also been considered as potential predictors of jury behavior. Fried et al. (1975), for example, have discussed the ideal types of thinkers desired by prosecutors and defense attorneys. Prosecutors understandably prefer individuals closed to new information, jurors who are dogmatic once they make a decision and who cling to strong opinions. The rationale behind this inference is the likelihood that these individuals will strongly believe in themselves and attempt to influence others on the jury. Persons in the military or in midlevel positions in organizations with established hierarchies are likely candidates for these traits. Defense attorneys, on the other hand, want individuals who can handle dissonant information and process *all* data received over the course of a trial. Hayes (1972) has recommended younger individuals and Katz (1968-1969) has suggested people with a wide variety of life experiences. All of these suggestions, however, come from folklore rather than research findings.

OUTSIDE DATA GATHERED ON MEMBERS OF THE JURY POOL

Network Model. As soon as the venire list is published, attorneys commonly review the names in order to identify individuals they, their clients, other attorneys, sheriffs, and so forth recognize as potentially favorable to their position. While this informal procedure may yield useful information in small jurisdictions, its usefulness is greatly diminished where jury pools are drawn from a large population or where the published list of names is available only at the last minute before *voir dire* begins. Depending upon their individual aims, some attorneys have gone so far as to consult police and other law enforcement records, IRS records, and private detective investigative records to provide information regarding the backgrounds of potential jurors.

The systematic jury selection approach has advocated use of a network of workers to collect information on venire members once the list is made public (e.g., Schulman, 1973). To avoid charges of jury tampering, personal information must come from observations of the jurors or contacts with individuals who might know the jurors. Typical ways to accomplish this include observation of the juror's residence and neighborhood, interviews with neighbors, and interviews with other individuals who have direct knowledge, such as a potential juror's minister or employer. In sparsely populated areas, community leaders and agency heads often have valuable data on venire members.

A variety of difficulties, some potentially serious, frequently plague this method (Berman & Sales, 1977; Suggs & Sales, 1978) although the National Jury Project (1979) has carefully outlined procedures for maximum effectiveness. Privacy issues seem paramount, as jurors who discover they are being investigated frequently become angry or frightened. Hostile attitudes toward the client frequently ensue. Because it is impossible to collect complete information—Schulman (1973) suggested that 400 workers are needed to provide background data on 70% to 80% of jurors in the pool—it is difficult for attorneys to know how to evaluate the available data. Furthermore, the accuracy of hearsay information collected from "acquaintances" is highly questionable. Personal data on jurors, filtered through the eyes of friends and acquaintances, may contain distortions due to jealousies, neighborhood disputes, disapproval, and other motivations on the part of the informants. The difficulties with the network model, combined with the hardships in its practical application, make this procedure one of the least attractive, most cumbersome, and least cost effective in terms of time expended and results obtained.

Group Dynamics Observation. Observations of jurors relating to other jurors also adds to the pot of already existing data. Several writers (e.g., Mullin, 1980) have indicated the need for observations based on the implications from jury decision-making studies. One reason for observing relationships is that juries homogeneous along demographic or attitudinal dimensions may be expected to respond in unison to the evidence presented, while heterogeneous juries are much more of an enigma (Fried et al., 1975). Of course, prosecutors and criminal defense attorneys generally hope for opposite juries; defense attorneys typically look for dissent and lack of agreement which may promote hung juries or, at least, well thought-out verdicts.

Another reason for observing juror interaction has been to determine which jurors exhibit leadership qualities. Saks and Hastie (1978) have reported the conclusion that more active jurors are more influential. Therefore, identified leaders may be a critical factor, especially in light of research findings that individuals from upper occupational classes frequently are chosen as jury forepersons and are statistically more likely to exhibit authoritarian tendencies. The National Jury Project (1979) has suggested that leaders who seem favorable to one's side may be extremely useful in influencing jury process, but has cautioned that not all leaders show overt, easily defined leadership characteristics. Indications to be screened for include: status and authority positions; intellectual and verbal abilities; decisiveness and strong will (e.g., self-confidence, social ease with other jurors, forcefulness in responses); and previous leadership training or experience. Mullin (1980) suggests some specific behaviors helpful in spotting leadership qualities as well as political attitudes, relationships between the sexes and races, cooperativeness, and homogeneity. She suggests that the outcome of a trial may hang on the selection of a "few key persons whose views are those desired and who also possess the ability to become leaders" (p. 11).

Independent thinkers may need to be in abundance to produce a hung jury as the literature suggests at least four individuals must disagree with the majority in their initial determinations (Saks & Hastie, 1978). People who will maintain opinions contrary to those of the group throughout deliberations are typically people who stubbornly hold their ground during *voir dire* questioning.

Other likely "hold outs" are those individuals proud of not conforming, extremely opinionated persons, and those antagonistic to figures in authority.

Individuals who are followers or who never make their own decisions might also be spotted by their interactional styles. Authoritarian personalities who are more likely to conform to authority figures or people who will follow a majority decision typically appear fairly passive, often seem quiet, may have a limited range of life experiences, can easily be swayed during *voir dire* questioning, seem to lack confidence, and thus are easily intimidated in the *voir dire*.

Berman and Sales (1977) have suggested a rule of thumb when faced with a choice between a persuasive person, whose predisposition is unknown or in doubt, and a persuadable follower, who is unfavorably disposed. The follower should be considered a safer bet due to his or her susceptibility to influence.

Subgroups of jurors who might form similar opinions based on perceived commonalities also may be spotted through observation of the venire. Seating patterns, sociometric contacts, choices for lunch partners, and car pooling all provide data regarding which individuals might form these subgroups (National Jury Project, 1979).

Where specific attitudes or issues may have direct bearing on a case, informal venire contacts may provide useful data. For example, racial and sex-role attitudes may often be assessed by observing the interaction of blacks and whites or men and women on the jury panel.

IN-COURT ASSESSMENT OF POTENTIAL JURORS

Voir Dire Questioning. Legal history has established the need for direct questioning of the venire as a means of implementing the constitutional right to a fair and impartial jury. *Voir dire* actually means "to speak the truth." Its effects appear far-reaching as several studies have concluded that the *voir dire* played some part in the decisions jurors made (e.g., Friend & Vinson, 1974; Kaplan, M. F., & Kemmerick, 1974).

However, what appears to be straightforward procedure is often fraught with complications, limitations, and confusing implications. Determination of how much questioning can occur, how specific the questions can be, and to what degree the questions must be directly related to the case at bar are all within the discretion of the trial judge. Therefore, personal experiences and biases of a judge, traditions of a particular locale, or the level of sophistication of procedures in an area may all differentially influence the extent to which questioning may occur. Limiting questions is especially problematic for jury selectors when indirect variables have been established as the best predictors of specific attitudes in a case. Probably the only cases in which an attorney may count on extensive *voir dire* are those involving capital punishment where a more careful examination of defendant's rights may be expected.

Frequently, a judge will not allow questions to be addressed to individuals, but will rather require that generic questions be addressed to the entire panel. Where an individual juror may respond (e.g., answer affirmatively to a question regarding employment in a hospital when the case is a malpractice suit), the judge usually asks that jury pool member his or her own perceptions of his or her ability to be fair. If a potential juror states a belief that he or she can be impartial, that person is kept in the jury pool.

Another difficulty attorneys often face is the decision of the judge to be the only one to ask questions of the jury pool, with questions being submitted by the attorneys for the judge's approval. Social scientists have given expert testimony in motions proceedings as to the necessity of either individual *voir dire* or attorney-conducted *voir dire*. Research to support their suppositions deals with demand characteristics, situational influences, influence of a powerful figure, social desirability aspects, and the need for privacy in eliciting sensitive information.

Should a defense team be fortunate enough personally to conduct an extensive *voir dire* with individual jurors, the focus of that effort becomes the specific questions used and the manner of interviewing needed to most effectively elicit attitudes. Additional goals of the *voir dire* which have been repeatedly suggested are: (a) education of the jurors as to the primary issues in the case and initiation of attitudes toward the legal concepts at stake in the trial, and (b) establishment of a beginning relationship between the juror and the attorney and his or her client (Bennett, 1977). Several authors have delineated in great detail the types of questions to ask and information to deliver during *voir dire* (e.g., Bennett, 1977; Mullin, 1980; National Jury Project, 1979; Suggs & Sales, 1978).

The reason for carefully probing a juror's attitudes is that demonstration of bias may result in dismissal of the juror from the panel "for cause." While jurors are unlikely directly to proclaim lack of fairness, skillful questioning may reveal the biases which they hold. At that point, jurors might admit an inability to be impartial or the attorney may ask the judge to dismiss the juror. When bias is clearly shown, and a juror is dismissed for cause, the defense team can use its peremptory strikes more judiciously to weed out individuals who disguise their biases, are very close-mouthed about their attitudes, or who seem to fit the profile of the least favorable juror.

Specific questions directed to potential jurors should seek the following data: (a) demographic and attitudinal factors shown by the pretrial survey to have predictive value; (b) awareness of pretrial publicity; (c) prejudicial attitudes regarding characteristics of the client (e.g., race, prison record, physical demeanor); (d) reactions toward the type of case (e.g., the specific crime or type of accident); (e) attitudes regarding the legal system and opposing sides in a trial; (f) knowledge of community attitudes toward the case; (g) attitudes toward evidence to be presented in the case; (h) ability to accept the relevant legal concepts such as the presumption of innocence; (i) knowledge of individuals involved in the case; (j) previous experience as a crime or tort victim or litigant on either side of a lawsuit; and (k) previous experience as a jury member.

In addition to the *content* of *voir dire* questions, jury selectors must also be concerned with the *manner* in which such questions are posed. Social scientists, especially those with clinical training, can be very helpful in phrasing questions and critiquing the attorney's style of delivery. Bennett (1977) has suggested that the best approach to questioning should include *empathy* for the juror's situation and ideas, *respect* for the person no matter how discrepant his or her feelings and attitudes are from the ones desired for the case, and *congruence*, or genuineness, of the interviewer in expressing the first two qualities.

As a rule, "open-ended" questions are most likely to elicit a wide range of relevant and pertinent responses from potential jurors. Questions which call for "yes-no" answers or which seem to require a certain response are "closed" questions. Leading questions of this type produce little additional information. When individuals feel the freedom to answer questions in their own particular style, when they feel they will not be judged for holding particular views, and when they feel there is no "right" answer to give, they will be most honest in revealing personal information. Under the best of conditions, some people still will not disclose sensitive information. The *ways* in which they respond (e.g., nonverbal cues), however, may be useful for inferring attitudes.

There are several types of open-ended questions. Bennett (1977) has suggested some major questioning styles for attorneys to use. *Summarizing* what the person has said and asking for *clarification* of an answer allows the juror to correct any misperception on the part of the examiner and to expand or qualify an answer. Both of these techniques increase the usefulness of an answer for prediction of attitudes. A summarizing statement or question may mention nonverbal cues the juror is emitting (e.g., "This topic seems to be somewhat upsetting for you"). If an attorney is willing to *self-disclose* (i.e., state his or her own thoughts and feelings), this approach has the potential for building rapport by personalizing and equalizing the relationship between attorney and juror. In addition, such an approach may be used to encourage willingness to reveal personal information. For example, an attorney might say, "I have been in positions myself where I felt on the spot and realized I did not know how much I wanted to let others know about me. I wonder if you might feel the same way." Mullin (1980) suggests the judicious use of silence by the interviewing attorney at the end of certain juror responses to encourage further disclosure. People will often try to fill silences with additional information. The added spontaneous, and often more uncomfortable, verbalizations frequently will be more revealing than the initial, more rehearsed and censored answer. The National Jury Project (1979) recommends that "open-ended" questions begin with "what," "why," or "how" because these words usually require the juror to do most of the talking.

Bennett (1977) has discussed the types of questioning which *decrease* revealed information. *Advice*, usually in the form of suggesting something the juror should feel or do, results in the juror feeling inferior or not listened to. The only place to use advice in the *voir dire* is in educating jurors as to legal concepts and ways to handle deliberations.

Similarly, *leading questions* are useless for giving people freedom to discuss their opinions. Such questions may be useful, however, in eliciting admissions of bias and for committing jurors to act on legal principles. The danger with leading questions, even for these purposes, is that the potential juror may feel forced to answer "yes" or "no" and, resentful, may act differently at a later time. The individual's true feelings may have been missed completely.

False reassurance inhibits further disclosure. If jurors are told they are not feeling certain emotions or not to feel some reaction, the effect is a denial of their feelings and a perception of being misunderstood. Should an attorney wish to cut off a juror's response, however, reassurance may be used. *Interpretation*, or analysis, rarely builds rapport or increases the data pool. Interpreting means making suppositions or inferences about a person from a minimum of data and then telling that person how he or she thinks. While some jurors may respond angrily, others may simply hide their resentment. Reactions are thus difficult to assess, no further knowledge is gained, and negative feelings may build toward the interviewer.

The educational component of the *voir dire* is the attorney's effort to familiarize jurors with legal concepts, issues in the particular case, and juror responsibilities (National Jury Project, 1979). Because the *voir dire* is a questioning process, education takes place through questions designed to provoke thought on the part of the juror. The understanding of well-known legal phrases, such as "innocent until proven guilty," should not be taken for granted. Rather, legal concepts should be carefully explored to insure that jurors understand and accept them. If the assumptions underlying the legal issues are not accepted, the judge should be asked to dismiss the juror for cause.

Thorough education of jurors regarding legal concepts and responsibilities through *voir dire* may include questions regarding: (a) burden of proof issues, (b) the right of a defendant not to testify, (c) presumption of innocence, (d) the need for jurors to individually decide what they believe (as the defense attorney might suggest) or the need for jurors to jointly decide issues (as the prosecution might suggest), (e) the meaning of reasonable doubt, and (f) the specific decisions jurors might have to make in the case. Anticipating the adversary party's trial tactics may lessen their impact. For example, seriously discussing the most troublesome aspects of a case during *voir dire* indicates to jurors that the attorney respects their natural concerns. Revelation of the most difficult parts of one's case also allows for determination of individual reactions with resulting challenges for cause or peremptory strikes.

Observation of Paralinguistics and Kinesics. Because communication is more than just the verbal content of a person's responses, paralinguistics and kinesics must also be carefully observed. In the *voir dire*, it is common for jurors to seek approval from society's symbols of fairness and justice (i.e., judges and attorneys). Jurors also report sometimes feeling as though *they* were on trial, especially when personal questions have been asked. Because of these pressures, the verbal content of jurors' responses may be deceptive, incomplete, or guarded.

Paralinguistic aspects of communication are the "other" parts of speech which do not constitute words, but are associated with verbal communications. *How* a person answers a question may do more to communicate his or her attitudes than do the words themselves. Aspects of the "how" include: pitch and tone of voice; disturbances in speech, such as stuttering or coughing; pauses in the flow of an answer; the amount of time taken to answer different questions; and amount of speech flow (Suggs & Sales, 1978).

Kinesics, on the other hand, considers the "body language" or nonverbal cues attached to verbal responses. Several authors have listed dimensions of body language considered important to observe: body movement, posture, movement of the hands, orientation of the body (toward or away from an object), facial cues, and eye contact (Frederick, 1978; Mullin, 1980; Suggs & Sales, 1978).

Verbal content is viewed as establishing factual information, while paralinguistics and kinesics are seen as expressing attitudes, emotions, attentiveness, feedback, and illustrations about the facts (Argyle, 1969). Recent research into nonverbal factors of communication supports the belief that deception may be discovered and truthfulness identified when people speak (Ekman & Friesen, 1969). Specifically, certain behaviors are related to shows of emotion, situational anxiety, and/or deception (Suggs & Sales, 1978). It is easy, however, to misinterpret nonverbal cues if observers assume that they can automatically infer what a nonverbal response means just because it occurs. The important task during the *voir dire* is to identify what observed changes in nonverbal communication actually mean.

To best understand nonverbal communication, observers must first note when and where the nonverbal shifts take place. Jurors should be watched to assess their nonverbal cues across questioning from different individuals (e.g., judge, opposing attorneys, defendant); across types of questions (e.g., factual demographics v. personal and sensitive information v. attitudes); and across different situations (e.g., sitting among the entire jury panel v. individual questioning in the *voir dire*). Any discrepancies and differences should be described and noted.

Second, observers must determine the *kind* of changes occurring. Are the changes indicative of greater ease and positive feelings, such as unclasping arms and moving the chair to directly face the speaker? Or are the changes suggestive of negative feelings toward an individual or anxiety regarding a specific question, such as discontinuing eye contact or hesitating before answering?

Third, observers should attempt to decide whether the nonverbal cues seem indicative of general personal styles (e.g., stiff posture of authoritarian personalities) or are a direct result of the current situation. Finally, they should assess whether congruence exists between the expressed verbal content and the paralinguistic and kinesic aspects of the communication. If not, which seems the most salient and believable? Which seems the most genuine?

Mullin (1980) has described a variety of body language cues denoting good rapport with the interviewer: eye contact that is "direct, continuous, and somewhat intense"; turning the entire body toward the interviewer; leaning forward; and absence of body movements typically signaling anxiety. Frederick (1978) has recommended rating the potential juror on paralinguistic and kinesic scales and converting these ratings to an overall score which would indicate the direction in which a juror leans. He stressed the importance of not relying upon only a single behavior, but rather examining the overall response pattern of observed behavior to guess at the favorability of a juror.

THE FINAL ANALYSIS AND DECISION

The jury selector's strategy will depend upon the number of peremptory strikes assigned to each side, whether challenges for cause have been effective with biased jurors, and whether strikes occur in a sequential or one-time format. It is crucial to have a good image of the opposing side's strategy for determining strikes since the same juror might be stricken by both sides due to different characteristics in the same person.

When jurors are selected sequentially, a decision must be made at the end of *voir dire* questioning of each individual to retain or reject that person as a juror. Because selectors do not know who else will be called from the venire, the decision must be made in light of that person's similarity to the ideal juror profile, the amount of personal bias compared to the community's range of bias, and the individual's characteristics compared to those of the general jury pool. In other words, the juror is chosen on the basis of the perceived odds of choosing a better or worse juror later.

In a system where all jurors are selected at the same time, a list is formed with more names from the venire than the necessary 12 jurors and additional alternates.

Following *voir dire* of all those on the list, each side independently ranks the potential jurors as to their desirability and submits the names of those they wish to strike. The first 12 individuals on the list who were not struck by either side comprise the jury. If both sides strike the same potential juror, each side has essentially lost a strike.

Mullin (1980) and the National Jury Project (1979) have suggested that extreme jurors are quite easy to spot and the greatest usefulness of carefully collected data lies in judiciously choosing among individuals who do not differ radically in overt characteristics. In making the final decisions, the National Jury Project (1979) has concluded that it is wise to carefully review the background and experiential information regarding the juror once again in light of the analysis of the case and the survey results. The network and investigation information should be consulted to determine its congruence or dissimilarity to the demographic predictions. Combining the findings with the in-court responses and behaviors of the potential juror should result in a rating for each person (e.g., on a scale of 1 to 5) as to his or her tendency to lean toward one side or the other. Observations of the group dynamics would next be included to evaluate each person's likely role in the final jury and whether he or she would be desirable or useful as a juror. This consideration might change the earlier assigned rating.

To compile the most comprehensive picture of jurors, all members of the jury selection team should be consulted in the final decision making. Reactions to each juror should be solicited from the client as well. To weigh the significance of stated data from each team member, opinions regarding a juror should be documented by specific behavioral examples. Even if information appears discrepant, team members should give their reports about a juror and leave in-depth discussion for a later time to resolve any confusion. Where consensus cannot be reached regarding a potential jury member, that person may either be ranked low in terms of desirability or struck due to the unpredictability of his or her profile.

Significant problems may arise at this stage of the process (Berman & Sales, 1977). Judges often set stringent time limits. If people working on different components of the jury selection procedures are not equally competent at collecting data, weighting of the data may be inaccurate. If certain individuals dominate the process, integration of the data may not occur. In fact, Berman and Sales (1977) assert that disillusionment is most apt to occur at this stage if data are loosely and uncertainly integrated, even if other processes have been rigorously coordinated and smoothly conducted.

THE STATE OF THE ART

There are many frustrations in store for those who wish to develop expertise in the field of jury selection. Finding litigants with the resources to allow for thorough use of available techniques is difficult. Recommending use of jury selection procedures may even appear unjustified when empirical proof of their value is lacking and outcome is unpredictable. Even when surrounded by piles of data, computer print-outs, observational materials, and inferences from minute behavioral changes, selectors must rely on their ability to utilize the information in accurate and effective ways. The myriad of factors involved in a trial will sometimes make even the most experienced and scientific selector of juries feel like relying on a coin toss.

One need look only at the dates of the majority of publications dealing with systematic jury selection to recognize that this field is barely out of its infancy. Without a doubt, further speculation and research will be directed toward jury selection, no matter what empirical and ethical issues surround it. An area such as this, with its potential for major impact on trial outcomes, is not going to be ignored or suppressed merely because of its controversial and difficult nature. Indeed the controversy and practical difficulties which currently surround systematic jury selection appear likely to encourage rather than discourage further experimentation, much of which seems bound to occur in the context of actual litigation.

A review article some 20 years from now may well scoff at the seemingly primitive methods developed when social scientists decided to make jury selection a "scientific" process. But however harshly they may ultimately be judged, the pioneering efforts of today's jury selectors have broken the ground and may well have provided the building blocks for more sophisticated and scientifically-based jury selection procedures—some of which may eventually have an extraordinarily profound impact upon our system of justice.

Diane R. Follingstad, Ph.D., a clinical and forensic psychologist, is an Associate Professor in the Clinical-Community Psychology program at the University of South Carolina. Dr. Follingstad is also in private practice, where she conducts forensic evaluations for both civil and criminal actions, consults with attorneys regrading jury selection, and helps prepare witnesses for courtroom testimony.

RESOURCES

Adkins, J. C. (1968-1969, December, January). Jury selection: An art? a science? or luck? *Trial Magazine*, pp. 37-39.

Adler, F. (1973). Socioeconomic factors influencing jury verdicts. *New York University Review of Law and Social Change, 3*, 1-10.

Adorno, T. W., Frenkel-Brunswik, E., Levinson, D. J., & Sanford, R. N. (1950). *The Authoritarian Personality.* New York: Harper and Row.

American Bar Association. (1974). *Standards Relating to the Administration of Criminal Justice.* Chicago: Author.

Argyle, M. (1969). *Social Interaction.* New York: Atherton Press.

Bennett, C. E. (1977). Psychological methods of jury selection in the typical criminal case. *Criminal Defense, 4*, 11-22.

Berk, R. A. (1976). Social science and jury selection: A case study of a civil suit. In G. Bermant, C. Nemeth, & N. Vidmar (Eds.), *Psychology and the Law* (pp. 283-297). New York: Lexington Books.

Berk, R. A., Hennessy, M., & Swan, J. (1977). The vagaries and vulgarities of "scientific" jury selection: A methodological evaluation. *Evaluation Quarterly, 1,* 143-158.

Berman, J., & Sales, B. D. (1977). A critical evaluation of the systematic approach to jury selection. *Criminal Justice and Behavior, 4,* 219-240.

Boehm, V. R. (1968). Mr. Prejudice, Miss Sympathy and the authoritarian personality: Application of psychological measuring techniques to the problem of jury bias. *Wisconsin Law Review, 1968,* 734-750.

Brodsky, S. (1977). *The Holiday Inn Caper: A Psychological Porthole Injury Selection.* Unpublished manuscript, University of Alabama, Tuscaloosa, AL.

Broeder, D. W. (1959). The University of Chicago jury project. *Nebraska Law Review, 38,* 744-760.

Broeder, D. W. (1965). *Voir dire* examinations: An empirical study. *Southern California Law Review, 38,* 503-528.

Bronson, E. J. (1970). On the conviction processes and representativeness of the death-qualified jury: An empirical study of Colorado veniremen. *Colorado Law Review, 42,* 1-32.

Brown, R. W. (1953). A determinant of the relationship between rigidity and authoritarianism. *Journal of Abnormal and Social Psychology, 48,* 469-476.

Campbell, S. (1972). The multiple functions of the criminal defense *voir dire* in Texas. *American Journal of Criminal Law, 1,* 255.

Center, R., Shomer, R., & Rodrigues, A. (1970). A field experiment in interpersonal persuasion using authoritative influence. *Journal of Personality, 38,* 392-403.

Chaikin, A. L., & Darley, J. M. (1973). Victim or perpetrator: Defensive attribution of responsibility and the need for order and justice. *Journal of Personality and Social Psychology, 30,* 268-275.

Christie, R. (1976). Probability vs. precedence: The social psychology of jury selection. In G. Bermant, C. Nemeth, & N. Vidmar (Eds.), *Psychology and the Law* (pp. 265-281). New York: Lexington Books.

Darrow, C. (1939, May). Attorney for the defense. *Esquire Magazine,* pp. 211-213.

Daugherty, M. (1976). *Juror Selection Methods of Trial Lawyers: Interviews with Ten Toledo Attorneys.* Unpublished manuscript, University of Toledo.

Diamond, S., & Zeisel, H. (1974). A courtroom experiment on juror selection and decision-making. *Personality and Social Psychology Bulletin, 1,* 276-277.

Ekman, P., & Friesen, W. V. (1969). Nonverbal leakage and uses to deception. *Psychiatry, 32,* 88-106.

Epstein, R. (1966). Aggression toward outgroups as a function of authoritarianism and imitation of aggressive models. *Journal of Personality and Social Psychology, 3,* 574-579.

Evenbeck, S. (1974). *Observers' Attributions of Causality.* Presented at the annual meeting of the Midwestern Psychological Association, Chicago, IL.

Frederick, J. T. (1978). Jury behavior: A psychologist examines jury selection. *Ohio Northern University Law Review, 5,* 571-585.

Fried, M., Kaplan, K., & Klein, K. (1975). Juror selection: An analysis of *voir dire.* In R. Simon (Ed.), *The Jury System in America: A Critical Overview* (pp. 47-66). Beverly Hills, CA: Sage Publications, Inc.

Friend, R. M., & Vinson, M. (1974). Leaning over backwards: Jurors' responses to defendants' attractiveness. *Journal of Communication, 24,* 124-129.

Goldberg, F. (1970). Toward expansion of Witherspoon: Capital scruples, jury bias, and use of psychological data to raise presumptions in the law. *Harvard Civil Rights Liberties Law Review, 5,* 53-69.

Grisham, T. L., & Lawless, S. F. (1973). Jurors judge justice: A survey of criminal jurors. *New Mexico Law Review, 3,* 352-363.

Harrington, D. C., & Dempsey, J. (1969). Psychological factors in jury selection. *Tennessee Law Review, 37,* 173-184.

Hayes, H. B. (1972). Applying persuasive techniques to trial proceedings. *South Carolina Law Review, 24,* 380.

Jurow, G. L. (1971). New data on the effect of a "death qualified" jury on the guilt determination process. *Harvard Law Review, 84,* 567-611.

Kairys, D., Schulman, J., & Harring, S. (1975). *The Jury System: New Methods for Reducing Prejudice.*

Philadelphia: National Jury Project and National Lawyers Guild.

Kallen, L. (1969). Peremptory challenges based upon juror background: A rational use? *Trial Lawyer's Guild, 13*, 143-165.

Kalven, H., & Zeisel, H. (1966). *The American Jury.* Boston: Little, Brown.

Kaplan, M. F., & Kemmerick, G. D. (1974). Juror judgment as information intergration: Combining evidential and nonevidential information. *Journal of Personality and Social Psychology, 31*, 493-499.

Katz, L. S. (1968-1969, December-January). The twelve man jury. *Trial Magazine*, pp. 39-42.

Keeton, R. E. (1973). *Trial Tactics and Methods* (2nd ed.). Boston: Little, Brown.

Long, R. E., & Ziller, R. C. (1965). Dogmatism and predecisional information search. *Journal of Applied Psychology, 49*, 376-378.

McConahay, J. B., Mullin, C. J., & Frederick, J. (1977). The uses of social sciences in trials with political and racial overtones: The trial of Joan Little. *Law and Contemporary Problems, 41*, 205-229.

McGuire, W. (1968). Personality and susceptibility to social influence. In E. F. Borgatta & W. W. Lambert, (Eds.), *Handbook of Personality Theory and Research* (pp. 1130-1187). Chicago: Rand McNally.

Mitchell, H., & Byrne, D. (1973). The defendant's dilemma: Effects of jurors' attitudes and authoritarianism of judicial decisions. *Journal of Personality and Social Psychology, 30*, 123-129.

Mullin, C. J. (1980). Jury selection techniques: Improving the odds of winning. In G. Cooke (Ed.), *The Role of the Forensic Psychologist* (pp. 141-162). Springfield, IL: C. C. Thomas Co.

National Jury Project. (1979). *Jurywork: Systematic Techniques.* National Jury Project, National Lawyers Guild, and the National Conference of Black Lawyers, Chicago, IL.

Padawer-Singer, A. M., Singer, A., & Singer, R. (1974). *Voir dire* by two lawyers: One essential safeguard. *Judicature, 57*, 386-391.

Phares, E., & Wilson, K. (1972). Responsibility attribution: Role of outcome severity, situational ambiguity, and internal-external control. *Journal of Personality, 40*, 392-406.

Reed, J. P. (1965). Jury deliberations, voting, and verdict trends. *Southwestern Social Science Quarterly, 65*, 361-374.

Rose, A. M., & Prell, A. E. (1955). Does the punishment fit the crime? A study in social valuation. *American Journal of Sociology, 61*, 247-259.

Rotter, J. B. (1966). Generalized expectancies for internal versus external control of reinforcement. *Psychological Monographs, 80*(1, Whole No. 609).

Saks, M. (1976). The limits of scientific jury selection: Ethical and empirical. *Jurimetrics Journal, Fall*, 3-22.

Saks, M., & Hastie, R. (1978). *Social Psychology in Court.* New York: Van Nostrand Reinhold Co.

Saks, M., Werner, C., & Ostrom, T. (1975). The presumption of innocence and the American juror. *Journal of Contemporary Law, 2*, 46-54.

Schulman, J. (1973). A systematic approach to successful jury selection. *Guild Notes, 2*, 13-20.

Schulman, J., Shaver, P., Colman, R., Emrich, B., & Christie, R. (1973, June). Recipe for a jury. *Psychology Today*, pp. 37-84.

Simon, R. J. (1967). *The Jury and the Defense of Insanity.* Boston: Little, Brown.

Sosis, R. (1974). Internal-external control and the perception of responsibility of another for an accident. *Journal of Personality and Social Psychology, 31*, 393-399.

Stephan, C. (1975). Selective characteristics of jurors and litigants: Their influence on juries' verdicts. In R. J. Simon (Ed.), *The Jury System in America: A Critical Overview.* Beverly Hills, CA: Sage.

Suggs, D., & Sales, B. D. (1978). The art and science of conducting the *voir dire. Professional Psychology, 9*, 367-388.

Tapp, J. L., & Keniston, A. (1976, September). *Wounded Knee—Advocate or Expert: Recipe for a Fair Juror?* Paper presented at the 89th Annual Convention of the American Psychological Association, Washington, DC.

Tapp, J. L., & Kohlberg, L. (1971). Developing senses of law and legal justice. *Journal of Social Issues, 27*, 65-69.

Tapp, J. L., & Levine, F. J. (1974). Legal socialization: Strategies for an ethical legality. *Stanford Law Review, 27,* 1-72.

Tivnan, C. (1975, November 16). Jury by trial. *New York Times Magazine,* pp. 30, 54.

Vidmar, N. (1974). Retributive and utilitarian motives and other correlates of Canadian attitudes toward the death penalty. *The Canadian Psychologist, 15,* 337-356.

Vidulich, R. N., & Kaiman, I. P. (1961). The effects of information source status and dogmatism upon conformity behavior. *Journal of Abnormal and Social Psychology, 63,* 639-642.

Wilson, W. (1964). *Belief in Capital Punishment and Jury Performances.* Unpublished manuscript, University of Texas, Austin, TX.

Zeisel, H., & Diamond, S. (1978). The effect of peremptory challenges on the jury and verdict. *Stanford Law Review, 30,* 491-531.

INTRODUCTION TO SECTION VII: LEGAL REGULATION OF PSYCHOLOGY, PSYCHIATRY, AND OTHER MENTAL HEALTH PRACTICE

Thus far, the chapters in this volume have emphasized the various ways in which psychology, psychiatry, and other mental health disciplines and behavioral sciences contribute to the legal system. The relationship between law and the mental health professions, however, is not simply a "one-way street." Mental health practice, like most professional activity in modern society, is heavily regulated by law. Today, more than at any time in the past, psychologists, psychiatrists, and other mental health clinicians must be aware of and conform their practices to not only professional standards of care but also the growing and often complex demands of the law. In this final section, two psychologists, both of whom are also attorneys, examine some of the more significant ways in which mental health practice is currently regulated by the law.

Robert Woody's chapter explains the general application of malpractice law to mental health professionals. Dr. Woody begins by describing the various theories of malpractice, noting that most malpractice claims against mental health clinicians are grounded upon a theory of negligence. He then describes the basic elements of proof in a negligence lawsuit, emphasizing the nature of the duty owed by clinicians to their patients. Finally, after alerting clinicians to the problem of vicarious liability and the demise of sovereign immunity, Dr. Woody offers a number of suggestions clinicians should find helpful in avoiding and defending against claims of professional malpractice.

After Dr. Woody's general introduction to the law of malpractice, Charles Ewing explores a number of specific legal issues to which mental health clinicians must be responsive in their everyday practices. Specifically, Dr. Ewing's chapter deals with informed consent to treatment, confidentiality and privacy, the assessment and treatment of "dangerous" and suicidal patients, and the legal limits of the clinician-patient relationship. Under this final rubric—legal limits of the clinician-patient relationship— Dr. Ewing details the legal system's response to a clinician's sexual involvement with patients, controversial treatment modalities, and patient abandonment.

PUBLIC POLICY, MALPRACTICE LAW, AND THE MENTAL HEALTH PROFESSIONAL: SOME LEGAL AND CLINICAL GUIDELINES

Robert Henley Woody

Malpractice, by definition, means a bad, wrongful, or inappropriate action by a professional. But beyond this simplistic starting point, definition of this term requires a complex social analysis. For professional malpractice is ultimately defined by public policies designed to safeguard society's human resources.

In the everyday pursuit of income, it is often easy for the professional to make false assumptions about his or her rights. It is sometimes believed, consciously or unconsciously, that membership in a recognized, duly licensed, and certified discipline conveys some inalienable right to self-determination in professional practices. Such a view is the first step toward malpractice. For, in fact, the professional has no such inalienable right. Professionalism is nothing more than a framework fashioned by society to categorize services for its members.

As society recognizes a profession, it imposes upon that discipline a concomitant responsibility or duty—a set of expectations as to what should and should not occur in professional practice. In other words, the *quid pro quo* for societal recognition of professionalism is professional accountability to society. When society judges professional practice to be substandard, it attaches legal liability. It is this interface between public policy and professionalism which creates the legal framework for malpractice.

This chapter examines some of the more significant legal theories under which a mental health professional may be held liable for professional malpractice—aspects of the law with which every clinician should be familiar. The emphasis here is upon broad legal principles rather than the elements of specific forms of malpractice, a number of which are covered in some detail in the following chapter. Among the legal principles to be discussed herein are negligence, standard of care, vicarious liability, and immunity from suit. Following an examination of these legal doctrines, the chapter concludes with some general remarks regarding the prevention and defense of malpractice suits against mental health professionals.

LEGAL THEORIES OF
PROFESSIONAL MALPRACTICE

In legal theory, there are a number of approaches to professional malpractice. Most malpractice claims are grounded upon a theory of negligence—that is, a claim that the professional failed to meet proper standards of care in rendering professional services, thereby breaching a legal duty to the recipient of such services. In analyzing over 300 lawsuits brought against psychotherapists, Hogan (1979) found that two-thirds of such suits were premised upon claims of negligence in treatment and/or diagnosis.

Yet, negligence is far from the only source of liability in professional medical or mental health services. In the area of medical malpractice (which generally encompasses malpractice by mental health professionals, whether or not they are physicians), King (1977) has noted that "claims against practitioners may also arise from intentional misconduct, breaches of contracts guaranteeing specific therapeutic result, defamation, invasion of privacy...and failures to prevent injuries to certain non-patients" (p. 4). Moreover, in the previously listed analysis of malpractice actions against psychotherapists, Hogan (1979) found that:

more than twenty-five types of actions were
brought including involuntary servitude, false
arrest, trespass, malicious infliction of emotional
distress, abuse of process, loss of liberty,
misrepresentation, libel, assault and battery,
malicious prosecution and false imprisonment. (p.
7)

Furthermore, Trent (1978) has identified 12 types of
claims filed against psychiatrists, including claims of: (a)
improper hospital commitment, (b) death, (c) pressing for
fee collection, (d) subpoenas to testify, (e) sexual relations
with patients, (f) adverse drug reactions, (g) unauthorized
release of confidential information causing damage to the
patient, (h) suicide, (i) improper administrative handling,
(j) electroconvulsive therapy (ECT), (k) improper
treatment, and (l) injury to a nonpatient during
professional services.

Each of these various types of legal action has its own
elements of proof (i.e., legal and factual particulars which
must be established by the party bringing the lawsuit).
Specification of the legal requirements for each cause of
action mentioned above is beyond the scope of this
chapter. Readers interested in examining the legal
elements of any particular cause of action are referred to
Prosser (1971). In general, however, it may be noted that:

The essential elements necessary to support a
malpractice action are fourfold. Ordinarily, a
plaintiff must demonstrate that: (1) a legal duty
existed between the practitioner and the injured
party; (2) the practitioner was derelict in that duty
(either through an action or through an omission);
(3) harm or injury of some sort; and (4) the harm
or injury was directly and proximately caused by
the professional's dereliction of duty. (Hogan,
1979, p. 8)

NEGLIGENCE

Since negligence is by far the most common basis for
malpractice lawsuits against mental health professionals,

it may be helpful to examine in some detail the elements of a negligence action, many of which, are common to any malpractice action.

The first element in a negligence action (indeed in any malpractice action) against a mental health professional is the *existence* of a duty owed by the professional (defendant) to the patient (plaintiff). The practitioner's duty ordinarily arises out of a professional relationship with the patient. The professional relationship is usually clear-cut and easily defined. Once the mental health professional accepts the patient for service, a legally defined relationship has been established and duty attaches. It should be noted, however, that subsequent alterations in the relationship between practitioner and patient may raise significant legal questions as to the existence of the relationship and, hence, the practitioner's duty.

In the mental health field perhaps the most common and troublesome "alteration" in the relationship between practitioner and patient is termination. For example, what if, after the service (e.g., psychotherapy) has begun, practitioner and patient jointly agree that the relationship should be personal rather than professional? Of course, the professional relationship can be terminated—indeed, most professional relationships are eventually terminated. In the mental health field, however, there are certain forms of relationship (e.g., the psychotherapist-patient relationship) in which inherent conditions, such as transference and countertransference, may provide conflicts which must be resolved therapeutically. If one of these conditions was the basis, consciously or unconsciously, for a decision to alter the relationship, it seems unlikely that the mental health professional would be exempted from the legally-defined relationship or absolved from the duties which accompany that relationship.

As a specific example, if a psychotherapist and patient mutually agreed to have a sexual relationship, there would be an abrogation of the professional relationship, but there would also be a violation of the therapist's duty to the patient.

The second element in a negligence action against a mental health professional is the *nature* of the duty owed by the practitioner to the patient. As a general matter, the nature of the practitioner's duty may be stated as follows. Professionals are required to (a) possess a reasonable degree of learning and skill common to their professions, (b) exercise reasonable care and diligence in the provision of services, (c) exercise their best judgment in the application of skills and knowledge to the patient's problems, (d) render services founded upon up-to-date information, and (e) conform their practices to methods approved by the profession to which they belong (Kramer, 1976). The specific nature of the professional's duty is closely related to the concept of standard of care, which will receive more detailed attention later in this chapter.

The third element to be proven in the negligence action is breach of duty by the mental health professional. Proof of this element is twofold. First, the plaintiff must prove that the allegedly negligent action or omission occurred. In the mental health field, where interactions between practitioner and patient are often not observed by anyone other than the parties themselves, proof that a negligent commission or omission actually occurred will often be difficult. Nevertheless, failure to prove that the alleged action or omission occurred will result in a complete denial of recovery by the plaintiff, regardless of any other evidence. In certain malpractice cases, the legal doctrine of *res ipsa loquitur* ("the thing speaks for itself") may be available to a plaintiff, but this doctrine is rarely applicable in suits against mental health professionals.

Second, having established that the action or omission took place, the plaintiff bears the burden of showing that the action or omission was indeed negligent—that is, that it violated the duty of care owed to him or her by the practitioner. Except where the alleged negligence is so gross as to be obvious to lay persons (which is rare in the mental health field) expert testimony by another practitioner of the same (or a closely related) profession is generally required.

The fourth element necessary to the negligence action is proof of harm. Even the most grossly negligent act or omission by a practitioner will not result in liability unless some harm occurs. The harm may be physical or emotional, serious or minimal, to the patient or to a third party. But in *every* case, actual harm must be proven. Given the nature of mental health practice, many resulting harms are subjective in nature (e.g., the worsening of the patient's already impaired emotional functioning) and difficult to prove. Nevertheless, here as in all negligence suits, the rule is "no harm, no liability."

The fifth and final element essential to recovery in a negligence suit (or any malpractice action) is proof of causation. It is not enough for the plaintiff to establish that he or she has been harmed and that the practitioner violated some duty of care owed to him or her. The plaintiff must establish that the practitioner's negligent act or omission was *both* a *cause in fact* and a *proximate cause* of the harm which he or she suffered.

An act of omission is a "cause in fact" of a harm when that harm would not have occurred *but for* the act or omission. Proof of *proximate* causation requires the plaintiff to further establish that the harm was the *direct* and *foreseeable* result of the practitioner's negligent act or omission.

STANDARD OF CARE

Establishing and maintaining a standard of care is probably the most important safeguard against legal action that can be taken by any mental health professional. The fundamental point is that the patient has a right to expect a certain quality of service. Thus, the professional must fulfill the legal "objective" requirements—that is, what the reasonable patient could expect of the typical professional. Of course, the "typical professional" is a fiction, and the quest for a definition is commonly the sum and substance of legal cases based on the standard of care issue.

The key is that all that is required is the possession and exercise of knowledge and skill common to members of the profession in good standing (Prosser, 1971). Furthermore, the professional has an obligation to keep abreast of scientific advances and to elevate the quality of practice within the bounds of reasonable expenditure of finances and personal effort. As Hogan (1979) states:

In determining whether a professional was derelict in her or his duty, the courts will ask whether the practitioner conformed to the standard of care required, measured by the degree of ability or skill possessed by other practitioners in the application of their skills; and the special or extraordinary skill of specialists, if the practitioner has represented himself or herself as such. (p. 8)

In summary, the professional does not have to be flawless. As Wilkinson (1982) observes:

An error in judgment is not actionable [when the clinician acted] in good faith, had made sufficient inquiry and examination into the cause and nature of the patient's disturbance, had exercised the requisite care in making the diagnosis and prescribing treatment, and otherwise had not deviated from generally accepted standards and practices. (p. 75)

At one time, the standard of care owed by any professional was determined strictly by reference to the immediate locale in which the professional practiced. This "locality rule" measured the performance of practitioners against that of nearby colleagues and was designed to protect rural practitioners and others who, by virtue of the location of their practices, would have difficulty keeping up with recent advances in their fields. With the advent of improved communications and the availability of professional journals and continuing education courses, however, courts and legislatures began to hold professionals to a national standard of care. Under current law, in many jurisdictions, mental health professionals, particularly those who hold themselves out as specialists, are most likely to be held to a national standard of care, as opposed to the standard of care maintained in the local community in which they practice.

When professionals hold special credentials, such as "board certification" in psychiatry or clinical psychology or national certification as a clinical social worker, such credentials have implications for the standard of care they must maintain. Instead of being compared to psychiatrists, psychologists, or social workers *in general*, the "certified" practitioner will be compared with fellow professionals holding the same (or comparable) status.

Professing to have expertise in a specific area of practice (e.g., sex therapy) may also elevate the standard of care to which a practitioner will be held, even though the practitioner making the claim does not have any special credential. For example, public policy (as reflected in various legal decisions) would seem to require that if mental health professionals claim to be able to perform sex therapy, they should meet the standards set by the American Association of Sex Educators, Counselors, and Therapists, even though they may not have acquired the status of Certified Sex Therapist from that organization (Woody, 1983b).

It is also worth noting that the standard of care may vary as a function of the theoretical "school" to which the mental health professional adheres. In order to invoke legal protection for mental health practice on the basis of one's particular school of thought, the school must be one generally recognized as legitimate. Prosser (1971) offers the following definition: "A 'school' must be a recognized one with definite principles, and it must be the line of thought of at least a respectable minority of the profession" (p. 163).

Even with this definition, however, there is uncertainty. Could the "definite principles" be without scientific basis (e.g., based upon religious appeal)? Probably not in psychiatry and psychology, since both these professions profess to have a scientific basis for their practices. Could the "respectable minority" be only a handful of practitioners? No clear-cut quantification is possible, but it is likely that a court would weigh not only the number, but both the academic background and the stature of those practitioners comprising the minority.

Judicial recognition of various schools of thought and practice may prove helpful to a clinician where there is doubt as to the standard of care. But such recognition certainly does *not* offer a clinician any *carte blanche* to an idiosyncratic determination of treatment methodologies. If there is any question as to what theory or school should apply in a given case, Glenn (1974) believes that the closest theoretical school of thought would likely be determinative for the court.

Given the necessity to encourage innovation, public policy does not categorically foreclose experimentation in psychiatry, psychology, and the other mental health disciplines. The state of the science (or art) can only be enhanced by reaching beyond the proven and seeking the improved. As Wilkinson (1982) notes:

> Difficulties arise when the psychiatrist [or other mental health professional] wishes to pursue a new treatment, but at the same time does not want to risk exposure to potential liability should the treatment prove ineffective, or even harmful to the patient. In such a situation, one must balance the need to protect the patient by assuring that only proven treatments are used, with the need to develop new methods that produce even better and more effective results. [U]nless modern psychiatry is allowed to explore new methods of treatment, the future growth of the profession and discovery of new cures will be greatly inhibited. (p. 76)

The willingness of some courts to indulge experimentation, however, should not be read as giving license to the reckless abandonment of knowledge and logic. Professional actions should always be predicated upon a scientific or academic rationale.

The balancing test invoked by Wilkinson has a time-honored place in law. Accordingly, a court would listen to the scientific rationale for an innovative procedure and would likely give the professional (if of respectable stature) the benefit of the doubt. But the court would still require that the risk not outweigh the possible benefits to the patient and society alike, and that the patient's rights to self-determination be honored.

It is helpful to both the professional and the patient to have the standard of care openly acknowledged and set forth in specific terms at the outset of treatment. A written statement of what services are to be provided and the qualitative conditions that will be maintained fosters a contract-like understanding between the professional and patient. Similarly, the professional should purposefully inform the patient about his or her qualifications, and should gain informed consent from the patient for all interventions. This meeting of the minds avoids subsequent misunderstandings. While contractual in nature, it does not, however, offer the professional any immunity from suit. Indeed, any attempt to get the patient to waive a right to sue in the event of professional negligence is likely to be found unconscionable and, therefore, invalid.

VICARIOUS LIABILITY

For the most part, mental health professionals are legally responsible only for their own malpractice. Given the team approach commonly employed in the provision of mental health services, however, it is important to note that professionals may acquire "vicarious liability"—that is, they may be held responsible for the acts of others, even if they had no contact at all with the patient. The concept of vicarious liability is well known to lawyers, particularly those who represent victims of alleged malpractice. As Shandell (1981) has urged trial lawyers: "The rule in medical malpractice is 'don't leave anybody out.' Sue everyone who may be liable" (p. 4).

How does a mental health professional acquire vicarious liability for malpractice? The primary fashion in which vicarious liability arises is through supervision of other mental health care providers. Mental health practitioners who provide on-going clinical supervision to other clinicians have a duty to stay informed of their supervisees' clinical performance, to insure that supervisees do not deviate from appropriate standards of care or create unreasonable risks of harm to patients, and to intervene to prevent harm to a patient under the care of a supervisee. Mental health professionals who employ other clinicians may also be held vicariously liable even if they do not directly supervise their employees' clinical work. The law recognizes a doctrine called *respondeat superior* ("let the master answer") under which an employer may be held to answer in money damages for the negligence of his or her employees.

Additionally, mental health professionals risk liability for the acts of others with whom they are merely associated in practice. The team approach in mental health care implies a duty to monitor the performance of fellow team members, and liability could attach to one team member as a result of the negligence of another team member. Outside of professional partnership arrangements (where clinicians are almost always liable for the malpractice of their partners), however, vicarious liability of this sort is unlikely unless the mental health professional was also directly involved in the treatment of the patient or had some supervisory responsibility for the clinical work of the treating clinician(s).

THE DEMISE OF IMMUNITY

At one time the doctrine of sovereign immunity precluded any legal action against a state. And since state-employed mental health professionals were agents of the state, they enjoyed an immunity from legal actions arising out of their employment-related activities. Recently, however, there has been a trend toward abrogating such all-inclusive protection of state employees. Well-publicized cases of abuse and society's increased demand for accountability by professionals have led many courts and legislatures to find that such protection from suit can no longer be justified. Thus, while most states continue to enjoy sovereign immunity (i.e., the state, itself, may not be sued without its consent), distinctions have been made between state employee functions which may give rise to legal action and those which remain immune from suit. Such distinctions commonly rest upon whether the employee's function was "discretionary" or "ministerial."

Discretionary functions are those that relate to policy making. Ministerial functions are those related to technical or service duties. In *National Bank of South Dakota v. Leir* (1982), the Court stated the general rule with regard to such functions:

Immunity extends to an employee who, while acting in the scope of his employment, exercises a discretionary function. [But] a state employee who fails to perform a merely ministerial duty is liable for the proximate results of his failure to any person to whom he owes performance of such duty. (p. 847)

For the most part, direct clinical activities of state-employed mental health professionals are deemed ministerial in nature. Since such professionals owe a duty of care to their patients, breach of that duty renders them subject to lawsuit despite the fact that they were acting as state employees at the time the duty was breached. A recent example of this emerging limit upon immunity is presented in *Frank v. State of Utah* (1980). In *Frank*, a state-employed psychologist was alleged to have negligently handled the case of a university student who committed suicide. In upholding the plaintiff's right to sue against a defense of immunity, the Utah Supreme Court held that the acts of the psychologist were ministerial, not discretionary, and, therefore, not protected by the common-law principle of sovereign immunity.

Even where a state-employed mental health professional acts in what appears to be a discretionary function, courts may still find reasons to disallow a claim of immunity from suit. In *Koepf v. County of York* (1977), for instance, the Nebraska Supreme Court considered claims of immunity asserted by various public employees in a wrongful death action. The suit was brought by the natural mother of an illegitimate child who had been removed from her custody and placed in foster care, where the child died. The Court held that immunity would extend to the county judge, the public prosecutor, and the sheriff for their roles in the removal and placement of the child, but refused to extend immunity to the social worker who had arranged the placement. The Court recognized that the process of making a foster care placement was discretionary in a literal sense, but found that the social worker's role did not reach the level of a basic policy decision and was, therefore, primarily ministerial. Consequently, the Court held, the social worker was subject to suit on a negligence theory.

AVOIDING AND
DEFENDING AGAINST CLAIMS
OF PROFESSIONAL MALPRACTICE

Obviously the first step in avoiding a malpractice suit is to become aware of the pertinent legal principles of malpractice, such as those described above. All clinicians should be fully aware of the potential for malpractice claims in every case they handle. They need not, however, indeed should not, overreact to this potential, but should always strive to conform all aspects of their practices to the standards of care applicable to their professions. As stated in the opening of this chapter, the view that professional status conveys some inalienable right to self-determination in clinical practice is the first step toward malpractice.

Conformity to applicable standards of care requires knowledge of those standards. Most professional organizations in the mental health field have both codes of ethics and written guidelines for the delivery of professional services. For example, the American Psychological Association has published not only the *Ethical Principles of Psychologists* (1981a) but also *Specialty Guidelines for the Delivery of Services by Clinical Psychologists* (1981b). Other professional groups have issued similar publications (see, e.g., American Psychiatric Association, 1981). If clinicians do nothing else to protect themselves from malpractice claims, they should become familiar with such publications and conform their practices to the standards dictated therein.

Even the strictest adherence to such professional standards and guidelines, however, will not insulate the clinician from the possibility of a lawsuit. As the following chapter indicates, legally imposed standards often go well beyond those set forth by the professions. Legally imposed standards are often more difficult to discern, but they clearly must be followed. Ignorance is no excuse, even for the busy clinician. There are a number of good publications to which the clinician can and should turn for guidance— see, for example, Barton and Sanborn (1978), Cohen (1979), Gutheil and Appelbaum (1982), and Sadoff (1982). When in doubt, of course, the clinician's best source of information and advice is a knowledgeable attorney.

In addition to becoming aware of and conforming to appropriate standards of care, the clinician should communicate those standards to his or her patients. Keeping patients well informed about treatment and what they have a right to expect from the clinician is a good defense against allegations of malpractice. Indeed, some clinicians (e.g., Brodsky, 1978; Schwitzgebel, 1975) have recommended a contractual approach whereby treatment is prefaced by an explicit agreement between clinician and patient specifying procedures to be followed, likely results, risks, fees, and the professional's responsibility to the patient. As indicated earlier, however, any attempt to secure a waiver by patients of their rights to sue the clinician in the event of negligence is likely to be unenforceable.

Clinicians should not only conform their own practices to appropriate standards of care but should also strive to assure similar conformity by team members, supervisees, partners, and others for whose malpractice they may be held to answer. In this regard, it is most prudent for clinicians to assume that they *will be* liable for the negligent acts of their team colleagues, supervisees, and partners. Such an assumption, while not always valid, will lead to the exercise of greater care by clinicians in their professional relationships and, therefore, to the minimization of the potential for malpractice claims.

Clinicians employed by governmental or government-funded agencies should likewise assume that they *will be* liable for acts of malpractice even though they may be committed in the scope of the clinician's governmental employment. Government-employed clinicians should conform their practices to the normally applicable standards of care for their professions and should always carry their own malpractice insurance.

Finally, all clinicians should take great care to assure contemporaneous written documentation of all aspects of care in every case. *Written* informed consent from the patient should be obtained wherever feasible and certainly in every case involving experimental or controversial treatments. Such informed consent should also be accompanied by a written understanding between clinician and patient as to the services to be provided and any conditions or exceptions thereto. It should be kept in mind, however, that such a "meeting of the minds," while contractual in nature, will not provide the clinician with any immunity from suit *per se*.

Written documentation in the form of clear and detailed clinical notes made at the time of treatment is also essential. Indeed, such documentation of what the clinician did or did not do to or for the patient—and when—often provides the best defense against allegations of malpractice. In this age of increasing litigiousness, it seems no exaggeration to assert that the clinician should regard every clinical record as a potential piece of evidence, perhaps crucial evidence, in a lawsuit.

Robert Henley Woody, Ph.D., Sc.D., J.D., is a Professor of Psychology at the University of Nebraska. An attorney and clinical/forensic psychologist, who maintains private practices in both disciplines, Dr. Woody is a Diplomate in Clinical Psychology, Forensic Psychology, and Psychological Hypnosis; a Fellow of the American Psychological Association, the American Association of Marriage and Family Therapy, the Society for Personality Assessment, and the American Society of Clinical Hypnosis; and a member of the Bar in both Nebraska and Florida.

RESOURCES

American Psychiatric Association. (1981). *The Principles of Medical Ethics with Annotations Especially Applicable to Psychiatry.* Washington, DC: Author.

American Psychological Association. (1981a). *Ethical Principles of Psychologists.* Washington, DC: Author.

American Psychological Association. (1981b). *Specialty Guidelines for the Delivery of Services by Clinical Psychologists.* Washington, DC: Author.

Barton, W. E., & Sanborn, C. J. (Eds.). (1978). *Law and the Mental Health Professions.* New York: International Universities Press.

Brodsky, S. L. (1978). Buffalo Bill's defunct now: Vulnerability of mental health professionals to malpractice. In W. E. Barton & C. J. Sanborn (Eds.), *Law and the Mental Health Professions* (pp. 119-132). New York: International Universities Press.

Cohen, R. J. (1979). *Malpractice, a Guide for Mental Health Professionals.* New York: Free Press.

Frank v. State of Utah, 613 P.2d 517 (Utah 1980).

Glenn, R. D. (1974). Standard of care in administering non-traditional psychotherapy. *University of California, Davis Law Review, 7,* 56-83.

Gutheil, T., & Appelbaum, P. (1982). *Clinical Handbook of Psychiatry and the Law.* New York: McGraw-Hill.

Hogan, D. B. (1979). *The Regulation of Psychotherapists, Volume III. A Review of Malpractice Suits in the United States.* Cambridge, MA: Ballinger Publishing.

King, Joseph H., Jr. (1977). *The Law of Medical Malpractice.* St. Paul, MN: West Publishing.

Koepf v. County of York, 251 N.W.2d 866 (Nebraska, 1977).

Kramer, C. (1976). *Medical Malpractice* (4th ed.). New York: Practising Law Institute.

National Bank of South Dakota v. Leir, 325 N.W.2d 845 (South Dakota, 1982).

Prosser, W. L. (1971). *Handbook of the Laws of Torts* (4th ed.). St. Paul, MN: West Publishing.

Sadoff, R. L. (1982). *Legal Issues in the Care of Psychiatric Patients.* New York: Springer.

Schwitzgebel, R. K. (1975). A contractual model for the protection of the rights of institutionalized mental patients. *American Psychologist, 30*, 815-820.

Shandell, R. E. (1981). *The Preparation and Trial of Medical Malpractice Cases.* New York: Law Journal Seminars-Press.

Trent, C. L. (1978). Psychiatric malpractice insurance and its problems: An overview. In W. E. Barton & C. J. Sanborn (Eds.), *Law and the Mental Health Professions* (pp. 101-117). New York: International Universities Press.

Wilkinson, A. P. (1982). Psychiatric malpractice: Identifying areas of liability. *Trial, 18*, 73-77, 89-90.

Woody, R. H. (1983a). Avoiding malpractice in psychotherapy. In P. A. Keller & L. G. Ritt (Eds.), *Innovations in Clinical Practice: A Source Book* (Vol. 2, pp. 205-216). Sarasota, FL: Professional Resource Exchange, Inc.

Woody, R. H. (1983b). Ethical and legal aspects of sexual issues. In J. D. Woody & R. H. Woody (Eds.), *Sexual Issues in Family Therapy* (pp. 153-167). Rockville, MD: Aspen Systems.

MENTAL HEALTH CLINICIANS AND THE LAW: AN OVERVIEW OF CURRENT LAW GOVERNING PROFESSIONAL PRACTICE

Charles Patrick Ewing

Psychology, psychiatry, and the other mental health professions have long histories of self-regulation. Each of these professions has its own set of self-imposed and largely self-enforced ethical standards, educational requirements, licensing prerequisites, and standards for professional practice (see e.g., American Psychiatric Association, 1981; American Psychological Association, 1981; Hogan, 1979).

In recent years, however, self-regulation of these professions has, in many aspects, been supplemented if not replaced by legal regulation. The courts, legislatures, and governmental administrative bodies have begun to fashion rules of law which now govern much of professional mental health practice.

While many such rules of law reflect no more than a legal codification of existing professional standards and requirements, much of the legal regulation of the mental health professions goes well beyond what these professions have long demanded of themselves. Thus, the contemporary practitioner can no longer be content merely to be aware of and follow the standards imposed by his or her profession. If for no other reason than self-protection, today's mental health clinician must be aware of and conform his or her practice to the growing and often complex demands of the law.

The purpose of this chapter is to provide mental health practitioners with a practical, understandable, and concise (though by no means comprehensive) overview of some of the current legal rules to which they must be responsive in their everyday practices. Issues to be considered include: (a) informed consent to treatment, (b) confidentiality and privacy, (c) the assessment and treatment of "dangerous" and suicidal individuals, and (d) legal limits of the clinician-patient relationship.

Before beginning to examine these issues, a note of caution is in order. Most of the legal rules which govern mental health practice have been fashioned by state courts and legislatures. Thus, such rules often vary considerably between and among jurisdictions. The discussion which follows will highlight those general rules which seem to have the most significant implications for everyday clinical practice. Many of the rules to be considered have been widely adopted among the states. The reader should *not*, however, assume that this discussion necessarily presents an accurate description of the law in the particular jurisdiction in which he or she practices.

Every mental health professional should become familiar with the laws pertaining to professional practice in his or her own state. In most states, licensing boards and state professional associations are an excellent source of information for the clinician who is uncertain as to the current state of the law governing his or her practice. In dealing with specific legal problems, the clinician's best source of advice is, of course, a knowledgeable attorney.

INFORMED CONSENT TO TREATMENT

THE DOCTRINE OF INFORMED CONSENT

The doctrine of informed consent today applicable to mental health practice has its roots in the common-law regulation of medical and surgical practice. This doctrine, which first emerged in case law in the late 1950s (see, e.g., *Salgo v. Leland Stanford Jr. University Board of Trustees*, 1957) and is still evolving in many jurisdictions, dictates in general terms the nature of information which must be given to patients so that they may decide for themselves whether to undergo a proposed treatment or procedure.

Stated broadly, the doctrine of informed consent requires the treating clinician to explain to the patient, prior to treatment, the nature of the patient's illness, the nature of the proposed treatment, the likelihood of success, available alternative treatments and their likelihood of success, and reasonably foreseeable risks of treatment and nontreatment. The doctrine further requires that the patient be competent to consent (i.e., have the necessary mental capacity to understand the information conveyed by the clinician and to weigh rationally the risks and benefits of the proposed treatment) and that the patient's consent be given voluntarily (i.e., free from significant coercion).

THE THREE ELEMENTS OF INFORMED CONSENT

Essentially, informed consent has three legal elements, all of which must be satisfied in every case but none of which has been clearly delineated by the law. These elements are (a) information, (b) competence, and (c) voluntariness.

Information. The doctrine of informed consent requires that the patient be given sufficient information on which to base a rational and informed decision. But how much information is sufficient?

To date, neither the courts nor the professions have provided mental health practitioners with particular guidelines regarding the sufficiency of information necessary to secure informed consent. For the most part, it appears that individual practitioners have a reasonable amount of leeway and that, as Sadoff (1982) has written, "in the practice of psychotherapy or mental health treatment it [is] an art to determine how much to tell the patient and what to withhold" (p. 8).

Generally, mental health clinicians may safely exercise their own discretion and tailor disclosure to the individual needs of the patient as long as they provide an honest and accurate appraisal of the main issues covered by the doctrine: namely, the patient's condition, the nature of the proposed treatment, likely benefits, foreseeable risks, and alternatives.

Perhaps the single issue which has most troubled many practitioners as well as some courts is the extent to which untoward side effects of the proposed treatment must be disclosed and explained to the patient. Certainly all *major* side effects should be disclosed and explained, even though their occurrence may be quite unlikely in a given case. Yet the clinician must exercise care not to frighten patients excessively and possibly deter them from accepting necessary treatment. Perhaps the best advice to the mental health professional is to resolve any doubt in favor of disclosure, being careful to present accurate data regarding the incidence of untoward side effects, presenting such data in a serious but matter-of-fact, nonthreatening fashion, and ultimately respecting the patient's autonomy with regard to the level of risk he or she is willing to accept.

Competence. Competence to consent to treatment has also not been clearly defined by the law and remains an issue to be approached by the clinician on a case-by-case basis. Some of the more general issues of legal competence have been addressed in earlier chapters (see, e.g., Chapter 2 on competence to stand trial and Chapter 8 on the right to refuse treatment). Generally, in the present context, competence refers to the patient's mental capacity to understand the information conveyed by the clinician and to make a rational choice regarding the proposed treatment.

The assessment of competence to consent to treatment is often a difficult and complex task and there is no "acid" test upon which the clinician may rely in order to insure informed consent. While there is a tendency to assume competence when a patient accepts the proposed treatment, such an assumption is not always warranted. As Halleck (1980) has observed, "Whenever a patient has a serious mental illness which interferes with his cognitive functioning, his perception, or his capacity to behave in a self-serving manner, the question of his competency to accept or refuse treatment is always at issue" (pp. 84-85). The "rule of thumb," as Gutheil and Appelbaum (1982) point out, "is that if there is any reason to doubt the patient's competency...a careful examination for competency should be conducted and recorded" (p. 162).

It is also worth noting that, as a rule, minors are *per se* incompetent to consent to treatment. In some jurisdictions there are exceptions for so-called "emancipated minors," but such exceptions vary significantly from state to state. Thus, clinicians are well advised to become familiar with the laws in their own jurisdiction before relying upon a minor's consent to treatment.

Voluntariness. In the eyes of the law, consent of any sort is not valid unless it is freely given. The voluntariness of consent to treatment is often an issue because many patients agree to seek mental health treatment only to avoid some threatened negative consequence such as loss of employment, revocation of probation or parole status, loss of child custody, and so forth. In these and other cases in which patients are responding in large measure to significant external coercion, it is difficult to assert that their consent to treatment is freely given.

As a legal matter, however, as long as the treating clinician is not directly involved in such coercion, it is rather unlikely that he or she would be subject to liability for treating a patient whose consent was something less than voluntary. Yet it is worth noting that regardless of the law, mental health professionals may have special ethical responsibilities in treating patients whose consent to treatment has been influenced by third party "coercion." For a discussion of some of the ethical concerns which arise in such cases, see Ewing (1983).

EXCEPTIONS TO THE DOCTRINE
OF INFORMED CONSENT

Implied Consent. Courts have long held that informed consent to treatment need not be obtained in certain emergency circumstances, generally cases in which immediate medical action is required to save the life or safeguard the health of a patient who is for some reason (e.g., unconsciousness) unable to give consent. In such cases, consent is said to be implied on the basis of what has been called the "reasonable person" test. The assumption underlying implied consent is that under the circumstances, a reasonable person would consent to treatment.

The *Restatement of Torts* (2d ed.) (American Law Institute, 1965) offers the following classic example of implied consent in an emergency situation. A man is run over by a train and taken unconscious to a nearby hospital where he is attended by a resident physician, who reasonably determines that the man will die unless his leg is amputated. The physician performs the amputation before the man regains consciousness and without procuring consent from anyone. As a rule, the man will be deemed to have consented to the amputation, given the life-threatening nature of the emergency.

In creating the fiction of implied consent, the courts have responded to the realities of emergency medical care, where life-threatening crises are relatively common. As a rule, however, the courts have been much less willing to apply this fiction to mental health emergencies. Indeed, as Gutheil and Appelbaum (1982) have observed, the only mental health emergency in which the courts have consistently granted such an exception to the requirement of informed consent is that in which a "violent, excited or self-mutilating psychotic patient [requires] immediate restraint and/or medication to prevent physical harm to self or others" (p. 163). As these authors further note, nonviolent patients, even though psychotic and in acute distress, may *not*, under several recent court decisions, "present a sufficiently emergent situation (from the legal viewpoint) to justify complete disregard for obtaining informed or substituted consent" (p. 163).

Substituted Consent. The law has also long recognized that under certain circumstances, consent to treatment may be given by someone other than the patient. For example, even in emergency situations such as those described above, consent may be, and in some cases must be, obtained from a close relative if one is at hand (Prosser, 1971). In the case of a minor patient, absent a life-threatening emergency, consent must be obtained from a parent or legal guardian (see, e.g., *Bonner v. Moran*, 1941).

In mental health practice, the issue of substituted consent is most likely to arise where a patient is incompetent to give informed consent. In such cases, the required informed consent clearly must be given by a third party, if treatment is to proceed. The problem for the law and the clinician in these cases has two major elements: (a) Whose consent may be substituted for that of the patient and (b) upon what basis is the substituted consent to be given?

From the time of the ancient Romans, the law has recognized the need for legally appointed guardians to oversee the affairs of the mentally ill (Robitscher, 1980). Under current law in most jurisdictions, any interested party may petition the appropriate court for appointment of a guardian to act on behalf of an incompetent individual. Within certain limits (e.g., the refusal to pursue potentially life-saving treatment, a decision generally reserved for the court, itself), the court-appointed guardian may consent to treatment on behalf of the incompetent individual. The identity and specific powers of the guardian are determined by the court, acting under applicable statutes and case law which vary among jurisdictions.

Appointment of a legal guardian, however, does not by itself resolve the issue of consent. The question remains whether the guardian should substitute his or her own judgment for that of the incompetent patient or, rather, base his or her judgment on what the guardian believes the patient would want, were the patient competent to decide. Outside of extreme cases involving life-threatening circumstances, the courts have rarely provided clear guidance on this issue. It does seem reasonably clear, however, that neither court nor guardian may consent to treatment which would not be "beneficial" to the incompetent individual (see, e.g., *In re Guardianship of Pescinski*, 1975).

Waiver of Consent. As a legal matter, the right of informed consent belongs to and, thus, may be waived by the patient. Waiver of a legal right, however, ordinarily must be knowing and intelligent. Thus, an incompetent patient may not waive his or her right to informed consent. Moreover, even with competent patients, a waiver will be valid only if the patient has been advised of his or her right to be told the necessary information and has affirmatively declined to hear such information.

APPLICATION OF THE DOCTRINE OF INFORMED CONSENT TO MENTAL HEALTH PRACTICE

Given its roots in the common-law regulation of medical and surgical practice, it is not surprising that in the context of mental health practice the doctrine of informed consent has been applied primarily to somatic treatment modalities such as psychosurgery, electroconvulsive therapy (ECT), and the prescription of psychotropic medications. By now, most clinicians who utilize such treatments are aware of and comply with the requirements of informed consent, although there continues to be debate (especially as regards medication side effects such as tardive dyskinesia) over how much a patient should be told. Any clinician who utilizes somatic therapies without regard for informed consent is clearly courting a potential lawsuit.

Psychotherapy, on the other hand, is rarely mentioned in legal discussions of informed consent. Many psychotherapists ignore the issue altogether or take for granted their patients' consent to treatment. For the most part, they do so with little legal risk, at least currently. Outside of cases in which psychotherapists have physically or sexually abused patients (see section entitled "Legal Limits of the Clinician-Patient Relationship" below), legal claims of harm resulting from psychotherapy have rarely been successful.

As a practical matter, it is extremely difficult to prove that psychotherapy was the proximate cause of a patient's alleged injury. Furthermore, as Pope, Simpson, and Weiner (1978) have pointed out, lawsuits arising out of psychotherapy are limited by the fact that there are no "standards of practice for psychotherapy, and therefore no measure of the adequacy of a psychotherapist's management of a case" (p. 593).

Yet, there is a growing consensus among mental health professionals that psychotherapy does hold "powerful potential for harm" (Robitscher, 1980). In a recent survey of mental health clinicians, respondents were virtually unanimous in the opinion that psychotherapy may have significant negative effects (Hadley & Strupp, 1976). Given this consensus and the almost boundless creativity of some tort lawyers in devising legal theories to support claims against mental health professionals, many psychotherapists would do well to rethink their current lack of concern for the doctrine of informed consent.

While legal guidelines regarding informed consent to psychotherapy are currently lacking, psychotherapists should act to protect themselves and their patients and will, in most cases, do so by providing patients with the following information prior to treatment. The psychotherapist should inform the patient that:

1. Psychotherapy may involve certain risks. Everstine et al. (1980), for example, suggest providing the patient with the following *written* statement:

    Psychotherapy may involve the risk of remembering unpleasant events and can arouse intense emotions of fear and anger. Intense feelings of anxiety, depression, frustration, loneliness, or helplessness may also be aroused. (p. 833)

2. Psychotherapy is not always effective and may, in some cases, result in deterioration rather than improvement of a patient's psychological functioning.

3. There are numerous forms of psychotherapy which vary not only in underlying theory and methods employed, but also in terms of time commitment and cost.

4. Current research has failed to demonstrate that any one form of psychotherapy is necessarily any more effective than any other.

5. Depending upon a patient's condition, there may be available alternatives to psychotherapy, such as medication or behavior modification.

6. Consent to psychotherapy, once given, may be rescinded by the patient at any time.

In addition, the prospective psychotherapy patient should be informed of his or her rights regarding confidentiality and privacy. Issues related to privacy and confidentiality are examined in detail in the next section of this chapter.

CONFIDENTIALITY AND PRIVACY

Confidentiality between patient and clinician has long been regarded as a cornerstone of effective mental health treatment. To succeed in the therapeutic role, the mental health professional must have access to a wide variety of information regarding the patient—often information which the patient would be quite reluctant to disclose in any other context. In order to gain such information, the clinician must be able to assure the patient that it will not be disclosed to anyone else without the patient's consent.

In the early days of modern mental health treatment, clinicians were generally able to give patients such assurances. Regulation of confidentiality and privacy was largely a matter of professional ethics and conscience. Most mental health professionals took confidentiality for granted. The categorical (though not always observed) rule was: Reveal nothing a patient tells you unless the patient requests otherwise.

In recent years, however, the regulation of confidentiality and privacy in mental health treatment has become a matter of law. Statutory and case law have made it clear that mental health patients have a legally protected right to confidentiality and privacy. Yet, the same body of law has made it equally clear that, as regards certain matters which may arise in mental health care, the patient has *no* right to confidentiality or privacy.

THE RIGHT TO CONFIDENTIALITY

Subject to a number of exceptions which will be detailed below, mental health professionals have an affirmative legal duty to preserve the confidences of their patients. For the most part, the clinician may not reveal any information regarding a patient without the patient's *informed* consent. Breach of confidentiality not only threatens to undermine the therapeutic relationship, but also may expose the clinician to civil liability for damages. Patients whose confidences are revealed by a clinician to their detriment and without their consent often have a legal cause of action against the clinician. Moreover, since the patient's cause of action may lie in defamation, invasion of privacy, or breach of fiduciary duty rather than professional malpractice, any damages awarded may not be covered by the clinician's malpractice insurance.

The extent and basis for the mental health professional's liability is well illustrated by a recent New York State Appellate Court decision. In *McDonald v. Clinger* (1982), a patient sued his psychiatrist, alleging that in the course of treatment he had revealed intimate details of his life and that the psychiatrist had divulged these details to the patient's wife without consent or justification. As a consequence, the patient alleged, he had lost his job and marriage, suffered financial losses, and experienced severe psychological distress which necessitated further treatment.

The Court held that a physician who enters into an agreement to provide medical attention, impliedly covenants to keep in confidence all disclosures made by the patient concerning the patient's physical and mental condition as well as all matters discovered by the physician in the course of examination and treatment. Additionally, the Court noted that "This is particularly and necessarily true of the psychiatric relationship [in which] 'the patient is called upon to discuss in a candid and frank manner personal material of the most intimate and disturbing nature'" (p. 804).

In upholding the patient's right to money damages, the Court further held that the psychiatrist's disclosures were actionable not only for breach of contract, a legal theory under which damages are limited to economic loss flowing directly from the breach, but also in tort (the law of civil, noncontractual, wrongs), under which the patient could recover for the deterioration in his marriage, loss of employment, and mental distress.

Lawsuits over disclosure of confidential information by mental health professionals are rare but seem to be increasing. Mental health clinicians are routinely faced with requests for disclosure of confidential information from a variety of sources. Thus, it is essential that clinicians understand the legally appropriate way in which to respond to such requests.

Most commonly, requests for disclosure of confidential information will be directed to the clinician by insurers, employers, schools, public agencies, health care professionals, and other institutions with which the patient is voluntarily associated. In such cases, it is often apparently advantageous to the patient to have certain confidential information released, and most patients will readily consent. Clinicians routinely handle such situations by having patients sign standard preprinted consent forms provided by the clinician or by the individual or institution seeking the information.

In many cases of this sort, such routine procedure adequately protects the patient's right to confidentiality and shields the clinician from legal liability for breach of confidentiality. Even in routine cases, however, the clinician should be certain to obtain the patient's *informed* consent to disclose the information sought by a third party. At the very least, securing informed consent to release confidential information requires careful discussion between patient and clinician.

In every case, the clinician should call the patient's attention to any possible adverse consequences of releasing the information and require the patient to specify exactly what information he or she is willing to have released. Under no circumstances should the clinician accept from a patient a "blank check" authorization to release information. If the clinician has any doubt as to the patient's willingness to have specific information (e.g., a diagnosis or clinical report) released, the clinician should first provide that information to the patient.

While patient consent to disclosure may be given orally, the better practice is to obtain written consent. Written consent both avoids misunderstandings between patient and clinician and provides a documentary record in the event the consent is later challenged.

Another common confidentiality issue which arises in mental health care is the sharing of patient information with colleagues and supervisors. Some have suggested that this practice, which is routine in many clinical settings, may continue "so long as the patient's privacy is protected by alteration of her name and other identifying data" (Gutheil & Appelbaum, 1982, p. 7). The better practice, however, therapeutically, ethically, and legally, is to obtain patient consent prior to any such sharing of confidential information.

Where a clinician intends to reveal confidential information outside of his or her immediate circle of colleagues—as, for example, through publication of a patient's case history—written informed consent of the patient seems essential, even if the clinician attempts to disguise the patient's identity. The clinician's liability for publication of such a case history without the patient's informed consent is illustrated by the case of *Doe v. Roe* (1975).

Dr. "Roe," a psychiatrist, had treated "Jane Doe" over an extended period of time and had discussed with "Doe" the possibility of publishing an account of "Doe's" therapy in book form. At times "Doe" agreed, but at other times she disagreed. According to Dr. "Roe's" testimony, "Doe's" consent was "there one day and not there another day."

Ultimately "Roe" published a book which disguised "Doe's" identity but described in detail intimate aspects of "Doe's" life and relationship with her husband. "Doe" instituted a lawsuit against "Roe" for breach of privacy, claiming that she was easily recognized because of the unusual facts of her case and because many of her associates knew that she had been in treatment with Dr. "Roe." After a number of years of litigation, "Doe" was awarded $20,000 in damages from "Roe" and her coauthor.

EXCEPTIONS TO THE RIGHT
TO CONFIDENTIALITY

While as a rule mental health professionals have an ethical and legal duty to protect patient confidences, there are a number of situations in which disclosure of confidential information is mandated by law. The first of these "exceptions" to the rule of confidentiality arises when a clinician is ordered by a court of appropriate jurisdiction to produce a patient's records or to testify regarding patient confidences. Even when responding to such a court order, however, the clinician must be certain that the information sought is not protected by some form of testimonial privilege.

Testimonial privilege, in this context, refers to the fact that in some jurisdictions, under some circumstances, communications between patients and certain mental health professionals are protected from disclosure, even under court order. To date, roughly two-thirds of the states provide some sort of physician-patient privilege, which naturally applies to psychiatrists. About one-fifth of the states provide a similar privilege for communications between patients and doctoral-level psychologists. Only a handful of states, however, provide such a privilege for communications between patients and other clinicians such as social workers, nurses, and counselors.

Where testimonial privilege is applicable, only the patient may decide whether to exercise it (and thus bar the clinician's testimony or production of records) or waive it (and thus allow the testimony or production of records). The clinician has no right to waive the privilege or to assert the privilege if the patient has waived it. While a patient's assertion of the privilege generally bars testimony or production of records by the clinician, there are numerous exceptions, which vary among the jurisdictions. Among the situations in which the testimonial privilege has been found inoperative, in at least some jurisdictions, are:

1. Cases in which the patient puts his or her mental condition in issue (e.g., where the patient is suing for damages based on a claim of psychological injury or is seeking child custody or visitation in a divorce suit).
2. Cases in which the patient-clinician communication arose during a court-ordered evaluation or an evaluation conducted solely for purposes of litigation.
3. Cases in which the patient is charged with a crime.

4. Cases involving litigation between patient and clinician, as in a malpractice suit or legal action by the clinician to collect an unpaid fee.

Numerous other exceptions to testimonial privilege have been recognized and the law in this area varies widely from state to state. Thus, the safest course for the clinician faced with a subpoena for records and/or testimony is to consult an attorney prior to making any disclosure of confidential information. And, of course, since the privilege belongs to the patient, he or she must be notified and given the opportunity to seek legal advice prior to any disclosure.

A second set of exceptions to the rule of confidentiality arises under (a) statutory law requiring mental health professionals to make disclosures of certain patient confidences, and (b) case law holding mental health professionals liable in tort actions for *not* breaching patient confidentiality.

The most common statutory exception to patient confidentiality in mental health care relates to information concerning child abuse. Most states now require physicians and other health care providers (including mental health professionals) to report to welfare authorities any reasonable suspicions of child abuse. While they are rarely, if ever, invoked, many statutes provide criminal sanctions for willful failure to report such suspicions. Thus, the clinician who learns of possible child abuse, even through an otherwise privileged patient communication, has a legal duty to report to the appropriate authorities what he or she has learned.

The most common case law exception to patient confidentiality in mental health care relates to threats of violence made by a patient. Probably the most widely known, and certainly the most controversial, case of this sort is *Tarasoff v. Board of Regents of the University of California* (1976). To state the facts of that case in an oversimplified fashion: A patient informed his psychotherapist (a psychologist) that he planned to kill a certain young woman. The psychologist informed the police, who briefly detained the patient but released him. No warning was ever given the intended victim or her

family.   The   patient   terminated   treatment   and
subsequently killed the young woman.

The   victim's   parents   brought   suit   against   the
psychotherapist's employer, the University. The suit was
originally dismissed, but on appeal by the plaintiffs, the
California Supreme Court held that the therapist had a
duty to warn the intended victim, and that the failure to
warn,   under   these   circumstances,   was   actionable
negligence.   In its landmark opinion, the Court stated
that:

> When a therapist determines or pursuant to the
> standards of his profession should determine that
> his patient presents a serious danger of violence to
> another, he incurs an obligation to use reasonable
> care to protect the intended victim against such
> danger. (*Tarasoff v. Board of Regents of the
> University of California*, 1976, p. 334)

In weighing the risk to the patient stemming from such a
breach of confidentiality against the risk to the patient's
potential victim, the Court held that "the protective
privilege ends where the public peril begins" (p. 347).

To date, the *Tarasoff* rule has not been widely
adopted in other jurisdictions (see Note, 1982).   The
Tarasoff decision does, however, have significant
persuasive value as a legal precedent and might well be
followed in future cases in other jurisdictions.   Thus, the
clinician who fails to heed its message may be acting at
his or her own peril.

As   regards   patient   threats   to   self   (i.e.,   suicidal
threats), clinicians clearly have a legal obligation to take
appropriate measures to prevent suicidal acting-out (see
"Assessment and Treatment of Suicidal and 'Dangerous'
Patients" below).   The clinician who fails to take such
measures may be liable for damages in a wrongful death
lawsuit should the patient succeed in committing suicide.
Appropriate preventive measures might be viewed as
including   a   warning   to   members   of   the   patient's
immediate family.   Certainly such a warning would not
be contrary to sound clinical practice.   Yet, the courts
have thus far *not* applied the *Tarasoff* "duty to warn" to
cases involving threats to self.   Indeed, in *Bellah v.*

Greenson (1978), a California Appeals Court explicitly refused to "further extend the holding of *Tarasoff*" to such cases. In that case, the parents of a suicide victim brought suit against a psychiatrist who had been treating the victim. In rejecting the parents' legal claim, the Court held that the "duty to warn" applies only "where the risk to be prevented is the danger of violent assault, and not where the risk of harm is self-inflicted" (p. 622).

ASSESSMENT AND TREATMENT
OF SUICIDAL AND "DANGEROUS" PATIENTS

Regardless of the applicability of the above-described duty to warn, mental health professionals may have special legal responsibilities in dealing with potentially suicidal or violent patients.

SUICIDAL PATIENTS

Successful lawsuits against mental health professionals whose patients have committed suicide are most likely to arise in the context of *inpatient* (i.e., hospital) care. As Sadoff (1982) has observed:

Hospitals are equipped with locked psychiatric wards with safety windows, quiet rooms, and seclusion to prevent such violent behavior. If it does occur in a hospital setting, there is presumed to have been a breakdown in security that led to the violent behavior and the ultimate damage. (p. 64)

Failure to take appropriate precautions to prevent suicidal acting-out by a *hospitalized* patient not infrequently results in malpractice liability for both the treating clinician and the institution (see, e.g., *Benjamin v. Havens, Inc.*, 1962; *Mounds Park Hospital v. VonEye*, 1957). On the other hand, successful malpractice suits stemming from the suicides of *outpatients* (at least those not recently released from a hospital) are quite rare. Nevertheless, the potential exists for successful wrongful death actions against outpatient therapists who fail to recognize a patient's obvious suicidal tendencies or neglect to take reasonable precautions to prevent a patient's suicide.

As regards "misdiagnosis" or failure to recognize clinical indications of suicidal intent, the likelihood of clinician liability is probably slight, except in cases of *gross* error. The difficulties inherent in assessing suicidal risk have long been noted by mental health professionals and are unlikely to be ignored altogether by the courts. Thus, as Halleck (1980) suggests, "As a rule...the [clinician] would not be held liable unless the indications for suicide had been very powerful, had been communicated to the [clinician], and he [or she] had failed to take them seriously in making a diagnosis and a treatment disposition" (p. 71).

Where suicidal indications are readily apparent and/or the clinician determines that the patient is at significant risk for suicide, the clinician is quite likely to be held to a duty to take reasonable precautions to prevent self-destructive behavior. What is reasonable will, of course, depend to a large extent upon the particular circumstances (e.g., level of risk, presence or absence of a stated plan, patient access to means of self-destruction, availability of familial and/or community support systems, etc.). Thus, it is difficult to formulate universal guidelines certain to prevent clinician liability in the event of suicide.

There are, however, a number of steps a conscientious clinician will take in dealing with a potentially suicidal patient—steps which, if taken, may well serve to shield the clinician from legal liability in the event of a patient's suicide:

1. In every case involving clear suicidal risk, the clinician should alert responsible "others" (such as close relatives of the patient) to the risk and instruct them as to necessary precautions (e.g., removing firearms, medications, and other means of destruction from the patient's access). Naturally, an attempt should be made to secure the patient's consent to notify others, but generally the clinician should do so even if the patient refuses consent. In the absence of consent, such notification represents a breach of confidentiality,

but is *extremely* unlikely to expose the clinician to liability if there is *any* reasonable basis for inferring suicidal potential. Indeed, under some state statutes (e.g., California Welfare and Institutions Code, Section 5328.1), notification of a patient's family members is permissible if "release of such information is in the best interests of the patient."

2. In treating suicidal patients, physicians should take great care in prescribing medications such as tricyclic antidepressants, monoamine oxidase inhibitors, barbiturates, and other drugs which may provide a means of suicide. As Halleck (1980) has observed:

> A relatively small overdose of any of these drugs can be fatal. Physicians are usually wise to restrict the amount of drugs available to suicidal patients. Conceivably a failure to do so could result in liability. (p. 73)

3. In all cases involving suicidal risk, the clinician should carefully consider whether hospitalization is required to prevent self-destructive acting-out. If hospitalization appears warranted and the patient refuses, the clinician may have a duty to see that commitment procedures are invoked.

4. Where hospitalization of a potentially suicidal patient does not appear warranted, the clinician should carefully clarify his or her continuing role in assisting the prevention of suicide. Elsewhere (Ewing, 1982), the author has advised that the clinician should:

> (A) Offer to be available to the patient and family members (or significant "others") by phone or in person as needed;
> (B) Make an appointment for an office visit within the next day or so and as needed thereafter;
> (C) Arrange a number of telephone "appointments" at which time the patient is to call the clinician (between office visits); and

> (D) Make the patient and family members
> (or "others") aware of the availability and
> location of emergency psychiatric services
> in the community. (p. 6)

5. Under no circumstances should the clinician "abandon" or unilaterally discharge from treatment an actively suicidal patient. If for some *compelling* reason a clinician is unable to continue treating such a patient, he or she should *immediately* arrange continued care by another clinician. Moreover, even if the patient insists upon terminating treatment, the clinician may have continuing responsibilities for prevention of suicide and should, in every such case, provide the patient with a good faith referral to another clinician or mental health agency.

6. In addition to taking the above-described steps or precautions, the clinician should be certain to document what was done on the patient's behalf. Appropriate documentation, which may prove vital in the later defense of a malpractice suit, should include a *contemporaneous* record of the following: (a) clinical indications of suicidal potential, (b) the clinician's assessment of risk and the basis for that assessment, (c) resources available to the patient outside the therapeutic relationship, (d) reasons for electing not to seek hospitalization of the patient, and (5) all steps taken by the clinician to prevent suicidal acting-out.

"DANGEROUS" PATIENTS

As John Monahan indicates in Chapter 1 of this volume, the assessment of a patient's potential for violence (or "dangerousness") is fraught with difficulties and uncertainties. Indeed, there is a growing body of research data which suggests that clinicians are unable accurately to predict future violent behavior (see Monahan, 1981). The American Psychiatric Association, Task Force on Clinical Aspects of the Violent Individual (1974) has taken the position that "Neither psychiatrists nor anyone else have demonstrated an ability to predict future violence or 'dangerousness'" (p. 20). The American Psychological Association, Task Force on the Role of Psychology in the Criminal Justice System (1978) has concluded that "the validity of psychological predictions of violent behavior, at least in the sentencing and release situations we are considering is extremely poor, so poor that one could oppose their use on the strictly empirical grounds that psychologists are not professionally competent to make such judgments" (p. 14).

Nevertheless, mental health professionals are at risk for liability in the event that one of their patients harms a third party. While lawsuits stemming from such harm to third parties have been successful primarily in cases involving patient escapes or discharges from mental institutions (see, e.g., *Hicks v. Holder*, 1982; *Merchants Bank & Trust Co. v. United States*, 1967), recently a growing number of lawsuits have been brought against *outpatient* clinicians whose patients have injured or killed third parties (Berreby, 1983).

While in the past it was thought that a clinician risked liability only when he or she "made a prediction of dangerousness and [failed] to take proper precautions" (Halleck, 1980, p. 76), as in the *Tarasoff* case described above, recent lawsuits against clinicians appear to be proceeding on a theory similar to that of products liability (see Chapter 13). As one plaintiffs' attorney has argued, speaking of clinicians who fail to foresee the future violence of their patients: "They're putting a lunatic into the stream of commerce. Everyone should be responsible for their product. [The patient] is their product. This is the implication of *Tarasoff* and of a sweeping movement across this country" (Berreby, 1983, p. 26).

Whether this attorney's position will be accepted by the courts remains to be seen, but the question is certain to arise as the courts struggle with now pending lawsuits. One particular series of lawsuits in which this question seems destined to be adjudicated is that arising out of John Hinckley's attempt to assassinate Ronald Reagan. Hinckley, it will be recalled, was acquitted of criminal charges by reason of insanity (see Chapter 3). The legal maneuvering over Hinckley's actions, however, did not end with his commitment to St. Elizabeth's Hospital.

As of this writing, one of Hinckley's victims (White House Press Secretary, James Brady) has brought, and another victim (Secret Service Agent, Timothy McCarthy) is considering bringing, legal action against a psychiatrist who treated Hinckley just months before the assassination attempt. According to a report in the *National Law Journal* (Berreby, 1983), this psychiatrist "gave his patient biofeedback exercises to do, prescribed Valium and eventually counseled Mr. Hinckley's parents to separate their family from their son" (p. 26). The same report indicates that at Hinckley's criminal trial, one of the expert witnesses testified that the psychiatrist had incorrectly diagnosed Hinckley's condition or had provided "totally inappropriate treatment." Finally, this report quotes McCarthy's attorney as having informed Hinckley's former psychiatrist that "we may have a claim against him" (p. 26).

The psychiatrist's situation in the Hinckley matter was, of course, markedly different from that encountered by the psychologist who treated Tarasoff's assailant. Hinckley's psychiatrist apparently had no clear-cut evidence of the likelihood of future violence (e.g., no threat) and no intended victim he could have warned. Whether a clinician will be held liable to third party victims for a failure to predict "dangerousness" under such circumstances remains to be seen.

In the event that liability is imposed in this and/or similar cases, it is to be hoped that the courts will provide standards of care to which mental health professionals may adhere in the future. For the moment, however, lacking any legal guidelines, the clinician's best line of defense would appear to be that of following the highest standards of care applicable to his or her profession, doing his or her best to evaluate a patient's potential for violence (see Chapter 1), and keeping *detailed* clinical records.

LEGAL LIMITS OF THE CLINICIAN-PATIENT RELATIONSHIP

The relationship between mental health clinician and patient is one founded upon trust. The patient has a moral and often legally enforceable right to trust the clinician to act in the patient's best interests. Ethical codes of all the mental health professions have long established the clinician's duty to so act. In recent years, many aspects of the clinician's duty to act in the patient's best interests have also been established as a matter of law.

Among those aspects of the clinician's legal duty which have the most significance in clinical practice are those related to: (a) sexual relations between clinician and patient, (b) the use of controversial treatment modalities, and (c) clinician "abandonment" of a patient.

SEXUAL RELATIONS WITH PATIENTS

The relationship between mental health clinician and patient is necessarily an intimate one. In individual psychotherapy, for example, patient and clinician spend many hours alone with each other, the patient is encouraged to reveal many of his or her innermost "secrets," and the clinician is expected to demonstrate warmth, empathy, and acceptance of the patient. Not surprisingly, the therapeutic relationship sometimes holds the potential for romantic or sexual involvement between patient and clinician. Mental health professionals have long recognized this potential and have spoken of it in terms of "transference and countertransference."

Yet, just as mental health professionals have long recognized this potential, they have also recognized that the clinician who takes advantage of it (i.e., engages in sexual relations with a patient) betrays the patient's trust, exploits the patient's vulnerabilities, and thereby undermines effective treatment. Some clinicians (e.g., McCartney, 1966; Shepard, 1971) have defended sexual relations with certain patients as therapeutic and beneficial. And confidential surveys have found that between 1% and 7% of clinicians have, in fact, engaged in sexual relations with their patients (Holroyd & Brodsky, 1977; Kardener, Fuller, & Mensch, 1973; Sadoff & Showell, 1981). The overwhelming bulk of professional sentiment, however, is vehemently opposed to any form of sexual contact between clinician and patient.

Such professional sentiment is clearly reflected in the current ethical standards of psychiatry, which state flatly that "Sexual activity with a patient is unethical" (American Psychiatric Association, 1981, Section 2.1), and those of psychology, which assert that "Psychologists do not exploit their relationships with clients...sexually or otherwise" (American Psychological Association, 1981, p. 636). Clearly a psychiatrist or psychologist who engages in sexual relations with a patient is subject to discipline by his or her professional organization for violation of professional ethics. But the sanctions to which such a clinician may be subject do not end with those imposed by professional organizations (e.g., censure, expulsion from membership, etc.). Proven instances of clinician-patient sexual relations can result in loss of license to practice as well as civil liability for money damages.

Perhaps the most widely publicized successful lawsuit against a psychiatrist alleged to have engaged in sex with a patient is *Roy v. Hartogs* (1976), which is described at length in Freeman and Roy (1976). The patient's allegation, denied by the psychiatrist, was that the psychiatrist had prescribed sexual relations as part of her psychotherapy and had filled the prescription during his sessions with her. Three other former patients testified that the psychiatrist had either engaged in or attempted sexual relations with them. A jury awarded the patient-plaintiff $250,000 for her deteriorated mental condition and an additional $100,000 punitive damages based upon a finding that the psychiatrist's malpractice had been deliberate. A New York State Appellate Court, however, subsequently found no basis for punitive damages and reduced the compensatory award to $25,000.

Despite the action of the Appellate Court, the clear message of *Roy v. Hartogs* is that clinicians who engage in sexual relations with their patients do so at considerable legal risk. More recently this message was reiterated by a California verdict which has yet to be tested on appeal. In *Walker v. Parzen* (1983), a jury ordered a psychiatrist to pay *$4.6 million* to a former patient with whom he had admitted having sexual intercourse during more than two years of psychotherapy.

Clinician-patient sex in the therapeutic context, however, is not the only grounds for clinician liability in mishandling a patient's "transference" and/or exploiting his or her trust and vulnerability. In *Zipkin v. Freeman* (1968), for example, a psychiatrist was held liable for inducing his patient to turn over her savings to him, leave her husband, and become his mistress. In *Anclote Manor Foundation v. Wilkinson* (1972), the Court upheld a malpractice verdict against a psychiatrist who told his patient that he would marry her after he divorced his wife. The patient subsequently divorced her husband and committed suicide. And in *Landau v. Werner* (1961), a British case, a patient was awarded the American equivalent of about $15,000 in a suit in which she alleged that her psychotherapist, with whom she had fallen in love, had exploited her feelings for him by meeting her outside the office (e.g., in restaurants, parks, and the patient's home) and discussing with her a possible weekend rendezvous. The Court, in making its award to the patient, made no finding as to sexual relations.

In view of this line of cases, it seems fair to conclude that a clinician who becomes romantically involved with a patient while treating that patient— regardless of whether the involvement includes sexual relations—may also be at significant risk for legal liability.

CONTROVERSIAL TREATMENT MODALITIES

As indicated earlier, any form of treatment requires the informed consent of the patient or of someone with the legal authority to speak for the patient. But even where such consent has been obtained, the clinician may be held liable for any actions—even those intended to be therapeutic—which exceed the scope of treatment to which consent has been given. Most lawsuits of this sort have charged the clinician with negligence (although the more appropriate legal rubric is that of "battery," the unconsented touching of another) and have stemmed from the use of controversial *physical* techniques as an adjunct to psychotherapy.

The leading cases of this sort both present somewhat extreme circumstances, yet should give pause to any clinician who contemplates the use of potentially painful or harmful physical procedures in the course of mental health treatment. The first of these cases dealt with a controversial form of psychotherapy for schizophrenics called "direct analysis." This technique, developed by John Rosen, a well-known psychiatrist, involved "a dramatic barrage of powerful maneuvers to persuade the patient to relinquish his psychiatric behavior—promising and rewarding, threatening and punishing, suggesting and instructing, coercing and rendering service, using group pressure, ridiculing and shaming" (May, 1975, p. 930).

While Rosen's "direct analysis" was apparently successful in a number of cases (Rosen, 1953) and "had some support among his fellows" (DeLeon & Borreliz, 1978, p. 470), its "dramatic barrage of powerful maneuvers" sometimes included physically striking a patient. One patient, allegedly struck by Rosen, sued him. The trial Court's verdict against Rosen was upheld by an appeals court, which found that "the very nature of the acts complained of bespeaks improper treatment" (*Hammer v. Rosen*, 1960, p. 380).

The second of these cases involved a much more controversial form of psychotherapy known as "rage reduction" or "Z" therapy (a variation of primal scream therapy). Z therapy included tickling the patient, presumably to release pent-up emotions. In *Abraham v. Zaslow* (1970), a Z therapy patient was awarded a judgment of $170,000 against her psychotherapist after she testified that her treatment had included being beaten, being held down, and having fingers stuck in her mouth, which led to bruises, acute kidney failure, and psychological harm.

In addition to liability for direct battery *of* a patient, it is conceivable that a clinician might be liable for encouraging or "prescribing" the battery of another *by* a patient. While such a course of action by a clinician seems rather unlikely, if not preposterous, a recent lawsuit has raised this very issue.

In *People v. Mentry* (1983), Betty Mentry, a 200-pound woman, was charged with manslaughter in the death of her 8-year-old son, which occurred while she was sitting on the boy. Mrs. Mentry was acquitted by a jury which apparently accepted her defense (i.e., that she sat on the child at the direction of a mental health counselor, who prescribed the technique as a means of reestablishing parental control over the youngster). According to Mrs.

Mentry's attorney, this technique was developed by Dr. Milton Erickson, a well-known psychiatrist, and described in the psychiatric literature.

While Mrs. Mentry's criminal trial ended in acquittal, she has pending (at the time of this writing) a $2.5 million malpractice suit against the clinic which employed the counselor who allegedly prescribed the unorthodox "treatment" (Ellison, 1983; Granelli, 1983; *Mentry v. Alum Rock Communications, Inc.*, 1983). If Mrs. Mentry's allegations are provable, the clinic may well be held liable in the death of her son.

Few clinicians are likely to engage in intentional battery of a patient or to encourage a patient to batter another. Yet, many clinicians do utilize recognized, though controversial, treatment modalities such as electroconvulsive therapy (ECT) and aversive conditioning, both of which present a risk of physical harm to patients. Clinicians who employ such modalities should be aware of the legal risks involved and the steps necessary to avoid such risks.

Many authorities regard ECT as a relatively safe and effective treatment in certain cases of severe depression. Yet, other commentators have challenged both its safety and efficacy, pointing out that ECT's beneficial effects are at best unsubstantiated and that its use may result in various forms of brain injury. Recently, the City of Berkeley, California passed an ordinance prohibiting the use of ECT in that jurisdiction. Subsequently, a Superior Court Judge enjoined enforcement of the ECT ban pending trial on the merits in a lawsuit brought by a local psychiatric group against the city (*Northern California Psychiatric Society v. City of Berkeley*, 1983; see Bishop, 1983 and Cunningham, 1983).

Regardless of the results of that trial, which "promises to be a lively debate over the scientific merits of ECT" (Cunningham, 1983, p. 17), this treatment modality is likely to remain the subject of legal controversy in Berkeley and elsewhere. Thus, clinicians who utilize ECT should take care not only to follow appropriate informed consent procedures (see "Informed Consent to Treatment" above), but also to exercise every reasonable precaution to prevent injury to the patient. Specifically, to avoid legal liability, psychiatrists should: (a) *not* use ECT without premedication, (b) carefully monitor the administration of neuroleptic drugs and keep dosages of such drugs to a minimum during the course of ECT, (c) see to it that patients are carefully watched to prevent injuries resulting from post-ECT confusion, and (d) take care to diagnose and treat any injuries (particularly fractures) resulting from ECT (Halleck, 1980, pp. 99-100).

Aversive conditioning, occasionally used by behavior modification clinicians, "involves the application of a negative reinforcer (aversive event) *at the same time* that the individual is performing the problem behavior...The procedure is termed *aversive* because of the nature of the aversive stimulus typically employed (emetics, electric shock, paralyzing drugs, imagination of noxious scenes)" (Rim & Masters, 1974, p. 354, emphasis in original).

Like ECT, aversive conditioning has its supporters and its critics. Also like ECT, it continues to be the subject of significant legal and professional controversy. A number of lawsuits have resulted from the use of aversive conditioning (involving administration of paralyzing drugs and emetics) with prison inmates. Courts in these cases have found that such treatment constitutes cruel and unusual punishment (see, e.g., *Knecht v. Gillman*, 1973 and *Mackey v. Procunier*, 1973).

To avoid potential legal liability, clinicians who utilize aversive conditioning should be *extremely* careful to obtain *truly* informed consent, should *carefully* follow *established* clinical procedures, and should *continuously* monitor patients for harmful effects. Furthermore, in employing aversive procedures, clinicians should be certain not to exceed the bounds of professional competence (e.g., the use of certain physically aversive stimuli such as emetics by a nonphysician might constitute unauthorized practice of medicine). Finally, clinicians who employ mechanical devices in aversive conditioning (or, for that matter, in any form of mental health treatment) have special responsibilities to insure their safe use. Specifically, such clinicians must: (a) "ensure that the device meets published performance and safety standards...and that it continues to conform to [such] standards;" (b) "be knowledgeable about the known side effects of the devices;" (c) "share that knowledge with prospective patients [and] obtain patients' permission to use the devices in treatment;" and (d) "be knowledgeable about what to do to prevent harm if medical accidents involving the devices do occur" (Schwitzgebel, 1978, p. 483).

ABANDONMENT

Once initiated, the mental health clinician-patient relationship continues until (a) it is terminated by mutual consent, (b) it is ended by the patient, (c) the clinician's services are no longer required, or (d) the clinician withdraws after giving the patient reasonable notice. The clinician who unilaterally terminates the relationship without giving the patient adequate notice may face liability for abandonment.

The vast majority of clinician-patient relationships are terminated by mutual consent or by the patient's failure to follow through on treatment. There are, however, many instances in which mental health clinicians unilaterally terminate the relationship. Robitscher (1980) cites, for example, the rash of poor practice occurring every June 30th when psychiatric residents tell their patients that they are leaving the clinic to pursue their training or practices elsewhere. And Gutheil and Appelbaum (1982) note that clinicians not infrequently terminate their relationships with patients who threaten them, patients they dislike, patients who do not cooperate with treatment, and patients who fail to pay for clinicians' services.

Aside from lawsuits stemming from premature release of a patient from a hospital (e.g., *Hicks v. Holder*, 1982; *Valenti v. United States*, 1982), legal claims arising out of abandonment by mental health clinicians are quite rare. Clinicians should realize, however, that if they do abandon a patient who later harms himself or herself or another, they could well find themselves held liable for malpractice.

There are a number of steps the clinician should take to avoid abandonment. First, the clinician should not unilaterally terminate any therapeutic relationship without giving reasonable notice to the patient. "Reasonable notice" cannot be defined precisely, but ordinarily in this context it means enough time to allow the patient to arrange care with another clinician. As a matter of good clinical practice, if not law, the clinician who wishes to terminate with a patient in need of further care should at least offer to refer the patient to another clinician and cooperate in providing necessary clinical data to the patient's new clinician—subject, of course, to the patient's consent to release such information.

Second, the clinician should make every effort to discuss termination with the patient and to minimize potentially harmful effects to the patient. The patient should be given not only adequate notice of the clinician's intention to terminate and reasons for the termination, but also the opportunity to discuss and "work through" unresolved concerns about termination. In some cases, this will require a number of appointments.

Third, as mentioned earlier, the clinician should be especially careful in terminating with a patient who is at risk for suicide or other violent acting-out. As a rule, the clinician should *not* terminate with such a patient until the risk has subsided unless it is *absolutely essential* to do so. Even then, the clinician should not merely make a good faith referral to another clinician, but should withdraw only when another clinician has assumed responsibility for the patient's care.

Finally, clinicians should be aware that they might be held liable for abandonment, even absent termination with a patient, if they fail, even briefly, to make themselves available to a patient in need of care. Obviously, no clinician can be available to patients at all times. Clinicians take vacations, leave town for conferences, and have other commitments which may take them away from their practices. They can and should arrange coverage by another clinician and should give all patients advance notice of such coverage.

Furthermore, the clinician should take care in selecting a covering clinician. As Gutheil and Appelbaum (1982) warn: "Although the primary clinician will not be responsible for the negligent acts of the covering clinician, he will be held liable for negligence in the selection of coverage" (p. 157). Thus, clinicians should entrust coverage of their practices only to clinicians they know to be capable of responding properly to patient needs.

Charles Patrick Ewing, J.D., Ph.D., is a clinical and forensic psychologist and an attorney. A recent graduate of Harvard Law School, Dr. Ewing is an Assistant Professor of Law and Adjunct Assistant Professor of Psychology at the State University of New York at Buffalo, where he teaches criminal law, juvenile law, and courses on the relationship of psychology and psychiatry to law. His professional interests and previous publications are in the areas of psychotherapy, professional ethics, and psychology and law.

RESOURCES

Abraham v. Zaslow, No. 245862 (Superior Court, Santa Clara County, California, October 26, 1970).

American Law Institute. (1965). *Restatement of Torts* (2d ed.). New York: Author.

American Psychiatric Association. (1974). *Report of the Task Force on Clinical Aspects of the Violent Individual* (Task Force Report No. 8). Washington, DC: Author.

American Psychiatric Association. (1981). *The Principles of Medical Ethics with Annotations Especially Applicable to Psychiatry.* Washington, DC: Author.

American Psychological Association. (1978). Report of the task force on the role of psychology in the criminal justice system. *American Psychologist, 33,* 1099. (Reprinted in J. Monahan (Ed.), *Who is the Client?* Washington, DC: American Psychological Association, 1980.)

American Psychological Association. (1981). Ethical principles of psychologists. *American Psychologist, 36,* 633.

Anclote Manor Foundation v. Wilkinson, 263 So.2d 256 (Fla. 1972).

Bellah v. Greenson, 81 Cal. App. 3d 614, 146 Cal. Rptr. 535 (1978).

Benjamin v. Havens, Inc., 60 Wash. 2d 196, 373 P.2d 109 (1962).

Berreby, D. (1983, January 17). Forcing therapists to pay. *National Law Journal,* at 1.

Bishop, K. (1983, January 10). Psychiatrists fight town over ban on electroshock. *National Law Journal*, at 3.

Bonner v. Moran, 126 F.2d 121 (D.C. Cir. 1941).

Cunningham, S. (1983). Superior court restarts electroshock in Berkeley. *APA Monitor, 14*, 17.

DeLeon, P., & Borreliz, M. (1978). Malpractice: Professional liability and the law. *Professional Psychology, 9*, 467.

Doe v. Roe, 324 N.Y.S.2d 71 (1971); *cert. dismissed*, 420 U.S. 307 (1975).

Ellison, K. (1983, March 14). Mother says she was told to sit on child who died. *National Law Journal*, at 4.

Everstine, L., Everstine, D. S., Heyman, G. M., True, R. H., Frey, D. H., Johnson, H. G., & Seiden, R. H. (1980). Privacy and confidentiality in psychotherapy. *American Psychologist, 35*, 828.

Ewing, C. P. (1982). Crisis intervention: Helping clients in turmoil. In P. A. Keller & L. G. Ritt (Eds.), *Innovations in Clinical Practice: A Source Book* (Vol. 1, pp. 5-15). Sarasota, FL: Professional Resource Exchange, Inc.

Ewing, C. P. (1983). Ethical issues in clinical practice. In P. A. Keller & L. G. Ritt (Eds.), *Innovations in Clinical Practice: A Source Book* (Vol. 2, pp. 399-410). Sarasota, FL: Professional Resource Exchange, Inc.

Freeman, L., & Roy, J. (1976). *Betrayal*. Briarcliff Manor, NY: Stein and Day.

Granelli, J. (1983, March 21). California mother acquitted in death of son. *National Law Journal*, at 29.

Gutheil, T., & Appelbaum, P. (1982). *Clinical Handbook of Psychiatry and the Law*. New York: McGraw-Hill.

Hadley, S., & Strupp, H. (1976). Contemporary views of negative effects in psychotherapy. *Archives of General Psychiatry, 33*, 1291.

Halleck, S. (1980). *Law in the Practice of Psychiatry: A Handbook for Clinicians*. New York: Plenum.

Hammer v. Rosen, 181 N.Y.S.2d 805 (1959); *modified*, 165 N.E.2d 756 (N.Y. 1960).

Hicks v. Holder, *National Law Journal*, October 11, 1982, at 4; *National Law Journal*, January 17, 1983, at 26, col. 1 (Civ. No. 81-1681, Cir. Ct., Alabama, 1982).

Hogan, D. (1979). *The Regulation of Psychotherapists* (Vols. 1-4). Cambridge, MA: Ballinger.

Holroyd, J., & Brodsky, A. (1977). Psychologists' attitudes and practices regarding erotic and nonerotic physical contact with patients. *American Psychologist, 32*, 843.

Kardener, S., Fuller, M., & Mensch, I. (1973). A survey of physicians' attitudes and practices regarding erotic and nonerotic contact with patients. *American Journal of Psychiatry, 130*, 1077.

Knecht v. Gillman, 488 F.2d 1137 (8th Cir. 1973).

Landau v. Werner, 105 Sol.J. 257 (Q.B. 1961).

Mackey v. Procunier, 477 F.2d 877 (9th Cir. 1973).

May, P. R. (1975). Schizophrenia: Overview of treatment methods. In A. M. Freedman, H. I. Kaplan, & B. J. Sadock (Eds.), *Comprehensive Textbook of Psychiatry* (Vol. I, pp. 923-938). Baltimore: Williams and Wilkins.

McCartney, J. (1966). Overt transference. *Journal of Sex Research, 2*, 227.

McDonald v. Clinger, 446 N.Y.S.2d 801 (1982).

Mentry v. Alum Rock Communications, Inc., No. 517164 (Superior Court, Santa Clara County, California, 1983).

Merchants Bank & Trust Co. v. United States, 272 F.Supp. 409 (D.N.D. 1967).

Monahan, J. (1981). *The Clinical Prediction of Violent Behavior.* Washington, DC: U. S. Government Printing Office.

Mounds Park Hospital v. VonEye, 245 F.2d 758 (8th Cir. 1957).

Northern California Psychiatric Society v. City of Berkeley, No. 566778-3 (Superior Court, Alameda County, California, filed January 13, 1983).

Note. (1982). Professional obligation and the duty to rescue: When must a psychiatrist protect his patient's intended victim? *Yale Law Journal, 91*, 1430.

People v. Mentry, No. 84637 (Superior Court, Santa Clara County, California, 1983).

In re Guardianship of Pescinski, 67 Wis.2d 4, 226 N.W.2d 180 (1975).

Pope, K., Simpson, S., & Weiner, M. (1978). Malpractice in outpatient psychotherapy. *American Journal of Psychotherapy, 32*, 593.

Prosser, W. (1971). *Handbook of the Law of Torts* (4th ed.). St. Paul, MN: West.

Rim, D. L., & Masters, J. C. (1974). *Behavior Therapy.* New York: Academic Press.

Robitscher, J. (1980). *The Powers of Psychiatry.* Boston: Houghton-Mifflin.

Rosen, J. (1953). *Direct Psychoanalysis* (Vols. 1-2). New York: Grune and Stratton.

Roy v. Hartogs, 381 N.Y.S.2d 587 (1976).

Sadoff, R. L. (1982). *Legal Issues in the Care of Psychiatric Patients.* New York: Springer.

Sadoff, R. L., & Showell, R. (1981, May). *Sex and Therapy: A Survey of Female Psychiatrists.* Paper presented at the annual meeting of the American Psychiatric Association, New Orleans, LA.

Salgo v. Leland Stanford Jr. University Board of Trustees, 317 P.2d 170 (Cal. App. 1957).

Schwitzgebel, R. K. (1978). Suggestions for the use of psychological devices in accord with legal and ethical standards. *Professional Psychology, 9,* 478.

Shepard, M. (1971). *The Love Treatment: Sexual Intimacy between Patients and Psychotherapists.* New York: Paperback Library.

Tarasoff v. Board of Regents of the University of California, 529 P.2d 553 (Cal. 1974); *modified,* 551 P.2d 334 (Cal. 1976).

Valenti v. United States, *National Law Journal,* January 17, 1983, at 26, col. 1 (D.Ill. 1982).

Walker v. Parzen, *National Law Journal,* July 20, 1981, at 5, col. 1 (Cal. 1981).

Zipkin v. Freeman, 436 S.W.2d 753 (Mo. 1968).

INDEX